The Marxists

The Marxists—For the past hundred years the marxists have posed the chief political alternative for capitalistic societies. They have been the successful revolutionaries of Russia, China, and Yugoslavia. They are now the technicians and philosophers whose appeals to the underdeveloped nations of Asia, Africa, and Latin America may be decisive.

Here they speak for themselves—in documents by the leading theorists from young Marx to Mao Tse-tung and Khrushchev.

As a guide through these theories, C. Wright Mills, author of such classic and best-selling studies as THE POWER ELITE, maps out the essential ideas of marxism, which he then examines critically. He sketches their historical development—the divisions and revisions, the successes and failures—and points to their implications for the present, and the future.

other books by C. WRIGHT MILLS

LISTEN, YANKEE: The Revolution in Cuba (1960)

IMAGES OF MAN (1960)—Edited with an Introduction

THE SOCIOLOGICAL IMAGINATION (1959)

THE CAUSES OF WORLD WAR THREE (1958)

THE POWER ELITE (1956)

CHARACTER AND SOCIAL STRUCTURE (1953)—with H. Gerth

WHITE COLLAR: The American Middle Classes (1951)

THE PUERTO RICAN JOURNEY (1950)—with C. Senior and R. Goldsen

THE NEW MEN OF POWER (1948)

FROM MAX WEBER: Essays in Sociology (1946)—Ed. and Tr. with H. Gerth

The Marxists C. Wright Mills

A LAUREL EDITION

Published by DELL PUBLISHING CO., INC.
1 Dag Hammarskjold Plaza, New York, N.Y. 10017

ISBN: 0-440-35470-6

This is an original Laurel book.

First printing—March, 1962
Second printing—December, 1963
Third printing—March, 1966
Fourth printing—March, 1968
Fifth printing—October, 1969
Sixth printing—March, 1970
Seventh printing—April, 1971
Eighth printing—October, 1972
Ninth printing—January, 1975
Tenth printing—August, 1977
Printed in U.S.A.

ACKNOWLEDGMENTS: I wish to thank Pablo Gonzales
Casanova, Carlos Fuentes, Enrique Gonzales Pedero, and
other friends at the University of Mexico for their criticisms
and aid. Earlier drafts have been read, in whole or in part, by
friends and colleagues to whom I am most grateful for their
generous help. They are, of course, absolved from any errors
or nonsense which may remain: Igor Alxandrov, Tom Bot-
tomore, Isaac Deutscher, Hans Gerth, Andrew Hacker, I. L.
Horowitz, Saul Landau, Sid Lens, Herbert Marcuse, Ralph Mili-
band, William Miller, George Mosse, George Novack, L. A.
Costa Pinto, Edward Thompson, William A. Williams.

contents

5. RULES FOR CRITICS

... in which some correct and some irrelevant grounds of criticism are sorted out, and the terms of criticism to be used in this book are stated.

6. CRITICAL OBSERVATIONS

... in which the major theories of Marx are examined critically and in light of relevant trends of contemporary societies; errors, ambiguities, and inadequacies of the intellectual structure are suggested.

7. ROADS TO SOCIALISM

... in which the major phases of marxism are each briefly characterized, politically and intellectually: the classic thinkers, the social democrats, the bolshevik pivot, the stalinist consolidation, critics of stalinism, soviet marxism and the new revisionists, marxism outside the bloc —and the over-all lines of marxist development are briefly summed up.

8. THE SOCIAL DEMOCRATS

... in which Karl Kautsky, Eduard Bernstein, and Rosa Luxemburg—representing the leading tendencies in the most important party of The Second International—discuss revolution and reform.

9. THE BOLSHEVIK PIVOT

... in which Nikolai Lenin is writing about an imperialist world, the party, the state, and the co-operation of workers with peasants; Leon Trotsky is developing the theory of the permanent revolution; how Lenin and Trotsky coincide in the bolshevism of October 1917 is explained.

10. THE STALINIST CONSOLIDATION

... in which Joseph Stalin is in 1924 defining what he is going to mean by "Leninism" and, near the end of his life, making a brief comment on base and superstructure and on the inevitability of war.

11. CRITICS OF STALINISM

... in which Rosa Luxemburg is giving an early warning; Trotsky is developing his theory of the nature of stalinist society; Rudolf Hilferding is writing on "state capitalism"; Franz Borkenau is characterizing the

12. SOVIET MARXISM AND THE NEW REVISIONISTS

...

12. MARXISM OUTSIDE THE BLOC

...

13. NEW BEGINNINGS

...

1. Ideals and Ideologies

This book is "a primer," a primer on marxisms, written mainly for those who do not really know these philosophies, and who do not pretend to know them. It is also written (hopefully, I suppose) for those who are already familiar with marxism but who believe that marxism as a whole has been "gobbled up by the communists" and accordingly is not for them; for those who hold to the notion that after all it is "merely ideology," and that, nowadays especially, ideology is at an end—or ought to be. It is also for those who are bored with politics and political philosophy, who have withdrawn to or never emerged from a strictly private life. If this book does no more than push such people a bit closer to the experience of being full citizens, it will have fulfilled its central purpose.

1

In reconsidering several varieties of marxism in terms appropriate to our own immediate times, I plan in the following pages to make a systematic inventory of what I take to be the essential ideas of classic marxism and then to criticize them. I shall follow this with some brief historical profiles of its main lines of development and uses. Rather than interrupt this presentation by lengthy quotations, I have arranged a selection of the most important marxist writings as independent chapters. In my criticisms I shall of course draw upon relevant work now available in those social sciences with which I am familiar. In order to keep this book to manageable length, I have not dealt here in any explicit and systematic way with interpretations and criticisms of marxism provided by other commentators. But I have tried to take other interpretations and criticisms into account, and I hope that I have remained aware of the most important of them.

Throughout I have tried to be objective, but I do not claim to be detached. No political philosopher can be detached; he can only pretend to be. And I do write this book in some part as a political philosopher, which only means: as one who is seeking, with his readers, political orientation. Accordingly, I shall try to be explicit about my own political and moral judgments.

As we read the marxists, a political comparison *is* in the minds of most of us, whether we are aware of it or not: the standards we generally tend to use are the standards we think of as "democratic" or "liberal" or those of "The Free World." We must state, and examine, these standards in order to examine marxism effectively. We must examine both "political liberalism"—the major alternative in political philosophy and in world reality, and the source of our values, assumptions and theories—and "social science" whose terms provide conventional grounds for criticism of marxism. My comments on liberalism will necessarily be brief, for my main concern in this book is with marxism.[1] But I hope to write in such ways that the assumptions of the liberal reader will rise to the surface, making him freer to clarify his political position.

Many of those who reject (or more accurately, ignore) marxist ways of thinking about human affairs are actually rejecting the classic traditions of their own disciplines. The "Social Science" in the name of which marxism is ignored or rejected is more often than not a social science having little or no concern with the pivotal events and the historic acceleration characteristic of our immediate times. It is a social science of the narrow focus, the trivial detail, the abstracted almighty unimportant fact.[2] A few differences between Marx's style of work and some leading types of contemporary social science will suffice to suggest their character. When marxists speak of "bourgeois social science," these are the sorts of things they mean (or ought to mean):

The social scientists study the details of small-scale

---

1. I have already made extended critiques of various liberal views which I am willing to let stand. For example, see *The New Men of Power* (1948), *White Collar* (1951), and *The Power Elite* (1956).
2. For an elaboration of this point of view, see *The Sociological Imagination* (1959); for a sampling of "the classic tradition in sociological thinking," see *Images of Man* (1960).

milieus; Marx studied such details too, but always within the structure of a total society. The social scientists, knowing little history, study at most short-run trends; Marx, using historical materials with superb mastery, takes as his unit of study entire epochs. The values of the social scientists generally lead them to accept their society pretty much as it is; the values of Marx lead him to condemn his society—root, stock and branch. The social scientists see society's problems as matters only of "disorganization"; Marx sees problems as inherent contradictions in the existing structure. The social scientists see their society as continuing in an evolutionary way without qualitative breaks in its structure; Marx sees in the future of this society a qualitative break: a new form of society—in fact a new epoch—is going to come about by means of revolution.

However, there is today no "marxist social science" of any intellectual consequence. There is just—social science: without the work of Marx and other marxists, it would not be what it is today; with their work alone, it would not be nearly as good as it happens to be. No one who does not come to grips with the ideas of marxism can be an adequate social scientist; no one who believes that marxism contains the last word can be one either. Is there any doubt about this after Max Weber, Thorstein Veblen, Karl Mannheim—to mention only three? We do now have ways —better than Marx's alone—of studying and understanding man, society, and history, but the work of these three is quite unimaginable without his work.

In the United States, the intellectual influences of marxism are often hidden; many of those whose very categories of thought are influenced by Marx are often unaware of the source of their own methods and conceptions. Many "western" social scientists would do more significant work if they paid closer attention to marxism as a major source of their disciplines. In the Soviet Union, on the other hand, many scholars are often ignorant of developments elsewhere that have come out of the conceptions and theories of Marx. Social scientists and reflective men are likely to be historically provincial and thus intellectually crippled by remaining or being forced to remain unaware of later developments in classic sociology.

Some day, perhaps, from either side, students of man, history and society will come to consider in more objective ways the enormously fruitful questions inherited from Marx and other marxists. In the meantime, although men of the soviet world are often not able to do this, we should not be deterred by any nation's political posture from trying to become aware of everything that has made us what we are.

Like many others just now, I am uneasily aware of the inadequacies of our inherited political philosophies. Both marxism and liberalism bear the trademarks of a period of human history that is ending; both are marred by inadequate attention to leading facts and problems with which the world scene now presents us. It it not the purpose of this book to work out a political philosophy adequate to the world era which we now enter. But it is my hope that it will serve my readers, and myself, as an *introduction* to nothing less than just such an effort.

2

Political philosophies are intellectual and moral creations; they contain high ideals, easy slogans, dubious facts, crude propaganda, sophisticated theories. Their adherents select some facts and ignore others, urge the acceptance of ideals, the inevitability of events, argue with this theory and debunk that one. Since in all political philosophies such a miscellany of elements is usually very much jumbled up, our first task is to sort them out. To do so, each of the following four points of view may be useful:

First of all, a political philosophy is itself a social reality: it is an *ideology* in terms of which certain institutions and practices are justified and others attacked; it provides the phrases in which demands are raised, criticisms made, exhortations delivered, proclamations formulated and, at times, policies determined.

Second, it is an ethic, an articulation of *ideals* which on various levels of generality and sophistication is used in judging men, events and movements, and as goals and guidelines for aspirations and policies.

Third, a political philosophy designates *agencies* of action, of the means of reform, revolution, or conservation. It contains strategies and programs that embody both ends and means. It designates, in short, the historical levers by which ideals are to be won or maintained after they have been won.

Fourth, it contains *theories* of man, society and history, or at least assumptions about how society is made up and how it works; about what is held to be its most important elements and how these elements are typically related; its major points of conflict and how these conflicts are resolved. It suggests the methods of study appropriate to its theories. From these theories and with these methods, expectations are derived.

A political philosophy tells us how to find out where we stand and where we may be going; it gives us some answers to these questions; it prepares us for the possible futures. To examine any political philosophy, then, we must examine it as an ideology, a statement of ideals, a designation of agency or agencies, and as a set of social theories. In this chapter, I shall pay attention mainly to ideologies and ideals; the points I shall try to make are these:

As ideology, liberalism and marxism have both been made vulgar and banal; each supplies clichés for the defense of a great-power state and for the abuse of the other bloc and all its works.

As statements of ideals, both carry the secular humanism of Western civilization. These ideals are the only ideals available that are at once part of a comprehensive political philosophy and proclaimed by both the leaders and the led of the most powerful nation-states of the world.

In their classic versions, liberalism and marxism embody the assurances and hopes, the ambiguities and fears of the modern age. Taken in all their varieties, they now constitute our major, even our only, political alternatives. Yet they are more than political philosophies: they are political realities of the first order, the proclaimed creeds of the two most powerful states in world history. Looking upon the USA and the USSR (and the blocs of nations around each), the rest of the world sees them in terms of these creeds; in these terms, the underdeveloped world thinks of them as alternative models for their own development.

From the standpoint of modern times, the differences between the classic versions of these political philosophies are often less important than what they have in common. Above all they are animated by common ideals: the major secular ideals that have been developed during the course of Western civilization. Both marxism and liberalism embody the ideals of Greece and Rome and Jerusalem: the humanism of the renaissance, the rationalism of the eighteenth century enlightenment. That is why to examine liberalism or marxism is to examine the politics of this humanist tradition; to find either or both ambiguous is to find this tradition ambiguous.

Liberalism and marxism have also each provided grand views of the nature of the social world, designated the agencies of historic change, and suggested programs for achieving these goals. For many decades now, within each advanced nation, they have confronted each other, differing about what their experts consider to be facts, and differing about the means they think necessary to reach their proclaimed goals. But these goals have not changed very much. First they were the goals of the English, the American, the French Revolutions; then they were the goals, reformulated to be sure, of the Russian Revolution; quickly they were again reformulated—in reaction, both liberal and marxist, to the consolidation of this revolution.[3]

The moral and political dilemmas of the marxists, and especially of the communists among them, overlap heavily the dilemmas of any liberal. Both share in the ideals of the big tradition; neither realizes them fully. And these ideals, as well as certain theoretical assumptions, are carried further and more consistently, are taken more seriously by several of the best marxists than by any liberal I know of. It is the crisis of this humanist tradition itself, I believe, that is at the bottom of our crisis in political orientation. One of the most direct ways to confront that crisis in all its aspects is to examine the ideas of Karl Marx —and the fate of these ideas.

What is most valuable in classic liberalism is most cogently and most fruitfully incorporated in classic marxism. Much of the failure to confront marxism in all its variety, is in fact a way of *not* taking seriously the ideals of liberalism itself, for despite the distortions and vulgarizations of Marx's ideas, and despite his own errors, ambiguities and inadequacies, Karl Marx remains the thinker who has articulated most clearly—and most perilously—the basic ideals which liberalism shares. Hence, to confront Marx and marxism is to confront this moral tradition.

3. For a scholarly, relevant, and exciting account of the eighteenth-century revolutions, see R. R. Palmer, *The Age of the Democratic Revolution* (Princeton, 1959).

There is of course no one liberalism and no one marxism. The work of Karl Marx and Friedrich Engels has been the chief ideological gadfly of liberalism, of social democracy, and later, of bolshevik and stalinist versions of the original doctrine. It has provided a major ideological basis for the criticism of liberal politics, capitalist economics—and of soviet politics and economics.

In the advanced capitalist countries of the nineteenth and early twentieth centuries, a great and often confused amalgamation of liberalism and marxism developed into a kind of ideological common denominator. In the process, both were modified and attenuated: marxism was revised, incorporating liberal elements; liberalism was adjusted to its critics and to changing realities, incorporating marxist elements. These modifications and mutual borrowings make up much of the history of recent and contemporary political philosophy—and political history. Within capitalist societies during the past one hundred years one of the non-revolutionary forms of marxism—social democracy—has been the major opposition movement in most of the advanced capitalist world. In attenuated forms, it has virtually replaced liberalism as opposition and critic from within.

In these societies today, the infirmity of political assurance and the collapse of political hope are very much a part of the crisis of the liberal outlook and of the liberal mood. In many parts of the soviet world, the same is true, although to a lesser degree and in a different way, of the marxist outlook and mood. Liberalism and marxism have become so central to events, to their making and to their suffering, that it is not too much to say that their crises are symptoms of the decline of what is still, rather curiously, called The Modern Epoch. Perhaps, too, this decline signals the onset of a new epoch in human history.

That new epoch—whatever else it may be—is truly a world epoch: the uses and the meanings of these contemporary creeds are now world-wide. Since the Russian Revolution and the consolidation of the soviet bloc, the encounter of liberalism with marxism has become a world encounter of nation-states. In political fact, the communist variety of marxism, seated in the soviet bloc, is now the leading form of marxism. In political fact, the North American variety of liberalism, seated in the United States, is now the leading form of liberalism.

Given the powerful means of history-making now at their disposal, these two states and the blocs they form are the most fateful organizations of public and private life that men now know, or indeed have ever known. That is why when we examine the political creeds they proclaim—explaining, comparing, criticizing them—we are not "merely talking about ideas"—whatever that phrase may mean. We are talking about decisive features of our recent past, our present, and our immediate future. We are also talking about the kinds of men and women who do and who will inhabit the earth. Only through the prism of one or another variety of these political philosophies can we now try seriously to know what is happening in the world and to orient ourselves to it.

But, it may be asked, what about conservatism? Well, what about it? Or, rather, where is it?

First, wherever "conservatism" prevails as the ascendant ideology of a state in power—as in Franco's Spain, Verwoerd's South Africa, Salazar's Portugal, or the Trujillos' Dominican Republic—it rests more upon police power than upon ideological consent. For well-known reasons, the days of such regimes are numbered in the underdeveloped world.

Second, in advanced capitalist societies, the ideological and intellectual functions performed by nineteenth-century conservatism are now usually performed by liberalism. In fact, there is no halfway coherent conservatism that is not a variety of liberalism, a restatement of Edmund Burke, or mere eccentricity. In the United States, at any rate, conservatism offers only a retrogressive utopia to circles best described as cranky, if not crackpot. Insofar as it is not that, conservatism is a defensive gesture of businessmen and politicians who would defend the *status quo* but who are without ideas with which to do so. As the *Wall Street Journal* has noted, conservatism "is hardly more than an instinctive belief that today's society is built on several thousands of years and that in those years men have found things they should fasten to." On that basis, we are all conservatives, and to be such is meaningless.[4]

4

To those who are truly possessed by a political philosophy, what is happening in the world in which they live seems altogether clear. An issue arises, or an issue is raised: the correct and proper view leaps readily to mind. By means of their philosophy, they are persuasively oriented. The positions they hold are easy to communicate. On various levels of sophistication, "the ideological message" seems obvious and compelling. The ideals in which they believe seem closely connected with the agencies of action they have chosen. And both ideal and agency fit into their theories of society and into what they imagine is going on within society.

This blissful condition seems rarely available in our time. In creeds that are mixed with history and held by tens of millions of people, each of the four elements of any political philosophy—ideology, ideal, agency, theory —are often curiously transformed and curiously related to each other, to their adherents and to the run of historical fact.

With success, the ideology usually becomes in due course vulgarized; there is vulgar liberalism and there is vulgar marxism. But vulgar or sophisticated, the ideological features seem to be the most variously useful and the most omnivorous element of any political philosophy. Many know only this one element—along with such features of ideal, agency, theory as it may loosely incorporate. Ideology, as the public face of a political philosophy, very often becomes simply myth or folklore; very often too, even a minimum of ideology withers away: all that is left is an empty and irrelevant rhetoric. Such ideological message as may once have prevailed is no longer persuasive. Indeed, it even becomes difficult to state clearly. Then it is often said of the political philosophy: "After

4. For one of the best attempts to define and elaborate a "new conservatism," see Peter Vierek, *Conservatism* (New York, 1956) from which the quote above is taken (page 186). For a critical account of varieties of conservatism today, see William J. Newman, *The Futilitarian Society* (New York, 1961).

In this book for reasons of convenience and limitations of space I have deliberately omitted any consideration of anarchism and syndicalism or their relationships with marxism. Perhaps this omission is justified by the fact that these doctrines are not now of immediate political significance.

all, it is more a general outlook or a sensibility than any dogmatic guideline."

Above all, with success, the ideals, especially the more insurgent ones, tend to become incorporated into the ideology of justification, and, in practical fact, to be identified with the agencies of action. To maintain these agencies becomes the going ideal; other ideals become "mere rhetoric"—campaign or revolutionary. As ideals, they are not connected with any agencies by which they might be realized. Yet even as rhetoric, they may be rigidly controlled, tied down tight into the ideological consolidation.

Often the theories are difficult to sort out from the other elements, for they tend to become merely assumptions used in discussions of the urgent goals, the necessary means, and the rhetoric of justification or of attack. As they are confused with these other elements, the theories grow fuzzy. Transformed into mere assumptions, they tend to become "merely ideological," and often—along with ideals—to become part of the ideological doubletalk so characteristic of our time. As theories, they become highly formal; it is not easy to see their relevance to the ideals proclaimed, the ideologies believed in, the agencies of historic action. For these ideals, ideologies, agencies are not "located" by the theories within an existing society and in the movement of its history.

At different phases and in different societies all these things have happened to varieties of liberal and of marxist political philosophy. But we must also ask: What happens when the adherents of a political philosophy are bypassed by history? when they become powerless grouplets, yet still cling to their philosophy?

The philosophy itself then tends to become concerned almost solely with ideals. It becomes a moral outlook, and not much else. This has happened, for example, among many ex-radical groups of fiercely anti-soviet persuasion who cling to "socialism." With distaste, they retreat from all "ideology"; they are uninterested in larger "theory," and they neither possess nor even try to designate agencies of action. They become interested in the "pragmatic" and the "piecemeal." Facts may be acknowledged, but only in a scattered way; they are not connected with each other or with larger theories and certainly not with definite programs. Something like this—I think it obvious

—is what has happened in our generation in many liberal and socialist circles of the NATO countries.

Other things have happened, too. In all ideological camps, the most politically useful (and the most confusing) of all grammatical moods is "the optative": what one hopes for is spoken of as though it were actually so. Among powerless groups, this mood is often expressed with extensive use of the most tricky word in the vocabulary of politics: that word, of course, is "We." Among the powerful, too, this mood appears, very often in what may be called the ideological incorporation of ideal and theories.

So the position of the political philosopher seems to be: heads you win, tails I lose. With success, horrid things happen to a political philosophy; and with failure they happen too.

This is of course the tension of political philosophy. It means that as a task at once intellectual and moral, political philosophy never ends. At least it cannot end so long as men *seek* political orientation. But of course most men do not: they merely accept the going folklore, liberal or marxist, as the accident of their geographic residence may determine.

5

Both liberalism and marxism have been insurgent creeds: in their several varieties they have been the rhetoric of movements, parties and classes on the road to power. And in due course, each has become a conservative creed: the ideology and the rhetoric of consolidated political and economic systems.

With their insurgent creed, liberals have denounced as a social system, feudalism and its remnants; they have denounced all forms of political absolutism. Marxists too have denounced feudalism and pre-industrial absolutism; but they have gone further, coming down hard against liberal capitalism as a type of economy which they have held to be the keystone of capitalist societies as a whole.

As an ideology, and on a world-wide scale, liberalism now becomes conservative. In its terms, liberals justify capitalist democracy, seated primarily in the richer nations of Western Europe and North America, and in Japan and Australia. In their stalinist variety, marxists have officially justified the Soviet Union and the states in various ways affiliated with it.

As a political "utopia," liberalism has been historically specific to the rising middle classes of advancing capitalist societies; marxism, the proclaimed creed of working class movements and parties. But in each case, as power is achieved, these political philosophies become official ideologies, become—in differing ways—engulfed by nationalism. In terms of each, the world encounter of the superstates is defined, and from either side, fought out. In the Soviet Union marxism has become ideologically consolidated and subject to official control; in the United States liberalism has become less an ideology than an empty rhetoric.

As a rhetoric, liberalism is commonly used by everyone who talks in public for every divergent and contradictory purpose. One spokesman can remain liberal and be *for*, another can remain liberal and be *against*, a vast range of contradictory political propositions. The businessman and the labor leader, the Democrat and the Republican, the General and the foot-soldier, the subsidized farmer and the subsidized watch-maker—all speak in the terms of the liberal rhetoric, defending their interests and making their demands. This means that liberalism as publicly used is without coherent content, that its goals have been made so formal and abstract as to provide no clear moral standards, that in its terms genuine conflicts of interest and ideal can no longer be stated clearly. Used by virtually all interests, classes, parties, it lacks political, moral, and intellectual clarity; this very lack of clarity is exploited by all interests. In this situation, as has often been noted, professional liberals, politicians and intellectuals make a fetish of indecision, which they call open-mindedness; of the absence of moral criteria, which they call tolerance; and of the formality—and hence political irrelevance—of the criteria, which they call speaking broadly.

The crisis of liberalism—and in turn, of political reflection in the United States—is due to liberalism's very success in becoming the official language for all public statement and debate, the political language of all mass communication. To this fact must be added the use of liberalism, since the New Deal period, as an administrative rationale: in close contact with power, liberalism has become more administrative and less political. It has become practical, flexible, realistic, pragmatic—as liberals assert—and not at all utopian. All of which means, I think, that as an ideology, as a rhetoric, liberalism has often become irrelevant to political positions having moral content.

In the soviet bloc, elements from marxism have become essential ingredients of an official creed subject to official interpretation, and the official guideline for all cultural and political life. In this form, marxism-as-ideology is *the* coin of all public transactions, the basic premise of an elaborate cultural and political apparatus that is oriented to the presumed interests of the one-party state. Since marxism enjoys an ideological monopoly, intellectual freedom is limited by official interpretations of it. From an image of the future, elaborated in nineteenth-century capitalist society, marxism has been transformed into the ideology of the soviet bloc.

Ideological uniformity and doctrinaire realignment have accompanied every phase and every turn of soviet political and economic development, domestic and foreign. There have been many such twists and turns, each of them duly proclaimed in the name of marxism. Politics and doctrine are closely linked; political directions often shift: it is not surprising that the doctrine itself has become banalized and, in the process, emptied of much of its moral force and intellectual cogency. It has often become a morally curious and intellectually empty ideology in which the communist-on-the-make must be expert—truly a red tape of an ideology which he must tie and untie and tie again, if he would act at all.

Moreover, such use of soviet marxism has been accompanied by its use as the one basic doctrine of the entire soviet cultural apparatus, which has had to swing into line with each shift in policy. In the course of such zig-zags, cultural workmen have been brutally eliminated. The political and status purge of intellectuals, artists, and scientists—as during Stalin's era—has thus accompanied the tight joining of culture and politics, both controlled by officials of party and of state.

Now these two folklores—the ideology of vulgar marxism and the rhetoric of abstracted liberalism—confront each other, each offering the world's publics various images

of the Soviet Union and of the United States, each pro-
viding the contrasting vocabularies, often in the same
words, with which leaders and led talk about their own
societies and about those of The Enemy.

Inside each country and around the world as well, a
vast and elaborate machinery of propaganda is kept busy
night and day grinding out these folklores, adapting them
to every turn of events and to events imagined; to threat
and counter-threat, to policies and to lack of policies.

In the folklore of liberalism, America is a free country
in which men at large truly govern their own affairs; Soviet
Russia is an absolute tyranny, monolithic and totalitarian,
in which men are forcibly held down and there is neither
freedom nor joy—and it is aggressive, too, out to conquer the world for its unchristian creed.

In the folklore of communism, the USSR is The Great
Step Forward of Humanity in the twentieth century; the
USA is a reactionary laggard in which the injustices of
capitalism are matched only by the hypocrisies of formal
democracy. It is run by warmongers, out to use military,
and any other means available, ruthlessly to expand and
consolidate their imperialistic domination.

In this realm of folklore, the ideas of Karl Marx and
of his intellectual followers are indeed in a sorry condition.

In soviet societies, the work of Marx—joined with that
of Lenin—is always celebrated and often vulgarized. Indeed marxism-leninism has become an official rhetoric
with which the authority of a one-party state has been defended, its expedient brutalities obscured, its achievements
proclaimed.

In capitalist societies, the ideas of Marx are ignored or
worse, ignorantly *identified* with "mere communist ideology." Thus, here too, the work of Marx, and of his followers, has become "marxism-leninism"—an official target
of confused and ignorant abuse, rather than an object of
serious study.

6

But all this *is* folklore. From both sides. All this is only
one aspect—the ideological—of liberalism and of marxism.
To be sure, even the folklore of each side contains glimpses
of truth and definitions of reality; but the point is that

back of each, there are sets of ideas that must be taken seriously if we are to understand even the uses of the folklores—not to mention the condition and the possible fate of the world today. Back of each of these ideologies there is much of the world's heritage of political ideas and moral ideals.

I must make one point clear: when in this book I use the term "West" or "Western civilization," I include Russia in it—historically and today. I do not use the term "Western" or "The West" in contrast to "The Communist Bloc" or "Communism.⁵ The territory of the Soviet Union of course sprawls into Asia, but its major historical developments have been in the European parts of the country. Culturally Russia has been in rather close contact with European societies, although historically it has lagged behind them.

Marxism itself, moreover, is as much a part of European culture as is Italian renaissance architecture. Marx and Engels were Europeans, and the leaders of the Russian Revolution were not exactly oriental peasants; many of them were topnotch intellectuals who spent much of their lives in West European capitals.

Finally, the Russians and most other leading nationalities in the Soviet Union—such as the Ukrainians—think of themselves as Europeans. Moreover, Asiatics—Indonesians, for example—usually think of Russia as among "the Western countries." Russia, concludes the geographer J. P. Cole, "can be included with the maritime empire builders of Western Europe as a carrier of European conquest and culture to the non-European world." ⁶

As far as ideals are concerned, classic liberalism and classic marxism practically exhaust the *political* heritage

5. The political intent of such classifications is to identify the present anti-soviet coalition of nations with "Western civilization." As for "The Free World," here is one statement, as of March, 1955: Of the 71 countries outside the communist bloc, some 49 were "outwardly or actually dictatorships or close oligarchies . . . of the remaining 22 nations, most of them truly have some claim to the adjective 'free' as far as their political governments are concerned, but, certainly as far as the economic control of several of them is concerned, it is oligarchic and a small percentage of the nation is living off the backs of the other 99 per cent."; Representative Thomas B. Curtis, *Congressional Record*, 1955, p. 1481. Materials prepared by "Legislative Reference Service," Library of Congress, USA.

6. J. P. Cole, *Geography of World Affairs* (London, 1959). See Appendix I for a cogent discussion of this point. Cf. also *The Causes of World War Three* (1960) pp. 29-35.

of Western civilization. Liberals have repeatedly asserted a secular humanism, stressing the priceless value of the individual personality and the right of each individual to be dealt with in accordance with rational and understandable laws, to which all power is to be subjected. They have seen man as the measure of all things: policies and events are good or bad, in terms of their effects upon men; institutions and societies are to be judged in terms of what they mean to and for the individual human being. Liberals have assumed that men should control their own fates. They have assumed that there are rational ways to acquire knowledge, and that the substantive reason of the individual, used freely, provides the way out. It is in terms of these values that their concern with consent to authority and their general opposition to violence should be understood.

The root principle of liberalism is not merely "freedom in general," but the specific, personal freedom of the individual, even the self-imposed obligation, to make *no* unconditional commitments to *any* organization. All loyalties to movements or organizations, parties or states, are, for the liberal, conditional upon his own principles and conscience.[7]

The works of Marx, and of many other marxists, clearly and consistently embody the secular humanism of the West, systematically, as deep and pervasive moral assumptions. As in the case of liberalism, one difficulty of showing that this is so lies in the uses and misuses of marxism as practiced. Another difficulty, peculiar to marxism, has to do with certain mannerisms and convictions of Marx himself. Living in the Victorian age, hating cant and spurning hypocrisy, Marx developed an image of himself as a "hard-headed and realistic" intellectual. He disliked the proclamation of grand ideals; he connected his ideals very closely with his analysis of the society that he felt was denying them, and with the agencies within that society

7. See L. T. Hobhouse, *Liberalism* (London, 1911)—the best twentieth-century statement of liberal ideals I know. It is necessary in this connection to say that the dogmatic celebration of American nationalism carried on by so many "liberal" intellectuals in the cold-war period has been a clear violation of classic liberal ideals. The ritualistic requirements of oaths of loyalty to the United States of America are at once tokens of the decline of democratic symbols of justification and of the cogency of liberalism as a creed.

which he expected to realize them. But the test of his moral position lies in what he wrote and in the assumptions that underlie every line of it.

1. Marx is a secular moralist, an atheist who thinks all religion an intellectual fraud and a political trap, another means of exploitation, psychic as well as material. Religion, as he conceives it, keeps men from coming to true self-consciousness of themselves, of their positions in society, and of their true interests as men. The ideals of a radical humanism in which man replaces God himself, accompanied by an Old Testament passion for human justice—these are among the mainsprings of Marx's career as a thinker and the moral grounds for his denunciation of what he saw as the degrading, crippling effects of capitalism.

2. Marx is a rationalist thinker: "To demand that men should abandon illusions about their condition is to demand that a condition that needs illusions should itself be abandoned." It cannot reasonably be denied that Karl Marx tried his best to practice this motto throughout his life's work. His belief in human reason, and in freedom as one of its conditions and consequences—these are the sources of his moral energy, the pivot of his thought, the key to his optimism, the basis of his expectation that the class of man in which "the human being has lost himself" should be abolished, and that men should come to experience themselves as truly human beings.

3. Marx is thoroughly and consistently humanist. A positive image of man, of what man might come to be, lies under every line of his analysis of what he held to be an inhuman society. His conception of "alienation" alone—his analysis of the meaning of work under capitalism—is enough to reveal his humanism. If it is not, then we need only consider his analysis of the pervasive and corrupting effects of cash as the supreme value of capitalist society. In Marx's view is it *because* proletarian men are so abstracted from humanity, so thoroughly alienated from their real natures, that they will struggle to emancipate themselves and, with themselves, all mankind. Marx is radical in the literal, the humanist, meaning of that term. Indeed, up to this day, who else has gone so far in this respect? He would eliminate all occupational stereotypes;

ideally, each man is to pursue not any one occupation; he is to engage himself in a variety of activities. Now a crippled fragment, man should become "the fully developed individual . . . to which the different social functions he performs are but so many modes of giving free scope to his own natural and acquired powers." [8]

4. Marx believed in human freedom, both in and of itself and as a condition for the use of man's reason. Thus he condemns "a censored press" in terms that parallel the condemnation by John Stuart Mill: it leads to "hypocrisy, the greatest of vices . . . the government hears only its own voice . . . surrenders to the illusion that it hears the voice of the people . . . The people on its side falls either into political superstition or else into indifference, and so turns completely away from the life of the state." Again and again, he speaks of and for "the free activity of men."

His ideal for the political community is one in which "true democracy prevails and the state itself disappears, as well as all classes." His ideal is "the realm of freedom," a conception by which he accepts and carries further the image of the classical *polis*. Slave as well as master are "true men—men in all their personal human dignity." [9] Foremost among the continuing tasks of Marx was the disclosure of the concrete conditions under which this freedom would be a genuine human reality.

From the liberal intellectual climate of his day, Marx assimilated these ideals—but with a difference. The moral bases of his criticism of liberal society are the ideals proclaimed by that society itself—taken seriously and made concrete. He accepts the ideals of liberty and equality inherited from the eighteenth-century enlightenment; from the ascendant bourgeoisie of his day, he takes over the rationalist, optimistic idea of progress itself, and reseats it in the lower depths of liberal society.

In brief: there is no positive *ideal* held by Marx that is not an altogether worthy contribution to the humanist tradition; that tradition, in turn, embodies the legacy of

---

8. *Capital,* (New York, Modern Library, no date) p. 534.
9. For documentation of Marx's ideals, see especially *The Economic and Philosophical Manuscripts of 1844* (Moscow, 1959); *The German Ideology* (New York, 1947); and "Critique of the Gotha Program." in *Selected Works,* Vol. II (New York, 1933); and the excerpts reprinted in Chapter 3 of this volume.

Classical, Judaic, and Christian images of man's estate. Considered morally, Karl Marx's principles are clearly among the animating principles of Western civilization.

I have not wished to imply that we may dismiss either liberalism or marxism merely because each has been made into banal rhetoric and vulgar ideology. The power of ideals displayed by liberalism and marxism, drawn from their common Western tradition, is too great. The very fact of their wide use limits the choices, and to some extent guides the decisions, of those in authority. For men are influenced in their use of the powers they possess by the rhetoric they feel they must employ, by the ideological coin in which they transact affairs with one another. The leaders as well as the led, even the hired myth-makers and hack apologists, are influenced by their own rhetoric of justification, by the ideological consolidation that prevails. In fact, from one limited point of view, the extent to which this is so is the extent to which ideas and ideals may influence the course of history.

Surely marxism has done just that. Beginning with quite marginal and seemingly insignificant groups of scholarly insurgents in the nineteenth-century capitals of Europe— a kind of man we do not know so well today—these ideas have come to be the guidelines for trade unions, parties, mass movements, nations, great blocs of states. In the heads of political intellectuals and revolutionary politicians, and of masses in the street—later, too, of bureaucrats and statesmen of every rank—the ideas of Marx and the slogans made up from them have guided actions of the greatest consequence. In terms of them, total societies and the ways of life of millions of people have been basically transformed. Today, these ideas inform the official creed of what were once among the most backward countries of Europe and Asia but which are now the ascendant powers of the Euro-Asiatic continent. At the same time, these ideas of Marx are also the source of the most bitter opposition to those powers which justify themselves In The Name Of Marx.

7

In this book I am concerned with marxism, but nonetheless I feel the need to make a brief comment on liberalism as agency and as theory—since in this chapter I have dealt mainly with ideals and ideology.[10]

As an articulation of ideals, liberalism remains compelling, but on each of the other three aspects of political philosophy—as ideology, as designation of historical agencies, and as a set of theories about man, society and history —its relevance is now largely historical only.

That liberalism has become the common denominator of political and moral rhetoric in America testifies to the compelling character of liberal ideals. But it also testifies to the fact that these ideals have been increasingly divorced from any historical agencies by which they might be realized. Of course, it is easier to agree upon abstract and general ends than upon the relevance and the necessity of specific means to such proclaimed ends. That is one reason liberalism is now more of a rhetoric than anything else.

It is doubtful that liberalism is in a position to designate the conditions under which the ideals it proclaims might be realized. It has been detached from any tenable theory of society and from any effective means of action. Accordingly, however engaging as a set of ideals, even these ideals in their abstracted and formal condition are no longer useful as guidelines to judgments about what is going on in the world, or as guidelines for those who would by the will of men consciously modify the course of historical events.

As a set of theories—or better, of assumptions about man, society, history—liberalism today is at a dead end. The optative mood has so thoroughly taken over that liberals often appear out of touch with the going realities. That is one reason it is so difficult to sort out distinctively liberal *theories* as such. Often failing to recognize facts that cry out to be recognized, liberalism is irrelevant to much that is happening in much of the world. Liberal ways of looking at these facts too often become mannerisms by which liberals avoid considering the structural conditions of social life and the need to change them. In fact, liberals have no convincing view of the structure of society as a whole—other than the now vague notion of it as some kind of a big balance. They have no firm sense of the history of

10. In order to get to the main concern of this book, at the risk of seeming dogmatic, I must deal with liberalism in a very brief manner. Elsewhere I have examined in considerable detail various features of liberalism; the major arguments of the present book do not necessarily rest upon acceptance of this brief comment on liberalism.

our times and of their nation's or of their generation's place within that history.

Liberalism has been the firm ideology of one class inside one epoch—the urban and entrepreneurial middle class. On a world-wide scale that class is now often simply not available and their epoch has now largely passed. If the moral force of liberalism is still abstractly stimulating, its sociological content is weak: its political means of action are unpromising, unconvincing, unimaginative. It has no theory of man in society, no theory of man as the maker of history. It has no political program adequate to the moral ideals it professes. Twentieth-century liberals have stressed ideals much more than theory and agency. But that is not all: they have stressed going agencies and institutions in such ways as to transform *them* into the foremost ideals of liberalism.

As a compelling, or even a useful, ideology, liberalism belongs to the heroic epoch of the middle classes of the already industrialized nations of capitalism; nowadays, as ideology and as rhetoric, it is much more useful as a defense of the *status quo*—in the rich minority of nations, and of these nations before the rest of the world—than as a creed for deliberate historical change.

To the world's range of enormous problems, liberalism responds with its verbal fetish of "Freedom" plus a shifting series of opportunistic reactions. The world is hungry; the liberal cries, "Let us make it free!" The world is tired of war; the liberal cries, "Let us arm for peace!" The peoples of the world are without land; the liberal cries, "Let us beg the landed oligarchs to parcel some of it out!" In sum: the most grievous charge today against liberalism and its conservative varieties is that they are so utterly *provincial,* and thus so irrelevant to the major problems that must now be confronted in so many areas of the world.

2. A Celebration of Marx [1]

During his lifetime what Karl Marx wrote was not widely read. But his ideas and moral temper, his vocabulary, even his stray notions, have since come to influence the course of world history. Whatever else marxism may be, it provides the foremost intellectual drama of our time, intellectual because its doctrine is used politically. For the same reason it is the foremost political drama. In marxism, ideas confront politics: intellectuals, politicians, passions, conceptions, the coldest analysis, the hottest moral condemnation—all meet. They meet—immediately, dramatically—and make history.

The intellectual value of classic marxism, and of marxism more generally, is not merely historical. It has a direct intellectual relevance today. Marx's work contains comprehensive statements about the elements and the structure of society to which attention must be paid—entirely apart from politics or ideology.

We cannot understand the history of any nation of consequence without considering Marx's ideas and what has happened to them. So important are they on a world scale that even of nations in which they have played little or no role, we must ask: Why not? And to ask and to answer such questions are among the most fruitful and revealing of endeavors.

To come to grips with marxism, whether that of the young Marx or of yesterday's Moscow slogan, forces us to confront: (1) every public issue of the modern world; (2) every great problem of social studies; (3) every moral

1. For convenience, I do not distinguish in this book between Marx and Engels, except on a few points of dubious interpretation made by Engels after Marx's death, I treat them "as one," under the name "Marx" and their work as "classic marxism." I do not know whether it is possible to sort out the contributions of each, but I rather think it is not a very useful thing to attempt. At any rate, it cannot be part of the work of such a short book as this one. For statements of their respective contributions, as well as much else about them, see the standard biographies: Franz Mehring, *Karl Marx* (New York, 1935) and Gustav Mayer, *Friedrich Engels* (London, 1936).

trouble encountered by men of sensibility today. Moreover, when we try to observe and to think within the marxist point of view, we are bound to see these issues, problems and troubles as inherently connected. We are forced to adopt an over-all view of the world, and of ourselves in relation to it.

1

In the present quarter of the twentieth-century, the soviet bloc embraces a variety of peoples which rival the British Empire at its height. But these peoples are developing at a faster historic tempo and in more thoroughgoing ways than those of the British Empire ever did. In every world region, intellectuals and politicians have for a hundred years thought and acted, and are now thinking and acting, in the name of Marx. Among the fabulous characters who participate in these circles, movements, parties, states there are: fanatics, but also cautious scholars; opportunists, but also altogether reliable men; men of loose life and rigorous reason, but also men of strict conformity and loose orthodox thought; pedantic bores, but also first-rate intellectuals and consummate politicians. There are leaders of unimaginable boldness, but also followers made silent and inactive by cowardice and threats.

What do these men have in common? Certainly not any "class position": this has varied greatly, despite a common self-identification with "working classes." Certainly not universal intelligence: many have fifth-rate minds. They have in common allegiance to a set of changing ideas.

For some men this allegiance has been and is an expedient cloak in the struggle for power, career, and privilege. But the marxists also include men and women who have taken these ideas so seriously that their external biographies as well as their inner lives have been shaped by them. Even the most opportunistic has been forced by his colleagues to consider expediencies in terms of principle. "The unity of theory and practice" is a marxist phrase which dictates to all its theorists and practitioners. Thus regardless of motive and use, ideas have mattered to the marxists and, in one way or another, these ideas are derived from what Karl Marx wrote.

What is at the heart of what he wrote? Why have his ideas had—and why do they have—such a deep and wide appeal to men and women of such different backgrounds? Although they appeal little to most people who live in advanced capitalist nations and who more likely than not have never been hungry or chronically ill by virtue of neglect and poverty, most of mankind is still subject to such conditions of life, and death. To them, as is frequently asserted, marxism is basically a politics of hunger; to them, that is "what marxism is all about." This ideological message underlies marxism as a political and intellectual force, yesterday and today. In marxism, ideal and agency, theory and ideology can be very closely connected, even confused; and the first three—ideal, agency, theory—can readily be converted into the Ideological Message of Marxism:

You do not have to be poor any longer. Everywhere men have always lived as exploiters and exploited. As long as the means of producing goods were not sufficient to provide for all, perhaps this evil condition was inevitable.

It is no longer inevitable.

You do not have to be poor.

You are poor not because of anything you have done or anything you have failed to do, not because of original Sin or the Will of God or because of bad luck. You are poor because of economic and political conditions. These conditions are called capitalism. At first, capitalism was a great progressive force in man's history; under it men built enormous facilities for the production of all the things they need.

You are poor and you are exploited and you are going to be exploited as long as capitalism prevails. For capitalism has ceased to be a progressive force; it has become an obstacle to Progress, to your progress. It enters into every feature of human life, private and public, and all of them it corrupts. Capitalism is the system that exploits you.

You do not have to be poor. The conditions that make you poor can be changed. They are going to be changed. Inside capitalism itself are the seeds of its own destruction. What will happen, whether you are yet aware of it or not, is that you are going to make a revolution. Those who rule over you and keep you poor will be overthrown. That is the next step forward in human progress. You are going to take that step. By the revolution you can abolish capitalism, root, stock and branch. By the revolution you can eliminate once and for all the exploitation of man by man; you can enter into a socialist society in which mankind conquers nature. And no man any longer will know poverty and exploitation.

It is rather difficult not to go on—so compelling is the message! And so it should be. Never mind now about the facts, the theories, the predictions: the hopes and ideals expressed in this message are firmly a part of Western civilization. Little wonder that clergymen regularly complain that the communists "have stolen our stuff." [2] Indeed, marxism as ideology is less a message than a "gospel," which in the literal sense means "glad tidings."

To understand this gospel, one must understand whom it attracts. The big answer to that question today is: it attracts many intelligent and alert people in the impoverished countries. Most of the world's population live in such hungry countries, and these countries are now very much in commotion. There is no longer any "unchanging East," no "primitively static Africa," no Latin America sitting in stupor in the sun. Their peoples are clamoring for the fruits of industrialization, and with good historical reason many reject the capitalist way of achieving them. Several varieties of marxism are among the models of industrialization available to them.

The Bolshevik Revolution offers a compelling model of development and modernization. Therein lies its present historical significance—at least if one believes that the leading long-run problem in world politics is what model the underdeveloped nations and territories will choose, economically, culturally, and politically. Marxism speaks to, as well as for, these people and in doing so, competes with liberalism.

The work of Marx taken as a whole is a savage, sustained indictment of one alleged injustice: that the profit, the comfort, the luxury of one man is paid for by the loss, the misery, the denial of another. If in societies founded in his name, as well as in capitalist societies of a sort he never knew, many have come to believe Marx mistaken about the form and the mechanism of this injustice, still for tens of millions of others, the indictment stands. Even it has to be reworked, extended, revised, even thor-

2. See, for example, Bishop James A. Pike, *New York Times*, 24 February 1961.

oughly remade, nonetheless it seems to many people an enormous truth.

There is one characteristic of marxism which I have already noted: in it ideal and agency are closely combined, even confused. Rather than proclaim ideals in abstraction, Marx argued that they *are* going to be realized because of the necessary development of capitalist society: the development of the struggles of the proletariat, climaxed by the proletarian revolution. This argument will be examined in later chapters. Here we need only note that this insistence on determination, as an intellectual strategy, provides much of the moral force and cogency of the ideological message.

2

The ideas of Marx and of other marxists are now an official part of the sino-soviet political world. But let us not forget that they are also an unofficial part of the world of any honest scholarship. It is the intellectual scope and brilliance of its theoretical content, as well as the political force of its ideological message, that has indeed made of Marx's ideas a specter that at once haunts and attracts the non-marxist world.

The history of social thought since the mid-nineteenth century cannot be understood without understanding the ideas of Marx. Without question, Marx belongs to the classic tradition in sociological thinking; in fact, it is difficult to name any other one thinker who within that tradition is as influential and as pivotal as he. He contributed the very categories dealt with by virtually all significant social thinkers of our immediate past. As is frequently remarked and often forgotten, the development of social inquiry and of political philosophy over the last century has in many ways been a more or less continuous dialogue with Marx. Often this sociological dialogue has been hidden, even unrecognized, by the several generations of thinkers involved in it; unrecognized or not, it has been a major thread in the historical development of the social thought of our times.

This is not to say that the last hundred years of sociological thinking has been politically marxist. Of course not. Max Weber, the foremost academic elaborator of Marx, was a classic liberal. Much of the work of Thorstein

Veblen may be considered an astute reworking of Marx for the academic American public of his day—and for the New Deal of the 1930's. Veblen's politics are masked by ironic distaste for the pronouncement of ideals, but probably he was at heart an anarchist and syndicalist. Karl Mannheim, with his sociology of knowledge, did more than anyone else to elaborate the theory of ideology, transforming Marx's unfinished insights into a sophisticated and indispensable method of inquiry. From his beginning as a revolutionary in Hungary, Mannheim, in Frankfurt and later in London, trekked politically to the position of a left-liberal who remained an unreconstructed opponent of marxism.

Every generation that is intellectually at work extracts from the ideas that it inherits those it needs, and so it is with the ideas of Marx. Everyone free to accept and reject will make his own selection. What needs to be said is quite simple: Karl Marx was *the* social and political thinker of the nineteenth century. Within the classic tradition of sociology, he provides us with the most basic single framework for political and cultural reflection. Marx was not the sole source of this framework, and he did not complete a system that now stands closed and finished. He did not solve all of our problems; many of them he did not even know about.

Yet to study his work today and then come back to our own concerns is to increase our chances of confronting them with useful ideas and solutions. Certainly to master the body of Marx's work, explicitly accepting or rejecting or modifying what we find in it, is to experience in our own intellectual development the central themes of social and political thinking developed in the last hundred years.

3

Marx conceived of a truly comprehensive social science; indeed, his work attempts to *be* "social science" all by itself. No social phenomenon is exempt from the theoretical reach of the model he constructed, and many things not usually considered objects of social science, even today, are embraced by his conceptions and theories. That is the first *contemporary* relevance of the legacy Marx has left: his encyclopedic scope, the reach of his attempted explanations. It ought, I believe, to be an especially attractive challenge, given the state into which much social study, especially in the United States, has lately fallen.

Marx is not inhibited by the boundary lines of academic disciplines or specialties. In his work, what are now called political science, social psychology, economics, sociology and anthropology are all used. They are used in such a way as to form a master view of (1) the structure of a society in all its realms; (2) the mechanics of the history of that society, and (3) the roles of individuals in all their psychological nuances.

Moreover, in marxism the elements of capitalist society form a working model of society; they are not left to interact in some loose and vague way. Rightly or wrongly, they are constructed, within the model, in close and specific interconnections with one another, and casual weights are assigned to each of them. These imputed connections and weights are of course the specific theories of Marx. Taken together, these theories make up his most general social theory: the theory of historical change and the place of revolution within it.

This structural view of a total society results from a classic sociological technique of thinking. With its aid Marx translated the abstract conceptions of contemporary political economy into the concrete terms of the social relations of men. Thus he related economic conceptions to sociological ones to form a model of modern bourgeois society. He then used this working model to develop a number of theories about what was happening within it and what was going to happen to it.[3]

This is a very important point—this analytic distinction between model and theory. A *model* is a more or less systematic inventory of the elements to which we must pay attention if we are to understand something. It is not true or false; it is useful and adequate to varying degrees. A *theory,* in contrast, is a statement which can be proved true or false, about the casual weight and the relations of the elements of a model.

Only in terms of this distinction can we understand why Marx's work is truly great, and also why it contains so much that is erroneous, ambiguous, or inadequate. His model is what is great; that is what is alive in marxism. He

3. For the point of view taken here toward structural and historical sociology, see *Images of Man,* from which I have adapted several points made here; cf. also *The Sociological Imagination.*

provides a classic machinery for thinking about man, society, and history. That is the reason there have been so many quite different revivals of marxism. Marx is often wrong, in part because he died in 1883, in part because he did not use his own machinery as carefully as we now can, and in part because some of the machinery itself needs to be refined and even redesigned. After all, obsolescence is part of history; as such it is part of the history of marxism.

Neither the truth nor the falsity of Marx's theories confirm the adequacy of his model. It can be used for the construction of many theories; it can be used for correcting errors in theories made with its aid. It is itself open to modifications, in ways that make it more useful as an analytic tool and empirically closer to the run of facts.

4

Marx took the view, and practiced it, that history is the shank of all well-conducted studies of man and society. In his working model of nineteenth century capitalism, in which he designates the characteristics of each institutional and psychological feature, he states the historical function that he thinks each fulfills. He uses this model not merely as "an anatomy of civil society" but in an active historical way to indicate the changing relations of the elements and forces of which the model is composed. His work thus contains a model, not only of a total social structure, but also of that structure in historical motion.

He is not concerned with the knife-edge present nor with the static model as such. He is concerned with trends having the span of a historically specific epoch, that of the "industrial capitalism" of his time. He projects trends he believes to be "secular," and so decisive, according to his model of social structure and his theory of history. Thus he presents an image of the probable future. This principle of historical specificity is, first, a rule for social inquiry and reflection; it is, second, a method for criticizing polemically other theories and conceptions; and, third, it is a theory of the nature of social life and of history.

1. As a rule of inquiry, it directs us to formulate regularities and trends we find in terms of a specific epoch, and it cautions us not to generalize beyond the confines of this epoch. We do not study "the general conditions of all social life"; we study "the specific historical form assumed

by them in present day bourgeois society,"[4] From this
principle it follows that we may not project quantitative
changes of the present into a future epoch, nor retrospec-
tively interpret past epochs in the terms of the present one.
We must think "epochally." Each epoch is a new type of
society; it creates new types of men and women, and neither
the society nor the men can be understood in terms of the
old epoch. All we can do is study the present epoch in an
attempt to discern within it those tendencies leading into
the next epoch.

2. As a method for criticizing conceptions, the principle
of historical specificity leads us to see that conceptions and
categories are not eternal, but are relative to the epoch
which they concern. They are historically specific: Thus,
"property" is one thing in a society of small entrepreneurs;
it is another thing in a society dominated by big corporations. Similarly, "freedom," "rent," "work," "population,"
"family," "culture," carry different meanings according to
the epoch with reference to which they are used. Perhaps
the fundamental charge against "bourgeois thinkers" made
by Marx is the unhistorical character of their very categories of thought.

3. As a theory of the nature of society and of history,
the principle of historical specificity holds that the history
of mankind may be, indeed must be, divided into epochs,
each defined by the structural form it assumes. All we can
mean by "laws" are the structural mechanics of change
characteristic of one epoch or another. Within an epoch
there are evolutionary changes; between one epoch and another, revolution. In world history, human society thus
evolves from one revolution to another, each revolution
marking off a new epoch. And each epoch must be examined as an independent historical formation, in terms of
categories suitable to it.

5

Marx's view of "the nature of human nature," his image
of man as he is and of how he might be, is worked out
with close reference to given types of society and specific
epochs of history. His views of human nature are fragmentary, it seems to me, but most of his assumptions about
the nature of man are in line with the most adequate as-

4. Cf. Karl Korsch, *Karl Marx* (New York, 1938), p. 38.

sumptions of contemporary social psychology. He emphasized that very little about society and history can be explained by reference to the innate limits or capacities of "human nature" as such. Human nature, according to Marx, is not an unchanging, inevitable anchor-point for any existing or possible institution. It is very much involved with the nature of specific societies—as well as with strata within societies. The principle of historical specificity includes the nature of human nature.

Thus of Jeremy Bentham, Marx writes: "With the driest naïveté, he takes the modern shopkeeper, especially the English shopkeeper, as the normal man. Whatever is useful to this queer normal man, and to his world, is absolutely useful. This yard-measure he applies to past, present, and future." [5]

Elsewhere and going further, Marx asserts: "This antagonism between modern industry and science, on the one side, modern misery and corruption on the other side, this antagonism between the forces of production and the social conditions of our epoch, is a tangible, overwhelming, and undeniable fact. Some parties may wish to get rid also of modern conflicts . . . [But] we know that the new form of social production, to achieve the good life, needs only 'new men.' " [6]

"Man" has an almost infinite potential. In his assumptions and reflections Marx carried forward the eighteenth-century tradition, in which man's human nature was considered in terms of a moral philosophy. In human nature, freedom and reason coincide, and both will flower in ways not before known when, under communism, "man" conquers nature and all the means for sustenance and for human growth are available to everyone. Just as Adam Smith's *Theory of Moral Sentiments* reminds us of George Herbert Mead's "social behaviorism," so Marx's 1844 manuscripts and other earlier works remind us of the most contemporary social psychology.

The conception of what social inquiry properly consists of, its aims and its methods, alone makes the work of Marx relevant as a framework for contemporary social inquiry. If a working philosophy is one that helps men to

5. *Capital, op. cit.* 668n.
6. Quoted by Karl Löwith, *Meaning in History* (Chicago, 1950), pp. 36-37.

work, then the marxism of Karl Marx is very much a working philosophy. By the use of his guidelines, especially the principle of historical specificity, we shall try to indicate how relevant classic marxism itself is to a critique of marxism today—in short, how open to revision within his own system the ideas of Marx really are.

3. The Classic Thinkers

The work of Marx as he left it when he died in 1883 is not very neat and nowhere does he summarize his ideas in a complete and systematic way. Moreover, much of what Marx wrote was written as polemics against the ideas of other men—many of them having today only slight historical interest. As with most complicated thinkers, there is no *one* Marx. The various presentations of his work which we can construct from his books, pamphlets, articles, letters written at different times in his own development, depend upon our point of interest, and we may not take any one of them to be The Real Marx. It is interesting to compare what thinkers from later generations, schools and parties have selected and stressed from the writings of Marx and Engels. A valuable book could easily be written about it. There is Marx the agitator—and accordingly compilations of the ideological message; Marx the economist—and so reprintings and condensations of *Capital;* and Marx the historian—more often neglected, perhaps, than any other. Of late, Marx the philosopher of history, the political sociologist, and The Young Marx as humanist and moralist, have been stressed. There is indeed no one Marx; every student must earn his own Marx.

Yet if the reader asks for the essentials of his ideas in a few sentences, no one has done it any better than Marx himself; here is what we may call his "summary," from the famous Preface to *A Contribution to the Critique of Political Economy.* In my next chapter, various terms which Marx uses here will be explained.

KARL MARX: *The Materialist Conception of History* [1]

I was led by my studies to the conclusion that legal re-

---

1. From *A Contribution to the Critique of Political Economy* (Chicago, 1904), pp. 11-13. First published 1859.

lations as well as forms of state could neither be understood by themselves, nor explained by the so-called general progress of the human mind, but that they are rooted in the material conditions of life, which are summed up by Hegel after the fashion of the English and French of the eighteenth century under the name "civic society;" the anatomy of that civic society is to be sought in political economy. . . . The general conclusion at which I arrived and which, once reached, continued to serve as the leading thread in my studies, may be briefly summed up as follows.

In the social production which men carry on they enter into definite relations that are indispensable and independent of their will; these relations of production correspond to a definite stage of development of their material powers of production. The sum total of these relations of production constitutes the economic structure of society—the real foundation, on which rise legal and political superstructures and to which correspond definite forms of social consciousness. The mode of production in material life determines the general character of the social, political and spiritual processes of life. It is not the consciousness of men that determines their existence, but, on the contrary, their social existence determines their consciousness. At a certain stage of their development, the material forces of production in society come in conflict with the existing relations of production, or—what is but a legal expression for the same thing—with the property relations within which they had been at work before. From forms of development of the forces of production these relations turn into their fetters. Then comes the period of social revolution. With the change of the economic foundation the entire immense superstructure is more or less rapidly transformed. In considering such transformations the distinction should always be made between the material transformation of the economic conditions of production which can be determined with the precision of natural science, and the legal, political, religious, esthetic or philosophic— in short ideological forms in which men become conscious of this conflict and fight it out. Just as our opinion of an individual is not based on what he thinks of himself, so can we not judge of such a period of transformation by its own consciousness; on the contrary, this consciousness must rather be explained from the contradictions of material life, from the existing conflict between the social forces of production and the relations of production. No social order ever disappears before all the productive forces, for which there is room in it, have been developed; and new higher relations of production never appear before the material conditions of their existence have matured in the womb of the old society. Therefore, mankind always takes up only such problems as it can solve; since, looking at the matter more closely, we will always find that the problem itself arises only when the material conditions necessary for its solution already exist or are at least in the process of formation. In broad outlines we can designate the Asiatic, the ancient, the feudal, and the modern bourgeois methods of production as so many epochs in the progress of the economic formation of society. The bourgeois relations of production are the last antagonistic form of the social process of production—antagonistic not in the sense of individual antagonism, but of one arising from conditions surrounding the life of individuals in society; at the same time the productive forces developing in the womb of bourgeois society create the material conditions for the solution of that antagonism. This social formation constitutes, therefore, the closing chapter of the prehistoric stage of human society. . . .

KARL MARX: *"The Method of Scientific Socialism"* [2]

After a quotation from the preface to my *Critique of Political Economy*, where I discuss the materialistic basis of my method, the writer goes on: "The one thing which is of moment to Marx is to find the law of the phenomena with whose investigation he is concerned; and not only is that law of moment to him, which governs these phenomena, in so far as they have a definite form and mutual connection within a given historical period. Of still greater moment to him is the law of their variation, of their development, i.e., of their transition from one form into another, from one series of connections into a different one. This law once discovered, he investigates in detail the ef-

2. From the preface to the second German edition, *Capital, op. cit.,* pp. 22-25. "The writer" refers to a reviewer, F. F. Kaufman.

fects in which it manifests itself in social life. Consequently, Marx only troubles himself about one thing; to show, by rigid scientific investigation, the necessity of successive determinate orders of social conditions, and to establish, as impartially as possible, the facts that serve him for fundamental starting points. For this it is quite enough, if he proves, at the same time, both the necessity of the present order of things, and the necessity of another order into which the first must inevitably pass over; and this all the same, whether men believe or do not believe it, whether they are conscious or unconscious of it. Marx treats the social movement as a process of natural history, governed by laws not only independent of human will, consciousness and intelligence, but rather, on the contrary, determining that will, consciousness and intelligence. . . .

If in the history of civilization the conscious element plays a part so subordinate, then it is self-evident that a critical inquiry whose subject-matter is civilization, can, less than anything else, have for its basis any form of, or any result of, consciousness. That is to say, that not the idea, but the material phenomenon alone can serve as its starting-point. Such an inquiry will confine itself to the confrontation and the comparison of a fact, not with ideas, but with another fact. For this inquiry, the one thing of moment is, that both facts be investigated as accurately as possible, and that they actually form, each with respect to the other, different momenta of an evolution; but most important of all is the rigid analysis of the series of successions, of the sequences and concatenations in which the different stages of such an evolution present themselves.

But it will be said, the general laws of economic life are one and the same, no matter whether they are applied to the present or the past. This Marx directly denies. According to him, such abstract laws do not exist. On the contrary, in his opinion every historical period has laws of its own. . . . As soon as society has outlived a given period of development, and is passing over from one given stage to another, it begins to be subject also to other laws. In a word, economic life offers us a phenomenon analogous to the history of evolution in other branches of biology. The old economists misunderstood the nature of economic laws when they likened them to the laws of physics and chemistry. A more thorough analysis of phenomena shows that social organisms differ among themselves as fundamentally as plants or animals. Nay, one and the same phenomenon falls under quite different laws in consequence of the different structure of those organisms as a whole, of the variations of their individual organs, of the different conditions in which those organs function, &c. Marx, e.g., denies that the law of population is the same at all times and in all places. He asserts, on the contrary, that every stage of development has its own law of population. . . . With the varying degree of development of productive power, social conditions and the laws governing them vary too. Whilst Marx sets himself the task of following and explaining from this point of view the economic system established by the sway of capital, he is only formulating, in a strictly scientific manner, the aim that every accurate investigation into economic life must have.

The scientific value of such an inquiry lies in the disclosing of the special laws that regulate the origin, existence, development, and death of a given social organism and its replacement by another and higher one. And it is this value that, in point of fact, Marx's book has."

Whilst the writer pictures what he takes to be actually my method, in this striking and [as far as concerns my own application of it] generous way, what else is he picturing but the dialectic method?

Of course the method of presentation must differ in form from that of inquiry. The latter has to appropriate the material in detail, to analyze its different forms of development, to trace out their inner connection. Only after this work is done, can the actual movement be adequately described. If this is done successfully, if the life of the subject-matter is ideally reflected as in a mirror, then it may appear as if we had before us a mere a priori construction.

My dialectic method is not only different from the Hegelian, but is its direct opposite. To Hegel, the life-process of the human brain, i.e., the process of thinking, which, under the name of "the Idea," he even transforms into an independent subject, is the demiurgos of the real world, and the real world is only the external, phenomenal form of "the Idea." With me, on the contrary, the ideal is nothing else than the material world reflected by the human mind, and translated into forms of thought.

KARL MARX: *Manifesto of the Communist Party* [3]

A specter haunts Europe—the specter of communism. All the powers of old Europe have entered into a holy alliance in order to lay this specter: pope and tsar; Metternich and Guizot; French radicals and German police.

Where is the opposition party which has not been stigmatized as communist by those who wield power? Where is the opposition party which has not hurled back this scandalous charge of communism in the teeth of its adversaries, whether progressive or reactionary?

Two things may be deduced from this:

1. Communism is already acknowledged by all the European powers to be itself a power.

2. It is time for the communists to make open proclamation of their outlook, their aims, their trends; and to confront the old wives' tale of a communist specter with a manifesto of their own party.

To this end, communists of various nationalities have foregathered in London and have drafted the following manifesto, which will be published in English, French, German, Italian, Flemish, and Danish.

1. *Bourgeois and Proletarians*

The history of all human society, past and present, has been the history of class struggles.

Freeman and slave, patrician and plebeian, baron and serf, guild-burgess and journeyman—in a word, oppressor and oppressed—stood in sharp opposition each to the other. They carried on perpetual warfare, sometimes masked, sometimes open and acknowledged; a warfare that invariably ended, either in a revolutionary change in the whole structure of society, or else in the common ruin of the contending classes.

In the earlier epochs of history, we find almost everywhere a complete subdivision of society into different ranks, a manifold gradation of social positions. In ancient Rome, we have: patricians, knights, plebeians, slaves. In the Middle Ages, we have: feudal lords, vassals, guild-bur-

3. Parts 1 and 2 Ryazanoff edition (New York, 1930), pp. 25-54. First published 1848. Reprinted by permission of International Publishers Co., Inc.

gesses, journeymen, serfs; and within each of these classes there existed, in almost every instance, further gradations.

Modern bourgeois society, rising out of the ruins of feudal society, did not make an end of class antagonisms. It merely set up new classes in place of the old; new conditions of oppression; new embodiments of struggle.

Our own age, the bourgeois age, is distinguished by this —that it has simplified class antagonisms. More and more, society is splitting into two great hostile camps, into two great and directly contraposed classes: bourgeoisie and proletariat.

From the serfs of the Middle Ages sprang the burgesses of the first towns; and from these burgesses sprang the first elements of the bourgeoisie.

The discovery of America and the circumnavigation of Africa opened up new fields to the rising bourgeoisie. The East Indian and the Chinese markets, the colonization of America, trade with the colonies, the multiplication of the means of exchange and of commodities in general, gave an unprecedented impetus to commerce, navigation, and manufacturing industry, thus fostering the growth of the revolutionary element in decaying feudal society.

Hitherto industrial production had been carried on by the guilds that had grown up in feudal society; but this method could not cope with the increasing demands of the new markets. Manufacture replaced guild production. The guildsmen were elbowed out of the way by the industrial middle class; the division of labor between the various guilds or corporations was superseded by the division of labor in the individual workshop.

The expansion of the markets continued, for demand was perpetually increasing. Even manufacture was no longer able to cope with it. Then steam and machinery revolutionized industrial production. Manufacture was replaced by modern large-scale industry; the place of the industrial middle class was taken by the industrial millionaires, the chiefs of fully equipped industrial armies, the modern bourgeoisie.

Large-scale industry established the world market, for which the discovery of America had paved the way. The result of the development of the world market was an immeasurable growth of commerce, navigation and land communication. These changes reacted in their turn upon industry; and in proportion as industry, commerce, navigation and railways expanded, so did the bourgeoisie develop, increasing its capitalized resources and forcing into the background all the classes that lingered on as relics from the Middle Ages.

Thus we see that the modern bourgeoisie is itself the product of a long course of development, of a series of revolutions in the methods of production and the means of communication.

Each step in the development of the bourgeoisie was accompanied by a corresponding political advance. An oppressed class under the dominion of the feudal lords, it became an armed and self-governing association in the commune; here an independent urban republic, there the taxable "third estate" under the monarchy; in the days of manufacture, the bourgeoisie was the counterpoise of the nobility in the semi-feudal or in the absolute monarchy and was the cornerstone of the great monarchies in general—to fight its way upward, in the end, after the rise of large-scale industry and the establishment of the world market, to exclusive political hegemony in the modern representative State. The modern State authority is nothing more than a committee for the administration of the consolidated affairs of the bourgeois class as a whole.

The bourgeoisie has played an extremely revolutionary role upon the stage of history.

Wherever the bourgeoisie has risen to power, it has destroyed all feudal, patriarchal, and idyllic relationships. It has ruthlessly torn asunder the motley feudal ties that bound men to their "natural superiors"; it has left no other bond betwixt man and man but crude self-interest and unfeeling "cash payment." It has drowned pious zeal, chivalrous enthusiasm, and humdrum sentimentalism in the chill waters of selfish calculation. It has degraded personal dignity to the level of exchange value; and in place of countless dearly-bought chartered freedoms, it has set up one solitary unscrupulous freedom—freedom of trade. In a word, it has replaced exploitation veiled in religious and political illusions by exploitation that is open, unashamed, direct, and brutal.

The bourgeoisie has robbed of their haloes various occupations hitherto regarded with awe and veneration. Doctor, lawyer, priest, poet, and scientist, have become its wage-laborers.

The bourgeoisie has torn the veil of sentiment from

the family relationship, which has become an affair of money and nothing more.

The bourgeoisie has disclosed that the brute force of the Middle Ages (that brute force so greatly admired by the reactionaries) found a fitting counterpart in excessive indolence. The bourgeoisie was the first to show us what human activity is capable of achieving. It has executed works more marvelous than the building of Egyptian pyramids, Roman aqueducts, and Gothic cathedrals; it has carried out expeditions surpassing by far the tribal migrations and the Crusades.

The bourgeoisie cannot exist without incessantly revolutionizing the instruments of production; and, consequently, the relations of production; and, therefore, the totality of social relations. Conversely, for all earlier industrial classes, the preservation of the old methods of production was the first condition of existence. That which characterizes the bourgeois epoch in contradistinction to all others is a continuous transformation of production, a perpetual disturbance of social conditions, everlasting insecurity and movement. All stable and stereotyped relations, with their attendant train of ancient and venerable prejudices and opinions, are swept away, and the newly formed becomes obsolete before it can petrify. All that has been regarded as solid, crumbles into fragments; all that was looked upon as holy, is profaned; at long last, people are compelled to gaze open-eyed at their position in life and their social relations.

Urged onward by the need for an ever-expanding market, the bourgeoisie invades every quarter of the globe. It occupies every corner; forms settlements and sets up means of communication here, there, and everywhere.

By the exploitation of the world market, the bourgeoisie has given a cosmopolitan character to production and consumption in every land. To the despair of the reactionaries, it has deprived industry of its national foundation. Of the old-established national industries, some have already been destroyed and others are day by day undergoing destruction. They are dislodged by new industries, whose introduction is becoming a matter of life and death for all civilized nations: by industries which no longer depend upon the homeland for their raw materials, but draw these from the remotest spots; and by industries whose products are consumed, not only in the country of manufacture, but the wide world over. Instead of the old wants, satisfied by the products of native industry, new wants appear, wants which can only be satisfied by the products of distant lands and unfamiliar climes. The old local and national self-sufficiency and isolation are replaced by a system of universal intercourse, of all-round interdependence of the nations. We see this in intellectual production no less than in material. The intellectual products of each nation are now the common property of all. National exclusiveness and particularism are fast becoming impossible. Out of the manifold national and local literatures, a world literature arises.

By rapidly improving the means of production and by enormously facilitating communication, the bourgeoisie drags all the nations, even the most barbarian, into the orbit of civilization. Cheap wares form the heavy artillery with which it batters down Chinese walls and compels the most obstinate of barbarians to overcome their hatred of the foreigner. It forces all the nations, under pain of extinction, to adopt the capitalist method of production; it constrains them to accept what is called civilization, to become bourgeois themselves. In short, it creates a world after its own image.

The bourgeoisie has subjected the countryside to the rule of the town. It has brought huge cities into being, vastly increasing the urban population as compared with the rural, and thus removing a large proportion of the inhabitants from the seclusion and ignorance of rural life. Moreover, just as it has made the country dependent on the town, so it has made the barbarian and the semi-barbarian nations dependent upon the civilized nations, the peasant peoples upon the industrial peoples, the East upon the West.

More and ever more, the bourgeoisie puts an end to the fractionization of the means of production, of property, and of population. It has agglomerated population, centralized the means of production, and concentrated ownership into the hands of the few. Political centralization has necessarily ensued. Independent or loosely federated provinces, with disparate interests, laws, governments, and customs tariffs, have been consolidated into a single nation, with one government, one code of laws, one national class interest, one fiscal frontier.

During its reign of scarce a century, the bourgeoisie

has created more powerful, more stupendous forces of production than all preceding generations rolled into one. The subjugation of the forces of nature, the invention of machinery, the application of chemistry to industry and agriculture, steamships, railways, electric telegraphs, the clearing of whole continents for cultivation, the making of navigable waterways, huge populations springing up as if by magic out of the earth—what earlier generations had the remotest inkling that such productive powers slumbered within the womb of associated labor?

We have seen that the means of production and communication which served as the foundation for the development of the bourgeoisie, had been generated in feudal society. But the time came, at a certain stage in the development of these means of production and communication, when the conditions under which the production and the exchange of goods were carried on in feudal society, when the feudal organization of agriculture and manufacture, when (in a word) feudal property relations, were no longer adequate for the productive forces as now developed. They hindered production instead of helping it. They had become fetters on production; they had to be broken; they were broken. Their place was taken by free competition, in conjunction with the social and political system appropriate to free competition—the economic and political dominance of the bourgeois class.

A similar movement is going on under our very eyes. Bourgeois conditions of production and communication; bourgeois property relations; modern bourgeois society, which has conjured up such mighty means of production and communication—these are like a magician who is no longer able to control the spirits his spells have summoned from the nether world. For decades, the history of industry and commerce has been nothing other than the history of the rebellion of the modern forces of production against the contemporary conditions of production, against the property relations which are essential to the life and the supremacy of the bourgeoisie. Enough to mention the commercial crises which, in their periodic recurrence, become more and more menacing to the existence of bourgeois society. These commercial crises periodically lead to the destruction of a great part, not only of the finished products of industry, but also of the extant forces of production. During the crisis, a social epidemic breaks out, an epidemic that would have seemed absurdly paradoxical in all earlier phases of the world's history—an epidemic of overproduction. Temporarily, society relapses into barbarism. It is as if a famine, or a universal, devastating war, had suddenly cut off the means of subsistence. Industry and commerce have, to all seeming, been utterly destroyed. Why is this? Because society has too much civilization, too abundant means of subsistence, too much industry, too much commerce. The productive forces at the disposal of the community no longer serve to foster bourgeois property relations. Having grown too powerful for these relations, they are hampered thereby; and when they overcome the obstacle, they spread disorder throughout bourgeois society and endanger the very existence of bourgeois property. The bourgeois system is no longer able to cope with the abundance of the wealth it creates. How does the bourgeoisie overcome these crises? On the one hand by the compulsory annihilation of a quantity of the productive forces; on the other, by the conquest of new markets and the more thorough exploitation of old ones. With what results? The results are that the way is paved for more widespread and more disastrous crises and that the capacity for averting such crises is lessened.

The weapons with which the bourgeoisie overthrew feudalism are now being turned against the bourgeoisie itself.

But the bourgeoisie has not only forged the weapons that will slay it; it has also engendered the men who will use these weapons—the modern workers, the *Proletarians*.

In proportion as the bourgeoisie, that is to say capital, has developed, in the same proportion has the proletariat developed—the modern working class, the class of those who can only live so long as their work increases capital. These workers, who are forced to sell themselves piecemeal, are a commodity like any other article of commerce, and are consequently exposed to all the vicissitudes of competition and to all the fluctuations of the market.

Owing to the ever more extended use of machinery and the division of labor, the work of these proletarians has completely lost its individual character and therewith has forfeited all its charm for the workers. The worker has become a mere appendage to a machine; a person from whom nothing but the simplest, the most monotonous, and the most easily learned manipulations are expected. The cost of production of a worker therefore amounts to little more than the cost of the means of subsistence he needs for his upkeep and for the propagation of his race. Now, the price of a commodity, labor not excepted, is equal to the cost of producing it. Wages therefore decrease in proportion as the repulsiveness of the labor increases. Nay more; in proportion as the use of machinery and the division of labor increases, so does the burden of labor increase—whether by the prolongation of working hours or by an increase in the amount of work exacted from the wage-earner in a given time (as by speeding-up the machinery, etc.)

Modern industry has transformed the little workshop of the patriarchal master into the huge factory of the industrial capitalist. Masses of workers, crowded together in the factory, are organized in military fashion. As rankers in the industrial army, they are placed under the supervision of a hierarchy of non-commissioned and commissioned officers. They are not merely the slaves of the bourgeois class, of the bourgeois State; they are in daily and hourly thraldom to the machine, to the foreman, and, above all, to the individual bourgeois manufacturer. The more frankly this despotism avows gain to be its object, the more petty, odious, and galling does it become.

In proportion as manual labor needs less skill and less strength, that is to say in proportion as modern industry develops, so the work of women and children tends to replace the work of men. Differences of age and sex no longer have any social significance for the working class. All are now mere instruments of labor, whose price varies according to age and sex.

When the worker has been paid his wages in hard cash, and for the nonce, has escaped from exploitation by the factory owner, he is promptly set upon by other members of the bourgeoisie: landlord, shopkeeper, pawnbroker, etc.

Those who have hitherto belonged to the lower middle class—small manufacturers, small traders, minor recipients of unearned income, handicraftsmen, and peasants—slip down, one and all, into the proletariat. They suffer this fate, partly because their petty capital is insufficient for the needs of large-scale industry and perishes in competition with the superior means of the great capitalists, and partly because their specialized skill is rendered valueless owing to the invention of new methods of production. Thus the proletariat is recruited from all classes of the population.

The proletariat passes through various stages of evolution, but its struggle against the bourgeoisie dates from its birth.

To begin with, the workers fight individually; then the workers in a single factory make common cause; then the workers at one trade combine throughout a whole locality against the particular bourgeois who exploits them. Their attacks are leveled, not only against bourgeois conditions of production, but also against the actual instruments of production; they destroy the imported wares which compete with the products of their own labor, they break up machinery, they set factories ablaze, they strive to regain the lost position of the medieval worker.

At this stage the workers form a disunited mass, scattered throughout the country, and severed into fragments by mutual competition. Such aggregation as occurs among them is not, so far, the outcome of their own inclination to unite, but is a consequence of the union of the bourgeoisie, which, for its own political purposes, must set the whole proletariat in motion, and can still do so at times. At this stage, therefore, the proletarians do not fight their own enemies; they attack the enemies of their enemies: the remnants of the absolute monarchy, the landlords, the non-industrial bourgeois, and the petty bourgeois. The whole historical movement is thus concentrated into the hands of the bourgeoisie; and every victory so gained is a bourgeois victory.

As industry develops, the proletariat does not merely increase in numbers: it is compacted into larger masses, its strength grows, it is more aware of that strength. Within the proletariat, interests and conditions of life become ever more equalized; for machinery obliterates more and more the distinctions between the various crafts, and forces wages down almost everywhere to the same low level. As a result of increasing competition among the bourgeois themselves, and of the consequent commercial crises, the workers' wages fluctuate more and more. The steadily accelerating improvement in machinery makes their livelihood increasingly precarious; more and more, the collisions between individual workers and individual bourgeois tend to assume the character of collisions between the respective classes. Thereupon the workers begin to form coalitions against the bourgeois, closing their ranks in order to maintain the rate of wages. They found durable associations which will be able to give them support whenever the struggle grows acute. Here and there, this struggle takes the form of riots.

From time to time the workers are victorious, though their victory is fleeting. The real fruit of their battles is not the immediate success, but their own continually increasing unification. Unity is furthered by the improvement in the means of communication which is effected by large-scale industry and which brings the workers of different localities into closer contact. Nothing more is needed to centralize the manifold local contests, which are all of the same type, into a national contest, a class struggle. Every class struggle is a political struggle. The medieval burghers, whose means of communication were at best the roughest of roads, took centuries to achieve unity. Thanks to railways, the modern proletariat can join forces within a few years.

This organization of the proletarians to form a class and therewith to form a political party, is perpetually being disintegrated by competition among the workers themselves. Yet it is incessantly reformed, becoming stronger, firmer, mightier. Profiting by dissensions among the bourgeoisie, it compels legislative recognition of some of the specifically working-class interests. That is how the Ten Hours Bill was secured in England.

Dissensions within the old order of society do much to promote the development of the proletariat. The bourgeoisie is ever at odds: at first with the aristocracy; then with those sections of the bourgeoisie whose interests conflict with the progress of industry; and at all times with the bourgeoisie of foreign lands. In these struggles, it is forced to appeal to the proletariat, to claim the help of the workers, and thus to draw them into the political arena. Consequently, the bourgeoisie hands on the elements of education to the proletariat, thus supplying weapons which will be turned against itself.

Furthermore, as we have seen, the advance of industry precipitates whole sections of the ruling class into the proletariat, or at least imperils their livelihood. These recruits to the proletariat also bring enlightenment into the ranks.

Finally, when the class war is about to be fought to a finish, disintegration of the ruling class and the old order of society becomes so active, so acute, that a small part of the ruling class breaks away to make common cause with the revolutionary class, the class which holds the future in its hands. Just as in former days part of the nobility went over to the bourgeoisie, so now part of the bourgeoisie goes over to the proletariat. Especially does this happen in the case of some of the bourgeois ideologists, who have achieved a theoretical understanding of the historical movement as a whole.

Among all the classes that confront the bourgeoisie to-day, the proletariat alone is really revolutionary. Other classes decay and perish with the rise of large-scale industry, but the proletariat is the most characteristic product of that industry.

The lower middle class—small manufacturers, small traders, handicraftsmen, peasant proprietors—one and all fight the bourgeoisie in the hope of safeguarding their existence as sections of the middle class. They are, therefore, not revolutionary, but conservative. Nay more; they are reactionary, for they are trying to make the wheels of history turn backward. If they ever become revolutionary, it is only because they are afraid of slipping down into the ranks of the proletariat; they are not defending their present interests, but their future interests; they are forsaking their own standpoint, in order to adopt that of the proletariat.

The slum proletariat, which is formed by the putrefaction of the lowest strata of the old society, is to some extent entangled in the movement of a proletarian revolution. On the whole, however, thanks to their conditions of life, the members of the slum proletariat are far more apt to become the venal tools of the forces of reaction.

For the proletariat, nothing is left of the social conditions that prevailed in the old society. The proletarian has no property; his relation to wife and children is utterly different from the family relations of bourgeois life; modern industrial labor, the modern enslavement by capital (the same in England as in France, in America as in Germany), has despoiled him of his national characteristics. Law, morality, and religion have become for him so many bourgeois prejudices, behind which bourgeois interests lurk in ambush.

The classes that have hitherto won to power have tried to safeguard their newly acquired position by subjecting society at large to the conditions by which they themselves gained their possessions. But the only way in which proletarians can get control of the productive forces of society is by making an end of their own previous method of acquisition, and therewith of all the extant methods of acquisition. Proletarians have nothing of their own to safeguard; it is their business to destroy all pre-existent private proprietary securities and private proprietary safeguards.

All earlier movements have been movements of minorities, or movements in the interest of minorities. The proletarian movement is an independent movement of the overwhelming majority in the interest of that majority. The proletariat, the lowest stratum of extant society, cannot raise itself, cannot stand erect upon its feet, without disrupting the whole superstructure comprising the strata which make up that society.

In form, though not in substance, the struggle of the proletariat against the bourgeoisie is primarily national. Of course, in any country, the proletariat has first of all to settle accounts with its own bourgeoisie.

In this outline sketch of the phases of proletarian development, we have traced the course of the civil war (which, though more or less concealed, goes on within extant society), have traced that civil war to the point at which it breaks out into open revolution, the point at which the proletariat, by forcibly overthrowing the bourgeoisie, establishes its own dominion.

As we have seen, all human society, past and present, has been based upon the antagonism between oppressing and oppressed classes. But before a class can be oppressed it must have a modicum of security for its vital conditions, so that within these it can at least carry on its slavish existence. In the days of serfdom, the serf worked his way up to membership of the commune; in like manner, under the yoke of feudal absolutism, the petty burgher became a bourgeois. But the modern worker, instead of rising as industry develops, sinks ever lower in the scale, and even falls into conditions of existence below those proper to his own class. The worker is becoming a pauper, and pauperism is increasing even more rapidly than population and wealth. This plainly shows that the bourgeoisie is no longer fitted to be the ruling class in society or to impose its own social system as supreme law for society at large. It is unfit to rule because it is incompetent to provide security for its slaves even within the confines of their slavish existence; because it has no option but to let them lapse into a condition in which it has to feed them instead of being fed by them. Society cannot continue to live under bourgeois rule. This means that the life of the bourgeoisie has become incompatible with the life of society.

The chief requisite for the existence and the rule of the bourgeoisie is the accumulation of wealth in the hands of private individuals; the formation and increase of capital. The chief requisite for capital is wage labor. Now, wage labor depends exclusively upon competition among the workers. The progress of industry, which the bourgeoisie involuntarily and passively promotes, substitutes for the isolation of the workers by mutual competition their revolutionary unification by association. Thus the development of large-scale industry cuts from under the feet of the bourgeoisie the ground upon which capitalism controls production and appropriates the products of labor. Before all, therefore, the bourgeoisie produces its own gravediggers. Its downfall and the victory of the proletariat are equally inevitable.

2. *Proletarians and Communists*

What position do communists occupy in relation to the general body of proletarians?

Communists do not form a separate party conflicting with other working-class parties.

They have no interests apart from those of the working class as a whole.

They do not put forward any sectarian principles in accordance with which they wish to mold the proletarian movement.

The only ways in which the communists are distinguished from other proletarian parties are these: on the one hand, in the various national struggles of the proletarians, they emphasize and champion the interests of the proletariat as a whole, those proletarian interests that are independent of nationality; and, on the other hand, in the various phases of evolution through which the struggle between the proletariat and the bourgeoisie passes, they always advocate the interests of the movement as a whole.

Thus, in actual practice, communists form the most resolute and persistently progressive section of the working-class parties of all lands whilst, as far as theory is concerned, being in advance of the general mass of the proletariat, they have come to understand the determinants of the proletarian movement and how to foresee its course and its general results.

The communists' immediate aims are identical with those of all other proletarian parties: organization of the proletariat on a class basis; destruction of bourgeois supremacy; conquest of political power by the proletariat.

The theories of the communists are not in any way based upon ideas or principles discovered or established by this or that universal reformer.

They serve merely to express in general terms the concrete circumstances of an actually existing class struggle, of a historical movement that is going on under our very eyes. The abolition of pre-existent property relations is not a process exclusively characteristic of communism.

Throughout the course of history, all property relations have been subject to continuous change, unceasing transformation.

For instance, the French Revolution abolished the feudal system of ownership and put the bourgeois system of ownership in its place.

The distinctive feature of communism is, not the abolition of property in general, but the abolition of bourgeois property.

Modern bourgeois property is, however, the final and most perfect expression of the method of production and appropriation which is based upon class conflicts, upon the spoliation of the many by the few.

In this sense, communists can sum up their theory in the pithy phrase: the abolition of private property.

We communists have been accused of wishing to abolish the property that has been acquired by personal exertion; the property that is supposed to be the foundation of individual liberty, activity, and independence.

Hard-won property, acquired by work; earned property! Are you talking about the petty-bourgeois or petty-peasant property which was the antecedent of bourgeois property? We do not need to abolish that kind of property, for industrial development has abolished it, or is doing so day by day.

Perhaps you are referring to modern bourgeois private property?

Does wage labor create property for the proletarianized worker? Not at all. It creates capital; and capital is the property which exploits wage labor, the property which can multiply itself—provided always that it produces a fresh supply of wage labor for further exploitation. Property in its contemporary form subsists upon the antagonism between capital and wage labor. Let us examine the two terms of this opposition.

The capitalist has, not merely a personal, but also a social position in the field of production. Capital is a collective product. It can only be set in motion by the joint activities of many members of society—in the last resort, only by the joint activities of all the members of society.

Thus capital is not a personal, but a social force.

Consequently, when capital is transformed into collective property, into property that belongs to all the members of society, the change is not effected by a transformation of private property into social property. The only change is in the social character of the property, which loses its class characteristics.

Now let us turn to wage labor.

The average price of wage labor is the minimum wage. This means the amount of the necessaries of life requisite to keep the worker alive as a worker. Therefore all that the worker can appropriate thanks to his activity suffices merely to support his bare existence and to reproduce his kind. We have no wish to abolish this personal appropriation of the product of labor, which is indispensable for the production of the immediate necessaries of life—an appropriation which does not leave any surplus that can be used as a means for wielding power over another's labor. All that we want to abolish is the deplorable character of this appropriation, of the system under which the worker lives only to increase capital, lives only in so far as his life serves the interest of the ruling class.

In bourgeois society, living labor is but a means for increasing the amount of stored labor. In communist society, stored labor is but a means for enlarging, enriching, furthering the existence of the workers.

In bourgeois society, therefore, the past rules the present; but in communist society the present rules the past. In bourgeois society, capital is independent and has individuality, whereas the living person is dependent and lacks individuality.

Yet the bourgeoisie declares that to make an end of this state of affairs means to make an end of individuality and freedom! That is true enough. Certainly we are concerned to make an end of bourgeois individuality, and bourgeois independence, and bourgeois freedom.

Within the framework of the bourgeois system of production, freedom means free trade, free buying and selling.

Of course, when trade disappears, free trade will disappear too. Chatter about free trade, like all the rest of the tall talk about freedom, has a meaning only as regards the trade that was not free, as regards the enslaved burgher of the Middle Ages. It has no bearing upon the communist abolition of trade, upon the communist abolition of the bourgeois system of production and of the bourgeoisie itself.

You are outraged because we wish to abolish private property. But, in extant society, private property has been abolished for nine-tenths of the population; it exists only because these nine-tenths have none of it. Thus you reproach us for wanting to abolish a form of property which can only exist on condition that the immense majority of the members of the community have no property at all.

In a word, you accuse us of wanting to abolish *your* property. Well, we do!

Your contention is that the individual will cease to exist from the moment when labor can no longer be transformed into capital, money, land rent; from the moment, in short, when it can no longer be transformed into a monopolizable social power; from the moment, that is to say, when individual property can no longer become bourgeois property.

You admit, therefore, that when you speak of individuals you are thinking solely of bourgeois, of the owners of bourgeois property. Certainly we wish to abolish individuals of that kind!

Communism does not deprive anyone of the power of appropriating social products. It only does away with the power of turning that appropriation to account as a means for the subjugation of another's labor.

The objection has been made that the abolition of private property will lead to the cessation of all activity and to the prevalence of universal sloth.

If this were true, bourgeois society would long since have perished of indolence; for in that society those who work do not acquire property, and those who acquire property do not work. The whole criticism amounts to nothing more than the tautologous statement that when there is no more capital there will be no more wage labor.

All the objections that have been urged against the communist method of producing and distributing material products, have likewise been urged against the communist method of producing and distributing mental products. Just as for the bourgeois the disappearance of class property is tantamount to the disappearance of production, so, for him, the disappearance of class culture is identical with the disappearance of culture as a whole.

The culture whose loss he bewails is, for the overwhelming majority, a culture which makes human beings into machines.

Please do not argue with us by using your bourgeois notions of liberty, culture, right, etc., as the standards by which to judge the abolition of bourgeois property. Your ideas are themselves the outcome of bourgeois methods of production and of bourgeois property relations; just as your "right" is only the will of your class writ large as law—a will whose trends are determined by the material conditions under which your class lives.

Your interests lead you to think that your methods of production, your property relations, are eternal laws of nature and reason, instead of being transient outcomes of the course of production. Earlier ruling classes, now fallen from power, shared this delusion. You understand that it was a delusion as regards the property of classical days, and as regards the property of feudal days; but you cannot see that it is no less a delusion as regards bourgeois property.

Abolition of the family! Even the extreme radicals hold up their hands in horror when they speak of this shameful communist proposal.

On what is the family, the bourgeois family, based to-day? On capital, on private gain. In its fully developed form, it exists only for the bourgeoisie, and it has two complements: one of these is the destruction of the family life of proletarians; the other is public prostitution.

Of course the bourgeois family will disappear with the disappearance of its complements, and the family and its complements will vanish when capital vanishes.

Do you reproach us for wanting to stop the exploitation of children by their parents? We plead guilty to the charge!

Our determination to replace domestic education by social, implies (you declare) a disregard of the most sacred of relationships.

But the education you provide, is it not socially determined? Is it not determined by the social conditions within whose framework you educate? Is it not determined directly or indirectly by society, acting through the schools, etc.? The influence of society upon education was not an original discovery of communists! They merely propose to change the character of the process, by withdrawing education from the influence of the ruling class.

Bourgeois phrasemaking about the family and education, about the intimate relations between parents and children, becomes more and more nauseating in proportion as the development of large-scale industry severs all the family ties of proletarians, and in proportion as proletarian children are transformed into mere articles of commerce and instruments of labor.

"But you communists want to make women common property!" shrieks the bourgeois chorus.

The bourgeois regards his wife as nothing but an instrument of production. He is told that the means of production are to be utilized in common. How can he help thinking that this implies the communization of women as well as other things?

He never dreams for a moment that our main purpose is to insure that women shall no longer occupy the position of mere instruments of production.

Besides, nothing could be more absurd than the virtuous indignation of our bourgeois as regards the official communization of women which the communists are supposed to advocate. Communists do not need to introduce community of women; it has almost invariably existed.

The members of the bourgeoisie, not content with having the wives and daughters of proletarians at their disposal (to say nothing of public prostitution), find one of their chief pleasures in seducing one another's wives!

Bourgeois marriage is in actual fact the community of wives. At worst, communists can only be charged with wanting to replace a hypocrital and concealed community of women by an official and frankly acknowledged community. Moreover, it is self-evident that the abolition of the present system of production will lead to the disappearance of that form of the community of women which results therefrom—to the disappearance of official and unofficial prostitution.

Communists have likewise been accused of wanting to do away with country, with nationality.

The workers have no country. No one can take from them what they have not got. Since the proletariat must first of all win political power, must make itself the ruling class, must raise itself to the position of a national class, must establish itself as the nation—it is, so far, still national, though by no means in the bourgeois sense of the term.

National distinctions and contrasts are already tending to disappear more and more as the bourgeoisie develops, as free trade becomes more general, as the world market grows in size and importance, as manufacturing processes and the resulting conditions of life become more uniform.

The rule of the proletariat will efface these distinctions and contrasts even more. United action, among civilized countries at least, is one of the first of the conditions requisite for the emancipation of the workers.

In proportion as the exploitation of one individual by another comes to an end, the exploitation of one nation by another will come to an end.

The ending of class oppositions within the nations will end the mutual hostilities of the nations.

The charges brought against communism upon religious or philosophical grounds, or (in general terms) upon ideological grounds, are not worth detailed consideration.

Is much perspicacity needed to understand that when changes occur in people's mode of life, in their social relations or social system, there will also be changes in their ideas and outlooks and conceptions—in a word, that their consciousness will change?

What does the history of ideas prove, if not that mental production changes concomitantly with material production? In every epoch, the ruling ideas have been the ideas of the ruling class.

It is customary to speak of ideas which revolutionize a whole society. This is only another way of saying that the elements of a new society have formed within the old one; that the break-up of the old ideas has kept pace with the break-up of the old social relations.

When the classical world was in its decline, the old religions were conquered by Christianity. When Christian ideas were put to flight by eighteenth-century rationalism, it was at the time when feudal society was fighting for very existence against the bourgeoisie, which was then the revolutionary class. The abstract ideas termed "freedom of conscience" and "religious liberty" were but the expression of the supremacy of free competition within the realm of knowledge.

The objector will say:

"It is true that religious, moral, philosophical, political, and legal notions have undergone changes in the course of historical development. Nevertheless (amid these changes), religion, morality, philosophy, political science, and law have persisted.

"Besides, there are eternal truths, such as liberty, justice, and the like, which are common to all social systems. But communism repudiates eternal truths, repudiates religion and morality instead of refashioning them, and is thus at odds with the whole course of historical evolution."

What does this accusation amount to? The history of all human society, past and present, has been the history of class antagonisms, and these have taken different forms in different epochs.

Whatever form it may have assumed, the exploitation of one part of society by the other has been a fact common to all past ages. No wonder, then, that the social consciousness of all the ages (despite manifold variations) has moved along lines of thought common to them all, along lines of thought that will necessarily persist until class oppositions have vanished from the face of the earth.

The communist revolution is the most radical breach with traditional property relations. Need we be surprised that it should imply a no less radical breach with traditional ideas?

Enough of these bourgeois objections to communism!

We have already seen that the first step in the worker's revolution is to make the proletariat the ruling class, to establish democracy.

The proletariat will use its political supremacy in order, by degrees, to wrest all capital from the bourgeoisie, to centralize all the means of production into the hands of the State (this meaning the proletariat organized as ruling class), and, as rapidly as possible, to increase the total mass of productive forces.

In the first instance, of course, this can only be effected by despotic inroads upon the rights of property and by despotic interference with bourgeois methods of production; that is to say by measures which seem economically inadequate and untenable, but have far-reaching effects, and are necessary as means for revolutionizing the whole system of production.

These measures will naturally differ from country to country.

In the most advanced countries they will, generally speaking, take the following forms:

1. Expropriation of landed property, and the use of land rents to defray State expenditure.

2. A vigorously graduated income tax.

3. Abolition of the right of inheritance.

4. Confiscation of the property of all émigrés and rebels.

5. Centralization of credit in the hands of the State, by means of a national bank with State capital and an exclusive monopoly.

6. Centralization of the means of transport in the hands of the State.

7. Increase of national factories and means of production, cultivation of uncultivated land, and improvement of cultivated land in accordance with a general plan.

8. Universal and equal obligation to work; organization of industrial armies, especially for agriculture.

9. Agriculture and urban industry to work hand-in-hand, in such a way as, by degrees, to obliterate the distinction between town and country.

10. Public and free education of all children. Abolition of factory work for children in its present form. Education and material production to be combined.

When, in the course of social evolution, class distinctions have disappeared, and when all the work of production has been concentrated into the hands of associated producers, public authority will lose its political character. Strictly speaking, political power is the organized use of force by one class in order to keep another class in sub-

jection. When the proletariat, in the course of its fight
against the bourgeoisie, necessarily consolidates itself into
a class, by means of a revolution makes itself the ruling
class, and as such forcibly sweeps away the old system of
production—it therewith sweeps away the system upon
which class conflicts depend, makes an end of classes, and
thus abolishes its own rule as a class.

The old bourgeois society, with its classes and class conflicts, will be replaced by an association in which the free
development of each will lead to the free development of
all.

KARL MARX: *The Revolutionary Transformation
of Capitalism* [4]

What does the primitive accumulation of capital, i.e.,
its historical genesis, resolve itself into? In so far as it is
not immediate transformation of slaves and serfs into wage-
laborers, and therefore a mere change of form, it only
means the expropriation of the immediate producers, i.e.,
the dissolution of private property based on the labour of
its owner. Private property, as the antithesis to social, collective property, exists only where the means of labor and
the external conditions of labor belong to private individuals. But according as these private individuals are laborers
or not laborers, private property has a different character.
The numberless shades, that it at first sight presents, correspond to the intermediate stages lying between these two
extremes.

The private property of the laborer in his means of
production is the foundation of petty industry, whether
agricultural, manufacturing or both; petty industry, again,
is an essential condition for the development of social
production and of the free individuality of the laborer
himself. Of course, this petty mode of production exists
also under slavery, serfdom, and other states of dependence.
But it flourishes, it lets loose its whole energy, it attains its
adequate classical form, only where the laborer is the private owner of his own means of labor set in action by himself: the peasant of the land which he cultivates, the arti-
san of the tool which he handles as a virtuoso.

This mode of production presupposes parceling of the

4. *Capital, op. cit.*, chapter 32, pp. 834-837. First published in 1867.

soil, and scattering of the other means of production. As it excludes the concentration of these means of production, so also it excludes co-operation, division of labor within each separate process of production, the control over, and the productive application of the forces of Nature by society, and the free development of the social productive powers. It is compatible only with a system of production, and a society, moving within narrow and more or less primitive bounds. To perpetuate it would be, as Pecqueur rightly says, "to decree universal mediocrity." At a certain stage of development it brings forth the material agencies for its own dissolution.

From that moment new forces and new passions spring up in the bosom of society; but the old social organization fetters them and keeps them down. It must be annihilated; it is annihilated. Its annihilation, the transformation of the individualized and scattered means of production into socially concentrated ones, of the pigmy property of the many into the huge property of the few, the expropriation of the great mass of the people from the soil, from the means of subsistence, and from the means of labor, this fearful and painful expropriation of the mass of the people forms the prelude to the history of capital. It comprises a series of forcible methods, of which we have passed in review only those that have been epoch-making as methods of the primitive accumulation of capital. The expropriation of the immediate producers was accomplished with merciless vandalism, and under the stimulus of passions the most infamous, the most sordid, the pettiest, the most meanly odious. Self-earned private property, that is based, so to say, on the fusing together of the isolated, independent laboring-individual with the conditions of his labor, is supplanted by capitalistic private property, which rests on exploitation of the nominally free labor of others, i.e., on wages-labor.

As soon as this process of transformation has sufficiently decomposed the old society from top to bottom, as soon as the laborers are turned into proletarians, their means of labor into capital, as soon as the capitalist mode of production stands on its own feet, then the further socialization of labor and further transformation of the land and other means of production into socially exploited and, therefore, common means of production, as well as the further expropriation of private proprietors, takes a new

form. That which is now to be expropriated is no longer
the laborer working for himself, but the capitalist exploiting many laborers.

This expropriation is accomplished by the action of the
immanent laws of capitalistic production itself, by the
centralization of capital. One capitalist always kills many.
Hand in hand with this centralization, or this expropriation
of many capitalists by few, develop, on an ever-extending
scale, the co-operative form of the labor-process, the conscious technical application of science, the methodical cultivation of the soil, the transformation of the instruments
of labor into instruments of labor only usable in common,
the economizing of all means of production by their use as
the means of production of combined, socialized labor, the
entanglement of all peoples in the net of the world-market,
and this, the international character of the capitalistic regime. Along with the constantly diminishing number of
the magnates of capital, who usurp and monopolize all advantages of this process of transformation, grows the mass
of misery, oppression, slavery, degradation, exploitation;
but with this too grows the revolt of the working-class, a
class always increasing in numbers, and disciplined, united,
organized by the very mechanism of the process of capitalist production itself. The monopoly of capital becomes
a fetter upon the mode of production, which has sprung
up and flourished along with, and under it. Centralization
of the means of production and socialization of labor at
last reach a point where they become incompatible with
their capitalist integument. This integument is burst
asunder. The knell of capitalist private property sounds.
The expropriators are expropriated.

The capitalist mode of appropriation, the result of the
capitalist mode of production, produces capitalist private
property. This is the first negation of individual private
property, as founded on the labor of the proprietor. But
capitalist production begets, with the inexorability of a
law of Nature, its own negation. It is the negation of negation. This does not re-establish private property for the
producer, but gives him individual property based on the
acquisitions of the capitalist era: i.e., on co-operation and
the possession in common of the land and of the means of
production.

The transformation of scattered private property, arising from individual labor, into capitalist private property

is, naturally, a process, incomparably more protracted, violent, and difficult, than the transformation of capitalistic private property, already practically resting on socialized production, into socialized property. In the former case, we had the expropriation of the mass of the people by a few usurpers; in the latter, we have the expropriation of a few usurpers by the mass of the people.

KARL MARX: *Theses on Feuerbach*[5]

1. The chief defect of all materialism up to now . . . is, that the object, reality, what we apprehend through our senses, is understood only in the form of the *object* or *contemplation;* but not as *sensuous human activity,* as *practice;* not subjectively. Hence in opposition to materialism the *active* side was developed abstractly by idealism—which of course does not know real sensuous activity as such. Feuerbach wants sensuous objects, really distinguished from the objects of thought: but he does not understand human activity itself as *objective* activity. . . . He therefore does not comprehend the significance of "revolutionary," of "practical-critical" activity.

2. The question whether objective truth is an attribute of human thought—is not a theoretical but a *practical* question. Man must prove the truth, i.e. the reality and power, the "this-sidedness" of his thinking in practice. The dispute over the reality or non-reality of thinking that is isolated from practice is a purely *scholastic* question.

3. The materialistic doctrine concerning the changing of circumstances and education forgets that circumstances are changed by men and that the educator himself must be educated. This doctrine has therefore to divide society into two parts, one of which is superior to society.

The coincidence of the changing of circumstances and of human activity or self-changing can only be comprehended and rationally understood as *revolutionary practice*.

4. Feuerbach starts out from the fact of religious self-estrangement, of the duplication of the world into a religious and a secular one. His work consists in resolving

5. From Appendix to *The German Ideology,* Parts I and III, *op. cit.,* pp. 197-199. Written 1845 and first published by Engels in 1888. Reprinted by permission of International Publishers Co., Inc.

the religious world into its secular basis. But that the secular basis raises itself above itself and establishes for itself an independent realm in the clouds can be explained only through the cleavage and self-contradictions within this secular basis. The latter must therefore in itself be both understood in its contradiction and revolutionized in practice. Therefore after, e.g., the earthly family is discovered to be the secret of the heavenly family, one must proceed to destroy the former both in theory and in practice.

5. Feuerbach, not satisfied with *abstract thought*, wants contemplation: but he does not understand our sensuous nature as *practical*, human-sensuous activity.

6. Feuerbach resolves the essence of religion into the essence of *man*. But the essence of man is no abstraction inherent in each separate individual. In its reality it is the *ensemble* (aggregate) of social relations.

Feuerbach, who does not enter more deeply into the criticism of this real essence, is therefore forced:

a. To abstract from the process of history and to establish the religious temperament as something independent, and to postulate an abstract—*isolated*—human individual.

b. The essence of man can therefore be understood only as "genus," the inward, dumb generality which *naturally* unites the many individuals.

7. Feuerbach therefore does not see that the "religious temperament" itself is a social product and that the abstract individual whom he analyzes belongs to a particular form of society.

8. All social life is essentially *practical*. All the mysteries which urge theory into mysticism find their rational solution in human practice and in the comprehension of this practice.

9. The highest point to which contemplative materialism can attain, i.e. that materialism which does not comprehend our sensuous nature as practical activity, is the contemplation of separate individuals and of civil society.

10. The standpoint of the old type of materialism is civil society, the standpoint of the new materialism is human society or social humanity.

11. The philosophers have only *interpreted* the world differently, the point is, to *change* it.

Modern socialism is, in its content, primarily the product of the perception on the one hand of the class antagonisms existing in modern society, between possessors and non-possessors, wage workers and capitalists; and on the other hand, of the anarchy ruling in production. In its theoretical form, however, it originally appears as a further and ostensibly more consistent extension of the principles established by the great French philosophers of the eighteenth century. Like every new theory, it had at first to link itself on to the intellectual material which lay ready to its hand, however deep its roots lay in material-economic facts.

The great men who in France were clearing the minds of men for the coming revolution themselves acted in an extremely revolutionary fashion. They recognized no external authority of any kind. Religion, conceptions of nature, society, political systems, everything was subjected to the most merciless criticism; everything had to justify its existence at the bar of reason or renounce all claim to existence. The reasoning intellect was applied to everything as the sole measure. It was the time when, as Hegel says, the world was stood upon its head; first, in the sense that the human head and the principles arrived at by its thought claimed to be the basis of all human action and association; and then later on also in the wider sense, that the reality which was in contradiction with these principles was in fact turned upside down from top to bottom. All previous forms of society and government, all the old ideas handed down by tradition were flung into the lumber-room as irrational; the world had hitherto allowed itself to be guided solely by prejudices; everything in the past deserved only pity and contempt. Now for the first time appeared the light of day, the kingdom of reason; henceforth, superstition, injustice, privilege and oppression were to be superseded by eternal truth, eternal justice, equality grounded in nature and the inalienable rights of man.

We know today that this kingdom of reason was nothing

6. From *Selected Works*, Vol. I (New York, no date), pp. 140-146, 155, 165-166, 185-188. Originally part of his book, *Anti-Duhring*, then issued as a separate pamphlet in 1880. Reprinted by arrangement with George Allen & Unwin Ltd.

more than the idealized kingdom of the bourgeoisie; that eternal justice found its realization in bourgeois justice; that equality reduced itself to bourgeois equality before the law; that bourgeois property was proclaimed as one of the essential rights of man; and that the government of reason, the Social Contract of Rousseau, came into existence and could only come into existence as a bourgeois-democratic republic. No more than their predecessors could the great thinkers of the eighteenth century pass beyond the limits imposed on them by their own epoch.

But side by side with the antagonism between the feudal nobility and the bourgeoisie, appearing on the scene as the representative of all the rest of society, was the general antagonism between the exploiters and the exploited, the rich idlers and the toiling poor. And it was precisely this circumstance that enabled the representatives of the bourgeoisie to put themselves forward as the representatives not of a special class but of the whole of suffering humanity. Still more: from its origin the bourgeoisie had been saddled with its antithesis: that capitalists cannot exist without wage workers, and in the same degree as the medieval burgher of the guild developed into the modern bourgeois, so the guild journeyman and the day-laborer outside the guilds developed into the proletarian. And although, on the whole, the bourgeoisie *in their struggle with the nobility* could claim to represent at the same time the interests of the different sections of workers of that period, yet in every great bourgeois movement there were independent outbursts of that class which was the more or less developed forerunner of the modern proletariat. For example, the Thomas Münzer tendency in the period of the Reformation and Peasant War in Germany; the Levellers, in the great English Revolution; in the great French Revolution, Babeuf. Alongside of these revolutionary armed uprisings of a class which was as yet undeveloped, the corresponding theoretical manifestations made their appearance; in the sixteenth and seventeenth centuries utopian portrayals of ideal social conditions; in the eighteenth century, actual communistic theories (Morelly and Mably). The demand for equality was no longer limited to political rights, but was extended also to the social conditions of individuals; it was not merely class privileges that were to be abolished, but class distinctions themselves. An ascetic communism, scorning all enjoyment of life and linked to Spartan conceptions, was the first form in which the new doctrine made its appearance. Then came the three great utopians: Saint-Simon, with whom bourgeois tendencies still had a certain influence, side by side with proletarian; Fourier; and Owen, who, in the country where capitalist production was the most developed, and under the influence of the antagonisms begotten of this, worked out his schemes for the removal of class distinctions systematically and in direct relation to French materialism.

It is common to all three of these that they do not come forward as representatives of the interests of the proletariat which in the meantime history has brought into being. Like the philosophers of the Enlightenment, they aim at the emancipation not first of all of a definite class, but of all humanity. Like them, they wish to establish the kingdom of reason and eternal justice; but their kingdom is spheres apart from that of the French philosophers. To them the bourgeois world based on the principles of these philosophers is also irrational and unjust, and therefore finds its way to the rubbish bin just as readily as feudalism and all earlier forms of society. If pure reason and justice have not hitherto ruled the world, this has been due only to the fact that until now men have not rightly understood them. What was lacking was just the individual man of genius, who has now arisen and has recognized the truth; the fact that he has now arisen, that the truth has been recognized precisely at this moment, is not an inevitable event, following of necessity in the chain of historical development, but a mere happy accident. He might just as well have been born five hundred years earlier, and would then have saved humanity five hundred years of error, strife and suffering.

We saw how the French philosophers of the eighteenth century, who paved the way for the revolution, appealed to reason as the sole judge of all that existed. A rational state, a rational society were to be established; everything that ran counter to eternal reason was to be relentlessly set aside. We saw also that in reality this eternal reason was no more than the idealized intellect of the middle class, just at that period developing into the bourgeoisie. When therefore the French Revolution had realized this rational society and this rational state, it became apparent that the new institutions, however rational in comparison with earlier conditions, were by no means absolutely rational. The rational state had suffered shipwreck. Rousseau's Social Contract had found its realization in the Reign of Terror, from which the bourgeoisie, who had lost faith in their own political capacity, had sought refuge first in the corruption of the Directorate, and ultimately in the protection of the Napoleonic despotism. The promised eternal peace had changed to an endless war of conquest. The rational society had fared no better. The antithesis between rich and poor, instead of being resolved in general well-being, had been sharpened by the abolition of the guild and other privileges, which had bridged it over, and of the benevolent institutions of the church, which had mitigated its effects; the "freedom of property" from feudal fetters, now become a reality, turned out to be for the small bourgeois and small peasants the freedom of selling this small property, which was being crushed by the overpowering competition of big property and big landed property, precisely to these great lords, and thus, for the small bourgeois and small peasants, became converted into freedom *from* property; the impetuous growth of industry on a capitalist basis raised the poverty and suffering of the working masses into a vital condition of society's existence. Cash payment became more and more, according to Carlyle's expression, the sole nexus in society. The number of crimes increased from year to year. And if the feudal depravities, formerly shamelessly flaunting in the light of day, though not abolished, were yet temporarily forced into the background, on the other hand the bourgeois vices, until then cherished only in privacy, now bloomed all the more luxuriantly. Trade developed more and more into swindling. The "fraternity" of the revolutionary motto was realized in the chicanery and envy of the competitive struggle. Corruption took the place of violent oppression, and money replaced the sword as the chief lever of social power. The "right of the first night" passed from the feudal lords to the bourgeois manufacturers. Prostitution assumed proportions hitherto unknown. Marriage itself remained, as before, the legally recognized form, the official cloak of prostitution, and was also supplemented by widespread adultery. In a word, compared with the glowing promises of the prophets of the Enlightenment, the social and political institutions established by the "victory of reason" proved to be bitterly disillusioning caricatures. The only thing still lacking was people to voice this disillusionment, and these came with the turn of the century. In 1802 Saint-Simon's *Geneva Letters* appeared; Fourier's first work was published in 1808, although the groundwork of his theory dated from 1799; on the first of January, 1800, Robert Owen took over the management of New Lanark.

The mode of outlook of the utopians for a long time governed the socialist conceptions of the nineteenth century and in part still govern them. Until quite recently it received the homage of all French and English socialists, and the earlier German communism, including Weitling, also belongs to it. To all these, socialism is the expression of absolute truth, reason and justice and needs only to be discovered to conquer the world by virtue of its own power; as absolute truth is independent of time and space and of the historical development of man, it is a mere accident when and where it is discovered. At the same time absolute truth, reason and justice are different for the founder of each different school; and as each one's special kind of absolute truth, reason and justice is in turn conditioned by his subjective understanding, his conditions of existence, the measure of his knowledge and intellectual training, so the only solution possible in this conflict of absolute truths is that they should grind each other down. And from this nothing could emerge but a kind of eclectic, average socialism, such as in fact dominated the minds of most socialist workers in France and England up to the present time; a mixture, admitting of the most manifold shades, of such of the critical observations, economic doctrines and delineations of future society made by the various founders of sects as excite the least opposition; a mixture which is the more easily produced the more its individual constituents have the sharp edges of precision rubbed off in the stream of debate, as pebbles are rounded in a brook. In order to make socialism into a science it had first to be placed upon a real basis. . . .

The materialist conception of history starts from the principle that production, and with production the exchange of its products, is the basis of every social order; that in every society which has appeared in history the distribution of the products, and with it the division of society into classes or estates, is determined by what is produced and how it is produced, and how the product is exchanged. According to this conception, the ultimate causes of all social changes and political revolutions are to be sought, not in the minds of men, in their increasing insight into eternal truth and justice, but in changes in the mode of production and exchange; they are to be sought not in the *philosophy* but in the *economics* of the epoch concerned. The growing realization that existing social institutions are irrational and unjust, that reason has become nonsense and good deeds a scourge, is only a sign that changes have been taking place quietly in the methods of production and forms of exchange, with which the social order, adapted to previous economic conditions is no longer in accord. This also involves that the means through which the abuses that have been revealed can be got rid of must likewise be present, in more or less developed form, in the altered conditions of production. These means are not to be *invented* by the mind, but *discovered* by means of the mind in the existing material facts of production.

Where then, on this basis, does modern socialism stand?

The existing social order, as is now fairly generally admitted, is the creation of the present ruling class, the bourgeoisie. The mode of production peculiar to the bourgeoisie —called, since Marx, the capitalist mode of production— was incompatible with the local privileges and the privileges of birth as well as with the reciprocal personal ties of the feudal system; the bourgeoisie shattered the feudal system, and on its ruins established the bourgeois social order, the realm of free competition, freedom of movement, equal rights for commodity owners, and all the other bourgeois glories. The capitalist mode of production could now develop freely. From the time when steam and the new tool-making machinery had begun to transform the former manufacture into large-scale industry, the productive forces evolved under bourgeois direction developed at a pace that was previously unknown and to an unprecedented degree. But just as manufacture, and the handicraft industry which had been further developed under its influence, had previously come into conflict with the feudal fetters of the guilds, so large-scale industry, as it develops more fully, comes into conflict with the barriers within which the capitalist mode of production holds it confined. The new forces of production have already outgrown the bourgeois form of using them; and this conflict between productive forces and mode of production is not a conflict which has arisen in men's heads, as for example the conflict between original sin and divine justice; but it exists in the facts, objectively, outside of us, independently of the will or purpose even of the men who brought it about. Modern socialism is nothing but the reflex in thought of this actual conflict, its ideal reflection in the minds first of the class which is directly suffering under it—the working class. . . .

The seizure of the means of production by society puts an end to commodity production, and therewith to the domination of the product over the producer. Anarchy in social production is replaced by conscious organization on a planned basis. The struggle for individual existence comes to an end. And at this point, in a certain sense, man finally cuts himself off from the animal world, leaves the conditions of animal existence behind him and enters conditions which are really human. The conditions of existence forming man's environment, which up to now have dominated man, at this point pass under the dominion and control of man, who now for the first time becomes the real conscious master of nature, because and in so far as he has become master of his own social organization. The laws of his own social activity, which have hitherto confronted him as external, dominating laws of nature, will then be applied by man with complete understanding, and hence will be dominated by man. Men's own social organization, which has hitherto stood in opposition to them as if arbitrarily decreed by nature and history, will then become the voluntary act of men themselves. The objective, external forces which have hitherto dominated history, will then pass under the control of men themselves. It is only from this point that men, with full consciousness, will fashion their own history; it is only from this point that the social causes set in motion by men will have, predominantly and in constantly increasing measure, the effects willed by men. It is humanity's leap from the realm of necessity into the realm of freedom.

In conclusion, let us briefly sum up our sketch of the course of development:

1. *Medieval Society*—Individual production on a small scale. Means of production adapted for individual use, hence primitively clumsy, petty, dwarfed in action. Production for immediate consumption, either of the producer himself or of his feudal lord. Only where an excess of production over his consumption occurs is such excess offered for sale and enters into exchange. Production of commodities, therefore, only in its infancy; but it already contains within itself, in embryo, *anarchy in social production*.

2. *Capitalist Revolution*—Transformation of industry,

at first by means of simple co-operation and manufacture. Concentration of the means of production, hitherto scattered, into large workshops. As a consequence, their transformation from individual into social means of production —a transformation which on the whole does not affect the form of exchange. The old forms of appropriation remain in force. The *capitalist* appears: in his quality of owner of the means of production he also appropriates the products and turns them into commodities. Production has become a social act, exchange and with it appropriation remain individual acts, the acts of separate individuals. *The social product is appropriated by the individual capitalist.* Fundamental contradiction, from which arise all the contradictions in which present-day society moves and which modern industry brings to light.

(a) Severance of the producer from the means of production. Condemnation of the worker to wage labor for life. *Antagonism of proletariat and bourgeoisie.*

(b) Growing emphasis and increasing effectiveness of the laws governing commodity production. Unbridled competitive struggle. *Contradiction between social organization in the individual factory and social anarchy in production as a whole.*

(c) On the one hand, perfecting of machinery, owing to competition, made a compulsory commandment for each individual manufacturer, and equivalent to a continually increasing displacement of workers: *industrial reserve army* —on the other hand, unlimited extension of production, likewise a compulsory law of competition for every manufacturer—on both sides, unheard of development of productive forces, excess of supply over demand, overproduction, glutting of the markets, crises every ten years, vicious circle: excess here of means of production and products, excess there of workers without employment and means of existence. But these two levers of production and of social well-being are unable to work together, because the capitalist form of production prevents the productive forces from working and the products from circulating, unless they are first turned into capital: which their very superabundance prevents. The contradiction has become heightened into an absurdity. *The mode of production rebels against the form of exchange.* The bourgeoisie is convicted of incapacity further to manage their own social productive forces.

(d) Partial recognition of the social character of the productive forces forced upon the capitalists themselves. Taking over of the great institutions for production and communication, first by *joint stock companies*, later by *trusts*, then by the *state*. The bourgeoisie shows itself to be a superfluous class; all its social functions are now performed by hired employees.

3. *Proletarian Revolution*—Solution of the contradictions. The proletariat seizes the public power and by means of this power transforms the socialized means of production, slipping from the hands of the bourgeoisie, into public property. By this act, the proletariat frees the means of production from the character of capital hitherto borne by them, and gives their social character complete freedom to assert itself. A social production upon a predetermined plan now becomes possible. The development of production makes the further existence of different classes of society an anachronism. In proportion as anarchy in social production vanishes, the political authority of the state also dies away. Man, at last the master of his own form of social organization, becomes at the same time the lord over nature, master of himself—free.

To carry through this world-emancipating act is the historical mission of the modern proletariat. And it is the task of scientific socialism, the theoretical expression of the proletarian movement, to establish the historical conditions and, with these, the nature of this act, and thus to bring to the consciousness of the now oppressed class the conditions and nature of the act which it is its destiny to accomplish.

4. Inventory of Ideas

The distinctive character of Marx's "scientific socialism," I think, lies in this: his images of the ideal society are connected with the actual workings of the society in which he lived. Out of his projections of the tendencies he discerns in society as it is actually developing he makes up his image of the future society (the post-capitalist society that he wants to come about). That is why he refuses, at least in his maturity, to *proclaim* ideals. Morally, of course, he condemns. Sociologically, he points to the results of that which he condemns. Politically, he directs attention to the agency of historical change—the proletariat—and he argues, with facts and figures, theories and slogans, that this developing connection between human agency and implicit goal is the most important trend in capitalist society. For by the development of this agency within it, capitalist society itself will be overthrown and socialism installed. The historical creation of the proletariat is the central thrust within the capitalist realm of necessity. That thrust is driving capitalism toward the revolutionary leap into the socialist epoch, into the realm of freedom.

This connection of ideal or goal with agency is at once a moral and an intellectual strategy. It sets Marx off from those he characterized as utopian socialists. This connection between built-in agency and socialist ideal is the political pivot around which turn the decisive features of his model of society and many specific theories of historical trend going on within it. It also provides a focus in social theory for the moral discontent registered in socialist aspirations; and on occasion, a new focus for liberal ideals as well. And it leads—as we shall presently see—to the direst ambiguities of marxian doctrine: this connection between ideal and agency has been at the bottom of the continual second thoughts, metaphysical squabbles, and major revisions by marxists who have come after Marx.

To explain the economic and psychological mechanics by which this built-in historical agency is developed, and how this development inevitably leads to the overthrow of capitalism—these are the organizing points of classic marxism. To explain delays in this development and find ways to facilitate and speed it up, or patiently to wait for it—these are the points from which subsequent varieties of marxism depart.

The remarkable coherence of Marx's system, the close correlation of its elements is in large measure a reflection of the consistency with which he holds in view the central thrust toward the development of the proletariat and its act of revolution. If we keep this in mind, we will not violate marxism as a whole. We must now attempt to set forth, for the moment without criticism, a brief inventory of the most important conceptions and propositions of classic marxism.[1]

1. The economic basis of a society determines its social structure as a whole, as well as the psychology of the people within it.

Political, religious, and legal institutions as well as the ideas, the images, the ideologies by means of which men understand the world in which they live, their place within it, and themselves—all these are reflections of the economic basis of society.

This proposition rests upon the master distinction within Marx's materialist model of society: the economic base (variously referred to as the mode of economic production, the substructure, the economic foundation) is distinguished from the rest of the society (called the superstructure or institutional and ideological forms). In the economic base, Marx includes the forces and the relations of production. In capitalism the latter means essentially the institution of private property and the consequent class relations between those who do and those who do not own it. The forces of production, a more complex conception, include both material and social elements: (a) natural resources, such as land and minerals, so far as they are used as objects of labor; (b) physical equipment such as tools, machines, technology; (c) science and engineering, the skills of men who

1. In this chapter, I do not quote Marx's phrases; the readings, I am hopeful, will have made these clear.

invent or improve this equipment; (d) those who do work with these skills and tools; (e) their division of labor, insofar as this social organization increases their productivity.

2. The dynamic of historical change is the conflict between the forces of production and the relations of production.

In earlier phases of capitalism, the relations of production facilitate the development of the forces of production. One cannot find a more handsome celebration of the work of capitalists in industrialization than in the pages of Marx's *Capital*. But in due course the capitalist organization of industry—the relations of production—come to fetter the forces of production; they come into objective contradiction with them. "Contradiction" I take to mean a problem that is inherent in and cannot be solved without modifying, or "moving beyond," the basic structure of the society in which it occurs. For Marx, "the basic structure" means the capitalist economy.

Continuous technological development and its full use for production conflicts with the interest of the property owners. The capitalists prohibit the utilization of new inventions, buying them up to avoid the loss of their investment in existing facilities. They are interested in increased productivity and in technical progress only as profits can thereby be maintained or increased. Thus capital itself is "the real historical barrier of capital production."

3. The class struggle between owners and workers is a social, political and psychological reflection of objective economic conflicts.

These conflicts lead to different reactions among the members of the different classes of bourgeois society. The "objective" contradiction within the capitalist economy, in brief, has its "subjective" counterpart in the class struggle within capitalist society. In this struggle the wageworkers represent the expanding forces of production and the owners represent the maintenance of the established relations of production (property relations mainly) and with them, the exploitation of the unpropertied class.

History is thus an objective sequence, a dialectic, a series of contradictions and of their resolutions. History is also a struggle between classes. These two ways of thinking are, within marxism, quite consistent. For Marx held that the revolution will result from the developing material forces of production as they come into conflict with the relations of production; this revolution will be realized by the struggle of the classes, a struggle caused by the objective, economic contradiction.

The point may be put more abstractly, in line with the "dialectical" method. In Marx's view, continual change— and change into its opposite—is inherent in all reality, and so in capitalist society. The dialectical method is a way of understanding the history of a social structure by examining its conflicts rather than its harmonies. In brief, and in ordinary language, the "laws of dialectics" are as follows: (a) if things change enough, they become different, qualitatively, from what they were to begin with; (b) one thing grows out of another and then comes into conflict with it; (c) history thus proceeds by a series of conflicts and resolutions rather than merely by minute and gradual changes.

4. Property as a source of income is the objective criterion of class: within capitalism the two basic classes are the owners and the workers.

Marx left unfinished his categories of social stratification. A few definitions and remarks are available in *Capital* along with his class analysis of historical events and remarks made in his more abstracted model of capitalist society. From all these, his conceptions and theories appear to be as follows:

The basic criterion of class is the relation of men to the means of production, an objective criterion having primarily to do with economic and legal fact. Those who own the means of production are bourgeoisie, those whom they hire for wages are proletariat. So defined, these terms point to aggregates of people, not to social organizations or psychological matters.

In this objective sense, Marx writes in *The German Ideology*, "the class . . . achieves an independent existence over and against individuals, so that the latter find their condition of existence predestined and hence have their position in life and their personal development assigned to them by their class, become subsumed under it."

This statement can be made empirically, as Max Weber later did, in a way that does not violate Marx's meaning. The chances for an individual to achieve that which he values, and even the values themselves, are dependent upon the objective, economic class-position he occupies. At least for statistical aggregates, this is so, irrespective of any psychological opinions or attitudes.

5. *Class struggle rather than harmony—"natural" or otherwise—is the normal and inevitable condition in capitalist society.*

Marx's denial of any theory of natural harmony is an affirmation that in capitalist society conflicts of interest are basic. By "basic" we are to understand: irremediable within the system: if one interest is fulfilled, the other cannot be. For Marx and for most marxists, the general and basic conflict of interest comes from the division between propertied and non-propertied classes. Whether these classes are aware of it or not, there is an inevitable conflict of interest between them, defined by the relation of each to the means of production. A contradiction of their basic interests prevails.

6. *Within capitalist society, the workers cannot escape their exploited conditions and their revolutionary destiny by winning legal or political rights and privileges; unions and mass labor parties are useful as training grounds for revolution, but are not a guarantee of socialism.*

Middle-class democracy is always and necessarily based upon economic inequalities and exploitation. Hence Marx continually warns against reformist illusions, and exposes them by reference to the objective contradiction between productive forces and productive relations. There is only one way out: the wageworkers must themselves, by their successful struggle as a property-less class against the property-owning class, resolve the objective contradiction. They themselves must liberate the constructive forces of production by overturning the entire superstructure that is rooted in the capitalist relations of production. The productive forces, now fettered by capitalist rigidity, will then go forward at an enormously accelerated rate of progress.

7. *Exploitation is built into capitalism as an economic system, thus increasing the chances for revolution.*

Whatever his wages may be, under capitalism the worker is economically exploited. That is the practical meaning of Marx's doctrine of "surplus value." Only human labor, for Marx, can create value. But by the application of his labor power, the worker produces a greater value than he is paid for by the capitalist for whom he works. The "surplus value" thus created is appropriated by the capitalist class, and so the worker under capitalism is exploited.

8. The class structure becomes more and more polarized, thus increasing the chance for revolution.

The composition of capitalist society will undergo these changes: (a) the bourgeoisie or middle class will decrease in numbers; (b) the wageworkers will increase in numbers; (c) all other "intermediary classes" will fade out of the political picture, as the society is polarized between bourgeoisie and proletariat. In general, by "intermediary" classes Marx means the petty bourgeoisie, those of small property; and not white collar employees.

9. The material misery of the workers will increase, as will their alienation.

The increasing misery of the wageworkers refers not only to the physical misery of their life conditions but also to the psychological deprivation arising from their alienation. It is essential to keep these separate, and to remember that for Marx the latter seemed the more important, that alienation could exist and deepen even if material standards of living were improved. However, he expected that the workers will increasingly suffer in both respects, although many latter-day marxists stress the psychological deprivation, the alienation of men at work.

It is to misunderstand Marx, I believe, to equate alienation with whatever is measured as "work dissatisfaction" by industrial psychologists in the USA today. Behind Marx's difficult conception of alienation there is the ideal of the human meaning he believes work ought to have and which he believes it will come to have in a socialist society.

According to Marx, wage work under capitalism is an activity by which men acquire the things they need. It is an activity undertaken for ulterior ends and not in itself a satisfying activity. Men are alienated from the process of their work itself, it is external to them, imposed by social conditions. It is not a source of self-fulfillment but rather a miserable denial of self. They do not "develop freely" their physical and mental energies by their work, but exhaust themselves physically and debase themselves mentally.

Moreover, in work the laborer gives over to the owner the control of his activity: "It is not his work, but work for someone else . . . in work he does not belong to himself but to another person." At work, men are homeless; only during leisure do they feel at home.

Finally, work results in the creation of private property; the product of the work belongs to another. The worker empties himself into this product; the more he works the greater his product, but it is not his. Private property, accordingly, causes him to be alienated. Thus the alienation of labor and the system of private property are reciprocal.

Alienation, working together with economic exploitation, leads to increasing misery—and so in due course, to the formation of the proletariat as a class-for-itself.

10. The wageworkers—a class-in-itself—will be transformed into the proletariat, a class-for-itself.

The first phase—a class-in-itself—refers to the objective fact of the class as an aggregate, defined by its position in the economy.

The second—a class-for-itself—refers to the members of this class when they have become aware of their identity as a class, aware of their common situation, and of their role in changing or in preserving capitalist society. Such class consciousness is not included in the objective definition of the term "class"; it is an expectation, not a definition. It is something that, according to Marx, is going to develop among the members of the classes. How it will develop he does not make as clear as why it will, for according to his analysis of their condition, as the interests of the two classes are in objective and irremediable conflict, their members will eventually become aware of their special interests and will pursue them.

Ideas and ideology are determined (as stated in proposition 1) by the economic bases of a society. The class consciousness of the proletariat will follow this rule. The ideas men come to have are generally determined by the stage of history in which they live, and by the class position they occupy within it. There is not, however, a universal and certainly not an immediate one-to-one correlation. The ideas of the ruling class in a given society are generally the ruling ideas of that epoch. Men who are not in this ruling class but who accept its definitions of reality and of their own interests are "falsely conscious." But in due course, true class consciousness will be realized among the proletariat.

The workers will become increasingly class conscious and increasingly international in their outlook. These economic and psychological developments occur as a result of the institutional and technical development of capitalism itself. In this process, the proletariat will abandon nationalist allegiances and take up loyalties to their own class, regardless of nationality. Like the relations of production, nationalism fetters their true interest which is to release the forces of production.

11. The opportunity for revolution exists only when objective conditions and subjective readiness coincide.

Neither the objective conditions for successful revolution nor revolutionary urges within the proletariat, in Marx's view, continuously increase. Both ebb and flow with the development of objective conditions and the resulting political and psychological ones. Sometimes Marx emphasizes the subjective factor of revolutionary class war, sometimes the underlying objective developments. Thus in 1850:

"Under the conditions of this general prosperity, when the productive forces of bourgeois society develop as abundantly as is at all possible within the existing bourgeois conditions, there can be no question of a real revolution. Such a revolution is only possible in those periods when the two factors, the modern productive forces and the bourgeois forms of production, come to contradict one another."

The proletariat must do the job by its own revolutionary action as a proletariat, but can succeed only under the correct objective conditions. Sooner or later, the will and the conditions will coincide. Many trends, already indicated, facilitate this. In addition, another rule points toward the proletarian revolution:

12. The functional indispensability of a class in the economic system leads to its political supremacy in the society as a whole.

This unstated premise of Marx is the underlying assumption, I believe, of the marxist theory of power. On this premise the capitalists have replaced the nobles, and capitalism has succeeded feudalism. In a similar manner, reasoned Marx, the proletariat will replace the bourgeoisie, and socialism replace capitalism. Old rulers who were once functionally indispensable are so no longer. In the course of capitalist development the bourgeoisie, like the feudal nobles before them, have become parasitical. They cannot help this. It is their destiny. And so they are doomed.

13. In all class societies the state is the coercive instrument of the owning classes.

This of course follows from the theory of power, just stated, and from the conception of the superstructure as economically determined. The state is seen as an instrument of one class and, in advanced capitalism, of a class that is in economic decline. The class of which the state is the coercive instrument is no longer economically progressive, no longer functionally indispensable, and yet it still holds power. It must, therefore, act increasingly by coercion.

14. Capitalism is involved in one economic crisis after another. These crises are getting worse. So capitalism moves into its final crisis—and the revolution of the proletariat.

As the proletariat are subjectively readied, the objective mechanics of capitalism moves the system into increasingly severe crises. The economic contradictions that beset it insure increasing crisis. This cannot be halted until the base of capitalism is abolished, for crisis is inherent in the nature of this system.

15. The post-capitalist society will first pass through a transitional stage—that of the dictatorship of the proletariat; then it will move into a higher phase in which true communism will prevail.

No one, Marx held, can say exactly what the nature of post-capitalist society will be. Only utopians and dreamers draw up detailed blueprints of the future. Just as he does not like to proclaim ideals, so Marx dislikes to go into explicit detail about the future. Either kind of discussion seems to him "idealistic" in the sense of "irrelevant" or "unrealistic." Nonetheless it is possible to find in the relevant texts, mainly his *Critique of the Gotha Program*, Marx's image of the future society:

The transitional stage may be equated with the revolution. The appropriating class will itself be expropriated, the owners' state will be broken up, the productive facilities transferred to society in order to permit a rational planning of the economy. In this first stage, society will be administered and defended against its enemies by a dictatorship of the revolutionary proletariat. This will probably be something like what he supposed the Paris Commune of 1871 to have been. Still "stamped with the birth-marks of the old society, the newborn society will be limited in many ways by inheritances from the old, capitalist society."

But history will not end there. A higher phase—that of communism—will develop; it will be characterized, first, by the fact that the proletariat as a revolutionary class (not just an aggregate of wageworkers) will form "the immense majority" of the population. The proletariat will be the nation; and so in the nation there will be no class distinctions and no class struggle. More than that, specialization of labor itself, as known under capitalism, with all its deformation of men, will not exist. The inherited opposition of manual and mental labor, the conflict between town and country, will disappear.

Second, the state will wither away, for the only function of the state is to hold down the exploited class. Since the proletariat will be virtually the total population, and thus cease to be a proletariat, they will need no state. Anarchy of production will be replaced by rational and systematic planning of the whole. Only in its second phase, when it has eliminated the remaining vestiges of capitalism and developed its own economic base, will society proceed on principles quite distinct from those of capitalism. Only then will men cease to govern men. Man will administer things. Public authority will replace state power. Only then will the ruling principle of communist society be: "From each according to his abilities, to each according to his needs."

16. *Although men make their own history, given the circumstances of the economic foundation, the way they make it and the direction it takes are determined. The course of history is structurally limited to the point of being inevitable.*

I have noted that in Marx's historical model of society the agency of change is intrinsically connected with socialist ideals. His major propositions and expectations have to do with the development of its historic agency, and with the revolutionary results of that development. Two general questions of interpretation arise when we confront this central view: (a) In general, does Marx believe in historical inevitability? (b) In connection with the mechanics of the central thrust, does he hold that the economic factor is the determining factor in capital society? These questions have been much argued over, as well they might be; for later marxists, notably Lenin, they have been of leading political urgency. Major party strategy has been debated in terms of different answers to them.

My answer to both questions is Yes. Classic marxism contains only one general theory of how men make history. Only in such terms as it provides do all the specific conceptions and theories of Marx make sense. That theory of history-making, very briefly, is as follows:

". . . each person follows his own consciously desired end, and it is precisely the resultant of these many wills operating in different directions and of their manifold effects upon the outer world that constitute history . . . the many individual wills active in history for the most part produce results quite other than those they intended—often quite the opposite: their motives [of individuals] therefore in relation to the total result are likewise only of secondary significance. On the other hand, the further question arises: what driving forces in turn stand behind these motives? What are the historical causes which translate themselves into these motives in the brains of these actors?" [2]

In the historical development of marxism, as we shall later see, there is always the tension between history as inevitable and history as made by the wills of men. It will not do, I think, to lessen that tension by "re-interpreting" or "explaining" what Marx plainly wrote on the theme. Politicians who must justify decisions by reference to founding doctrine may need to do that. We do not. It is better to try to keep the record straight, and to designate departures from classic marxism as departures.

Aside from the documentary evidence, I believe that Marx is a determinist for the following reasons:

(a) The question of the historical agency is clearly bound up with the problem of historical inevitability and with the ideal of socialism. However ambiguous assorted quotations may make the point seem, classic marxism does differ from utopian socialism and from liberalism precisely on this

2. F. Engels, *Ludwig Feuerbach* (New York, 1935), pp. 58-59.

point. It may be that in arguing against utopian socialism and against liberalism Marx stresses the idea of inevitability. Be that as it may, I am less concerned with *why* he held this view than with the fact that he did.

(b) Marx's refusal to preach ideals and his reluctance to discuss the society of the future makes no sense otherwise. Because he did believe in the historical inevitability, as he saw it, he can treat socialism not as an ideal, a program, a choice of means, or as a matter of or for political decision. He can treat it as a matter for scientific investigation.

(c) He did not try to persuade men of any new moral goals, because he believed that the proletariat would inevitably come to them. "In the last analysis," social existence determines consciousness. Historical developments will implant these goals into the consciousness of men, and men will then act upon them. The individual has little choice. If his consciousness is not altogether determined, his choice is severely limited and pressed upon him by virtue of his class position and all the influences and limitations to which this leads.

(d) Historically, the idea of Progress has been fully incorporated into the very ethos of marxism. Marx re-seats this idea—in the development of the proletariat. This becomes the gauge for moral judgments of progress and retrogression. Generally in his temper and in his theories of the master trends of capitalism in decline Marx is quite optimistic.[3]

17. The social structure, as noted in proposition number 1, is determined by its economic foundations; accordingly, the course of its history is determined by changes in these economic foundations.

I have held this point until the end, because it is a point of great controversy. There is a tendency among some marxists to attempt to "defend" Marx's economic determinism by qualifying it. They do this in the manner of Engels' later remarks (made in letters) about the interplay of various factors, or by opposing to it a vague sociological pluralism, by which everything interacts with everything and

---

3. Despite its earlier notions of progress, liberalism is no longer congenial to ideas of historical inevitability. Such notions collide too obviously with its basic principle of liberty for the individual and the celebration of voluntary associations. Later liberals—at least its more knowledgeable spokesmen—tend to be rather pessimistic about the idea of progress itself; later marxists do not.

no causal sequence is ever quite determinable. Neither line of argument, even when put in the abstruse terms of "dialectical materialism," seems very convincing or helpful. Moreover, to dilute the theory in these ways is to transform it from a definite theory, which may or may not be adequate, into equivocation, a mere indication of a problem.

Marx stated clearly the doctrine of economic determinism. It is reflected in his choice of vocabulary; it is assumed by, and fits into, his work as a whole—in particular his theory of power, his conception of the state, his rather simple notions of class and his use of these notions (including the proletariat as the agency of history-making). We may of course assume with Engels that he allows a degree of free-play among the several factors that interact, and also that he provides a flexible time-schedule in which economic causes do their work. But in the end—and usually the end is not so very far off—economic causes are "the basic," the ultimate, the general, the innovative causes of historical change.

To Marx "economic determinism" does *not* mean that the desire for money or the pursuit of wealth, or calculation of economic gain is the master force of biography or of history. In fact, it does not pertain directly to *motives* of any sort. It has to do with the social—the class—context under which motives themselves arise and function in biography and in history. The *causes* of which Marx writes are causes that lie behind the motives which propel men to act. We must understand this in the terms of his model of history-making: "Marx examines the causal nature of the resultants of individual wills, without examining the latter in themselves; he investigates the laws underlying *social* phenomena, paying no attention to their relation with the phenomena of the individual consciousness." [4]

Such are the bare outlines of classic marxism. In summary, it consists of a model of maturing capitalist society and of theories about the way this society and the men within it are changing. In this society, the productive facilities are owned privately and used to make private profit; the rest of the population works for wages given by those who own. It is a society that is changing because its forces of production come into increasing conflict with the or-

4. Nikolai Bukharin, *Economic Theory of the Leisure Class* (New York, 1927), p. 40.

ganization of its economy by the owners and by their state.

At bottom, developments of its economic basis—in particular its economic contradictions—are making for changes in all its institutions and ideologies. Increasingly resulting in crisis, increasingly deepening the exploitation of men by men, these contradictions are causing the development of the historical agency which upon maturity is destined to overturn capitalism itself. That agency is the proletariat, a class which within capitalism is being transformed from a mere aggregate of wageworkers into a unified and conscious class-for-itself, aware of its common interests, and alert to the revolutionary way of realizing them.

The objective or institutional conflicts are a fact of capitalist life, but may not yet be reflected fully as the class struggle of owners and workers. Now a minority, concerned only with their immediate interests, the workers are growing more and more exploited, more alienated, more miserable, and more organized; in their ranks what men are interested in is coming to coincide with what is to men's interest; and the workers are becoming more numerous. They are coming to be "the self-conscious independent movement of the immense majority" in pursuit of their real and long-run interests. They are coming to true self-consciousness because self-consciousness itself is being changed by the relations of production men enter into independent of their will. And having become self-conscious, they cannot pursue their interests, they cannot raise themselves up, "without the whole super-incumbent strata of official society being sprung into the air." [5]

That is why when the time is ripe, when capitalism is mature and the proletariat ready, the revolution of the proletariat by the most politically alert sector of the proletariat is going to occur. Then bourgeois institutions and all their works will be smashed. In turn, the post-capitalist society of socialism will evolve into the communist realm of freedom.

Comprehending every feature of man's activities, human and inhuman, Marx's conception is bitterly filled with sheer intellect and with brilliant leaps of the mind; it is at once analysis, prophecy, orientation, history, program. It is "the most formidable, sustained and elaborate indictment ever delivered against an entire social order, against its rulers,

5. Löwith, *op. cit.*, p. 41.

its supporters, its ideologists, its willing slaves, against all whose lives are bound up with its survival." [6]

No sooner were its outlines stated than it began to be revised by other men who were caught up in the torment of history-making. Then the intellectual beauty of its structure, the political passion of its central thrust began to be blunted by the will of political actors and the recalcitrance of historical events.

6. Isaiah Berlin, *Karl Marx* (New York, 1959), p. 21.

5. Rules for Critics

Critics often confuse the marxism of Marx with that of later marxists, and they tend to mix up their political and their intellectual points. By sorting out the several distinct kinds of information and argument relevant to "making up one's mind about marxism" I shall also be able to make clear the grounds for my own criticism.

1

To judge from its practitioners and from its critics there seem to be at least three intellectual types: Vulgar Marxism, Sophisticated Marxism, and Plain Marxism.

Vulgar Marxists (as we have seen) seize upon certain ideological features of Marx's political philosophy and identify these parts as the whole. This is true of adherents as well as of critics. We need here say no more about this type.

Sophisticated Marxists are much more complicated. They are mainly concerned with marxism as a model of society and with the theories developed with the aid of this model. Empirical exceptions to theories are relegated to subsidiary importance; new theories are made up to account for these exceptions in such a way as to avoid revision of the general model. These theories are then read back into the texts of Marx. It is always possible to save a theory by attaching to it supplementary hypotheses; if the theory is assumed to be true, then of course one can find explanations for deviant facts—so that they do not "really" contradict the theory. Some of this, no doubt, is quite all right: it is merely an elaboration and refinement of the theory. But there comes a time when the supplementary hypotheses become so bulky, the deviant facts so overwhelming, that the whole theory or even the model becomes clumsy. At that point marxism becomes "sophisticated" in a useless and obscurantist sense.

For example: (1) It is true, admits the sophisticated marxist, that wageworkers in advanced capitalist societies are not revolutionary; they are not even as yet a class-conscious proletariat. (2) But, he argues, that is because of the intensive capitalist propaganda, the misleaders of labor who dominate the trade unions, the "labor aristocracy" that is bought off by the imperialist powers, the traitors who run the social democratic labor parties.

The admissions of fact (statement 1) seem to disprove the basic theory, the proletarianization of the workers, but are they supplementary explanations (2) contained within the theory, or do they constitute new theories? The explanations suggest the decisive, and possibly autonomous role of the cultural apparatus as part of the superstructure in the formation and persistence of political ideologies; the problem of the mediation between base and superstructure; the role of political and social organization in the life of an economic class; the durability of monopoly capitalism as an economic system and its political stability as a type of society; the effects upon Marx's expectations of occupational and income differentiation among the wageworkers with a consequent need for more refined categories of class itself. At the least these are extreme modifications of the basic theory.

The style of the most sophisticated marxists leads them to treat Marx's predictions, not as empirical statements about what is going to happen, but in close terms to his *model,* always with the qualification "other things being equal." For example, they see in Volume I of *Capital,* where the theory of increasing misery is set forth, an abstracted model into which Marx later introduces more empirical elements. So they conclude that Marx is not really mistaken about increasing misery. This is confused and confusing strategy. It is generally correct if it is used *only* to judge or to praise Marx as a historical figure, and a careful thinker. It is incorrect and misleading if it is used to assert or to imply the relevance of Marx's work on any specific point of reference in present-day society.

Sophisticated marxists generally are commited to current marxist practice on political as well as on intellectual grounds. Consequently, they tend to incorporate into "marxism" the whole tradition of sociology, before and after Marx. Some know very little but Marx; they have not availed themselves of the sociological tradition as a whole within which the big conversation with Marx is one very important feature, but only one. For them, there is no "social science" of much worth; there is only marxist social science. Thus, they tend to stretch and to bend marxist ideas to fit new facts, and to confuse Marx's general model with specific theories. Even when Marx's terminology is obviously ambiguous and plainly inadequate they are often reluctant to abandon it. At its best, this style of thinking is tedious and hampers analysis unnecessarily. At its worst, it becomes a substitute for reflection and inquiry, a sophisticated sloganeering.

Plain Marxists (whether in agreement or in disagreement) work in Marx's own tradition. They understand Marx, and many later marxists as well, to be firmly a part of the classic tradition of sociological thinking. They treat Marx like any great nineteenth-century figure, in a scholarly way; they treat each later phase of marxism as historically specific. They are generally agreed that Marx's work bears the trademarks of the nineteenth-century society, but that his general model and his ways of thinking are central to their own intellectual history and remain relevant to their attempts to grasp present-day social worlds. This is the point of view, for example, of Isaac Deutscher in his biographies and in his analysis of the soviet world, and of Joan Robinson in her *Essay on Economics and Marxism*. It is, of course, the point of view taken in the present essay.

Other attempts to characterize the plain marxists include such phrases as Edward Thompson's *the marxisans,* George L. Mosse's *the marxists of the heart,* and what many writers refer to as *the marxian tradition,* as opposed to any rigid or institutionalized marxism. Included among plain marxists, although by no means exhausting the list, are such varied thinkers as the later William Morris, Antonio Gramsci, Rosa Luxemburg, G. D. H. Cole, Georg Lukàcs, Christopher Cauldwell, Jean-Paul Sartre, the later John Strachey, Georges Sorel, Edward Thompson, Lezlo Kolokowski, William A. Williams, Paul Sweezy, and Erich Fromm.

Politically, the plain marxists have generally been among the losers. They may have been through The Party, of one sort or another, yet as plain marxists they have really stood outside it; they have not been enchurched. They may have simply been theorists, not political actors. And there is another point of distinction, the intellectual (which, of course, varies from one man to another): in their work, plain marxists have stressed the humanism of marxism, especially of the younger Marx, and the role of the superstructure in history; they have pointed out that to underemphasize the *interplay* of bases and superstructure in the making of history is to transform man into that abstraction for which Marx himself criticized Feuerbach. They have been "open" (as opposed to dogmatic) in their interpretations and their uses of marxism. They have stressed that "economic determinism" is, after all, a matter of degree, and held that it is so used by Marx in his own writings, especially in his historical essays. They have emphasized the volition of men in the making of history—their freedom—in contrast to any Determinist Laws of History and, accordingly, the lack of individual responsibility.

In brief, they have confronted the unresolved tension in Marx's work—and in history itself: the tension of humanism and determinism, of human freedom and historical necessity.

By no means is the distinction between plain marxists and the others who have worked in Marx's name an either-or classification: a man can be both—one or another at different times or simultaneously as he plays different roles: for example, the ideological and the theoretical. Lenin and Trotsky, as we shall see, are especially ambiguous in this way. Stalin was not: he was not a plain marxist in any sense or at any time. On the other hand, many plain marxists of scholarly mien today are not ambiguous either: they are plain marxists and—politically as well as intellectually —nothing else. The plain marxists are men who, although in great travail, nonetheless have confronted the world's problems; they are unable to take the easy ways out. But this book is not about them. In my selections I have stressed the marxists who have won power, or come close to it. This does not imply any lack of esteem for those who have lost; it is just that one can do only so much in one book.

2

A fundamental difference among scholars in their attitude toward "marxism" lies in whether or not they see the practices and proclamations of stalinism as continuous with the doctrines of Marx or as distinct from them, a betrayal in moral and political terms, and a set of errors in intellectual terms. The word around which the differences very often revolve is "socialism" itself. Is the Soviet Union today socialist or is it not? More generally, what is socialism and what is not?

In examining definitions of socialism two of the suggested criteria for considering political philosophies may be helpful. If we refer to a complex set of ideals into which are jammed all sorts of values—moral, political, human—and all sorts of imagined social and economic arrangements, we can readily condemn partial realizations, or partial attempts at realization, as misleading or even as downright anti-socialist distortion. Many critics who define socialism by reference only to ideals, see the USSR as anything but socialist.

At the opposite extreme are critics who use the criterion of institutional agencies. Before the Revolution this agency meant the working class, after it the abolition of private property in the means of production and the establishment of central economic planning. In these terms the Soviet Union is socialist. Both attitudes are correct, given the terms of their definitions.

But what is the proper distinction? Can one really be a marxist and yet approve the USSR? Can one really be a marxist and *not* approve? To attempt a final definition is to engage in a controversy of concern only to those with a vested interest either in justifying or in condemning the USSR. In most such controversies the disputants are attempting to steal whatever prestige and authority the word "socialism" or the word "Marx" may have, and to monopolize it for their own views. Many of them have been in personal need of the ideological support of orthodoxy; this assurance has also been needed for urgent political reasons. From the standpoint of many other political philosophies, "marxism" has a curious intellectual history, because it has been so mixed up with practice and hence so heavily ideological.

The most fruitful approach is to attempt answers to such questions as: (1) Was the course of events in the Soviet Union "inevitable" *because* of the acceptance of the ideas of Marx by its changing power elite as well as by considerable other sections of the Soviet population? (2) Is its

present character inevitably going to continue in the foreseeable future? (3) Does the course of affairs in the USSR
prove that attempts in other countries to follow Marx's
ideas will end in the same way?

My answer to each of these is: No. My reasons will, I
hope, become clear later on in this book. I know I am disappointing many kinds of marxists who would ask rather:
Which of the various interpretations of Marx that have
been developed since Marx died is closest to his original
intention? Was Stalin *the* (or even *a*) legitimate heir of
Marx? Was Lenin? Were the social democrats? The answer
of course is: No one was, at least not altogether.

But judging from what he did write, considered as a
whole, I think these interpretations are "deviations" from
Marx. Leninism in particular, though in several ways
"based on Marx," differs profoundly from others of his
theories and from the range of political action expected and
from the policy most clearly derivable from him. Certainly
the same is true of stalinism. And of social democracy.
And of trotskyism. It is quite impossible, I think, to infer
from Marx's work what views or practices he would have
favored at various times between 1883 when he died, and
today.

It is possible to contrast what Marx wrote with the practice of those who have acted politically in his name, and
with the results of their practice. These Lessons from the
Practice of Others inform us that the classic statement
has been modified by practitioners, no matter how insistent, and boring, their protestations of "orthodoxy" may be.

Only those who are possessed by the fantasy—and the
political urgencies—of immutable certainties, can believe
that Marx, or Marx *and* Lenin, could have anticipated by
their wisdom the present-day theoretical needs of China,
the USA, Russia, Cuba, Poland, France, Yugoslavia, Australia—as these countries exist and struggle today. So far
as intellectual history is concerned, the notion of eternal
orthodoxy is absurd—although at times—as under stalinism—there really is no intellectual history, only a codifi-
cation of inherited ideas and their official interpretation
for expedient internal and international use.

3

There are many other orientations to marxism. One of

them is a type of social thinking that rejects that classic tradition of sociology—and so, marxism along with it. Marx, if he is considered at all, figures as one of "the social philosophers" who, in the dreary textbooks, are paraded as "predecessors" of The Real Social Science. Or, more crudely, such social scientists hold that the significance of marxism is entirely ideological and political, whereas their own work is politically neutral and morally pure—in one word, objective. Social Science is really (i.e., only) Science; marxism is really (i.e., only) Ideology.

Marx is also dismissed as "only a philosopher," and thus not part of "empirical social science." Marx, especially given his terminology, can of course be read in basic continuity with Hegel. He can also be read in continuity with empirical social study and the most careful speculation. For he is both a philosopher and an empirical sociologist.

He is also a revolutionary, a moralist, a very scholarly man, and much else. He is a speculator of audacity about virtually every realm of man and society in history. He is also full of genuine murk. I do not know which is The Real Marx, but fortunately for us the question of The Real Marx is not a dogmatic question subject to political decision. We are able freely to use whatever of his we feel the need of, and to reject what we do not.

Marxism is at once an intellectual and a moral criticism. In its documents, in its very conceptions, the two *are* often difficult to separate, but it *is* a political philosophy *and* at the same time it is definitely social science.

One can compare the expectations stated by Marx, or derivable from his work, with what has actually happened and what has not. (The same can be done with any other marxist.) In such attempts, again one asks: To what extent have Marx's expectations come about? What predictive or orienting value do they have, and what predictive value are they likely to have?

Such lessons from historical events are not as easy to draw as many critics seem to believe, for the meanings of events are usually ambiguous. Moreover, of a theory addressed to an epoch, any criticism is made difficult by a certain vagueness or flexibility about what is short- and what is long-run. Yet surely enough time has now elapsed to permit us to judge Karl Marx's expectations without encountering at every turn a rebuttal: "Wait a while; it may happen yet." The way to handle the problem of the short-run and the long-run is the way of Marx himself: to specify the historical span. Two points should always be kept in mind:

First, Marx was generally an analyst of long-run forces and trends. Our immediate times (let us say, 1945 to 1965) should not be considered as "the normal," or as a closed-off span of time in terms of which to judge his predictions. To do so eliminates major facts of our century: the capitalist depression of the thirties, the rise of fascism out of one specific form of capitalism, and the two World Wars. Yet given the accelerated pace of history, it is hardly useful to speculate further than a decade or so into the future.

Second, historical events used to refute theories, like any facts, do not explain themselves; to comprehend them we must consider a longer historical span; only then can we consider the nature of the mechanisms that have produced and support them. This we must do, for Marx is concerned not only with what is or is not going to happen, but with *why*, with the underlying structural mechanism of events and trends. Accordingly, to confront his theories adequately, we too must go into the "why"; in doing so we must consider whether or not it is necessary to modify the model of society set forth by Marx, or to modify merely one of his theories.

4

Here then are some obvious rules for critics which I shall try to follow: I am not going to argue over definitions as such, especially definitions of emotive terms, but will break them up into distinct and empirically answerable questions, using neutral terms having clear and unambiguous meanings. I shall examine each phase and type of marxist development in terms of its historical specifics, keeping distinct each phase of the history of marxist theory and practice; only after that considering—carefully—the movement as a whole. In brief, I will try to work as a plain marxist, avoiding the ways of sophisticated and vulgar marxists. My own values I shall try to recognize and state explicitly. I will do my best to avoid the optative mood. When accepting or rejecting some theory, I shall distinguish features of it in accordance with the criteria of any political philosophy (ideology, ideal, theory, agency), and for each stage of marxist development, I shall try to state carefully the relations among them. In criticizing the predictions of Marx or any marxist, I shall pay close attention to the time-span appropriate to understanding his work. If the time-span is not designated by the thinker in question, I shall criticize this as an un-marxist slip, and then consider, as a separate problem, the relevance of his expectations to present-day realities. I shall try to confront the fact as opposed to the expectation, the trend versus the theory; but also I shall consider the structural mechanics back of the fact or trend.

Perhaps all these rules may be summed up in one self-admonition, drawn from the practice of Karl Marx himself; understand and use consistently the principle of historical specificity. Any man can think only *within* his own times; but he can think *about* the past and the future, thus attempting to expand "his time," constructing out of its materials the image of an epoch. That—to a brilliant extent— is what Karl Marx did. In his work, the awareness of an epoch becomes available. Intellectually, what he provided was a general model of his social reality. Perhaps it was the best approximation available in its time of its time. Its inaccuracies of detail, its inadequacies of specific theory, are themselves fruitful errors.

That is why Marx's work still lives. It is being used in belief and practice. Living marxism realizes that neither marxists nor non-marxists, or anti-marxist scholars, have done much with it of late, in any rigorous intellectual way, but that this may be due less to anything inherent in the ideas than to political expediencies and other factors extraneous to marxism as theory. Such marxism is a lively part of any viable contemporary social science.

Dead marxism is just the opposite. It means to call upon Marx (or Lenin, or Trotsky, or whoever) as Authority; to treat their texts, or even their phrases, as sacred. Dead marxism is the view that it is all true, and that it contains all that men need to know.

So, I suppose the master rule for critics is: be a plain and live critic of plain and live marxism.

6. Critical Observations

The usefulness of any criticism depends upon agreement about what is being criticized—and that is an interpretation. The usefulness also depends upon the rules that are being followed—and these ought to be made explicit. The observations that follow are criticisms of Marx as I interpret his work (chapter 4) and are in accordance with the rules for critics (chapter 5).[1]

1. The economic basis of a society determines its social structure as a whole as well as the psychology of the people within it.

2. The dynamic of historical change is the conflict between the forces of production and the relations of production.

3. The class struggle between owners and workers is a social, political and psychological reflection of objective economic conflicts.

Exactly what is included and what is not included in "economic base" is not altogether clear, nor are the "forces" and "relations" of production precisely defined and consistently used. In particular: "science" seems to float between base and superstructure; and it is doubtful that either base or superstructure can be used (as Marx does) as units, for both are composed of a mixture of many elements and forces. Superstructure is a residual category for Marx, something into which to dump everything that is left over.

The distinction of base and superstructure itself is by

---

1. I shall follow the same order of points as in my inventory, with a preliminary comment (or counter-statement) elaborated in greater or lesser detail. This brief critique does not depend upon any positive alternative. Accordingly, I shall only suggest the outlines of a more adequate social model now available for capitalist society and its historical drift and thrust.

no means clear-cut. The institutional organization of a society, including relations of production, certainly penetrates deeply into technological implements and their scientific developments, including forces of production, shaping their meaning and their role in historical change. Many factors that cannot clearly be considered "economic" enter into what Marx seems to mean by "mode of production" or "economic base." That marxists hold such a wide variety of interpretations also seems to support my point. Moreover, the problem of mediation—exactly *how* the base determines the superstructure—is not worked out well. By what mechanisms and under precisely what conditions are economic conflicts "reflected" into psychological and political struggle is a question to which we shall return. Given the fundamental character of these conceptions, their looseness does lend a certain imprecision to the model as a whole.

4. Property as a source of income is the objective criterion of class: within capitalism, the two basic classes are the owners and the workers.

In the modern age, the "estates" of the medieval order were generally replaced by economic classes. This represents a shift in the prevailing principle of stratification and is one of the major points in the very definition of the two epochs. Various features of this shift from status to class, when generalized, are standard in sociological reflection.

Now, Marx's model stripped away all status remnants, defining the position of men within capitalist society solely in terms of their relation to the means of production, to the sources of their income. In part, this is due to his method of abstraction, and in part to his expectations about the development of capitalism. As method, it is a fruitful simplification if "class" is then used as *one* dimension of stratification. As substantive prediction, it has turned out to be mistaken.

In a similar way, later thinkers have abstracted and emphasized other dimensions, such as status, power, and occupation, and they have refined and elaborated the conception of economic class itself. Each of these methods for understanding the stratification of a society is most fruitfully used, first as a distinct, analytical tool; after that for empirical, historical inquiry of the several kinds of changing relations between each.

But Marx did not systematically confront such problems. In his few comments on the conception of class, as in his general expectations, he stuck to the simplification. In his historical studies he was more adequate, but on the whole his simplification becomes misleading and unfruitful.

Property as an objective criterion of class is indispensable to the understanding of the stratification of capitalist society. Alone it is inadequate and misleading, even for understanding economic stratification. In addition to property classes, which depend on the kinds and the sizes of property involved, we can usefully classify people who own no property in the means of production according to income classes.

Of course many specific combinations of sources and amounts of income are of decisive consequence for the political psychology of both higher and lower classes. For example, although the shift from owners to managers as the immediate controllers of corporate property does not mean that property becomes less important, these changes have led to a "corporate rich" stratum which cannot be understood solely in terms of property ownership.

The simple property versus wages distinction does not permit us to understand thoroughly even the *economic* facts of stratification today. Perhaps we could, had Marx's expectation of the polarization of naked class structure come about, but it has not and in all probability will not in the advanced capitalist societies. Be that as it may: to depend upon this distinction alone leads to further inadequacies of conception.

It enters his confusion—or at the very least, his ambiguity—about the relationship of "class consciousness" and other "subjective factors," with objective material circumstances. Without using other criteria than property, "class consciousness" (or its absence) cannot be explained, nor the role of ideology in political and class consciousness understood. In capitalist societies, among the immense majority who are propertyless, distinctions of status and occupation lead to or away from just those psychological and political consequences of economic stratification expected by Marx. To name only the most obvious, white collar employees, like factory workers, are without property and many receive less income; none the less to treat them together as one stratum, on the criterion of property alone, is to abdicate any real effort to understand one of the most consequential facts of stratification in all advanced capitalist societies.

5. Class struggle rather than harmony—"natural" or otherwise—is the normal and inevitable condition in capitalist society.

"Natural harmony" is indeed a myth, which classical economists (and eighteenth-century philosophers) used in their apologetics for capitalism and their hopeful views of progress. Yet it does not follow that class struggle is either normal or inevitable. To assert the first is to make a moral judgment rather than to state an empirical proposition; to assert the second is to ignore the increasing institutionalization of conflicts of economic interests. It is possible within capitalism for considerable periods, to transform class struggle into administrative regulations, just as it is possible to stabilize capitalism itself, subsidizing its deficiencies, defaults, and absurdities, by economic, military and political means. In brief, economic conflicts are not necessarily "contradictions" in Marx's sense, and they do not necessarily lead to the open political struggle of classes.

Perhaps this is most readily illustrated by the character and role of labor unions. Insofar as labor unions represent "classes," and labor-management controversy "class struggle," the object of the struggle has become to receive a greater share of the product, rather than to change capitalism as a social structure. Under such conditions, class struggle in Marx's sense, or in any reasonable meaning that can be given to it, does not necessarily grow sharper, more open, more political in form. On the contrary, it is often fragmented in occupational divisions of ever-increasing complexity. In the slump-boom cycle, the class struggle is intermittent and sometimes altogether absent. Above all, in the political economy as a whole, it has been institutionalized and limited to objectives whose realization lies within the bounty of the capitalist system. Collaboration is as much a fact of class history as is struggle. There are many varieties and many causes of both—historically specific causes which include more than economic conditions.

6. Within capitalist society, the workers cannot escape their exploited condition and their revolutionary destiny by winning legal or political rights and privileges; unions and mass labor parties are useful as training grounds for the revolution, but are not a guarantee of socialism.

The general fact is that rights and privileges, both economic and political, have been won, and that neither unions nor mass labor parties have generally served as such "training grounds." Organizations of wageworkers have been incorporated within the routines of twentieth-century capitalism. Their aims, their functions and their results have been firmly stabilized. They do not "normally" reveal, as Marx held, spontaneous anti-capitalism, much less the attempt to organize a new society. They are economic organizations operating within capitalism, and their policies do not transcend their businesslike function.

Moreover, in some advanced countries—notably, the United States—decisive unionization came about very late and in considerable part was achieved under the legal and political umbrella of a state generally dominated by middle and upper class interests. Such militancy as the unions displayed in their organizing stage declined, and then came to be widely accepted by capitalists. In fact, one of their functions has come to be part of the management of the labor force, a disciplining agent in the plant, in the firm, and even in the industry. They have become bureaucratic organizations which in the main work to stabilize relations between wageworkers and owners and managers of the means of production.[2]

7. Exploitation is built into capitalism as an economic system, thus increasing the chances for revolution.

The first part of the sentence I believe sound as a moral judgment—arguments about "theories of value" quite apart. But it is a moral judgment, disguised as an economic statement. The major and rather obvious point, however, is this: conditions which may be judged (rightly or wrongly) as exploitation have not, as yet, increased the chances for proletarian revolutions in any advanced capitalist society.

8. The class structure becomes more and more polarized, thus increasing the chance for revolution.

The polarization has not occurred; in the course of capitalism's history, the class structure has not been simpli-

2. For convenience of presentation, I am delaying my discussion of labor parties until we come to discuss Social Democracy. See chapter **7** below.

fied, as Marx expected, into two classes. On the contrary, the opposite trend has been general—and the more "advanced" the capitalism, the more complex and diversified has the stratification become.

The wageworkers in advanced capitalist societies have leveled off as a proportion of the labor force—in the USA, for example, this occurred before World War I. With automation, the trend certainly may be expected to continue. The intermediary or middle classes have not dwindled away. Their internal composition has changed, dramatically and drastically. They have become predominantly a New Middle Class of Salaried Employees, rather than an Old Middle Class of Entrepreneurs. As a whole their proportion to the working population has grown enormously.

In the twentieth century this has happened in all advanced capitalist countries. Among entrepreneurial farmers, a drastic decline in numbers; among free professionals, a leveling off; among small businessmen, a leveling off but also a great turnover with a high rate of bankruptcy and of new starts. The most decisive change is the expansion of the new middle class of salaried employees: salaried professionals, managers, office workers and sales personnel have composed the growing strata.

From a marxist point of view, these white collar employees can only be considered "a new proletariat," for they do not own the means of production with which they work, but work for wages or salaries. But to consider them in this category is seriously to limit one's understanding of them as a new set of strata. They are a new twentieth-century pyramid, superimposed upon and overlapping the older entrepreneurial-wageworker pyramid of nineteenth-century capitalism. Their higher-level managers have joined the property owners and with them constitute a corporate rich of a sort Marx did not know. Their middle and lower levels cannot be adequately understood as "merely" a new sort of proletariat.[3] They simply do not fit into the scheme of stratification provided by classic marxism, nor any scheme that is recognizably marxist; their very existence contradicts the expected two-class polarization of modern capitalism.

9. The material misery of the workers will increase, as will their alienation.

3. Cf. *White Collar.*

Economic or material misery has not increased inside the advanced capitalist world. On the contrary, the general fact has been an increase in material standards of living. Wageworkers have generally improved their economic condition, decreased their hours of work, abolished such cruel practices as child labor with which Marx was familiar, gained by their unions varying degrees of control over working conditions in factories, and, because of mechanization have much less brutal, physical toil to do than workers did in the nineteenth century.

Such facts are qualified in a decisive way by the mass unemployment of depression periods; and there is, even in the middle of general prosperity, much economic misery. But, as a whole, the secular trend of advanced capitalism in the twentieth century has been against Marx's expectation of increasing material misery—and for reasons that are not firmly a part of Marx's model of capitalism.

The improvement in the material standards of living is due (a) to institutional reforms of a political nature: the development of welfare programs by the state, and of the welfare state itself, which subsidizes and alleviates the economic deficiencies of the capitalist system. It is due (b) to the economic and political roles within capitalism played by labor unions and, in some countries, by labor parties. These agencies of the wageworkers have been reformist, and they have succeeded in putting through considerable reforms. Prosperity is also due (c) to the development of a seemingly permanent war economy which is, from an economic point of view, sheer waste on an enormous scale. And naturally the increased or continued standards of living rest upon (d) all those political, economic and military mechanisms on which the mid-twentieth-century stabilization of capitalism rests. (These will be discussed below, point 14.)

The relative weight of each of these, and of other mechanisms of capitalist prosperity and increased living standards, is of course controversial, but together, in one proportion or another, they have refuted Marx's expectation of increasing material misery within advanced capitalist societies. Moreover, they are not given sufficient weight in Marx's model of this society.

The shift of critical emphasis, by marxists and by non-marxists, is from material misery to psychological deprivation, or alienation. This emphasis is well within the orbit

of Marx's mind, especially of the young Marx, but as part
of marxist thinking it now lacks the solidity of its old ac-
companiment, material exploitation. New mechanisms of
"exploitation" have to be added. The increased time for leisure is dominated and even expropriated by the machinery
of amusement, for example. The chance really to experience, to reason and, in due course, the very capacity to
reason are often expropriated.

To read back into Marx these kinds of ideas, in the detail in which we know them, is going too far. They are not
there. Although Marx knew the subtleties of psychic exploitation, he did not know many that we know. The
mechanisms, the scope, the locale, and the effects of modern alienation do not necessarily contradict anything he
wrote but he did not describe them. Moreover, these psychic exploitations are not, we suspect, rooted in capitalism
alone and as such. They are also coming about in non-
capitalist and post-capitalist societies. They are not necessarily rooted either in the private ownership or in the
state ownership of the means of production; they may be
rooted in the facts of mass industrialization itself.

However that may be, the marxist conception of alienation, brilliant and illuminating as it is, remains, like class
consciousness, a quite rationalist conception. In these conceptions are mixed moral judgments; indeed, into his conception of "alienation," Marx has jammed his highest and
most noble image of man—and his fiercest indignation
about the crippling of man by capitalism. And he has the
strong tendency to impute, in an optative way, these judgments to the psychological realities of the work men do
and the life men lead. Often these are not the realities men
experience. The question of the attitude of men toward the
work they do, in capitalist and in non-capitalist societies,
is very much an empirical question, and one to which we
do not have adequate answers. At any rate, to say the
least, the condition in which Marx left the conception of
alienation is quite incomplete, and brilliantly ambiguous.

The case for alienation, then, is much more convincing
than that for material misery, although the variety and
the causes of alienation go beyond Marx's cryptic and
not too clear comments about it. Moreover, alienation does
not necessarily, or even usually, result in revolutionary
impulses. On the contrary, often it seems more likely to

be accompanied by political apathy than by insurgency of
either the left or right.

The psychological alternatives for men in capitalist society are no more polarized than is the class structure. Not
conservatism *or* insurgency, proletarian *or* bourgeois, but
social apathy, a developed and mature political indifference, is often the determining psychological condition.
Such apathy is not readily explained in terms of Marx's
rationalist model of ideological forms and class consciousness, or by his conception of alienation.

*10. The wageworkers, a class-in-itself, will be trans-
formed into the proletariat, a class-for-itself.*

In advanced capitalism this has occurred only episodically and partially. It tends to occur in earlier rather than
in later phases of industrialization, and in a situation in
which political repression coincides with economic exploitation. But neither the mechanisms nor the full mixture
of conditions under which it tends to occur are adequately
stated by Marx. In fact, they cannot be so stated in his
(economic) categories of stratification; for they involve
certain (autocratic) political conditions as well as considerations of the status and the occupational composition of
economic classes.

But for Marx the structural development of capitalism
—the growth of factories, of their enlarged scale and concentration, etc.—leads to the psychological and political
development of the proletariat, to its unity, its consciousness, its revolutionary insurgency. He was quite clearly
wrong.

Neither "consciousness" nor "existence" altogether determines the other. They interact, as Marx more or less in-
consistently knew. But "intervening variables" are also at
work: the means of mass communication, the machinery of
amusement, the cultural apparatus—in brief, features of the
ideological superstructure. Such variables mediate the relations of "existence" and "consciousness"; they affect
each of these and they affect their interplay. They can
play and often do play an autonomous role in the development of class consciousness or the lack of it. Existence
itself is subject to the definitions of reality carried by the
cultural apparatus. Consciousness itself, even self-identity, is
also subject to these stereotypes and meanings.

In his notion of class, Marx tends to confuse the objective fact of it, a statistical aggregation of people, with the psychological developments that may occur within its membership. He seems to believe that class consciousness is a necessary psychological consequence of objective economic development, which includes the polarization of owners and workers. To Marx there is no ambiguity about this because the psychological and political results are, in some way not fully explained, the product of economic changes. But the connections between economic facts and psychological changes are not well considered as empirical questions.

The conditions under which class consciousness of the sort Marx had in mind does occur are not fully known, but it is certain that they include more than economic developments in general, or relations to the means of production in particular. This is true even if we assume that economic developments are the prime movers of all historical change. The mechanisms by which such changes in the economic base lead to psychological changes are not worked out by Marx (or by later marxists).

If we agree with Marx that ideas must be connected with material interest to have any effect—must become justifications or criticisms—this is not to agree that ideas are accordingly mere "reflections" of such interests. In a satisfactory model of social structure we must allow a considerable degree of autonomy to the formation and role of ideas. We must trace the ways in which ideas are related to individuals and to institutions with more sophistication than Marx was able to achieve in his general model. In such work we are not limited (for the social bases to which we may impute ideas) to economic classes, however defined, still less to only two such classes.

The inadequacy of Marx's notion of "class interests" is of great moral importance. He does not consider the difference between (a) What Is to the Interests of Men according to an analysis of their position in society, and (b) What Men Are Interested In according to the men themselves. Nor does he confront fully (as we must since Lenin), the moral meaning of the political uses of this distinction. (This is the moral root of problems of leninism and of the meaning of democracy and freedom.)

Marx himself is able to avoid these problems because of

a confusion in his very categories of stratification, and because of the optative mood of his statements. By "to the interest of" Marx means, I take it, long-run general and rational interests. And to him, consciousness of such interests is revolutionary class consciousness. All else is temporary, partial, irrational, not yet fully developed.

But the fact is that men are often concerned with temporary rather than long-run interests, and with particular interests, of occupational trades, for example, rather than the more general interests of their class. Also it is a matter of intellectual controversy and of moral judgment to determine what is temporary or durable, and it is certainly in part a moral judgment to decide what is "rational," and whether or not class interests are the only, or even the main, rational interests. Marx's view of class consciousness is however as utilitarian and rationalist as anything out of Jeremy Bentham. "Class consciousness" is the marxian counterpart to liberalism's image of "man as citizen."

Two possibilities must be considered. First, revolutionary class consciousness in which what is to men's interests is also what they are interested in; objective conditions and subjective development coincide. This point of coincidence between economic and psychological trends is the political target of classic marxism and it is also assumed to be an inevitable product of the course of capitalist history.

But second, there are some occasions when men are *not* interested in what is to their rational interests (however judged) and others when they *are* interested in what is not to their interests. Such men, according to Marx, are "falsely conscious," and they are in this irrational state because objective and subjective developments do not as yet coincide. He assumes that capitalist history will do away with false consciousness. Obviously it has not.

11. The opportunity for revolution exists only when objective conditions and subjective readiness coincide.

Obviously true—and a truism. As already indicated, the two processes have not coincided in any advanced capitalist society, even the most advanced in the worst depression so far—the USA in the 1930's.

12. The functional indispensability of a class in the economic system leads to its political supremacy in the society as a whole.

This assumption, which underlies Marx's theory of power, seems to be drawn from the history of the bourgeoisie. Becoming functionally supreme within the feudal system, the bourgeoisie broke out of it to form the new society of capitalism. Likewise, reasoned Marx, within advanced capitalism, as the bourgeoisie becomes parasitical, and capitalism beset by contradictions, the workers will become the functionally indispensable class. Accordingly, they too will smash the system that hampers its own functioning; they too will become the ascendant class. Behind the marxian theory of power, in short, there is a grand—and false—historical analogy of bourgeoisie with proletariat, of the transition from feudalism to capitalism with that from capitalism to socialism.

"The ancient slave," Professor Bober has noted, "did not erect the feudal system, nor the serf or journeyman the capitalist system. History does not demonstrate that the exploited class of one society is the architect of the next social organization."[4] Capitalism did not come about because of a class struggle between exploited serfs and nobles or between journeymen and exploiting guildmasters. The economy and the society of the bourgeoisie grew up as an independent structure within feudalism.

In eighteenth-century France, the bourgeoisie became economically and politically powerful enough to gain control over the government, to smash the status and legal privileges of the nobles, and to reconstruct the social structure in accordance with bourgeois interests in an extended free market and a redistribution of taxation burdens. But, these successes of the middle classes were caused by their very wealth, which in the end made it impossible for governments lacking their support to govern.

In contrast, capitalists and wageworkers *are* part of the same economic and social structure: within capitalism, wageworkers are *not* representatives of any independent economic system. As already indicated, what capitalist and wageworkers fight over is the distribution of the product, not the capitalist system of production as such. In contrast with the bourgeoisie (which before the French Revolution was expanding in size and in importance), the

4. M. M. Bober, *Karl Marx's Interpretation of History*, Second Edition, Revised (Harvard Economic Studies, Vol. 31; Cambridge, Mass., 1948), p. 340.

wageworkers of advanced twentieth-century capitalism have in both respects declined.

In addition to the falseness of the historical analogy on which it rests, this theory of power seems too formal to be a useful guide to investigation. More than that, it is often misleading. It obscures the organizational connection between classes and political institutions, and the role of political ideas and ideals, as well as of military force, in capturing and using the power of the state.

The notion is upset, for example, by the fact of Nazi Germany where, on any reasonable account, parasitical and functionally useless elements of German society gained political power. There are of course many other instances of the military seizure and political maintenance of the powers of the state. Economic indispensability does *not* necessarily, and certainly does not automatically, lead to political power. Economic parasitism does not automatically lead to loss of political power.

13. In all class societies, the state is the coercive instrument of the owning classes.

This is true only in part and on occasion. It is certainly not an exhaustive statement of the functions or the interests served by the state in the full variety of advanced capitalist societies. In societies with propertied classes, the state can not adequately be understood as "merely" the instrument of such classes. In societies without propertied classes, the state does not appear to wither away, nor does it miraculously change all its functions and meanings merely because those who dominate society by means of it talk ideologically of the class "interests" the state serves.

Allied with Marx's conception of the state, and its theory of power, is the phrase "the ruling class." As with the conception of the state, this phrase enables those who use it to smuggle in by means of definition A Theory: the theory that the top economic class is also necessarily the top political group. I say "smuggle in" because use of the phrase, ruling class, implies what ought to be examined. To examine the theory, to test it, we must use more clear-cut and distinct terms. Although it was not developed as a criticism of Marx, I have suggested "the power elite" as a useful, unloaded term.

There is more to the difference (ruling class versus

power elite) than mere terminology. The latter conception leaves empirically open the question of economic determinism and the problem of the relative weight of upper economic classes within the higher circles. If the political order and the military establishment are given their due place alongside the economic system, it follows that our conception of the higher circles in capitalist society must be seen as more complex than the rather simple "ruling class" of Marx, and especially later marxists.

This is *not* a matter of something called "elite theory" (whatever that might be) versus "class theory." Both are *structural* conceptions, defined by reference to the institutional positions men occupy and, accordingly, to the means of power that are available to them. It is the shape, the variety, the relations, the weight of such institutions and such positions within them that is at question. And these are not questions that can be solved by definition.

The element of truth—and it is a large and important truth—in Marx's theory of the state is his general conception of the powers of property. Property does provide not merely control over things, but also control over men. This power is exercised in many different spheres of life, and some of them certainly through the state. But two points must be considered.

First, the powers of property in capitalism are restricted by labor unions, which also act through the state, and by other forces that do countervail against the naked political and economic powers of property.

Second, to nationalize property does not necessarily eliminate "the powers of property." It may in fact increase the actual exploitation of men by men in all social spheres; it may be more difficult to oppose exploitation or to do away with it. Marx generally assumed that, with the abolition of propertied classes, democratic mechanisms would accompany the collectivization. For us today, this must, to say the least, be taken as an open question.

Together, these two points raise serious questions about the adequacy of Marx's conception of the state. The source of his error is his economic determinism and his neglect of political and military institutions as autonomous and originative—matters I shall examine later. Here it is sufficient to note that if we *define* the state as a "committee of the ruling class" or "of propertied classes," we cannot very well *test*, within various societies, the range of relations between economic classes and political forms. But if we focus first in a clear-cut and unilateral way upon the means of political rule, and *define* the state, with Max Weber, simply as an organization that "monopolizes legitimate violence over a given territory," then we can be historically specific and empirically open in our reflections. And that is what we ought to do: make of the state an object of inquiry, rather than a theory closed up in a slogan.

This is a matter of comparative and historical inquiry, but even without any such close analysis it is obvious that quite different political systems can and do coexist with similar capitalist economic bases: the United States in 1920, Nazi Germany, England in the 1940's, Sweden today. Surely it is careless to lump all these together as "committees of the propertied classes."

14. Capitalism is involved in one economic crisis after another. These crises are getting worse. So capitalism moves into its final crisis—and the revolution of the proletariat.

The slump-boom cycle is a foremost economic fact about the history of capitalism. But it is a very real question whether or not this cycle is inherent in capitalism, as presently organized in individual nation-states and on an international scale. The political role of the state, in direct and indirect economic actions, of unions and of labor parties, of the economic brinkmanship of military preparation—these and other developments transform the problem of crisis from a problem of seemingly inevitable economic mechanisms into political and military issues of international and domestic scale.

On the stabilization of advanced capitalism, in general, I think we have now to say: Not yet proved one way or another, still in balance. By no means may we rule out severe economic crisis; the general model of crisis set forth by Marx is instructive. *But* to prove Karl Marx's theories correct or incorrect on this point, it is not enough to show that capitalism is in trouble, or even that it is subject to severe crises. To proceed in that way would be to treat Marx as a mere prophet, rather than as the social analyst he was. We must ask: What are the causes of the trouble, the nature of the crises? And what are their results? To these questions Marx is an inadequate guide.

The mechanics of such stabilization as does prevail—and the instabilities too, as well as the possible downfall—are not due to the internal, economic developments Marx foresaw. The mechanics of stabilization now very much include imperialist mechanics of a sort Marx did not foresee and, above all, the threat of competition with an economically developed, politically consolidated, militarily strong non-capitalist structure—the sino-soviet bloc—about which Marx clearly had nothing to say.

Considered internally, the problems of capitalist crisis are political and military issues rather than economic problems as such. These issues exist because what must be done economically is politically repugnant to the most powerful capitalist interests. War preparation as a means of *economic* brinkmanship is more often more to their taste.

Advanced capitalism, in its political, military and economic forms, has been stabilized on an international scale. Self-corrections within it, of a politically facilitated kind, are at work, not only within but also between the advanced capitalist economies. International aid and support has been available among capitalist societies—for political and military reasons, no doubt—but with the economic result of capitalist prosperity for both North America and Western Europe. Most United States aid since World War II has been used to help resuscitate the capitalist economies of already advanced societies, not to industrialize non-industrial areas. This postwar reconstruction of the advanced capitalist systems (former allies and former enemies alike) has tended to consolidate them as an economic bloc at high levels of economic activity, and to stabilize this bloc politically and militarily on an international scale. The major political meaning of this work lay in the military postures that have been assumed by the USA and USSR. Given that posture, the USA aided the world capitalist recovery and boom, directly by military aid and indirectly by assuming most of the "burden" of military preparation for a possible World War III.

In the meantime, regardless of causes, advanced capitalism has not collapsed in economic crisis; crises or slumps have indeed occurred, but these appear more episodic than secular. Moreover, in overcoming them in non-marxian ways, capitalist society as known to Marx has been changed into other forms, many of them not expected by Marx.

What has come to prevail is a politically and militarily organized capitalism. Its managers *have* alleviated economic crisis, and there has been especially since World War II began, an economic boom on an unprecedented scale.

Marx did not see clearly and adequately the nature of capitalism's monopoly form and the political and military manner of its stabilization. In this monopoly form it has not remained merely "an anarchy of production." Vast sectors of it have been highly rationalized by private corporations, trade associations, and state intervention. Capitalism and bureaucracy, in brief, are not polar opposites. They have been integrated. The anarchy of production has not been generalized; to a considerable extent, it has been rationalized.

The operation of the most advanced capitalist economies at high levels is also due, in considerable part, to "artificially stimulated demands;" built into them is systematic waste on an enormous scale, a scale not even Marx fully grasped. The "status obsolescence" of perfectly serviceable commodities is one example; the change of automobile models by Detroit costs more than several years of "the whole of the productive investment program of all of India." [5] The economic waste of mass advertisement, not to speak of the preparation for war, are further examples.

But this is just the point: Marx did not know that despite all this waste, in part because of it, the engines of capitalist production and productivity could continue and even increase. He saw the waste, the fraud, the contradictions, but he underestimated the fabulous capacities (technical, economic, political) of fully developed capitalism as we know it today.

The gap between possible and actual production in advanced capitalism is indeed, as Marx saw clearly, enormous. This contradiction, objectively speaking, has grown greater and probably will continue to do so, for scientific possibilities *are* restricted by waste, fraud, inefficiency, and short-run profit-seeking. But it is a political gap rather than an "economic contradiction." Increasingly a matter of moral evaluation and an object of political decision, it has *not* resulted even during severe economic depression, in any "proletarian upsurge" to resolve it.

5. Thomas Balogh, *The New Statesman*, 12 December 1959.

Marx assumes that capitalism is a dynamic system largely determined by economic forces at work within it. As such, his model is a brilliant description, analysis and prediction. But the fact is that "other forces" *have* interfered with the economic mechanics. Some of these are within it—in particular political and military forces; some are outside it—in particular the world consolidation of the sino-soviet bloc as a counter-force to world capitalism. The fate of capitalism as a system now depends upon these forces as well as upon its own internal economic mechanics.

15. The post-capitalist society will first pass through a transitional stage—that of the dictatorship of the proletariat; then it will move into a higher phase in which true communism will prevail.

About this, we have no information: a proletarian revolution of the sort Marx had in mind has never occurred. The revolutions "made in his name" have occurred in types of society quite different than those he had in mind. These we shall consider when we examine post-Marx marxism.

16. Although men make their own history, given the circumstances of the economic foundations, the way they make it and the direction it takes are determined. The course of history is structurally limited to the point of being inevitable.

The general model of history-making set forth by Marx and Engels is (a) a generalization applied to the whole of society of the economic model of the market of classic capitalism, in which events are the unintended results of innumerable deciders (buyers and sellers determining prices, for example). It is also (b) a generalization from one historically specific phase of capitalism—in the main, Victorian Great Britain—to the whole of the capitalist epoch, and perhaps to all previous history as well.

The historic facts now at hand suggest the need for an additional model. These facts are: the increased scope and the centralization of the means of power in every major institutional order of society, political, economic, military. Because of these facts we must construct another model in which events may be understood in closer and in more conscious relation to the decisions and lack of decisions of powerful elites, political and military as well as economic. We must apply this model, with appropriate modifications, to the understanding of soviet types of society, to underdeveloped countries, as well as to advanced capitalist societies.

The categories of political, military and economic elites are thus as important (or more so) to the analysis and understanding of our times as the mechanics of economic classes and other more impersonal forces of history-making.

The marxist model of history is brilliantly constructed and, for one phase of one type of society, it is generally the most appropriate. But taken alone and used universally, it is an undue generalization and as such, inadequate. It assumes a society in which the typical units are small in scale and their mode of interaction, like that of the free market economy, autonomous. In marxist terms, such a society is referred to as "the kingdom of necessity." Marx also refers, of course, to the "kingdom of freedom," to the post-capitalist realm in which men will be masters of their own fate and intention will more closely coincide with resultant event. The realm of necessity still does prevail; and Marx's model of it is useful in all types of society, in much of advanced capitalism, as well as in the undeveloped world. The realm of freedom is still an ideal only; as Marx envisaged it, it exists nowhere.

But these are not the only two models of history-making available; and we cannot suppose that the second is the only alternative to the first. Further models are needed for advanced capitalism as well as for other types of society.

The sequence of epochs Marx imagined, is not necessarily going to happen. The sequence (from feudalism to capitalism and from capitalism to socialism) is the big historical framework of Marx's theory and expectation. We must now modify it: out of advanced capitalism nowhere has socialism, of any sort recognizable as marxist, come; out of feudalism socialism of one type has sprung directly. In this type, moreover, the assumed coincidence of the individual's interests with those of his community—the realm of freedom—is not the unambiguous case.

So these epochs themselves—feudalism, capitalism, socialism—need revision: the capitalism that prevails is not the capitalism Marx knew; the post-capitalist societies that have arisen do not conform to Marx's expectations, either in their origins or in their character. The socialism, much less the communism, that Marx expected is certainly not, as yet, the society that has come about out of one type of feudalism, in the sino-soviet zone.

17. The social structure, as noted in proposition number 1, is determined by its economic foundations; accordingly, the course of its history is determined by changes in these economic foundations.

The economic means are only one means of power, and they may themselves be shaped, in fact determined, by political and military means and in accordance with military and political aims and interest. "Political determinism" and "military determinism" are often as relevant as, or more relevant than, "economic determinism" to the explanation of many pivotal events in the mid-twentieth century.

The economic determinism of Marx (and along with it, the inevitability of history with which it is closely linked) is usually placed in opposition to the "moral determination" of liberals and of utopian socialists. Both views, I think, are historically specific to the period between the French Revolution and the First World War, and in particular to Great Britain and the United States. Neither can be taken as universal. Both must be reconsidered in the light of events in our own present time and immediately foreseeable future. And we are *not*, of course, limited to either moral or economic determinism.

Since Marx's day, the social structures of capitalism have changed to such an extent as to require a new statement of the causal weight of economic institutions, and of their causal relations with other institutions. In view of the history of marxist movements, the developments in advanced capitalism, and the conditions and prospects of the underdeveloped world—economic determinism has come to seem a fundamental (although a most fruitful) error in Marx's work. The view that economic causes are the supreme causes within capitalism is directly linked with the erroneous expectations about the role of the wageworker, the over-formal theory of power, and the oversimplified conception of the state.

Since the First World War, it has become increasingly clear that political forms may drastically modify—and even, on occasion, determine—the economies of a society. Not the mode of economic production but the mode of political action may well be decisive. As more and more areas of social life, private as well as public, become objects of political organization, a struggle, for political ideals and for the political and military means of action and decision must, along with economic means, be seen as keys to man's making of history.

This does not mean that economic powers are minor, or that they are not translated into effective political and military power. But it does mean that with the expansion of the state, economic powers are now often defensive and limited, and that they are not the all-sufficient key to the understanding of political power or to the shaping of total social structures.

Many twentieth-century economic developments must themselves be explained by changes in political and military forces. I do not mean to replace "economic determinism" by "political determinism" or "military determinism," but only to suggest that the causal weight of each of these types is not subject to any historically universal rule. It must be historically determined in the case of any given society.

In various capitalist societies, political policies have greatly modified the economic base—and the social effects of economics upon all strata of the population. The welfare state is not "determined" by the mode of economic production, although of course it is made possible by economic developments. What is politically possible within present-day capitalist economies undoubtedly is wider than Marx's doctrine would lead us to expect. Just how wide it is, we cannot predict, but there is nothing inherent in the capitalist economic system that prohibits *political* history-making, including reform and deliberate change of the economy itself.

Within the present era of capitalism, the arena of conflict and the motor of historic change is less the economic base as such than the political and economic institutions joined into the political economy. This kind of political capitalism Marx neither knew nor foresaw. He did not grasp the almost neo-mercantilist form it has taken, nor the extent and effects of politically controlled and subsidized capitalism. The subsidies have been direct and indirect, of a welfare and of a military nature. That they may be considered subsidies of the economic defaults of capitalism does not alter my point: it strengthens it.

The political forces that have modified capitalism in

some countries are reforms carried out in Marx's name; in others, as in the New Deal, they are liberal forces, often led by upper class circles and strongly influenced by the weight of those "intermediary classes" that were, according to Marx, supposed to dwindle away. In part, too, the modifications are of course concessions made by monopoly capitalists in pursuit of their own interests. Capitalists have more political control over economic forces and so can perpetuate their role in political capitalism, thus upsetting the marxist anticipations of economic crisis and its expected results.

In brief, we must generalize Marx's approach to economics. We come then to focus—as did Marx—upon the changing techniques of economic production. But we also focus—as did Max Weber—upon the techniques of military violence, of political struggle and administration, and upon the means of communication—in short, upon *all* the means of power, and upon their quite varied relations with one another in historically specific societies.

So we may speak in a thoroughly marxist manner of the appropriation and monopolization of such political and military means. The emphasis upon the economy must be treated as a convenience of method. We must always try to distinguish its causal weight in the society as a whole, but we must leave open the possibilities of more political and more military autonomy than did Marx.

I think this is a necessary and useful refinement and elaboration of the general model of society drawn up by Marx. It then becomes possible to do *whatever* marxists may wish by way of arguing and investigating economic determinism. But economic determinism becomes one hypothesis to be tested in each specific epoch and society. Military determinism and political determinism may also be so tested. Given the present state of our knowledge, no one of the three should automatically be assumed to predominate uniformly among history-making factors in all societies, or even in all types of capitalist societies.

There is one implication of economic determinism quite detrimental to the present-day usefulness of Marx's work: the role of the nation-state and of nationalism in history. That nationalism would decline and internationalism come to be paramount in the ideology and political policies pursued by wageworkers—these expectations have turned out to be quite wrong. This is revealed within socialist movements and communist states, within capitalist societies, and within colonial and underdeveloped areas.

Within capitalism, internationalism as a current has generally declined in force since Marx's time. The wageworkers have certainly been no less nationalist than have middle and upper classes. The most dramatic blow to the idea of "internationalism," especially in Germany, was struck by The Second International at the time of the First World War. On August 4, 1914, European "socialism" gave way to "nationalism" in a decisive way.

One meaning of such facts for the marxist model is that classes are only one basis in terms of which consciousness —and specifically, passionate consciousness—of interest may be formed; many other bases interfere with it, however strong at times it may be. Nationalism is only the most obvious example of this more general fact. Yet it *is* a grievous one. Nationalism, contrary to Marx's general assumption, has increased in importance as a political and economic force, as a military form, and as a basis of men's consciousness. In the making of history today, nation-states—and supra-national blocs of states—are the most immediate forms of organization, political consciousness and militant will. Classes, and particularly alliances of classes, do of course operate by means of nation-states, but the political and military powers resting in these political structures and upon nationalist consciousness often reshape classes and alliances of classes. Economic differences are greater between one nation-state and another than between classes within the advanced capitalist nations. Whatever the practice of later marxists may reveal, the idea does not form a systematic part of the work of Karl Marx.

To summarize, at the center of Marx's thought—indeed of all varieties of marxism—there is this proposition: of all the elements and forces of capitalist society it is the wageworkers who are destined to be the dynamic political actors in the maturity and in the decline of capitalism. Virtually every feature of marxism, as we have noted, finds its place as an explanation of why this process goes on and why it must go on.

Intellectually, that is the heart of marxism. The theories of trend, noted in our inventory, lie immediately back of this labor metaphysic and support it as the central proposition about what is going on in the advanced capitalist world.

Morally, too, marxism is an affirmation of the processes by which the wageworkers are becoming a revolutionary proletariat, and a celebration of the revolutionary drama they are going to enact.

Politically, the history of the marxists is at bottom a set of strategies and efforts to further these processes, and so to make possible or to insure the enactment of that drama.

This being so, it must immediately be said that Marx's major political expectation about advanced capitalist societies has collapsed: the central agency which he designates has not developed as expected; the role he expected that agency to enact has not been enacted. The trends supposed to facilitate the development and the role of the agency have not generally come off—and when they have occurred, episodically and in part, they have not led to the results expected.

Wageworkers in advanced capitalism have rarely become a "proletariat vanguard"; they have not become the agency of any revolutionary change of epoch. To a very considerable extent they have been incorporated into nationalist capitalism—economically, politically, and psychologically. So incorporated, they constitute within capitalism a dependent rather than an independent variable. The same is true of labor unions and of labor parties. These organizations function politically and economically in a reformist manner only, and within the capitalist system. Class struggle in the marxist sense does not *prevail;* conflicts of economic interests have quite generally been institutionalized: they are subject to indirect and bureaucratic decision, rather than to open and political battle. There are, of course, basic class conflicts of interest. But there is little class struggle over them.

These points form a serious charge against Marx; they carry implications for the categories and the model which he set forth. To put it in another way, not only have the expectations of Marx failed to come about in any advanced capitalist society, but there are very good reasons to expect that they are not going to come about in the manner and on the scale expected by Marx. It is not merely a matter of an empirical miss: it rests upon theoretical deficiencies of his categories and in his general model of capitalism.

Such, after all, is only to be expected in view of the fact

that Marx's model as a whole, and in virtually all of its parts, is built upon and around the labor metaphysic. Since this labor metaphysic provides the central thrust and the major political expectation of classic marxism, its collapse entails the collapse of much else in his thinking.

Behind the labor metaphysic and the erroneous views of its supporting trends there are deficiencies in the marxist categories of stratification; ambiguities and misjudgments about the psychological and political consequences of the development of the economic base; errors concerning the supremacy of economic causes within the history of societies and the mentality of classes; inadequacies of a rationalist psychological theory; a generally erroneous theory of power; an inadequate conception of the state.

Even being as generous as possible in our application to Marx's work of his own principle of historic specificity, we find him too wrong on too many points. The political, psychological and economic expectations clearly derivable from his work seem increasingly unreal, his model as a whole increasingly inadequate. His theories bear the stamp of Victorian capitalism. It is little wonder: that is what they are about. We must accuse him of dying, his work unfinished, in 1883.

Of course it is easy to confront nineteenth-century doctrine with twentieth-century events—so many decades have passed since Marx's work was done. Such easy hindsight about such work as his may make one feel cheap; but it is inevitable for any possible advance in social reflection and inquiry. Classic marxism today is less an adequate definition of advanced capitalist realities than a political statement in the optative mood.

But we must now ask: Has the value of Marx's *method* of work been destroyed? My answer to this should already be clear: No. His method is a signal and lasting contribution to the best sociological ways of reflection and inquiry available.[6]

6. I do *not* refer to the mysterious "laws of dialectics," which Marx never explains clearly but which his disciples claim to use. The outsider must note that among the dialecticians there is no agreement on the meaning of dialectics. But consider, for a moment, the "three laws":

First, quantitative changes produce qualitative changes, and vice versa. The polemic that Marx makes with this "law" is against those who believe that there are no "leaps" (that is, revolutions) in history, but only a minute series of gradual changes. In our revolutionary epoch it is no longer necessary to "refute" such a view by reference to pretentious "laws." It is obvious that if anything changes enough, it becomes something different than what it was to begin with. (Cont'd on p. 130).

But has the value of his general *model* of society and of history been destroyed by the run of historical events that have overturned specific theories and expectations? My answer to this question is, substantively: Yes. The model as Marx left it is inadequate. One can use it only with great intellectual clumsiness and wasted sophistication, and often only with doubletalk. For us today, the work of Marx is a beginning point, not a finished view of the social worlds we are trying to understand. So far as our own orienting political philosophy and our own social theories are concerned, we may not know just where we stand but there is little doubt that we are somewhere "beyond Marx." Proof for

---

Second, "the negation of the negation": one thing grows out of another and then does battle with it. In turn, the newly grown produces in itself "the seeds of its own destruction." Marx's texts are full of metaphors from the reproductive cycle and the hospital delivery-room. Things are pregnant; there are false alarms; wombs and midwives abound. And finally, there is bloody birth. Thus the proletariat, born from the womb of capitalism, in turn makes capitalist society "pregnant with revolution." But there is no clear-cut method for recognizing "negation"; one should not mistake metaphors of style for a method of thinking, much less for "a general scientific law of nature." The substantive content is merely this: that things (sometimes) grow out of others and (sometimes) in due course displace them.

Third, the "law" that marxists consider the most important: "the interpenetration of opposites," which I take to mean that there are objective contradictions and resolutions in the world. This is clearly to confuse logic with metaphysics: one can say that the *statements* men make are often contradictory. One cannot say that trees or rocks, or, for that matter, classes "contradict" one another. Men can believe that positive and negative charges of electricity contradict each other, but this clearly is to anthropomorphize electricity.

The simple truth about the "laws of dialectics," as discerned in Marx, is that they are ways of talking about matters *after* these matters have been explained in ordinary ways of discourse and proof. Marx himself never *explained* anything by the "laws of dialectics," although he did not avoid, on occasion, the dialectical vocabulary of obscurantism. "Dialectics" was, after all, the vocabulary of the Hegelian-trained man, and Marx did put this vocabulary to good substantive use: in terms of dialectics he rejected the absurdity of eighteenth-century views of "natural harmony"; achieved a sense of the fluidity and many-sided nature of history-making; saw the "universal interconnection" of all its forces; consistently maintained an awareness of perennial change, of genuine conflict, of the ambiguous potentialities of every historical situation.

We may also understand that if not for Marx, for many marxists, mere reference to "dialectical" serves to let one out of the determinist trap. But for self-appointed "insiders" it is all too often an intellectually cheap way to mysterious insights, a substitute for the hard work of learning. Perhaps their insistence upon this language is due mainly to their having become disciples before having read much else. For us, the "dialectical method" is either a mess of platitudes, a way of doubletalk, a pretentious obscurantism—or all three. The essential error of "the dialectician" is the know-it-all confusion of logic with metaphysics; if the rules of dialectics were "the most general laws of motion" all physical scientists would use them every day. On the other hand, if dialectics is the "science of thinking," then we are dealing with the subject-matter of psychology, and not with logic or method at all. As a guide to thinking, "dialectics" can be more burdensome than helpful, for if everything is connected, dialectically, with everything else, then you must know "everything" in order to know anything, and causal sequences become difficult to trace.

this, fragmentary but nonetheless decisive, has been suggested in the present chapter.

But there is one further question. "Marxism" certainly does not end with Marx. It begins with him. Later thinkers and actors have used, revised, elaborated his ideas, and set forth quite new doctrines, theories and strategies. In one way or another, these are indeed "based upon Marx," although they can be identified with classic marxism only by those who feel they must distort intellectual and political history for their unmarxist need for certainty through orthodoxy. That is not the question. The question is: Are any of these later theories adequate as political orientation and useful for social inquiry today? Let us examine the most important and influential of these.

7. Roads to Socialism

The intellectual history of marxism is characterized by tortuous and savage controversies. To many outsiders they often appear sectarian as well. But for the thinkers and politicians engaged in them, these controversies have been and are truly agonizing and of the most vital intellectual importance. The intellectual work of Marx and of post-Marx marxists, is no calm debate in scholarly circles; it occurs in close connection with decision and event. It consists of a continuous series of doctrinal battles fought with close attention to personal need and political defeat, moral aspiration and again defeat. And it is connected with historic questions of supreme human importance. Each revision, elaboration, rebuttal, deviation is geared to political and economic developments first within one nation, then another, and now within the world as a whole.

Each of the several major phases into which the development of marxism may conveniently be divided is at once a political stage and an intellectual pivot. As we quickly pass them in preliminary review in the present chapter we must pay attention to the immediate political *context* of each phase, and to the *agencies* of historical change that each emphasizes.

In the 1840's, among western thinkers with generally socialist objectives, several reform programs competed with each other and with various liberal doctrines. These provided the intellectual and political context for the ideas of the young Marx. Many small groups and utopian colonies, as well as publics and schools, existed under the general name of "socialism." A welter of German doctrines, English views, French ideologies prevailed. And there were many projects and "projectors." They all denounced the power that monopoly of property gave some men over other men. But about programs, they differed greatly. Some favored large industrial enterprises; others, small communities of agrarian and craft workmen. Some wanted property to be parceled out in small units; others wanted it concentrated and held in large collective ownership. Some wanted equality of income for all men; others wanted income distributed according to need or service, or left to the workings of free markets. Some would abolish all inheritance; others regarded inheritance as necessary for family and economic continuity. Some wanted the technically efficient to rule economic affairs; others wanted a purer democratic rule.[1]

If we try to sort out all these "roads to socialism," three main tendencies appear during the nineteenth century: (1) some men withdrew, as it were, into utopian communities within which to practice or at least to try out their anti-capitalist principles; (2) some appealed to the powerful on the basis of reason and in terms of such ideals as justice; (3) others thought of making a socialist revolution. Among these revolutionaries, some had in mind a more or less spontaneous uprising of exploited masses or perhaps direct action by labor unions. Others thought of the revolution as the conspiracy of a small, tightly-knit party. In between, at different times someone held almost every view imaginable.

When in the late nineteenth century, the right to vote became more nearly universal and labor unions more effective and secure, a fourth road to socialism appeared: (4) through the work of trade unions, pressure groups, co-operatives, and legal parties might come a series of victories at the polls, the resultant parliamentary legislation bringing socialism.

Karl Marx rejected the first road (the isolated socialist community) and the second (the moral-utopian appeal to the powerful); the fourth (the social democratic way) he never really considered, although Engels did confront the question at the end of his life.

We should remember that during their lifetimes, Marx and Engels were in close touch with various political circles and parties; they wrote letters and manifestoes; they made speeches to small groups of people, insurgent scholars and stray, often immigrant, workmen. But neither was a direct

political leader of any consequence.[2] They were intellectuals
—political intellectuals. As such, throughout his lifetime
Marx remained a revolutionary socialist. Although he
learned much about practical revolution-making from his
experience of 1848, and by his careful study of the Paris
Commune of 1871, he could not, or at least did not, spell
out clearly the *manner* of the proletarian revolution. Other
men came to spell it out differently, each in the name of
Marx, and much disagreement about "the roads to socialism" persists.

The ideas of Marx did of course become involved in
political action; in fact, his work as a whole became the
basis for all important left-wing activities and thought.
Almost immediately its influence spread in two directions,[3]
and this political split of marxism, in one form or another,
has remained decisive:

The Social Democratic: a mass party claiming socialism
as its objective, advocating education of the working class
so that its members will understand the reasons they should
vote themselves into power. In general, social democracy is
about how to install socialism in advanced capitalist nations having parliamentary political systems.

The Bolshevik: a small party of professional revolutionaries which prepares above all for the conquest of state
power, hits quickly at opportune moments, enlisting the
support of larger circles and of masses on immediate issues.
In general, bolshevism is about how to make a revolution
in an economically backward country having a despotic
government.

Leaving aside for the moment theoretical judgments
about which of these is more in line with the ideas of Marx,
which is the most "orthodox," let us consider the historical
facts and interpretations. Social democracy as displayed in
Eduard Bernstein's legal and evolutionary socialism con-
tends that a socialist party enrolling a major section of the

2. In London in 1864, a group of British and French trade unionists—
and Karl Marx—founded "The International Working Men's Association"
which soon included delegates from other nations of Europe. The Association was full of turbulent rivalry, notably between Marx and M. A.
Bakunin, the Russian anarchist. Perhaps its organizational peak was The
Hague Congress of the early seventies. There 65 delegates gathered: 18
Frenchmen, 15 Germans; the rest were scattered, with one Dane, one
Irishman, one Pole. Among them were tailors and printers, teachers and
shoemakers, and one "porcelain painter." See H. H. Gerth's admirably
edited volume, *The First International: Minutes of The Hague Conference
of 1872*, with Related Documents (Madison, 1958).
3. The third is that of anarchism and syndicalism, which, as I have
already noted, I cannot consider in this book. See Irving L. Horowitz,
Radicalism and the Revolt against Reason (London and New York, 1961).

electorate and linked with trade unions and co-operatives can achieve socialism within a democratically constituted polity by use of constitutional means—that is, without a revolution. Bolshevism, as displayed in the works of Lenin and Trotsky, rests politically upon the felt need to create and to use a small, tightly organized and disciplined party of revolutionaries as "the vanguard of the working class." Perhaps elsewhere the working class, if properly educated, might put through the revolution by their votes, but in Russia, Lenin's type of party did put through the revolution, against the remnants of the ramshackle tsarist regime, against the liberals led by A. F. Kerensky, against the Russian social democrats, and against the armies and the boycotts of capitalist Europe, America and Japan.

1

In the latter half of the nineteenth century, there developed in Western Europe mass labor parties and powerful trade unions. These parties were loosely organized in The Second International, which between 1899 and 1914 represented "orthodox marxism" to the world. The central party was in Germany. In many ways it was the prototype of the social democratic version of marxism: in ideology, revolutionary; in practice, reformist.

In the 1890's this party became the seat of what one might call The Socialist Revisionaries, the first coherent specification of marxism as a significant political practice. This revisionism is most notably developed as a variety of marxism by Eduard Bernstein. He was answered in the name of orthodoxy by Karl Kautsky,[4] and in the name of revolutionary socialism by Rosa Luxemburg.

Since then, with interruptions and many modifications, the social democratic direction of marxism has been ascendant among the varieties of socialism in the more advanced capitalist countries of Western and Central Europe. In Chapter 8 Bernstein and Kautsky and Luxemburg will speak for themselves. In the present chapter, we shall merely characterize Eduard Bernstein's outlook, which in the end, (in fact before World War I) had come to prevail as "Social Democracy."

4. I am aware that Kautsky believed in parliamentary action only— even before his shift of view in 1918.

As labor unions and socialist parties grew in size and in power, they became agencies of reform rather than levers for revolution. The revolution could wait, and the notion of the inevitability of a gradual drift toward a socialist society served to shore up hopes while waiting. In the meantime, social democratic parties, along with trade unions and consumers' co-operatives, and, on occasion, in alliance with non-socialist parties, made such economic and political gains as they could.

Bernstein's was the most explicit acknowledgment of the fact that the movement became everything. To maintain it, to advance it, *is* to build socialism. Accordingly, there is no need to smash the democratic state. By using this state, the workers and their parties can make and are making great, immediate advances; they can also progress toward the "revolutionary change." Revolution becomes a rhetoric; force is judged unnecessary, even futile; marxism becomes "a democratic socialist reform party," and socialism is to come about in Imperial Germany as an "emancipation through economic organization," although of course this requires political as well as economic struggle. Did not Engels write in his *Preface to the Class Struggle in France* that the working class must be educated for democracy? that the German socialists were demonstrating to comrades everywhere "how to use universal suffrage"?[5] Trade unions and consumers' co-operatives are "democratic elements in industry." As instruments of piecemeal reform, they work; moreover, if they win strong contracts, do they not win "a real kind of part ownership in the industry"?

The general strike—the mass strike for political as well as economic ends—was not ruled out by Bernstein. It is a technical weapon in the realistic struggle for socialism, useful no doubt in special circumstances. After all, given modern weapons, the days of street fights and barricades are over, the workers cannot win battles in such ways. But the mass political strike can be used to exert "the strongest pressure upon government and public opinion." To be sure, its chances of success are slim; it must be used sparingly and only at critical moments, only when the workers' actions through legal channels are blocked, and it must be

5. A good work on Eduard Bernstein and related matters is the scholarly volume by Peter Gay, *The Dilemma of Democratic Socialism* (New York, 1952) to which I am indebted for most of the quotations in this section. See especially pp. 217ff. See also Carl Schorske, *German Social-Democracy* (Cambridge, Mass., 1955).

carefully prepared by the party and by the unions. It need not be a universal stoppage of work. As a matter of fact, reasoned Bernstein, "in a thoroughgoing democracy the political strike will be an outmoded weapon." That it is still a live option testifies to how far removed we are from that democracy.

Such were the historical levers looked to by the leading socialist revisionary. The choice of these, and more generally the management of social democratic parties to which they led, were accompanied by revisions of marxist ideas, and rested upon going facts about the agencies themselves. As for the ideas, Bernstein's briefest summary runs as follows: "Peasants do not shrink; middle class does not disappear; crises do not grow ever larger; misery and serfdom do not increase. There *is* increase in insecurity, dependence, social distance, social character of production, functional superfluity of property owners." [6]

In the first decade of the twentieth century, three interpretations of Marx developed in the Social Democratic Party of Germany: the "orthodox," the "revisionist," and the "radical." But the First World War was the crucial test for all proclaimed "radicals" or revolutionaries. Confronted by this test in Germany, the revisionists and the orthodox became for all practical purposes, actively or passively, one and the same: They supported the war; by 1919 they were opposing the bolsheviks. The group that remained revolutionary—the radicals—*did* oppose the war and did support, although certainly not uncritically, the bolshevik victory in tsarist Russia.

The anti-bolsheviks in the German party were led, in their theories, by the orthodox Karl Kautsky who was joined by Bernstein. Kautsky who, in his stand for "pure" marxism, had once polemicized mightily against Bernstein now found himself wringing his hands. When the war broke out, he was trying to figure out what Marx would have said and done, were *He* still alive. Bernstein, on the other hand, who had openly abandoned revolution as a means of achieving power, had perhaps a less grievous travail. Bernstein's counterparts throughout Western Europe joined him. Thus in World War I, the social democrats fought for whichever country they happened to live in, and thus, insofar as they were composed of working classes, they killed off one another.

6. *Ibid.*, p. 244.

The First World War and the Bolshevik Revolution, these two events literally separated the revolutionaries from the reformists. The only thing that the social democrats have succeeded in nationalizing is socialism itself.

From Bernstein's view, there was no great moral problem. By supporting the war the workers would come out better than ever: Kaiserism would be weakened if Germany lost, or else the Kaiser would reward the loyal support of the German working class by allowing them still more power and social security.

Kautsky had finally to conclude that, according to historical and dialectical materialism, the conditions for revolution were not yet ripe in Germany. Therefore the German workers could not effectively oppose the war. If conditions in industrially advanced Germany were not ripe, imagine the horror he felt when the audacious bolsheviks not only tried but succeeded in making a revolution in backward Russia.

Rosa Luxemburg was the leader of the revolutionary wing of the German party; we shall read her attack on Bernstein in chapter 8 and in chapter 11 her critique of bolshevism.[7]

2

Tsarist Russia stood in sharp contrast to Western Europe, and accordingly the development of "socialism" assumed a quite different character there. Russia was a semi-feudal autocracy, having no significant parliamentary life or any other democratic forms. Its population was largely rural and illiterate; its capitalism was both feeble and curious in its development. Although its working class was concentrated, it was small, and attempts to organize it were harshly suppressed. In tsarist Russia there could be no mass parties, no labor unions, no co-operatives of the sort or on the scale of Western Europe.

The "socialist movement" in Russia had developed as an answer to *rural* misery, and was, accordingly, not marxist. These early revolutionaries—they were called Narodniks or Populists—aimed to liberate the peasants. But as capitalism began to develop in Russia, especially during the 1890's, Russian followers of Marx came to challenge the narod-

7. Further discussion of Rosa Luxemburg will be found below, this chapter, section 4.

niks. In 1895, led by Georg Plekhanov,—perhaps he might be called the Kautsky of Russia—the Russian Social Democratic Labor Party was formed. There followed a period of struggle against the narodniks who were not equal to the marxists' intellectual brilliance. But by 1903, the marxists themselves had begun to fight, and two wings emerged in the Russian Social Democratic Labor Party: the majority (bolshevik), led by Lenin, and the minority (menshevik). This division did not represent the actual majority and minority strengths, but nonetheless the labels stuck.

The mensheviks generally stood with the moderates of The Second International, waiting for capitalism to develop in Russia so that the working class could grow and thus ultimately overthrow the system. In the meantime, the party too would grow and the workers would become educated for the day of the coming.

Lenin argued that this was all nonsense. If you want to make a revolution in Russia, he said in effect, you have to make some revolutionaries, a tightly organized group ready to act when the moment arrives. After the collapse of tsarism in the war, and after the February Revolution of 1917, the bolsheviks began to gain ascendancy over other socialist parties. They did not have a settled long-range program. They said: *Stop fighting the war. Give the land to the peasants. Give everyone food. Peace. Land. Bread.*

They acted quickly and decisively in the insurrection of October 1917. By then it was not very difficult for them to seize power in the major cities. In the summer and fall of 1917, the two most brilliant Russian revolutionaries who had previously held conflicting views came together to solidify bolshevism. Taken together, the doctrines of Lenin and of Trotsky coincided to make up bolshevism as theory, strategy, ideology. And the revolution they led is *the* pivotal event in the *political* history of marxism. The fact of it, the way in which it occurred, where it occurred, how it was subsequently consolidated—these are the pivots around which all marxist argument since 1917 has revolved.

What are the distinctive traits of bolshevism—as doctrine and as practice—up to the death of Lenin in 1924? In chapter 9, below, we shall read some writings from Lenin and Trotsky. Here, I wish merely to outline what seem to me the essential points of bolshevism.

1. A socialist revolution can occur in a backward country which has a weak capitalist development as well as in a mature capitalist nation.

2. A disciplined, tightly organized party of professional revolutionaries, illegal if need be, "represents" (or replaces) the proletariat as the spontaneous historical agency of this revolution.

3. In such countries alongside the worker stands the peasant. The Russian peasant is an ally of the Russian worker. The bolshevik party will stand for the interests of both, because, due to peculiar Russian circumstances, the Russian peasantry is a revolutionary class.

4. Politically and morally, violence and conspiracy are justified, first against the tsarist police state (which knows nothing of "liberal freedom") and later against the counter-revolutionaries (who come to be defined as those who oppose the bolshevik rule). Morality means doing what has to be done to make a revolution—provided you accept morally its historical consequences. For bolsheviks, the end—the accomplishments of the revolution—determines and justifies the means of the revolution as an act.

5. The capitalist world has entered its imperialist phase, an age dominated by great financial networks of monopoly capitalists. This is the last stage of capitalism. It is a period of continual warfare for the division of the world among the capitalist powers.

6. On a world-wide scale, the capitalist system is using itself up; it cannot sustain itself. In order to acquire new markets, world-wide monopoly capitalism requires the export of *capital,* and not merely the export of finished consumer goods. Only in this way can new markets now be acquired by the capitalists.

7. This imperialism means that the world is divided up among the major capitalist powers; therefore, the backward countries can never develop economically in the manner of the already established capitalist powers. For example, a bourgeois class will never be strong in such countries as Russia, China, or India. Russian industry in particular is controlled by French and British capitalists who will not allow its further development.

8. For these reasons, and especially because of this uneven development caused by imperialism, the Russian proletariat, small though it may be, must make its revolution

before it is swallowed up completely by the imperialists. It is the weakest link in the chain; the bolsheviks will now smash that link.

9. Furthermore, the imperialists have produced just the situation that shows the workers of backward nations what imperialism really is. Imperialism has produced war, and increased colonial exploitation. The workers of such colonies will come to act against imperialism precisely when the big capitalist countries are busy fighting and so weakening each other. By their action, the workers of underdeveloped lands will provide to decisive sections of the working class of the imperialist nations themselves a moral inspiration to do the same, to make the proletarian revolution.

10. The bolshevik party, the agency by which the revolution is firmly led if not made, must maintain its structure as a revolutionary organization after it has won the power of the state. It will be the only party because it is the only true "representative of the workers and the peasants." Within this party there may be much disagreement, but once a decision is reached by the small controlling group, then all party members must accept it; any public disagreement after such a decision has been reached amounts to treason.[8]

11. Having won power in Russia, bolsheviks are actively to encourage other revolutions, both in advanced capitalist societies and in pre-industrial societies. Since the bolsheviks had been able to make a revolution, it seemed obvious to them that they were correct. Therefore, any party that hopes to be successful must follow their organization and their tactics, with some consideration given to historical and national differences.

12. Both in the winning of state power, and after the victory, bolsheviks hold that it is necessary to destroy completely the old state and set up a completely new state machinery.

8. This idea of political monopoly is a controversial, historical point, but the facts seem to be as follows: the dogma of the single party was less an essential principle of Lenin and Trotsky than a response to the activities of other parties during the civil war in the young Soviet Union. Even after October, 1917, the bolsheviks sought the collaboration of other parties, from the socialist revolutionaries, of various tendencies, to the mensheviks. Only when these parties engaged in "counter-revolutionary" activity, did the bolsheviks declare them illegal, and this was regarded as a temporary, military measure to be abandoned as soon as the civil war ended. The dogma of the single party, the prohibition of factions within that party, and eventually the totalitarian rule by one man, became, in due course, basic features of stalinism.

Such, crudely, is the bolshevism of Lenin and Trotsky of the October days. Their work is a brilliant series of attempts to adapt the ideas of Marx to revolutionary purposes in a society that is the very opposite of the kind of society Marx had written about. Bolshevik theorists confronted problems Marx never confronted; bolshevik practitioners solved these problems in ways with which Marx may or may not have agreed. But what is certain is that Marx never even confronted them in the manner of the bolsheviks. The soviet insistence that bolshevism is, in one way or another, "orthodox marxism" should not obscure the fact that, taken as a whole, bolshevism is a distinct theory and has a quite different political orientation.

The bolsheviks do, of course, use the categories of Marx as well as various elements of his general model of society; in particular, they do stick to his nineteenth-century views when they consider twentieth-century capitalist societies. Their rhetoric is drawn from his rich and often telling vocabulary of invective; and the ideals Marx formulated, the bolsheviks proclaim. Everything is done In His Name, but the doing is *not* in line with his theory or with his political orientation. Whatever "orthodox marxism" may reasonably be taken to mean, it does not include bolshevik practice. Nonetheless, the bolsheviks of Russia made a revolution in the name of marxism. We must, I believe, consider Russian bolshevism, as we must consider Victorian marxism, concretely, as a historically specific political philosophy.

Much of marxism after Marx is an attempt to explain why the wageworkers of advanced capitalist societies have *not* generally become proletarianized, much less performed the act of the proletarian revolution. But with bolshevism this is not the central point, if only because bolshevism as theory is not generally *about* "advanced capitalist societies" and as practice it does not occur in such societies. It is about a backward, predominantly agricultural society that is autocratic as well as pre-industrial. It is also a search for ways to further actively the process of proletarianization, and so the advent of socialism in political ways. And as a successful revolution, bolshevism became the point upon which all other marxian movements in all nations have had to focus. All marxists have had to confront it in every way and this is, of course, as we shall see, still the case today.

In 1924 Lenin died.

No revolution had succeeded in Western Europe.

In 1929, Trotsky was expelled from Russia.

These three facts meant the end of original bolshevism, and much of the original ethos of "leninism" as well. During the late twenties and thirties Stalin—and stalinism —won out in the Soviet Union and in the parties of The Third International. Stalinism is more important as political fact than for any theoretical contribution to the development of the ideas of Marx and Engels or of Lenin and Trotsky. Nonetheless it *is* a distinct variety of marxism, one in which theory and practice are at once closely unified and brutally segregated. Stalinism grew out of what Stalin felt were the practical day-to-day expediencies, even though it rested on the long-range decision to industrialize and modernize at breakneck pace. Each of its elements arose to justify a policy or to guide a decision for some specific occasion. As theory goes, it is a patchwork of rationalized solutions. But it is a coherent patchwork, sewn together with a single thread—the need to consolidate and industrialize the Soviet nation-state. If only in response to the high theoretical capacities of Stalin's opponents, to the theoretical traditions of marxism and of bolshevism, and to the felt need for "orthodoxy," stalinism is a doctrinal development. It is a consolidation of some of the bolshevik doctrine under specific conditions. It is not "the only possible consolidation," but it is one of them.

Briefly, stalinism is based upon one fact and upon two decisions. The fact is this: revolutions of a bolshevik type —or of any type—did not come off in the advanced capitalist nations. The first decision is: we must go it alone; we must build socialism in the Soviet Union. The second decision, virtually forced by the first, is: by means of political agencies and military powers, we must build the economic basis for socialism. In tsarist Russia, capitalism had not built this economic base. One of the major historical functions of stalinism was to help make an industrial revolution in a backward country. It suggests the means used—political tyranny and police coercion—a totalitarian system combining, in Barrington Moore's apt phrase, "progress and tyranny."

For stalinists, one goal—heavy industrialization and rapid modernization—was not only necessary but necessary immediately. Stalin was able—and this is the substance of stalinism—to organize all social activities toward these ends. A cultural and intellectual organization was created for the purpose of adapting art, literature, the social and economic sciences, toward the emergency goal. And contrariwise, all those who did not accept this as *necessary*, or who opposed it, were at the least severely condemned, and at the most murdered. The result was the production of a literature and art, which more and more began to identify the ideal with the person who proclaimed it. Unity was the password. Work was the order. Therefore, no possible disagreements could be allowed, artistically or intellectually or politically. That would divert needed energy.

The theme of unity soon provided the basis for merging separate institutions and organizations into the image of this one man, Stalin the Tyrant. The more unity was obtained, the more severe was the punishment for disunity, and soon for suspected disunity. There resulted the purges, the executions, the forced labor, the doubletalk; thus the total identification of one individual with a gigantic process he had helped to begin and still led, a process which came to form, as it were, its own institutions and its own ideologies. The cost in human life and in brain power was enormous, but stalinism worked: it *was* the means of rapidly industrializing a backward country, isolated and threatened by enemies and potential enemies, outside and within.

Stalinism cannot be explained by "the power hunger of Stalin" or as the inevitable result of the fact of the Bolshevik Party organization as it existed up through the Civil War in Russia. Certainly it cannot be explained, as in classic marxism, by the functional need of the state to hold down the unpropertied classes in the interests of the propertied. I think it must be understood as *one possible series of responses* to three major conditions:

First, the need for social, economic and political order in order to consolidate the revolution. By "the need for order" I mean the need politically to override what men are immediately interested in, for what those in power judge to be to their interest. Specifically, the demands of the peasants had to be balanced with those of the workers, and of course all those who were against the ascendancy of the ruling circle had to be put down.

Second, the desperate need to defend the new state against its external enemies. However exaggerated by Stalin's apologists, this threat was genuine. It was a fact at the beginning of the Revolution, immediately after it, and certainly it was a fact with new force from the advent of Hitler's control of Nazi Germany.

Third, the need to accomplish these aims under the prevailing conditions, to construct heavy basic industry swiftly, and to enforce the labor discipline and consumption sacrifices which such priority to heavy industry required. In stalinist Russia, the cruel work of earlier capitalist managers elsewhere passed into political hands. It is debatable, but worth mentioning, that these tasks were all the more difficult in the absence of disciplined work habits and industrial routines among the soviet peoples.

It is rather easy with some historical perspective to see that in all probability the Soviet Union could not have survived World War II had she not been intensively industrialized and a large number of her farms mechanized. A peasant population had been trained for a warfare of machines. The industries of course also supplied the war machines. Ten years before Hitler's lunge, Stalin had said: "We are 50 or 100 years behind the advanced countries. We must make up this lag in 10 years. Either we do it or they crush us." [9]

The price paid by Russia for victory over the Nazis *almost* made it a pyrrhic victory: millions dead, cities devastated, industries destroyed, and a people weary and impoverished. So were the peoples of Western Europe, but their rehabilitation, especially in Germany, was decisively helped by massive aid from the United States of America (which had known *no* devastation or great loss in the war). Stalin's Russia was not aided in this way; its rehabilitation was "aided" by a combination of *booty imperialism* among the vanquished nations, and a continuation of the stalinist way of *enforced industrialization*.

The booty imperialism consisted of simply taking equipment to Russia, levying reparations, and directly exploiting the labor forces of other countries. The enforced indus-

9. This quotation is from Isaac Deutscher, *Stalin* (New York, 1949), p. 549ff. from which I am taking several points made in this section. Stalin's speech, from which the quote is taken, was delivered in 1931 before The First Conference of Industrial Managers.

trialization consisted of planned economic development, as before the war, but now including the East European nations as well as the USSR herself. Gradually however this economic imperialism has declined, the enforced industrialization having become the major means of economic advance.

This international development of stalinism into a bloc did not of course confirm the original Trotsky-Lenin outlook. First of all, contrary to these early bolshevik expectations and hopes, revolution still did not occur in London and Berlin, in the advanced capitalist societies, but in Warsaw and Bucharest, in countries generally not advanced industrially. Second, these Eastern European revolutions, with the exception of Yugoslavia, were not made from below by working classes, certainly not by any internationally minded proletariat, but generally from above and from the outside, their chief historical lever being the Red Army, either in fact or by threat. They were in part revolutions, in part conquest; but they were managed and then defended by the great power-state of the area, the USSR.

The isolation of the Soviet Union from outside influences, so characteristic a feature of the stalinist era, has been, among other things, a Russian variety of economic protectionism, which all newly industrializing powers have used, against competition from more industrialized nations. In considerable part, the isolation was due to "Western" actions, but for Stalin's Soviet Union it served economic, social and political functions. Because of the enforced manner and the painful tempo of the industrialization, the soviet ruling circles felt the need to keep the soviet peoples from knowing about the higher standards of living outside Russia. To prevent comparisons, they lied about the soviet condition and about conditions abroad, often in the most fantastic manner. They also conjured up the hideous picture of foreign conspirators working at home and abroad, in the manner of the United States McCarthyites. But in Stalin's Russia, "McCarthyism" was taken much further. There was the travesty of the frame-up trial, the horrible injustices of the purges, the prison camps, and murder and all the rest of it.

Stalinism with all its deceit and cruelty did perform the positive function of industrialization and of military protection. It also served to protect the despotic means used

and the deception of the soviet peoples that the practice
of these means involved and required.[10]

In 1917 the Russian bolsheviks set up The Third International in defense of their own revolution, in support of
revolutions abroad, and as a counterbalance to The Second
International. The history of all communist parties outside
the Soviet Union, from the Revolution until the end of
World War II, goes on within or with close reference to
(pro or con) this Third International, which in 1943 was
formally dissolved. For a quarter of a century, from the
late twenties until the mid-fifties, stalinism and finally
Stalin himself dominated world marxist practices and
theories.

Outside the Soviet Union to be sure, there were social
democratic, as well as communist parties, and there was
Trotsky. The social democrats, when they did gain power,
for example in Germany's Weimar Republic, quickly surrendered any marxist heritage or any other socialist heritage; Germany in the 1920's under the social democrats,
and Great Britain in the late 1940's, remained capitalist by
any definition of the term. In the rest of Europe, during
and after the Second World War social democrats did not
gain power; generally, I think it must be agreed that they
have been more vociferous in their criticism of stalinism
than of the "class" enemies in their own countries.

So it is with reference to stalinism, positively or negatively judged, that marxism must be considered during the
second quarter of the twentieth century.

4

Trotskyism and social democracy have been the two
major centers of marxist opposition to the course of the
Soviet Revolution under Stalin, and to the role of the parties of The Third International. But both were on the
outside looking in. (They could hardly have been elsewhere, since the stalinist consolidation permitted no internal opposition.)

Leon Trotsky, driven to Turkey, France, Norway and
finally Mexico, established in the late thirties what was
optimistically—very optimistically—called The Fourth International. It was never important as a political reality,

10. *Cf. ibid.*, pp. 559ff.

but it did become a theoretical center of marxian controversy concerning the nature of soviet society as well as of other world-historical problems. During the inter-war period, these three types of marxism—social democracy, stalinism, trotskyism (The Second, The Third, and The Fourth International)—engaged in bitter doctrinal and political combat. Out of their controversies, ideas developed. Each claimed descent from Marx; each accused the others of having deviated from the original doctrine.

No marxist, including Marx himself and Lenin, filled so many revolutionary roles so brilliantly as did Leon Trotsky. Of his lifework, as of Lenin's, it truly can be said that theory and practice were intricately and continuously related. Trotsky's several visions and revisions, criticisms of and contributions to marxism, cover the range of its development over the first forty years of the twentieth century. To the encounter of revolution and reform, of orthodoxy and revisionism, he added a kind of revolutionary revisionism which he called the Permanent Revolution. He engaged in the intellectually marvelous, early controversies about the prospects of the revolution in Russia, in Europe, and in America as well: the bolshevik versus menshevik versus narodnik arguments over revolutionary strategies. The painful and immediate decisions of the Revolution itself, then the fearful, precarious civil war which followed; finally, first in Russia and then from exile, Trotsky's essays, attacks, critiques were in the middle of it all.

Early in his career Trotsky worked out some of the essentials of what became the most serious and cogent attempt to reconcile Marx's theory with bolshevik practice—his "theory of the permanent revolution." Toward the end of his life, Trotsky provided the most thorough-going theory of the society presided over by Stalin.[11] In between, he wrote a sensitive book of literary criticism, a three-volume history of the Russian Revolution, which is one of the truly great historical works of the twentieth century, and a torrent of pamphlets and letters.

Politically, he was at the decisive points of action from the beginning of the century until he was exiled by Stalin in 1929. He led the Petrograd Soviet in 1905 and again in 1917. During the Civil War he formed and led the Red

11. Parts of each of these works we shall read in chapters 9 and 11.

Army and, as stalinism took hold, he became in due course the center of the opposition.

Yet even with his truly amazing range, Trotsky too, as a thinker and as a politician, was historically tied down: he lived before and during the events of the Revolution, contributing mightily, as already indicated, to bolshevism as theory and practice. But after his exile, Trotsky became a revolutionary without a revolutionary context, a bureaucrat without a bureaucracy, a politician without a party. He had the will, the motive, but neither the means nor the opportunity—the two are always relative—to make a revolution.

Rosa Luxemburg, whom we have already mentioned among the extreme left of the German Social Democratic Party, was along with Trotsky and Lenin perhaps the most complicated of the twentieth-century marxists. She was not a harsh critic of stalinism for she died before Stalin's triumph; but she was a friendly critic of bolshevism. Politically, Rosa Luxemburg seems to me to have occupied a peculiar, and a powerless, position between The Second and The Third Internationals. She opposed the German branch of The Second International's participation in World War I. She accepted Lenin's and Trotsky's Revolution, but with early and important reservations. She was, first of all and continuously, a revolutionary (as the leaders and the theoreticians of The Second International were not) but she was also passionately for democracy and for freedom in all the decisive meanings of these terms.

These two views, "For The Revolution" *and* "For Freedom," fuse in her belief in the revolutionary spontaneity of the proletariat masses. She is in this respect a very close follower of the basic ideas of Karl Marx. His ambiguity at this point is hers. On no point is this clearer than in her view that democratic procedures and the socialist revolution *must* coincide. She had one foot in The Second International, one foot in The Third, and her head, I am afraid, in the cloudier, more utopian reaches of classic marxism. What I have called, in my criticisms of Marx, the labor metaphysic was for Rosa Luxemburg both a final fact and an ultimate faith.

This woman, now glorified by many social democrats, especially in the United States, because of her early criticism of bolshevism, was revolutionary to the core. She saw the pluses as well as the minuses of the Revolution, but she felt that the pluses far outweighed the minuses. In many ways, Rosa Luxemburg's attitude toward the Revolution in 1917 was similar to many North and Latin American Fidelistas' view of the Cuban Revolution in 1961: the pluses far outweigh the minuses, but there is worry over the minuses.

There is no way to prove or to disprove that Rosa Luxemburg would have done as Lenin did had she been in his place, but it is true, I think, as Max Shachtman insightfully pointed out in 1938, that it was in considerable part the difference in countries that accounted for the differences between Lenin and Luxemburg. "Just as Lenin's views must be considered against the background of the situation in Russia, so must Luxemburg's polemic against them be viewed against the background of the situation in Germany. . . . Where Lenin stressed ultra-centralism, Luxemburg stressed democracy and organizational flexibility. Where Lenin emphasized the dominant role of the professional revolutionist, Luxemburg countered with emphasis on the mass movement and its elemental upsurge. . . . Why? Because these various forces played clearly different roles in Russia and in Germany. The 'professional revolutionists' whom Luxemburg encountered in Germany were not, as in Russia, the radical instrument for gathering together loose and scattered local organizations, uniting them into one national party. . . . Quite the contrary. In Germany, 'the professionals' were the careerists, the conservative trade union bureaucrats, the lords of the ossifying party machine, the reformist parliamentarians, the whole crew who finally succeeded in disemboweling the movement." [12]

It is this that led Rosa Luxemburg to repudiate "centralism" or tight organization and to found her appeal in the grassroots of the movement from which she hoped the militancy would spring. In 1919 Rosa Luxemburg was murdered by German officers.

Social democrats, as I have already noted, began their criticism of bolshevism in October 1917, and have not yet stopped. For them, in all truth, nothing much has changed. Meanwhile the revolution made by the bolsheviks has passed through the major burdens of its stalinist phase. Ac-

12. Max Shachtman, "Lenin and Rosa Luxemburg," *The New International*, May 1938, p. 143.

cordingly, we must now examine "soviet marxism" after the death of Stalin.

5

"Marxism-leninism," as it now prevails in the countries of the soviet bloc, is not a freely developed or a freely developing set of theories worked out by politically detached philosophers. It is an attempt to justify in terms of various elements drawn from the legacy of Marx and Lenin decisions and policies made by the political and intellectual elite of a great-power state. It has to do more with ideology, with statements of ideals, and with political strategy and decisions, domestic and international; it has less to do with theories of society, of history, of human nature.

It would, however, be a great mistake to think marxism-leninism today is therefore "merely ideology." It *is* ideology, but with a difference: it is bolshevik ideology, drawing upon Marx's ideas, and this does mean something. It means, first, that its practitioners are likely to be at least mediocre theorists and second, that they are likely to call upon and use (in their domestic political struggles and in their international encounters) theorists who are not necessarily mediocre at all. It means, third, that the terms of their competition with one another, and with outsiders, are the terms of marxist and bolshevik theory: they are called upon by one another to justify, in terms of these theories, their arguments over policy.

Perhaps the central question to be asked about marxism-leninism today is this: it does provide ideological justification for policies, but is it also in any real sense a theoretical guideline to the *formulation* of policy? The question is as important for communists as for anti-communists; and among anti-communists and non-communists it is very much a point of disagreement. I think the answer is: Yes, to an ungaugable but politically significant extent, marxism-leninism has been and is a theoretical guideline. To understand this is essential for anyone who would understand the character as well as the political structure and the world-historical meaning of the soviet bloc today.

Inside the Bloc, and in the accepted orthodox communist parties outside it, a great turmoil followed the death of Stalin and, still more, the 1956 "secret speech "of Khrushchev denouncing Stalin. In chapter 12, we shall read some contemporary examples of marxism-leninism: from Khrushchev's criticism of Stalin in 1956; from Mao Tse-tung's booklet on "contradictions;" from a discussion of stalinism by Togliatti—the leader of the biggest communist party outside the sino-soviet bloc. In the meantime, there is one "variety" of marxism which we must consider—the so-called "new revisionism," which has succeeded that championed by Bernstein.

The second wave of revisionism and the reactions to it are separated from the first wave by over half a century of enormous defeats and enormous victories and, above all, by the fact of the stalinist consolidation of the bolshevik revolution in the Soviet Union. Inside the Bloc, the arguments of the 1950's were not free-for-all debates among intellectuals, attached to circles and parties that had nowhere assumed power. They occurred with close reference to "soviet marxism" whose spokesmen and men of power were keeping close watch. More often than not, the participants were ignorant of the works and authentic ideas of Trotsky. Arguments went on in the "freezes" as in the "thaws." They appeared under literary disguises, as ingenious fables and paradoxical stories. And the intellectuals who carried on these arguments frequently did so at the very real risk of death, and always at the risk of political downfall. It was a curious juncture in the history of marxism—and a curious fate for the immensely creative ideas of Karl Marx, the Marx who devoured books in the British Museum, and wrote them in a kind of frenzy few men of the Victorian age ever knew.

When World War II ended in 1945 the Soviet Union lay prostrate. As already noted, she had borne the heaviest share of losses in defeating the Nazis. Many of her cities had been blown up, much of her farmland devastated, millions of her younger men and women dead. Surely one of the least expected events of the postwar era was the speed and the vigor with which the Soviet Union reconstructed herself. In only a few years she emerged far stronger than anyone hoped, or dreaded. Militarily, and in due course politically and economically as well, she controlled almost all of Eastern Europe. In a few years, in a genuine revolution of her own making, China, with her multitude of peoples and enormity of potential power, joined the Bloc.

"Socialism in one country" became "socialism in one bloc."

In an attempt to rationalize inter-party relations, the Communist International or "Comintern" was transformed into the Communist Information Agency or "Cominform." For communist parties throughout the world there was no change in their relationship with the Soviet Union. They continued to be dominated by her. To them she was the first and the only "true workers' state." Accordingly, she had to be defended at any costs.

All soviet policy was *ipso facto* correct. Since it was made by "the socialist state" it could provide the answer, it was the model, regardless of each nation's peculiarities. So to follow the Moscow Line was not necessarily "conspiratorial." Much of the information was open to anyone who cared to listen. Moscow spoke through the Cominform; the other parties listened, and tried to act accordingly. It is debatable but it does seem to me that the idea of "a secret conspiracy" is often fabricated by overstaffed and perhaps even slightly paranoid secret-police forces in nations outside the Bloc. By 1946, the cold war was clearly in progress. In 1947, the United States, adopting the Marshall Plan to undermine soviet prestige and morale, offered aid, with conditions of course, to the soviet bloc. Stalin reacted by hardening the line. Here was an open issue of the cold war, and the Cominform made it clear that each party must accept The Line.

Marshal Tito of Yugoslavia had been growing increasingly dissatisfied with the dogmas of stalinism: the revolution in Yugoslavia was, after all, the only indigenous revolution in Eastern Europe, and the majority of the Yugoslav Partisans, led by the communists, were determined to "go it in their own way." They agreed to accept Marshall Plan aid, without any important strings attached. This led to a complete break with the Soviet Union. Tito now became, in soviet propaganda, not only "a tool and willing puppet of imperialism" but the "worst enemy of the working class." Communists in many countries published silly books under titles such as "Tito's Plot Against Europe." At any rate, Yugoslavia became in 1948 a country governed according to marxian and bolshevik ideals, but outside the Bloc. Yet Yugoslav socialism, in theory and in practice, represents in many ways—and perhaps essentially —an attempt to resuscitate the very ethos of original bolshevism.

After Stalin's death, Khrushchev managed to narrow the split, superficially, but soon it widened again. Certainly today, in 1961, there is little ideological friendship between the Soviet government—to say nothing of China—and the Yugoslavs. When the eighty-one Communist Parties met in Moscow in November 1960, the Yugoslav Party, or "League" as it is called, was not invited. Moreover, it was fiercely attacked with the rhetoric and invective of the stalinist era. This does not indicate "merely a political grudge"; it reveals profound differences in theory and practice: how to achieve socialism and then communism. That is the issue involved in the Yugoslav-China dispute.

Tito's break with Stalin was the first real revolt within the Bloc; but by 1956 Khrushchev was faced with a series of nationalist rebellions of "our own roads to socialism." Seen as a whole these constitute the second revisionism. Here are some of the key events in its development.

In 1949, Mao Tse-tung's movement came to power in China. Although this "road" was duly explained with ambiguous marxist-leninist phrases, it was clearly something new. A peasant army liberated Peking, and while some analysts might argue that there had been in 1917 a growing Russian working class, no one could reasonably claim that the Chinese Revolution of 1949 was made by any industrial proletariat.

In the same year, the Soviet Union responded to the military alliance of NATO by forming The Warsaw Pact. Lines already had become harder; internal repression, a soviet counterpart of McCarthyism, increased, partly in response to the cold war and partly in an effort to consolidate political power in the newly stalinized states.

But 1953 brought the end of the Korean War, the death of Stalin, and the riots of workers and students against the East German government. Dissatisfaction throughout Eastern Europe became more vocal. In 1956 there were riots in Posnan, Poland; and at the Twentieth Party Congress in Russia Khrushchev made his denunciation of Stalin, if not really of stalinism. The anguished cry of Polish intellectuals and their new beginnings were heard; in Hungary there was violent as well as intellectual revolt. In its bloody aftermath, soviet tanks commanded the streets of Budapest.

The second revisionist wave inside the Bloc has not yet resulted in any signal contributions to the development of marxism. However, in the very center of soviet power it has undoubtedly influenced several very important shifts of policy. The revisionist upsurge in Poland, for example, has not produced any alternative programs, any intellectual development of marxian doctrine or even new critiques of it, or so my own interviews in Krakow and Warsaw, as well as readings, indicate. The theoretician and official, Adam Schaff, is probably correct when he asserts (as quoted in *The Reporter* of October 29, 1959): "We are not afraid to discuss a revision of marxism, but we are definitely opposed to the liquidation of marxism. The revisionists failed to carry their point in Poland because their philosophy was based entirely on negation. They had no positive program to offer the people."

That is probably true. Yet it would certainly be churlish of us to condemn these New Revisionists because of it. It is clear that it has been the intellectuals and the labor leaders of the advanced countries outside the Bloc who have been and who are in default. They have quite generally accepted the Cold War—and done nothing to help those who would break out of it. They did not give real support to those socialists who fought in Hungary; they did nothing to support the Polish "revisionists." This is not to say that had they done so they could have helped to break up orthodoxy and increase the pace of democratization. The important point is that they have no right to sneer at those people inside the Bloc who have thought and acted against stalinism.

By 1956 it was clear that the second wave of revisionism had made a profound impact on the ruling circles of the soviet bloc countries, including the USSR itself. Regardless of how one may judge their intellectual contributions, there is no question about the fact that the revisionists did represent a real breaking away from stalinist orthodoxy and repression. For this alone, the "revisionist" of the 1950's should be honored among marxists. Moreover, the best of the "revisionists"—as they were called by orthodox stalinists—did not abandon socialism as an ideal or as a type of economy. They did not—as did Milovan Djilas of Yugoslavia—go over to what amounts to liberalism or at most a watered-down social democracy. The Poles, in particular, never gave up being either Poles or socialists in the full revolutionary sense of both "Polish" and "socialist."

6

In the postwar period, the center of social democratic thinking and rethinking has been Great Britain. And perhaps the leading man, the most interesting marxist, has been G. D. H. Cole. For what he represented during the 1950's, and especially after the Twentieth Congress in 1956, is a kind of "social democratic revisionism." I mean by this phrase the attempt, often desperate but always honest, of non-communist, left-wing socialists to *confront* morally, intellectually, and politically the post-Stalin soviet world, and somehow to make "social democracy" a socialism with immediate and obvious freedom built into it, a live and vigorous movement, and a real new beginning in the advanced capitalist societies.

In his pamphlet, "Is This Socialism?," G. D. H. Cole asked: "What is the use of winning an election, except as a means to an end? To win an election without a policy is the surest way of losing the next, and of spreading dismay and disillusionment among one's supporters. If the end is no longer Socialism but something else—what else? If it is still Socialism, let us tell the electors frankly how we propose to advance towards it." [13]

In 1956 Professor Cole wrote a pamphlet, "World Socialism Restated," selections from which you will read in Chapter 13. It contained bold statements of how socialists ought to view the post-Stalin soviet bloc, as well as local communist parties. The center of controversy, it was attacked by trotskyists and by social democrats as a new call for a "popular front" and as "fellow-traveling."

In order to indicate the level and the substance of the discussion that has been going on in Great Britain, I reproduce here a paragraph or so of Peter Shore's comment on Cole's pamphlet and something of Cole's response.

"What, then, should be our attitude to Communism?" Shore asks in summary. "It must begin with the recognition that Communism has proved to be the most speedy, effective and in some ways attractive instrument yet devised for transforming primitive into modern societies. It is speedy because, with iron political control, it can hold down mass consumption to the subsistence level while it accumulates capital. It is attractive, particularly to na-

13. Reprinted, in part, in *Dissent*, Autumn, 1954, p. 331.

tionalist sentiment, because it can carry through the process of accumulation with the minimum recourse to external aid. Furthermore, when all its repulsive features are weighed, Communism remains an infinitely superior system of social organization to the feudalism which, with minor exceptions, it has so far replaced. Professor Cole speaks for most of us when he says he is 'on the side' of the Russian Revolution, the Chinese Revolution, and the Viet Minh. We are for them, in the last resort, simply because we know that it is better to live in the twentieth century than in the thirteenth—and because there was no instrument other than Communism for effecting the change."

"But, most important of all [Democratic Socialism], must regain its self-confidence. [It] is not a pusillanimous and half-hearted version of Communism, as some have come to believe, but a radically different political creed. Its job is not simply to destroy capitalism and feudalism, but—and it is likely to prove far more difficult—to destroy the new bases for inequality and class rule that are now developing. In its quest for a classless and civilized society, democracy, it will find, is not an encumbrance but a sheer necessity." [14]

G. D. H. Cole replied: "Finally I come back to what is, I think, the main issue between Mr. Shore and me. Capitalism, I agree, is not the *only* enemy; but I hold it to be still the principal enemy. . . . I agree . . . that the socialization of the means of production does not itself suffice to make a country Socialist. I do however hold that such socialization at any rate of most of the means of production is an indispensable condition of socialism—of course, including as socialization a variety of forms of national, regional, local and co-operative ownership; for I see serious dangers in the concentration of most of the ownership in the hands of a single body, the state. The Soviet Union as I see it made a great stride towards socialism by abolishing private ownership of the means of production, but still falls a long way short of being fully Socialist because of its anti-Socialist practice in respect of economic inequality." [15]

In the postwar era, *outside* the soviet bloc in the pre-

14. "The World of G. D. H. Cole," *The New Statesman and Nation,* 25 August 1956, pp. 205 and 206.
15. *The New Statesman and Nation,* September 8, 1956.

industrial world there has developed what may be called "revolutionary revisions"—in such places as Ghana, Indonesia, Guinea and Cuba. These are indeed "different roads to socialism" under a variety of conditions and occurring on the basis of individual national histories. Nonetheless, all past marxist thought has been important to these revolutions; even if not in their beginnings, it tends to become so in the due course of their developments.

These revolutions differ from the October 1917 Revolution in many respects—but one is very important indeed: these new nations can expect, and increasingly they will get, economic (and if need be military) aid from the established soviet bloc. Accordingly, they are finding ever closer ties with the established countries of the Bloc. They constitute the most important arena of the Cold War. In them, one can see most nakedly the world confrontation—morally and economically, intellectually and politically—of the capitalist bloc and the soviet bloc.

One final supposition must be made about these new revolutions: There is reason to suppose that not only the USA power elite but also that of the USSR has often been startled by the revolutionary euphoria, social exuberance and political tactics of such revolutionaries, as for example, Cuba's. This is due not only to the Soviet Union's suspicion that such countries might exploit and exacerbate the Moscow-Peking rift, but also to the fact that the Russian Revolution, being over forty years old, has developed in its ruling circles a tradition of patience and of the slow maturation which attends long-range planning.

But all these are "further questions." The historical facts of marxist practice so far do not automatically provide us with the answers to them. In the next six chapters some of the followers of Marx will "speak for themselves."

8. The Social Democrats

KARL KAUTSKY: *What a Social Revolution Is* [1]

There are few conceptions over which there has been so much contention, as over that of revolution. This can partially be ascribed to the fact that nothing is so contrary to existing interests and prejudices as this concept, and partially to the fact that few things are so ambiguous.

As a rule, events cannot be so sharply defined as things. Especially is this true of social events, which are extremely complicated, and grow ever more complicated the further society advances—the more various the forms of co-operation of humanity become. Among the most complicated of these events is the Social Revolution, which is a complete transformation of the wonted forms of associated activity among men.

It is no wonder that this word, which every one uses, but each one in a different sense, is sometimes used by the same persons at different times in very different senses. Some understand by Revolution barricades, conflagrations of castles, guillotines, September massacres and a combination of all sorts of hideous things. Others would seek to take all sting away from the word and use it in the sense of great but imperceptible and peaceful transformations of society, like, for instance, those which took place through the discovery of America or by the invention of the steam engine. Between these two definitions there are many grades of meaning.

Marx, in his introduction to the "Critique of Political Economy," defines social revolution as a more or less rapid transformation of the foundations of the juridical and political superstructure of society arising from a change in its economic foundations. If we hold close to this definition we at once eliminate from the idea of social revolution

1. From *The Social Revolution* (Chicago, 1902), pp. 5-20, 26-37, 80-84.

"changes in the economic foundations," as, for example, those which proceeded from the steam engine or the discovery of America. These alterations are the causes of revolution, not the revolution itself.

But I do not wish to confine myself too strictly to this definition of social revolution. There is a still narrower sense in which we can use it. In this case it does not signify either the transformation of the juridical and political superstructure of society, but only some particular form or particular method of transformation.

Every socialist strives for social revolution in the wider sense, and yet there are socialists who disclaim revolution and would attain social transformation only through reform. They contrast social revolution with social reform. It is this contrast which we are discussing today in our ranks. I wish here to consider social revolution in the narrow sense of a particular method of social transformation.

The contrast between reform and revolution does not consist in the application of force in one case and not in the other. Every juridical and political measure is a force measure which is carried through by the force of the State. Neither do any particular forms of the application of force, as, for example, street fights, or executions, constitute the essentials of revolution in contrast to reform. These arise from particular circumstances, are not necessarily connected with revolutions, and may easily accompany reform movements. The constitution of the delegates of the third Estate at the National Assembly of France, on June 17, 1789, was an eminently revolutionary act with no apparent use of force. This same France had, on the contrary, in 1774 and 1775, great insurrections for the single and in no way revolutionary purpose of changing the bread tax in order to stop the rise in the price of bread.

The reference to street fights and executions as characteristic of revolutions is, however, a clue to the source from which we can obtain important teachings as to the essentials of revolution. The great transformation which began in France in 1789 has become the classical type of revolution. It is the one which is ordinarily in mind when revolution is spoken of. From it we can best study the essentials of revolution and the contrast between it and reform. This revolution was preceded by a series of efforts at reform, among which the best known are those of Turgot. These attempts in many cases aimed at the same things which the revolution carried out. What distinguished the reforms of Turgot from the corresponding measures of the revolution? Between the two lay the conquest of political power by a new class, and in this lies the essential difference between revolution and reform. Measures which seek to adjust the juridical and political superstructure of society, to changed economic conditions, are reforms if they proceed from the class which is the political and economic ruler of society. They are reforms whether they are given freely or secured by the pressure of the subject class, or conquered through the power of circumstances. On the contrary, those measures are the results of revolution if they proceed from the class which has been economically and politically oppressed and who have now captured political power and who must in their own interest more or less rapidly transform the political and juridical superstructure and create new forms of social co-operation.

The conquest of the governmental power by an hitherto oppressed class, in other words, a political revolution, is accordingly the essential characteristic of social revolution in this narrow sense, in contrast with social reform. Those who repudiate political revolution as the principal means of social transformation or wish to confine this to such measures as have been granted by the ruling class are social reformers, no matter how much their social ideas may antagonize existing social forms. On the contrary, anyone is a revolutionist who seeks to conquer the political power for an hitherto oppressed class, and he does not lose this character if he prepares and hastens this conquest by social reforms wrested from the ruling classes. It is not the striving after social reforms but the explicit confining of one's self to them which distinguishes the social reformer from the social revolutionist. On the other hand, a political revolution can only become a social revolution when it proceeds from an hitherto socially oppressed class. Such a class is compelled to complete its political emancipation by its social emancipation because its previous social position is in irreconcilable antagonism to its political domination. A split in the ranks of the ruling classes, no matter even if it should take on the violent form of civil war, is not a social revolution. In the following pages we shall only discuss social revolution in the sense here defined.

A social reform can very well be in accord with the interests of the ruling class. It may for the moment leave their social domination untouched, or, under certain circumstances, can even strengthen it. Social revolution, on the contrary, is from the first incompatible with the interests of the ruling class, since under all circumstances it signifies annihilation of their power. Little wonder that the present ruling class continuously slander and stigmatize revolution because they believe that it threatens their position. They contrast the idea of social revolution with that of social reform, which they praise to the very heavens, very frequently indeed without ever permitting it to become an earthly fact. The arguments against revolution are derived from the present ruling forms of thought. So long as Christianity ruled the minds of men the idea of revolution was rejected as sinful revolt against divinely constituted authority. It was easy to find proof texts for this in the New Testament, since this was written at the time of the Roman Empire, during an epoch in which every revolt against the ruling powers appeared hopeless, and all independent political life had ceased to exist. The revolutionary classes, to be sure, replied with quotations from the Old Testament, in which there still lived much of the spirit of the primitive pastoral democracy. When once the judicial manner of thought displaced the theological, a revolution was defined as a violent break with the existing legal order. No one, however, could have a right to the destruction of rights, a right of revolution was an absurdity, and revolution in all cases a crime. But the representatives of the aspiring class placed in opposition to the existing, historically descended right, the right for which they strove, representing it as an eternal law of nature and reason, and an inalienable right of humanity. The re-conquest of these latter rights, that plainly could have been lost only through a violation of rights, was itself impossible without a violation of rights, even if they came as a result of revolution.

Today the theological phrases have lost their power to enslave, and, most of all, among the revolutionary classes of the people. Reference to historical right has also lost its force. The revolutionary origin of present rights and present government is still so recent that their legitimacy can be challenged. Not alone the government of France, but the dynasties of Italy, Spain, Bulgaria, England and Holland, are of revolutionary origin. The kings of Bavaria and Wurtemburg, the grand duke of Baden and Hesse, owe, not simply their titles but a large share of their provinces, to the protection of the revolutionary *parvenu* Napoleon; the Hohenzollerns attained their present positions over the ruins of thrones, and even the Hapsburgers bowed before the Hungarian revolution. Andrassy, who was hung in effigy for high treason in 1852, was an imperial minister in 1867, without proving untrue to the ideas of the national Hungarian revolution of 1848.

The bourgeoisie was itself actively engaged in all these violations of historical rights. It cannot, now, since it has become the ruling class, well condemn revolution in the name of this right to revolution, even if its legal philosophy does everything possible to reconcile natural and historical rights. It must seek more effective arguments with which to stigmatize the revolution, and these are found in the newly-arising natural science with its accompanying mental attitude. While the bourgeoisie were still revolutionary, the catastrophic theory still ruled in natural science (geology and biology). This theory proceeded from the premise that natural development came through great sudden leaps. Once the capitalist revolution was ended, the place of the catastrophic theory was taken by the hypothesis of a gradual imperceptible development, proceeding by the accumulation of countless little advances and adjustments in a competitive struggle. To the revolutionary bourgeoisie the thought of catastrophes in nature was very acceptable, but to the conservative bourgeoisie these ideas appeared irrational and unnatural.

Of course I do not assert that the scientific investigators had all their theories determined by the political and social needs of the bourgeoisie. It was just the representatives of the catastrophe theories who were at the same time most reactionary and least inclined to revolutionary views. But everyone is involuntarily influenced by the mental attitude of the class amid which he lives and carries something from it into his scientific conceptions. In the case of Darwin we know positively that his natural science hypotheses were influenced by Malthus, that decisive opponent of revolution. It was not wholly accidental that the theories of evolution (of Darwin and Lyell) came from England, whose history for 250 years has shown nothing more than revolutionary beginnings, whose point the ruling class have always been able to break at the opportune moment.

The fact that an idea emanates from any particular class, or accords with their interests, of course proves nothing as to its truth or falsity. But its historical influence does depend upon just these things. That the new theories of evolution were quickly accepted by the great popular masses, who had absolutely no possibility of testing them, proves that they rested upon profound needs of those classes. On the one side these theories—and this gave them their value to the revolutionary classes—abolished in a much more radical manner than the old catastrophic theories, all necessity of a recognition of a supernatural power creating a world by successive acts. On the other side—and this pleased most highly the bourgeoisie—they declared all revolutions and catastrophes to be something abnormal, contrary to the laws of nature, and wholly absurd. Whoever seeks today to scientifically attack revolution does it in the name of the theory of evolution, demonstrating that nature makes no leaps, that consequently any sudden change of social relations is impossible; that advance is only possible through the accumulation of little changes and slight improvements, called social reforms. Considered from this point of view revolution is an unscientific conception about which scientifically cultured people only shrug their shoulders.

It might be replied that the analogy between natural and social laws is by no means perfect. To be sure, our conception of the one will unconsciously influence our conception of the other sphere as we have already seen. This is, however, no advantage and it is better to restrain rather than favor this transference of laws from one sphere to another. To be sure, all progress in methods of observation and comprehension of any one sphere can and will improve our methods and comprehension in others, but it is equally true that within each one of these spheres there are peculiar laws not applying to the others.

First of all must be noted the fundamental distinction between animate and inanimate nature. No one would claim on the ground of external similarity to transfer without change a law which applied to one of these spheres to the other. One would not seek to solve the problem of sexual reproduction and heredity by the laws of chemical affiliation. But the same error is committed when natural laws are applied directly to society, as for example when

competition is justified as a natural necessity because of
the law of the struggle for survival, or when the laws of
natural evolution are invoked to show the impossibility of
social revolution.

But there is still more to be said in reply. If the old catastrophic theory is gone forever from the natural sciences,
the new theory which makes of evolution only a series of
little, insignificant changes meets with ever stronger objections. Upon one side there is a growing tendency toward
quietistic, conservative theories that reduce evolution itself to a minimum, on the other side facts are compelling
us to give an ever greater importance to catastrophes in
natural development. This applies equally to the geological theories of Lyell and the organic evolution of Darwin.

This has given rise to a sort of synthesis of the old catastrophic theories and the newer evolutionary theories, similar to the synthesis that is found in Marxism. Just as Marxism distinguishes between the gradual economic development and the sudden transformation of the juridical and
political superstructure, so many of the new biological
and geological theories recognize alongside of the slow
accumulation of slight and even infinitesimal alterations,
also sudden profound transformations—catastrophes—that
arise from the slower evolution.

A notable example of this is furnished by the observations of de Vries reported at the last Congress of Natural
Sciences held at Hamburg. He has discovered that the species of plants and animals remain unchanged through a
long period; some of them finally disappear, when they
have become too old to longer adapt themselves to the
conditions of existence, that have in the meantime been
changing. Other species are more fortunate; they suddenly
"explode," as he has himself expressed it, in order to give
life to countless new forms, some of which continue and
multiply, while the others, not being adapted to the conditions of existence, disappear.

I have no intention of drawing a conclusion in favor of
revolution from these new observations. That would be to
fall into the same error as those who argue to the rejection
of revolution from the theory of evolution. But these observations at least show that the scientists are themselves
not wholly agreed as to the part played in organic and
geologic development by catastrophes, and for this reason

it would be an error to attempt to draw from either of these hypotheses any fixed conclusions as to the role played by revolution in social development.

If in spite of these facts such conclusions are still insisted upon, then we can reply to them with a very popular and familiar illustration, which demonstrates in an unmistakable manner that nature does make sudden leaps: I refer to the act of birth. The act of birth is a leap. At one stroke a fetus, which had hitherto constituted a portion of the organism of the mother, sharing in her circulation, receiving nourishment from her, without breathing, becomes an independent human being, with its own circulatory system, that breathes and cries, takes its own nourishment and utilizes its digestive tract.

The analogy between birth and revolution, however, does not rest alone upon the suddenness of the act. If we look closer we shall find that this sudden transformation at birth is confined wholly to functions. The organs develop slowly, and must reach a certain stage of development before that leap is possible, which suddenly gives them their new functions. If the leap takes place before this stage of development is attained, the result is not the beginning of new functions for the organs, but the cessation of all functions—the death of the new creature. On the other hand, the slow development of organs in the body of the mother can only proceed to a certain point, they cannot begin their new functions without the revolutionary act of birth. This becomes inevitable when the development of the organs has attained a certain height.

We find the same thing in society. Here also the revolutions are the result of slow, gradual development (evolution). Here also it is the social organs that develop slowly. That which may be changed suddenly, at a leap, revolutionarily, is their functions. The railroad has been slowly developed. On the other hand the railroad can suddenly be transformed from its function as the instrument to the enrichment of a number of capitalists, into a socialist enterprise having as its function the serving of the common good. And as at the birth of the child, all the functions are simultaneously revolutionized—circulation, breathing, digestion—so all the functions of the railroad must be simultaneously revolutionized at one stroke, for they are all most closely bound together. They cannot be gradually and successively socialized, one after the other, as if, for example,

we would transform today the functions of the engineer
and fireman, a few years later the ticket agents, and still
later the accountants and bookkeepers, and so on. This fact
is perfectly clear with a railroad, but the successive socialization of the different functions of a railroad is no less
absurd than that of the ministry of a centralized state.
Such a ministry constitutes a single organism whose organs must co-operate. The functions of one of these organs cannot be modified without equally modifying all the
others. The idea of the gradual conquest of the various
departments of a ministry by the Socialists is not less
absurd than would be an attempt to divide the act of birth
into a number of consecutive monthly acts, in each of
which one organ only would be transformed from the
condition of a fetus to an independent child, and meanwhile leaving the child itself attached to the navel cord
until it had learned to walk and talk.

Since neither a railroad nor a ministry can be changed
gradually, but only at a single stroke, embracing all the
organs simultaneously, from capitalist to socialist functions, from an organ of the capitalist to an organ of the
laboring class, and this transformation is possible only
to such social organs as retain a certain degree of development, it may be remarked here that with the maternal
organism it is possible to scientifically determine the moment when the degree of maturity is attained, which is not
true of society.

On the other hand, birth does not mark the conclusion
of the development of the human organism, but rather the
beginning of a new epoch in development. The child comes
now into new relations in which new organs are created,
and those that previously existed are developed further in
other directions; teeth grow in the mouth, the eyes learn
to see; the hands to grasp, the feet to walk, the mouth to
speak, etc. In the same way a social revolution is not the
conclusion of social development, but the beginning of a
new form of development. A socialist revolution can at a
single stroke transfer a factory from capitalist to social
property. But it is only gradually, through a course of slow
evolution, that one may transform a factory from a place
of monotonous, repulsive, forced labor into an attractive
spot for the joyful activity of happy human beings. A socialist revolution can at a single stroke transform the
great bonanza farms into social property. In that portion

of agriculture where petty industry still rules, the organs of social and socialist production must be first created, and that can come only as a result of slow development.

It is thus apparent that the analogy between birth and revolution is rather far-reaching. But this naturally proves nothing more than that one has no right to appeal to nature for proof that a social revolution is something unnecessary, unreasonable, and unnatural. We have also, as we have already said, no right to apply conclusions drawn from nature directly to social processes. We can go no further upon the ground of such analogies than to conclude: that as each animal creature must at one time go through a catastrophe in order to reach a higher stage of development (the act of birth or of the breaking of a shell), so society can only be raised to a higher stage of development through a catastrophe. . . .

Among the great nations of modern times England is the one which most resembles the Middle Ages, not economically, but in its political form. Militarism and bureaucracy are there the least developed. It still possesses an aristocracy that not only reigns but governs. Corresponding to this, England is the great modern nation in which the efforts of the oppressed classes are mainly confined to the removal of particular abuses instead of being directed against the whole social system. It is also the State in which the practice of protection against revolution through compromise is farthest developed.

If the universal armament of the people did not encourage great social revolutions, it did make it much easier for armed conflict between the classes to arise at the slightest opportunity. There is no lack of violent uprisings and civil wars in antiquity and the Middle Ages. The ferocity with which these were fought was often so great as to lead to the expulsion, expropriation and oftentimes to the extermination of the conquered. Those who consider violence as a sign of social revolution will find plenty of such revolutions in earlier ages. But those who conceive social revolution as the conquest of political power by a previously subservient class and the transformation of the juridical and political superstructure of society, particularly in the property relations, will find no social revolution there. Social development proceeded piecemeal, step by step, not through single great catastrophes but in countless little broken-up apparently disconnected, often interrupted, ever renewing, mostly unconscious movements. The great social transformation of the times we are considering, the disappearance of slavery in Europe, came about so imperceptibly that the contemporaries of this movement took no notice of it, and one is today compelled to reconstruct it through hypotheses.

Things took on a wholly different aspect as soon as the capitalist method of production was developed. It would lead us too far and would be only to repeat things well known if I were here to go into the mechanism of capitalism and its consequences. Suffice it to say that the capitalist method of production created the modern State, made an end to the political independence of communities and at the same time their economic independence ceased, each became part of a whole, and lost its special rights and special peculiarities. All were reduced to the same level, all were given the same laws, the same taxes, same courts, and were made subject to the same government. The modern State was thus forced to become a National State and added to the other equalities the equality of language.

The influence of governmental power upon the social life was now something wholly different from what it was through antiquity or the Middle Ages. Every important political change in a great modern State influences at once with a single stroke and in the profoundest manner an enormous social sphere. The conquest of political power by a previously subject class must, on this account, from now on, have wholly different social results than previously.

As a result the power at the disposal of the modern State has grown enormously. The technical revolution of capitalism reaches also to the technique of arms. Ever since the Reformation the weapons of war have become more and more perfect, but also more costly. They thus become a privilege of governmental power. This fact alone separates the army from the people, even in those places where universal conscription prevails, unless this is supplemented by popular armament, which is not the case in any great State. Most important of all, the leaders of the army are professional soldiers separated from the people, to whom they stand opposed as a privileged class.

The economic powers also of the modern centralized State are enormous when compared with those of the earlier States. They comprehend the wealth of a colossal sphere whose technical means of production leave the higher culture of antiquity far behind.

The modern State also possesses a bureaucracy far more centralized than that of any previous State. The problems of the modern State have grown so enormously that it is impossible to solve them without an extensive division of labor and a high grade of professional knowledge. The capitalist manner of production robs the ruling class of all the leisure that they previously had. Even if they do not produce but are living from the exploitation of the producing classes, still they are not idle exploiters. Thanks to competition, the motive force of present economic life, the exploiters are continuously compelled to carry on an exhausting struggle with each other, which threatens the vanquished with complete annihilation.

The capitalists have therefore neither time nor leisure, nor the previous culture necessary for artistic and scientific activity. They lack even the necessary qualifications for regular participation in governmental activities. Not only in art and science but also in the government of the State the ruling class is forced to take no part. They must leave that to wageworkers and bureaucratic employees. The capitalist class reigns but does not govern. It is satisfied, however, to rule the government.

In the same way the decaying feudal nobility before it satisfied itself by taking on the forms of a royal nobility. But while with the feudal nobility the renunciation of its social functions was the product of corruption, with the capitalists this renunciation arises directly from their social functions and is an essential part of their existence.

With the help of such a powerful government a class can long maintain itself, even if it is superfluous. Yes, even if it has become injurious. And the stronger the power of the State, just so much the more does the governing class rest upon it, just so much more stubbornly will it cling to its privileges and all the less will it be inclined to grant concessions. The longer, however, it maintains its domination in this manner, the sharper become class antagonisms, the more pronounced must be the political collapse when it finally does come, and the deeper the social transformation that arises out of it, and the more apt the conquest of political power by an oppressed class to lead to revolution.

Simultaneously the warring classes become more and more conscious of the social consequences of their political struggle. The capitalist system of production tends to greatly accelerate the march of economic evolution. The economic transformation for which the century of invention has prepared the way is continued by the introduction of machines into industry. Since their introduction our economic relations are subject to continual change, not only by the rapid dissolution of the old but by the continuous creation of the new. The idea of the old, of the past, ceases to be equivalent to the tested, to the honorable, to the inviolable. It becomes synonymous with the imperfect and the outgrown. This idea is transplanted from the economic life into the field of art and science and politics. Just as in earlier days people clung without reason to the old, so today one gladly throws the old aside without reason just because it is old. And the time which is necessary in order to make a machine, an institution, a theory outgrown becomes ever shorter. And if in former days men worked with the intention of building for eternity with all the devotedness that flows from such a consciousness, so today one works for the fleeting effect of a moment with all the frivolity of this consciousness. So that the creation of today is within a short time not simply unfashionable but also useless.

The new is, however, just that thing that one observes, criticizes and investigates the most closely. The ordinary and the commonplace pass as a matter of course. Mankind studied the causes of eclipse much earlier than the rising and setting of the sun. In the same way the incentive to investigate the laws of social phenomena was very slight so long as these phenomena were the ordinary, the matter-of-course, the "natural." This incentive must at once be strengthened as soon as new, hitherto unheard of formations appeared in the social life. It was not the old hereditary feudal economics, but rather the newly appearing capitalist economics that first roused scientific observation at the beginning of the seventeenth century.

Economic science was encouraged still more by another motive. Capitalist production is mass production, social production. The typical modern capitalist state is the great state. Modern economics, like modern politics, must deal with mass phenomena. The larger the number of similar appearances that one observes, the greater the tendency to notice the universal—those indicating a social law—and the more the individual and the accidental disappear, the easier it is to discover the laws of social movements. The mathematical mass-observation of social phenomena, statistics, and the science of society that rises from political economy and reaches its highest point in the materialistic conception of history, has only been possible in the capitalist stage of production. Now for the first time classes could come to the full consciousness of the social significance of their struggles, and for the first time set before themselves great social goals, not as arbitrary dreams and pious wishes destined to be shattered on the hard facts, but as results of scientific insight into economic possibilities and necessities. To be sure this scientific thought can err, many of its conclusions can be shown to be illusions. But however great these errors may be, it cannot be deprived of the characteristic of every true science, the striving after a uniform conception of all phenomena under an indisputable whole. In social science this means the recognition of the social whole as a single organism in which one cannot arbitrarily and for itself alone change any single part. The socially oppressed class no longer directs its theoretical criticism against individual persons and tendencies, but against the total existing society. And just because of this fact every oppressed class which conquers political power is driven to transform the whole social foundations.

The capitalist society which sprang from the revolution of 1789 and its outcome was foreseen in its fundamental outlines by the physiocrats and their English followers.

Upon this distinction between the modern states and society and the organizations of antiquity and the Middle Ages rests the difference in the manner of their development. The former was predominantly unconscious, split up into local and personal strifes and the rebellion of countless little communities at different stages of development; the latter grows more and more self-conscious and strives toward a great recognized social goal which has been determined and is propagated by scientifically critical work. Political revolutions are less frequent, but more comprehensive and their social results more extensive.

The transition from the civil wars of antiquity and the Middle Ages to social revolutions in the previously used sense of the word was made by the Reformation, which belonged half to the Middle Ages and half to modern times. On a still higher stage was the English revolution of the middle of the seventeenth century, and finally the great French revolution becomes the classical type of social revolution, of which the uprisings of 1830 and 1848 were only faint echoes.

Social revolution in the sense here meant is peculiar to the stage of social development of capitalist society and the capitalist state. It does not exist previous to capitalism, because the political boundaries were too narrow and social consciousness too undeveloped. It will disappear with capitalism because this can only be overthrown by the proletariat, which as the lowest of all social classes can use its domination only to abolish all class domination and classes and therewith also the essential conditions of social revolution.

There now arises a great question, a question that today affects us profoundly, because it has the greatest influence upon our political relations to the present: Is the time of social revolution past or not? Have we already the political conditions which can bring about a transition from capitalism to socialism without political revolution, without the conquest of political power by the proletariat, or must we still expect an epoch of decisive struggles for the possession of this power and therewith a revolutionary epoch? Does the idea of social revolution belong with those antiquated ideas which are held only by thoughtless echoers of outgrown conceptions or by demagogical speculators upon the applause of the unthinking masses, and which every honest modern person who dispassionately observes the facts of modern society must put aside?

That is the question. Certainly an important question which a couple of phrases will not serve to dismiss.

We have discovered that social revolution is a product of special historical conditions. They presuppose, not simply a highly developed class antagonism, but also a great national state rising above all provincial and communal peculiarities, built upon a form of production that operates to level all local peculiarities, a powerful military and bureaucratic state, a science of political economy and a rapid rate of economic progress.

None of these factors of social revolution have been decreasing in power during the last decade. Many of them, on the contrary, have been much strengthened. Never was the rate of economic development more rapid. Scientific economics make, at least, a great extensive, if not intensive growth, thanks to the newspapers. Never was economic insight so broadly dispersed; never was the ruling class, as well as the mass of people, so much in a condition to comprehend the far-reaching consequences of its acts and strivings. This alone proves that we shall not make the tremendous transition from capitalism to socialism unconsciously, and that we cannot slowly undermine the dominion of the exploiting class without this class being conscious of this, and consequently arming themselves and using all their powers to suppress the strength and influence of the growing proletariat.

If, however, the insight into social relations was never so extensive as today, it is equally true that the governmental power was never so strong as now, nor the military, bureaucratic and economic forces so powerfully developed. It follows from this that the proletariat, when it shall have conquered the governmental powers, will have thereby attained the power to at once bring about most extensive social changes. It also follows from this that the personal governing class with the help of these powers can continue its existence and its plundering of the laboring class long after its economic necessity has ceased. The more, however, that the ruling classes support themselves with the State machinery and misuse this for the purposes of exploitation and oppression, just so much more must the bitterness of the proletariat against them increase, class hatred grow, and the efforts to conquer the machinery of State increase in intensity.

* * *

I do not wish to be understood as holding democracy superfluous, or to take the position that co-operatives, unions, the entrance of social democracy into municipalities and parliaments, or the attainment of single reforms, is worthless. Nothing would be more incorrect. On the contrary, all these are of incalculable value to the proletariat. They are only insignificant as means to avoid a revolution.

This conquest of political power by the proletariat is of the highest value exactly because it makes possible a higher form of the revolutionary struggle. This struggle is no longer, as in 1789, a battle of unorganized mobs with no political form, with no insight into the relative strength of the contending factors, with no profound comprehension of the purposes of the struggle and the means to its solution; no longer a battle of mobs that can be deceived and bewildered by every rumor or accident. It is a battle of organized, intelligent masses, full of stability and prudence, that do not follow every impulse or explode over every insult, or collapse under every misfortune.

On the other hand, the elections are a means to count ourselves and the enemy, and they grant thereby a clear view of the relative strength of the classes and parties, their advance and their retreat. They prevent premature outbreaks and they guard against defeats. They also grant the possibility that the opponents will themselves recognize the untenability of many positions and freely surrender them when their maintenance is no life-and-death question for them. So that the battle demands fewer victims, is less sanguinary and depends less upon blind chance.

Neither are the political acquisitions that are gained through democracy and the application of its freedom and rights to be undervalued. They are much too insignificant to really restrict the dominion of capitalism and to bring about its imperceptible transition into socialism. The slightest reform or organization may be of great significance for the physical or intellectual *re-birth of the proletariat* that, without them, would be surrendered helpless to capitalism and left alone in the misery that continuously threatens it. But it is not alone the relief of the proletariat from its misery that makes the activity of the proletariat in Parliament and the operation of the proletarian organizations indispensable. They are also of value as a means of practically familiarizing the proletariat with the problems and methods of national and municipal government and of great industries, as well as to the attainment of that intellectual maturity which the proletariat needs if it is to supplant the bourgeoisie as ruling class.

Democracy is also indispensable as a means of ripening the proletariat for the social revolution. But it is not capable of preventing this revolution. Democracy is to the proletariat what light and air are to the organism; without them it cannot develop its powers. But we must not be so occupied with observing the growth of one class that we cannot see the simultaneous growth of its opponent. Democracy does not hinder the development of capital, whose organization and political and economic powers increase at the same time as does the power of the proletariat. To be sure, the co-operatives are increasing, but simultaneously and yet faster grows the accumulation of capital; to be sure, the unions are growing, but simultaneously and faster grows the concentration of capital and its organization in gigantic monopolies. To be sure, the socialist press is growing (to only mention here a point which cannot be further discussed), but simultaneously grows the partyless and characterless press that poisons and unnerves ever wider popular circles. To be sure, wages are rising, but still faster rises the mass of profits. Certainly the number of socialist representatives in Parliament is growing, but still more sinks the significance and efficaciousness of this institution, while simultaneously Parliamentary majorities, like the government, fall into ever greater dependence on the powers of the high finance.

So beside the resources of the proletariat develop also those of capital, and the end of this development can be nothing less than a great, decisive battle that cannot end until the proletariat has attained the victory.

The capitalist class is superfluous and the proletariat, on the other hand, has become an indispensable social class. The capitalist class is not in a condition either to elevate the proletariat nor to root it out. After every defeat the latter rises again, more threatening than before. Accordingly the proletariat, when it shall have gained the first great victory over capital that shall place the political powers in its hands, can apply them in no other way than to the abolition of the capitalist system. So long as this has not yet happened, the battle between the two classes will not and cannot come to an end. Social peace inside of the capitalist system is a Utopia that has grown out of the real needs of the intellectual classes, but has no foundation in reality for its development. And no less of a Utopia is the imperceptible growth of capitalism into socialism. We have not the slightest ground to admit that things will end differently from what they began. Neither the economic nor the political development indicates that the era of revolution which characterizes the capitalist system is closed. Social reform and the strengthening of the proletarian organizations cannot hinder it. They can at the most operate to the end that the class struggle in the higher developed grades of the battling proletariat will be transformed from a battle for the first conditions of existence to a battle for the possession of dominion.

EDUARD BERNSTEIN: *The Case for Reformism* [2]

... Whilst tradition is essentially conservative, criticism is almost always destructive. At the moment of important action, therefore, criticism, even when most justified by facts, can be an evil, and therefore be reprehensible.

To recognize this is, of course, not to call tradition sacred and to forbid criticism. Parties are not always in the midst of rapids when attention is paid to one task only.

For a party which has to keep up with a real evolution, criticism is indispensable and tradition can become an oppressive burden, a restraining fetter.

But men in very few cases willingly and fully account for the importance of the changes which take place in their traditional assumptions. Usually they prefer to take into account only such changes as are concerned with undeniable facts and to bring them into unison as far as can be with the traditional catchwords. The method is called pettifogging, and the apologies and explanations for it are called cant.

Cant—the word is English, and is said to have been first used in the sixteenth century as a description of the saintly sing-song of the Puritans. In its more general meaning it denotes an unreal manner of speech, thoughtlessly imitative, or used with the consciousness of its untruth, to attain any kind of object, whether it be in religion, politics, or be concerned with theory or actuality. In this wider meaning cant is very ancient—there were no worse "canters," for example, than the Greeks of the past classic period—and it permeates in countless forms the whole of our civilized life. Every nation, every class and every group united by theory or interest has its own cant. It has partly become such a mere matter of convention, of pure form, that no one is any longer deceived by its emptiness, and a fight against it would be shooting idly at sparrows. But this does not apply to the cant that appears in the

2. From *Evolutionary Socialism* (New York: B. W. Huebsch, 1911), pp. 220-224. First published 1899.

guise of science and the cant which has become a political battle cry.

My proposition, "To me that which is generally called the ultimate aim of socialism is nothing, but the movement is everything," has often been conceived as a denial of every definite aim of the socialist movement, and Mr. George Plekhanov has even discovered that I have quoted this "famous sentence" from the book *To Social Peace*, by Gerhard von Schulze-Gävernitz. There, indeed, a passage reads that it is certainly indispensable for revolutionary socialism to take as its ultimate aim the nationalization of all the means of production, but not for practical political socialism which places near aims in front of distant ones. Because an ultimate aim is here regarded as being dispensable for practical objects, and as I also have professed but little interest for ultimate aims, I am an "indiscriminating follower" of Schulze-Gävernitz. One must confess that such demonstration bears witness to a striking wealth of thought.

When eight years ago I reviewed the Schulze-Gävernitz book in *Neue Zeit*, although my criticism was strongly influenced by assumptions which I now no longer hold, yet I put on one side as immaterial that opposition of ultimate aim and practical activity in reform, and admitted—without encountering a protest—that for England a further peaceful development, such as Schulze-Gävernitz places in prospect before her, was not improbable. I expressed the conviction that with the continuance of free development, the English working classes would certainly increase their demands, but would desire nothing that could not be shown each time to be necessary and attainable beyond all doubt. That is at the bottom nothing else than what I say today. And if anyone wishes to bring up against me the advances in social democracy made since then in England, I answer that with this extension a development of the English social democracy has gone hand in hand from the Utopian, revolutionary sect, as Engels repeatedly represented it to be, to the party of political reform which we now know. No socialist capable of thinking, dreams today in England of an imminent victory for socialism by means of a violent revolution—none dreams of a quick conquest of Parliament by a revolutionary proletariat. But they rely more and more on work in the municipalities and other self-governing bodies. The early contempt for the trade union movement has been given up; a closer sympathy has been won for it and, here and there also, for the co-operative movement.

And the ultimate aim? Well, that just remains an ultimate aim. "The working classes have no fixed and perfect Utopias to introduce by means of a vote of the nation. They know that in order to work out their own emancipation—and with it that higher form of life which the present form of society irresistibly makes for by its own economic development—they, the working classes, have to pass through long struggles, a whole series of historical processes, by means of which men and circumstances will be completely transformed. They have no ideals to realize, they have only to set at liberty the elements of the new society which have already been developed in the womb of the collapsing bourgeois society." So writes Marx in *Civil War in France*. I was thinking of this utterance, not in every point, but in its fundamental thought in writing down the sentence about the ultimate aim. For after all what does it say but that the movement, the series of processes, is everything, whilst every aim fixed beforehand in its details is immaterial to it. I have declared already that I willingly abandon the form of the sentence about the ultimate aim as far as it admits the interpretation that every general aim of the working class movement formulated as a principle should be declared valueless. But the preconceived theories about the drift of the movement which go beyond such a generally expressed aim, which try to determine the direction of the movement and its character without an ever-vigilant eye upon facts and experience, must necessarily always pass into Utopianism, and at some time or other stand in the way, and hinder the real theoretical and practical progress of the movement.

Whoever knows even but a little of the history of German social democracy also knows that the party has become important by continued action in contravention of such theories and of infringing resolutions founded on them. What Engels says in the preface to the new edition of *Civil War* with regard to the Blanquists and Proudhonists in the Paris Commune of 1871, namely that they both had been obliged in practice to act against their own theory, has often been repeated in another form. A theory or declaration of principle which does not allow attention being paid at every stage of development to the actual interests of the working classes, will always be set aside just as all forswearing of reforming detail work and of the support of neighboring middle class parties has again and again been forgotten; and again and again at the congresses of the party will the complaint be heard that here and there in the electoral contest the ultimate aim of socialism has not been put sufficiently in the foreground.

In the quotation from Schulze-Gävernitz which Plekhanov flings at me, it runs that by giving up the dictum that the condition of the worker in modern society is hopeless, socialism would lose its revolutionary point and would be absorbed in carrying out legislative demands. From this contrast it is clearly inferred that Schulze-Gävernitz always used the concept "revolutionary" in the sense of a struggle having revolution by violence in view. Plekhanov turns the thing round, and because I have not maintained the condition of the worker to be hopeless, because I acknowledge its capability of improvement and many other facts which bourgeois economists have upheld, he carts me over to the "opponents of scientific socialism."

Unfortunately for the scientific socialism of Plekhanov, the Marxist propositions on the hopelessness of the position of the worker have been upset in a book which bears the title, *Capital: A Criticism of Political Economy*. There we read of the "physical and moral regeneration" of the textile workers in Lancashire through the Factory Law of 1847, which "struck the feeblest eye." A bourgeois republic was not even necessary to bring about a certain improvement in the situation of a large section of workers! In the same book we read that the society of today is no firm crystal, but an organism capable of change and constantly engaged in a process of change, that also in the treatment of economic questions on the part of the official representatives of this society an "improvement was unmistakable." Further that the author had devoted so large a space in his book to the results of the English Factory Laws in order to spur the Continent to imitate them and thus to work so that the process of transforming society may be accomplished in ever more humane forms. All of which signifies not hopelessness, but capability of improvement in the condition of the worker. And, as since 1866, when this was written, the legislation depicted has not grown weaker but has been improved, made more general, and has been supplemented by laws and organizations working in the same direction, there can be no more doubt today than formerly of the hopefulness of the position of the worker. If to state such facts means following the "immortal Bastiat," then among the first ranks of these followers is—Karl Marx.

Now, it can be asserted against me that Marx certainly recognized those improvements, but that the chapter on the historical tendency of capitalist accumulation at the end of the first volume of *Capital* shows how little these details influenced his fundamental mode of viewing things. To which I answer that as far as that is correct it speaks against that chapter and not against me.

One can interpret this chapter in very different kinds of ways. I believe I was the first to point out, and indeed repeatedly, that it was a summary characterization of the tendency of a development which is found in capitalist accumulation, but which in practice is not carried out completely and which therefore need not be driven to the critical point of the antagonism there depicted. Engels has never expressed himself against this interpretation of mine, never, either verbally or in print, declared it to be wrong. Nor did he say a word against me when I wrote, in 1891, in an essay on a work of Schulze-Gävernitz on the questions referred to: "It is clear that where legislation, this systematic and conscious action of society, interferes in an appropriate way, the working of the tendencies of economic development is thwarted, under some circumstances can even be annihilated. Marx and Engels have not only never denied this, but, on the contrary, have always emphasized it." If one reads the chapter mentioned with this idea, one will also, in a few sentences, silently place the word "tendency" and thus be spared the need of bringing this chapter into accord with reality by distorting arts of interpretation. But then the chapter itself would become of less value the more progress is made in actual evolution. For its theoretic importance does not lie in the argument of the general tendency to capitalistic centralization and accumulation which had been affirmed long before Marx by bourgeois economists and socialists, but in the presentation, peculiar to Marx, of circumstances and forms under which it would work at a more advanced stage of evolution, and of the results to which it would lead. But in this respect actual evolution is really always bringing forth new arrangements, forces, facts, in face of which that presentation seems insufficient and loses to a corresponding extent the capability of serving as a sketch of the coming evolution. That is how I understand it.

One can, however, understand this chapter differently. One can conceive it in this way, that all the improvements mentioned there, and some possibly ensuing, only create temporary remedies against the oppressive tendencies of capitalism, that they signify unimportant modifications which cannot in the long run effect anything substantially against the critical point of antagonisms laid down by Marx, that this will finally appear—if not literally yet substantially—in the manner depicted, and will lead to catastrophic change by violence. This interpretation can be founded on the categoric wording of the last sentences of the chapter, and receives a certain confirmation because at the end reference is again made to the *Communist Manifesto,* whilst Hegel also appeared shortly before with his negation of the negation—the restoration on a new foundation of individual property negatived by the capitalist manner of production.

According to my view, it is impossible simply to declare the one conception right and the other absolutely wrong. To me the chapter illustrates a dualism which runs through the whole monumental work of Marx, and which also finds expression in a less pregnant fashion in other passages— a dualism which consists in the fact that the work aims at being a scientific inquiry and also at proving a theory laid down long before its drafting; a formula lies at the basis of it in which the result to which the exposition should lead is fixed beforehand. The return to the *Communist Manifesto* points here to a real residue of Utopianism in the Marxist system. Marx had accepted the solution of the Utopians in essentials, but had recognized their means and proofs as inadequate. He therefore undertook a revision of them, and this with the zeal, the critical acuteness, and love of truth of a scientific genius. He suppressed no important fact, he also forbore belittling artificially the importance of these facts as long as the object of the inquiry had no immediate reference to the final aim of the formula to be proved. To that point his work is free of every tendency necessarily interfering with the scientific method.

For the general sympathy with the strivings for emancipation of the working classes does not in itself stand in the way of the scientific method. But, as Marx approaches a point when that final aim enters seriously into the question, he becomes uncertain and unreliable. Such contradictions then appear as were shown in the book under consideration, for instance, in the section on the movement of incomes in modern society. It thus appears that this great scientific spirit was, in the end, a slave to a doctrine.

Nothing confirms me more in this conception than the anxiety with which some persons seek to maintain certain statements in *Capital*, which are falsified by facts. It is just some of the more deeply devoted followers of Marx who have not been able to separate themselves from the dialectical form of the work ... who do this. At least, that is only how I can explain the words of a man, otherwise so amenable to facts as Kautsky, who, when I observed in Stuttgart that the number of wealthy people for many years had increased, not decreased, answered: "If that were true then the date of our victory would not only be very long postponed, but we should never attain our goal. If it be capitalists who increase and not those with no possessions, then we are going ever further from our goal the more evolution progresses, then capitalism grows stronger, not socialism."

That the number of the wealthy increases and does not diminish is not an invention of bourgeois "harmony economists," but a fact established by the boards of assessment for taxes, often to the chagrin of those concerned, a fact which can no longer be disputed. But what is the significance of this fact as regards the victory of socialism? Why should the realization of socialism depend on its refutation? Well, simply for this reason: because the dialectical scheme seems so to prescribe it; because a post threatens to fall out of the scaffolding if one admits that the social surplus product is appropriated by an increasing instead of a decreasing number of possessors. But it is only the speculative theory that is affected by this matter; it does not at all affect the actual movement. Neither the struggle of the workers for democracy in politics nor their struggle for democracy in industry is touched by it. The prospects of this struggle do not depend on the theory of concentration of capital in the hands of a diminishing number of magnates, nor on the whole dialectical scaffolding of which this is a plank, but on the growth of social wealth and of the social productive forces, in conjunction with general social progress, and, particularly, in conjunction with the intellectual and moral advance of the working classes themselves.

Suppose the victory of socialism depended on the constant shrinkage in the number of capitalist magnates, social democracy, if it wanted to act logically, either would have to support the heaping up of capital in ever fewer hands, or at least to given no support to anything that would stop this shrinkage. As a matter of fact it often enough does neither the one nor the other. These considerations, for instance, do not govern its votes on questions of taxation. From the standpoint of the catastrophic theory a great part of this practical activity of the working classes is an undoing of work that ought to be allowed to be done. It is not social democracy which is wrong in this respect. The fault lies in the doctrine which assumes that progress depends on the deterioration of social conditions.

In his preface to the *Agrarian Question,* Kautsky turns upon those who speak of the necessity of a triumph over Marxism. He says that he sees doubt and hesitation expressed, but that these alone indicate no development. That is so far correct in that doubt and hesitation are no positive refutation. They can, however, be the first step toward it. But is it altogether a matter of triumphing over Marxism, or is it not rather a rejection of certain remains of Utopianism which adhere to Marxism, and which are the cause of the contradictions in theory and practice which have been pointed out in Marxism by its critics? This treatise has become already more voluminous than it ought to have been, and I must therefore abstain from going into all the details of this subject. But all the more I consider it my duty to declare that I hold a whole series of objections raised by opponents against certain items in Marx's theory as unrefuted, some as irrefutable. And I can do this all the more easily as these objections are quite irrelevant to the strivings of social democracy.

We ought to be less susceptible in this respect. It has repeatedly happened that conclusions by followers of Marx, who believed that they contradicted the theories of Marx, have been disputed with great zeal, and, in the end, the supposed contradictions were proved for the most part not to exist. Amongst others I have in my mind the controversy concerning the investigations of the late Dr. Stiebling on the effect of the concentration of capital on the rate of exploitation. In his manner of expression, as well as in separate items of his calculations, Steibling made some great blunders, which it is the merit of Kautsky to have discovered. But on the other hand the third volume of *Capital* has shown that the fundamental thought of Stiebling's works—the decrease of the rate of exploitation with the increasing concentration of capital did not stand in such opposition to Marx's doctrine as then appeared to most of us, although his proof of the phenomenon is different from that of Marx. Yet in his time Stiebling had to hear (from Kautsky) that if what he inferred was correct, the theoretical foundation of the working class movement, the theory of Marx, was false. And as a matter of fact those who spoke thus could refer to various passages from Marx. An analysis of the controversy which was entered into over the essays of Stiebling could very well serve as an illustration of some of the contradictions of the Marxist theory of value.

Similar conflicts exist with regard to the estimate of the relation of economics and force in history, and they find their counterpart in the criticism on the practical tasks and possibilities of the working class movement which has already been discussed in another place. This is, however, a point to which it is necessary to recur. But the question to be investigated is not how far originally, and in the further course of history, force determined economy and vice versa, but what is the creative power of force in a given society.

Now it would be absurd to go back to the prejudices of former generations with regard to the capabilities of political power, for such a thing would mean that we would have to go still further back to explain those prejudices. The prejudices which the Utopians, for example, cherished rested on good grounds; indeed, one can scarcely say that they were prejudices, for they rested on the real immaturity of the working classes of the period as a result of which, only a transitory mob rule on the one side or a return to the class oligarchy on the other was the only possible outcome of the political power of the masses. Under these circumstances a reference to politics could appear only to be a turning aside from more pressing duties. Today these conditions have been to some extent removed, and therefore no person capable of reflecting will think of criticizing political action with the arguments of that period.

Marxism first turned the thing round, as we have seen, and preached (in view of the potential capacity of the industrial proletariat) political action as the most important duty of the movement. But it was thereby involved in great contradictions. It also recognized, and separated itself thereby from the demagogic parties, that the working classes had not yet attained the required maturity for their emancipation, and also that the economic preliminary conditions for such were not present. But in spite of that it turned again and again to tactics which supposed both preliminary conditions as almost fulfilled. We come across passages in its publications where the immaturity of the workers is emphasized with an acuteness which differs very little from the doctrinairism of the early Utopian socialists, and soon afterward we come across passages according to which we should assume that all culture, all intelligence, all virtue, is only to be found among the working classes —passages which make it incomprehensible why the most extreme social revolutionaries and physical force anarchists should not be right. Corresponding with that, political action is ever directed toward a revolutionary convulsion expected in an imminent future, in the face of which legislative work for a long time appears only as a *pis aller* —a merely temporary device. And we look in vain for any systematic investigation of the question of what can be expected from legal, and what from revolutionary action.

It is evident at the first glance that great differences exist in the latter respect. But they are usually found to be this: that law, or the path of legislative reform, is the slower way, and revolutionary force the quicker and more radical. But that only is true in a restricted sense. Whether the legislative or the revolutionary method is the more promising depends entirely on the nature of the measures and on their relation to different classes and customs of the people.

In general, one may say here that the revolutionary way (always in the sense of revolution by violence) does quicker work as far as it deals with removal of obstacles which a privileged minority places in the path of social progress: that its strength lies on its negative side.

Constitutional legislation works more slowly in this respect as a rule. Its path is usually that of compromise, not the prohibition, but the buying out of acquired rights. But it is stronger than the revolution scheme where prejudice and the limited horizon of the great mass of the people appear as hinderances to social progress, and it offers greater advantages where it is a question of the creation of permanent economic arrangements capable of lasting; in other words, it is best adapted to positive social-political work.

In legislation, intellect dominates over emotion in quiet times; during a revolution emotion dominates over intellect. But if emotion is often an imperfect leader, the intellect is a slow motive force. Where a revolution sins by over-haste, the every-day legislator sins by procrastination. Legislation works as a systematic force, revolution as an elementary force.

As soon as a nation has attained a position where the rights of the propertied minority have ceased to be a serious obstacle to social progress, where the negative tasks of political action are less pressing than the positive, then the appeal to a revolution by force becomes a meaningless phrase. One can overturn a government or a privileged minority, but not a nation. When the working classes do not possess very strong economic organizations of their own, and have not attained, by means of education on self-governing bodies, a high degree of mental independence, the dictatorship of the proletariat means the dictatorship of club orators and writers. I would not wish that those who see in the oppression and tricking of the working men's organizations and in the exclusion of working men from the legislature and government the highest point of the art of political policy should experience their error in practice. Just as little would I desire it for the working class movement itself.

One has not overcome Utopianism if one assumes that there is in the present, or ascribes to the present, what is to be in the future. We have to take working men as they are. And they are neither so universally pauperized as was set out in the *Communist Manifesto*, nor so free from prejudices and weaknesses as their courtiers wish to make us believe. They have the virtues and failings of the economic and social conditions under which they live. And neither these conditions nor their effects can be put on one side from one day to another.

Have we attained the required degree of development of the productive forces for the abolition of classes? In face of the fantastic figures which were formerly set up in proof of this and which rested on generalizations based on the development of particularly favored industries, socialist writers in modern times have endeavored to reach by carefully detailed calculations, appropriate estimates of the possibilities of production in a socialist society, and their results are very different from those figures. Of a general reduction of hours of labor to five, four, or even three or two hours, such as was formerly accepted, there can be no hope at any time within sight, unless the general standard of life is much reduced. Even under a collective organization of work, labor must begin very young and only cease at a rather advanced age, if it is to be reduced considerably below an eight-hours' day. Those persons ought to understand this first of all who indulge in the most extreme exaggerations regarding the ratio of the number of the non-propertied classes to that of the propertied. But he who thinks irrationally on one point does so usually on another.

But he who surveys the actual workers' movement will also find that the freedom from those qualities which appeared Philistine to a person born in the bourgeoisie, is very little valued by the workers, that they in no way support the morale of proletarianism, but, on the contrary, tend to make a "Philistine" out of a proletarian. With the roving proletarian without a family and home, no lasting, firm trade union movement would be possible. It is no bourgeois prejudice, but a conviction gained through decades of labor organization, which has made so many of the English labor leaders —socialists and non-socialists—into zealous adherents of the temperance movement. The working class socialists know the faults of their class, and the most conscientious among them, far from glorifying these faults, seek to overcome them with all their power.

We cannot demand from a class, the great majority of whose members live under crowded conditions, are badly educated, and have an uncertain and insufficient income, the high intellectual and moral standard which the organization and existence of a socialist community presupposes. We will, therefore, not ascribe it to them by way of fiction. Let us rejoice at the great stock of intelligence, renunciation, and energy which the modern working class movement has partly revealed, partly produced; but we must not assign, without discrimination to the masses, the millions, what holds good, say, of hundreds of thousands. . . . I confess willingly that I measure here with two kinds of measures. Just because I expect much of the working classes I censure much more everything that tends to corrupt their moral judgment than I do similar habits of the higher classes, and I see with the greatest regret that a tone of literary decadence is spreading here and there in the working class press which can only have a confusing and corrupting effect. A class which is aspiring needs a sound morale and must suffer no deterioration. Whether it sets out for itself an ideal ultimate aim is of secondary importance if it pursues with energy its proximate aims. The important point is that these aims are inspired by a definite principle which expresses a higher degree of economy and of social life, that they are an embodiment of a social conception which means in the evolution of civilization a higher view of morals and of legal rights.

From this point of view I cannot subscribe to the proposition: "The working class has no ideas to realize." I see in it rather a self-deception, if it is not a mere play upon words on the part of its author.

And in this mind, I, at the time, resorted to the spirit of the great Königsberg philosopher, the critic of pure reason, against the cant which sought to get a hold on the working class movement and to which the Hegelian dialectic offers a comfortable refuge. I did this in the conviction that social democracy required a Kant who should judge the received opinion and examine it critically with deep acuteness, who should show where its apparent materialism is the highest—and is therefore the most easily misleading—ideology, and warn it that the contempt of the ideal, the magnifying of material factors until they become omnipotent forces of evolution, is a self-deception, which has been and will be exposed as such at every opportunity by the action of those who proclaim it. Such a thinker, who with convincing exactness could show what is worthy and destined to live in the work of our great champions, and what must and can perish, would also make it possible for us to hold a more unbiased judgment on those works which, although not starting from premises which today appear to us as decisive, yet are devoted to the ends for which social democracy is fighting. . . . it is not every epoch that produces a Marx, and even for a man of equal genius the working class movement of today is too great to enable him to occupy the position which Marx fills in its history. Today it needs, in addition to the fighting spirit, the co-ordinating and constructive thinkers who are intellectually enough advanced to be able to separate the chaff from the wheat, who are great enough in their mode of thinking to recognize also the little plant that has grown on another soil than theirs, and who, perhaps, though not kings, are warm-hearted republicans in the domain of socialist thought.

ROSA LUXEMBURG: *Reform or Revolution* [3]

Can the Social-Democracy be against reforms? Can we contrapose the social revolution, the transformation of the existing order, our final goal, to social reforms? Certainly not. The daily struggle for reforms, for the amelioration of the condition of the workers within the framework of the existing social order, and for democratic institutions, offers to the Social-Democracy the only means of engaging in the proletarian class war and working in the direction of the final goal—the conquest of political power and the suppression of wage-labor. Between social reforms and revolution there exists for the Social-Democracy an indissoluble tie. The struggle for reforms is its means; the social revolution, its aim.

It is in Eduard Bernstein's theory . . . that we find, for the first time, the opposition of the two factors of the labor movement. His theory tends to counsel us to renounce the social transformation, the final goal of the Social-Democracy and, inversely, to make of social reforms, the means of the class struggle, its aim. Bernstein himself has very clearly and characteristically formulated this viewpoint when he wrote: "The final goal, no matter what it is, is nothing; the movement is everything."

But since the final goal of socialism constitutes the only decisive factor distinguishing the Social-Democratic movement from bourgeois democracy and from bourgeois radicalism, the only factor transforming the entire labor movement from a vain effort to repair the capitalist order into a class struggle against this order, for the suppression of this order—the question: "Reform or Revolution?" as it is posed by Bernstein, equals for the Social-Democracy the question: "To be or not to be?" In the controversy with Bernstein and his followers, everybody in the Party ought to understand clearly it is not a question of this or that method of struggle, or the use of this or that set of tactics, but of the very existence of the Social-Democratic movement.

Upon a casual consideration of Bernstein's theory, this may appear like an exaggeration. Does he not continually mention the Social-Democracy and its aims? Does he not

3. (New York, 1937), pp. 4-5, 7-10, 24, 26-27, 29, 50-53. First published, 1899.

repeat again and again, in very explicit language, that he too strives toward the final goal of socialism, but in another way? Does he not stress particularly that he fully approves of the present practice of the Social-Democracy?

That is all true, to be sure. It is also true that every new movement, when it first elaborates its theory and policy, begins by finding support in the preceding movement, though it may be in direct contradiction with the latter. It begins by suiting itself to the forms found at hand and by speaking the language spoken hereto. In time, the new grain breaks through the old husk. The new movement finds its own forms and its own language.

To expect an opposition against scientific socialism, at its very beginning, to express itself clearly, fully and to the last consequence on the subject of its real content; to expect it to deny openly and bluntly the theoretic basis of the Social-Democracy—would amount to underrating the power of scientific socialism. Today he who wants to pass as a socialist, and at the same would declare war on Marxian doctrine, the most stupendous product of the human mind in the century, must begin with involuntary esteem for Marx. He must begin by acknowledging himself to be his disciple, by seeking in Marx's own teachings the points of support for an attack on the latter, while he represents this attack as a further development of Marxian doctrine. On this account, we must, unconcerned by its outer forms, pick out the sheathed kernel of Bernstein's theory. This is a matter of urgent necessity for the broad layers of the industrial proletariat in our Party.

No coarser insult, no baser aspersion, can be thrown against the workers than the remark: "Theoretic controversies are only for academicians." Some time ago Lassalle said: "Only when science and the workers, these opposite poles of society, become one, will they crush in their arms of steel all obstacles to culture." The entire strength of the modern labor movement rests on theoretic knowledge.

But doubly important is this knowledge for the workers in the present case, because it is precisely they and their influence in the movement that are in the balance here. It is their skin that is being brought to market. The opportunist theory in the Party, the theory formulated by Bernstein, is nothing else than an unconscious attempt to assure predominance to the petty-bourgeois elements that have entered our Party, to change the policy and aims of our Party in their direction. The question of reform and revolution, of the final goal and the movement, is basically, in another form, but the question of the petty-bourgeois or proletarian character of the labor movement.

It is, therefore, in the interest of the proletarian mass of the Party to become acquainted, actively and in detail, with the present theoretic controversy with opportunism. As long as theoretic knowledge remains the privilege of a handful of "academicians" in the Party, the latter will face the danger of going astray. Only when the great mass of workers take the keen and dependable weapons of scientific socialism in their own hands, will all the petty-bourgeois inclinations, all the opportunist currents come to naught. The movement will then find itself on sure and firm ground. "Quantity will do it."

* * *

If it is true that theories are only the images of the phenomena of the exterior world in the human consciousness, it must be added, concerning Eduard Bernstein's system, that theories are sometimes inverted images. Think of a theory of instituting socialism by means of social reforms in the face of the complete stagnation of the reform movement in Germany. Think of a theory of trade union control over production in face of the defeat of the metal workers in England. Consider the theory of winning a majority in Parliament, after the revision of the constitution of Saxony and in view of the most recent attempts against universal suffrage. However, the pivotal point of Bernstein's system is not located in his conception of the practical tasks of the Social-Democracy. It is found in his stand on the course of the objective development of capitalist society, which, in turn, is closely bound to his conception of the practical tasks of the Social-Democracy.

According to Bernstein, a general decline of capitalism seems to be increasingly improbable because, on the one hand, capitalism shows a greater capacity of adaptation, and on the other hand, capitalist production becomes more and more varied.

The capacity of capitalism to adapt itself, says Bernstein, is manifested first in the disappearance of general crises, resulting from the development of the credit system, employers' organizations, wider means of communication and informational services. It shows itself secondly, in the tenacity of the middle classes, which hails from the growing differentiation of the branches of production and the elevation of vast layers of the proletariat to the level of the middle class. It is furthermore proved, argues Bernstein, by the amelioration of the economic and political situation of the proletariat as a result of its trade union activity.

From this theoretic stand is derived the following general conclusion about the practical work of the Social-Democracy. The latter must not direct its daily activity toward the conquest of political power, but toward the betterment of the condition of the working class within the existing order. It must not expect to institute socialism as a result of a political and social crisis, but should build socialism by means of the progressive extension of social control and the gradual application of the principle of co-operation.

Bernstein himself sees nothing new in his theories. On the contrary, he believes them to be in agreement with certain declarations of Marx and Engels. Nevertheless, it seems to us that it is difficult to deny that they are in formal contradiction with the conceptions of scientific socialism.

If Bernstein's revisionism merely consisted in affirming that the march of capitalist development is slower than was thought before, he would merely be presenting an argument for adjourning the conquest of power by the proletariat, on which everybody agreed up to now. Its only consequence would be a slowing up of the pace of the struggle.

But that is not the case. What Bernstein questions is not the rapidity of the development of capitalist society, but the march of the development itself and, consequently, the very possibility of a change to socialism.

Socialist theory up to now declared that the point of departure for a transformation to socialism would be a general and catastrophic crisis. We must distinguish in this outlook two things: the fundamental idea and its exterior form.

The fundamental idea consists of the affirmation that capitalism, as a result of its own inner contradictions, moves toward a point when it will be unbalanced, when it will simply become impossible. There were good reasons for conceiving that juncture in the from of a catastrophic general commercial crisis. But that is of secondary importance when the fundamental idea is considered.

The scientific basis of socialism rests, as is well known, on three principal results of capitalist development. First, on the growing anarchy of capitalist economy, leading inevitably to its ruin. Second, on the progressive socialization of the process of production, which creates the germs of the future social order. And third, on the increased organization and consciousness of the proletarian class, which constitutes the active factor in the coming revolution.

Bernstein pulls away the first of the three fundamental supports of scientific socialism. He says that capitalist development does not lead to a general economic collapse.

He does not merely reject a certain form of the collapse. He rejects the very possibility of collapse. He says textually: "One could claim that by collapse of the present society is meant something else than a general commercial crisis, worse than all others, that is a complete collapse of the capitalist system brought about as a result of its own contradictions." And to this he replies: "With the growing development of society a complete and almost general collapse of the present system of production becomes more and more improbable, because capitalist development increases on the one hand the capacity of adaptation and, on the other,—that is at the same time, the differentiation of industry."

But then the question arises: "Why and how, in that case, shall we attain the final goal? According to scientific socialism, the historic necessity of the socialist revolution manifests itself above all in the growing anarchy of capitalism, which drives the system into an impasse. But if one admits with Bernstein that capitalist development does not move in the direction of its own ruin, then socialism ceases to be objectively necessary. There remain the other two mainstays of the scientific explanation of socialism, which are also said to be consequences of capitalism itself: the socialization of the process of production and the growing consciousness of the proletariat. It is these two matters that Bernstein has in mind when he says: "The suppression of the theory of collapse does not in any way deprive socialist doctrine of its power of persuasion. For, examined closely, what are all the factors enumerated by us that make for the suppression or the modification of the former crises? Nothing else, in fact, than the conditions, or even in part the germs, of the socialization of production and exchange."

Very little reflection is needed to understand that here too we face a false conclusion. Where lies the importance of all the phenomena that are said by Bernstein to be the means of capitalist adaptation—cartels, the credit system, the development of means of communication, the amelioration of the situation of the working class, etc.? Obviously, in that they suppress or, at least, attenuate the internal contradictions of capitalist economy, and stop the development or the aggravation of these contradictions. Thus the suppression of crises can only mean the suppression of the antagonism between production and exchange on the capitalist base. The amelioration of the situation of the working class, or the penetration of certain fractions of the class into the middle layers, can only mean the attenuation of the antagonism between Capital and Labor. But if the mentioned factors suppress the capitalist contradictions and consequently save the system from ruin, if they enable capitalism to maintain itself—and that is why Bernstein calls them "means of adaptation"—how can cartels, the credit system, trade unions, etc. be at the same time "the conditions and even, in part, the germs" of socialism? Obviously only in the sense that they express most clearly the social character of production.

But by presenting it in its capitalist form, the same factors render superfluous, inversely, in the same measure, the transformation of this socialized production into socialist production. That is why they can be the germs or conditions of a socialist order only in a theoretic sense and not in an historic sense. They are phenomena which, in the light of our conception of socialism, we know to be related to socialism but which, in fact, not only do not lead to a socialist revolution but render it, on the contrary, superfluous.

There remains one force making for socialism—the class consciousness of the proletariat. But it, too, is in the given case not the simple intellectual reflection of the growing contradictions of capitalism and its approaching decline. It is now no more than an ideal whose force of persuasion rests only on the perfection attributed to it.

We have here, in brief, the explanation of the socialist program by means of "pure reason." We have here, to use simpler language, an idealist explanation of socialism. The objective necessity of socialism, the explanation of socialism as the result of the material development of society, falls to the ground.

Revisionist theory thus places itself in a dilemma. Either the socialist transformation is, as was admitted up to now, the consequence of the internal contradictions of capitalism, and with the growth of capitalism will develop its inner contradictions, resulting inevitably, at some point, in its collapse (in that case the "means of adaptation" are ineffective and the theory of collapse is correct); or the "means of adaptation" will really stop the collapse of the capitalist system and thereby enable capitalism to maintain itself by suppressing its own contradictions. In that case socialism ceases to be an historic necessity. It then becomes anything you want to call it, but is no longer the result of the material development of society.

The dilemma leads to another. Either revisionism is correct in its position on the course of capitalist development, and therefore the socialist transformation of society is only a utopia, or socialism is not a utopia, and the theory of "means of adaptation" is false. There is the question in a nutshell.

* * *

The production relations of capitalist society approach more and more the production relations of socialist society. But on the other hand, its political and juridical relations establish between capitalist society and socialist society a steadily rising wall. This wall is not overthrown, but is on the contrary strengthened and consolidated by the development of social reforms and the course of democracy. Only the hammer blow of revolution, that is to say, the conquest of political power by the proletariat can break down this wall. . . . It is not true that socialism will arise automatically from the daily struggle of the working class. Socialism will be the consequence of (1), the growing contradictions of capitalist economy and (2), of the comprehension by the working class of the unavoidability of the suppression of these contradictions through a social transformation. When, in the manner of revisionism, the first condition is denied and the second rejected, the labor movement finds itself reduced to a simple corporative and reformist movement. We move here in a straight line toward the total abandonment of the class viewpoint.

This consequence also becomes evident when we investigate the general character of revisionism. It is obvious that revisionism does not wish to concede that its standpoint is that of the capitalist apologist. It does not join the bourgeois economists in denying the existence of the contradictions of capitalism. But, on the other hand, what precisely constitutes the fundamental point of revisionism and distinguishes it from the attitude taken by the Social-Democracy up to now, is that it does not base its theory on the belief that the contradictions of capitalism will be suppressed as a result of the logical inner development of the present economic system.

We may say that the theory of revisionism occupies an intermediate place between two extremes. Revisionism does not expect to see the contradictions of capitalism mature. It does not propose to suppress these contradictions through a revolutionary transformation. It wants to lessen, to attenuate, the capitalist contradictions. So that the antagonism existing between production and exchange is to be mollified by the cessation of crises and the formation of capitalist combines. The antagonism between Capital and Labor is to be adjusted by bettering the situation of the workers and by the conservation of the middle classes. And the contradiction between the class State and society is to be liquidated through increased State control and the progress of democracy.

It is true that the present procedure of the Social-Democracy does not consist in waiting for the antagonisms of capitalism to develop and in passing on, only then, to the task of suppressing them. On the contrary, the essence of revolutionary procedure is to be guided by the direction of this development, once it is ascertained, and inferring from this direction what consequences are necessary for the political struggle. Thus the Social-Democracy has combated tariff wars and militarism without waiting for their reactionary character to become fully evident. Bernstein's procedure is not guided by a consideration of the development of capitalism, by the prospect of the aggravation of its contradictions. It is guided by the prospect of the attenuation of these contradictions. He shows this when he speaks of the "adaptation" of capitalist economy.

* * *

Revisionism is nothing else than a theoretic generalization made from the angle of the isolated capitalist. Where does this viewpoint belong theoretically if not in vulgar bourgeois economics?

All the errors of this school rest precisely on the conception that mistakes the phenomena of competition, as seen from the angle of the isolated capitalist, for the phenomena of the whole of capitalist economy. Just as Bernstein considers credit to be a means of "adaptation," so vulgar economy considers money to be a judicious means of "adaptation" to the needs of exchange. Vulgar economy, too, tries to find the antidote against the ills of capitalism in the phenomena of Capitalism. Like Bernstein, it believes that it is possible to regulate capitalist economy. And in the manner of Bernstein, it arrives in time at the desire to palliate the contradictions of capitalism, that is, at the belief in the possibility of patching up the sores of capitalism. It ends up by subscribing to a program of reaction. It ends up in a utopia.

The theory of revisionism can therefore be defined in the following way. It is a theory of standing still in the socialist movement, built, with the aid of vulgar economy, on a theory of a capitalist standstill.

* * *

Bernstein's book is of great importance to the German and the international labor movement. It is the first attempt to give a theoretic base to the opportunist currents common in the Social-Democracy.

These currents may be said to have existed for a long time in our movement, if we take into consideration such sporadic manifestations of opportunism as the question of subsidization of steamers. But it is only since about 1890, with the suppression of the anti-Socialist laws, that we have had a trend of opportunism of a clearly defined character. Vollmar's "State Socialism," the vote on the Bavarian budget, the "agrarian socialism" of South Germany, Heine's policy of compensation, Schippel's stand on tariffs and militarism, are the high points in the development of our opportunist practice.

What appears to characterize this practice above all? A certain hostility to "theory." This is quite natural, for our "theory," that is, the principles of scientific socialism, impose clearly marked limitations to practical activity—insofar as it concerns the aims of this activity, the means used in attaining these aims, and the method employed in this activity. It is quite natural for people who run after immediate "practical" results to want to free themselves from such limitations and to render their practice independent of our "theory."

However, this outlook is refuted by every attempt to apply it in reality. State socialism, agrarian socialism, the policy of compensation, the question of the army, all constituted defeats to our opportunism. It is clear that, if this current is to maintain itself, it must try to destroy the principles of our theory and elaborate a theory of its own. Bernstein's book is precisely an effort in that direction. That is why at Stuttgart all the opportunist elements in our party immediately grouped themselves about Bernstein's banner. If the opportunist currents in the practical activity of our party are an entirely natural phenomenon which can be explained in light of the special conditions of our activity and its development, Bernstein's theory is no less natural an attempt to group these currents into a general theoretic expression, an attempt to elaborate its own theoretic conditions and to break with scientific socialism. That is why the published expression of Bernstein's ideas should be recognized as a theoretic test for opportunism, and as its first scientific legitimation.

What was the result of this test? We have seen the result. Opportunism is not in a position to elaborate a positive theory capable of withstanding criticism. All it can do is to attack various isolated theses of Marxist theory and, just because Marxist doctrine constitutes one solidly constructed edifice, hope by this means to shake the entire system, from the top of its foundation.

This shows that opportunist practice is essentially irreconcilable with Marxism. But is also proves that opportunism is incompatible with socialism (the socialist movement) in general, that its internal tendency is to push the labor movement into bourgeois paths, that opportunism tends to paralyze completely the proletarian class struggle. The latter, considered historically, has evidently nothing to do with Marxist doctrine. For, *before Marx* and independently from him, there have been labor movements and various socialist doctrines, each of which, in its way, was the theoretic expression, corresponding to the conditions of the time, of the struggle of the working class for emancipation. The theory that consists in basing socialism on the moral notion of justice, on a struggle against the mode of distribution, instead of basing it on a struggle against the mode of production, the conception of class antagonism as an antagonism between the poor and the rich, the effort to graft the "co-operative principle" on capitalist economy—all the nice notions found in Bernstein's doctrine—already existed before him. And these theories were, *in their time*, in spite of their insufficiency, effective theories of the proletarian class struggle. They were the children's seven-league boots, thanks to which the proletariat learned to walk up on the scene of history.

But after the development of the class struggle and its reflex in its social conditions had led to the abandonment of these theories and to the elaboration of the principles of scientific socialism, there could be no socialism—at least in Germany—outside of Marxist socialism, and there could be no socialist class struggle outside of the Social-Democracy. From then on, socialism and Marxism, the proletarian struggle for emancipation and the Social-Democracy, were identical. That is why the return to pre-Marxist socialist theories no longer signifies today a return to the seven-league boots of the childhood of the proletariat, but a return to the puny worn-out slippers of the bourgeoisie.

Bernstein's theory was the *first*, and at the same time, the *last* attempt to give a theoretic base to opportunism. It is the last, because in Bernstein's system, opportunism has gone—negatively through its renunciation of scientific socialism, positively through its marshaling of every bit of theoretic confusion possible—as far as it can. In Bernstein's book, opportunism has crowned its theoretic development (just as it completed its practical development in the position taken by Schippel on the question of militarism), and has reached its ultimate conclusion.

Marxist doctrine cannot only refute opportunism theoretically. It alone can explain opportunism as a historic phenomenon in the development of the party. The forward march of the proletariat, on a world historic scale, to its final victory is not, indeed, "so simple a thing." The peculiar character of this movement resides precisely in the fact that here, for the first time in history, the popular masses themselves, *in opposition to* the ruling classes, are to impose their will, but they must effect this outside of the present society, beyond the existing society. This *will* the masses can only form in a constant struggle against the existing order. The union of the broad popular masses with an aim reaching beyond the existing social order, the union of the daily struggle with the great world transformation, that is the task of the Social-Democratic movement, which must logically grope on its road of development between the following two rocks: abandoning the mass character of the party or abandoning its final aim, falling into bourgeois reformism or into sectarianism, anarchism or opportunism.

In its theoretic arsenal, Marxist doctrine furnished, more than half a century ago, arms that are effective against both of these two extremes. But because our movement is a mass movement and because the dangers menacing it are not derived from the human brain but from social conditions, Marxist doctrine could not assure us, in advance and once for always, against the anarchist and opportunist tendencies. The latter can be overcome only as we pass from the domain of theory to the domain of practice, but only with the help of the arms furnished us by Marx.

"Bourgeois revolutions," wrote Marx a half century ago, "like those of the eighteenth century, rush onward rapidly from success to success, their stage effects outbid one another, men and things seem to be set in flaming brilliants, ecstasy is the prevailing spirit; but they are short-lived, they reach their climax speedily, and then society relapses into a long fit of nervous reaction before it learns how to appropriate the fruits of its period of feverish excitement. Proletarian revolutions on the contrary, such as those of the nineteenth century, criticize themselves constantly; constantly interrupt themselves in their own course; come back to what seems to have been accomplished, in order to start anew; scorn with cruel thoroughness the half-measures, weaknesses and meanness of their first attempts; seem to throw down their adversary only to enable him to draw fresh strength from the earth and again to rise up against them in more gigantic stature; constantly recoil in fear before the undefined monster magnitude of their own objects—until finally that situation is created which renders all retreat impossible, and conditions themselves cry out: 'Hic Rhodus, hic salta!' Here is the rose. And here we must dance!"

This has remained true even after the elaboration of the doctrine of scientific socialism. The proletarian movement has not as yet, all at once, become social-democratic, even in Germany. But it is becoming more social-democratic, surmounting continuously the extreme deviations of anarchism and opportunism, both of which are only determining phases of the development of the Social-Democracy, considered as a process.

For these reasons we must say that the surprising thing here is not the appearance of an opportunist current but rather its feebleness. As long as it showed itself in isolated cases of the practical activity of the party, one could suppose that it had a serious practical base. But now that it has shown its face in Bernstein's book, one cannot help exclaiming with astonishment: "What? Is that all you have to say?" Not the shadow of an original thought! Not a single idea that was not refuted, crushed, reduced into dust, by Marxism several decades ago!

It was enough for opportunism to speak out to prove it had nothing to say. In the history of our party that is the only importance of Bernstein's book.

Thus saying good-by to the mode of thought of the revolutionary proletariat, to dialectics and to the materialist conception of history, Bernstein can thank them for the attenuating circumstances they provide for his conversion. For only dialectics and the materialist conception of history, magnanimous as they are, could make Bernstein appear as an unconscious predestined instrument, by means of which the rising working class expresses its momentary weakness but which, upon closer inspection, it throws aside contemptuously and with pride.

9. The Bolshevik Pivot

NIKOLAI LENIN: *Backward Europe and Advanced Asia* [1]

The conjunction of these words seems paradoxical. Who does not know that Europe is advanced and Asia backward? But the words taken for the title for this article contain a bitter truth.

In civilized and advanced Europe, with its brilliantly developed machine industry, its rich all-round culture and its constitution, a historical moment has supervened when the commanding bourgeoisie, out of fear for the growth and increasing strength of the proletariat, is supporting everything backward, effete and medieval. The obsolescent bourgeoisie is combining with all obsolete and obsolescent forces in order to preserve tottering wage slavery.

Advanced Europe is commanded by a bourgeoisie which supports everything backward. Europe is advanced today not *thanks to,* but *in spite of* the bourgeoisie, for the proletariat alone is adding to the million-strong army of champions of a better future, it alone is preserving and propagating implacable enmity toward backwardness, savagery, privilege, slavery and the humiliation of man by man.

In "advanced" Europe, the *sole advanced* class is the proletariat. The living bourgeoisie, on the other hand, is prepared to go to any length of savagery, brutality and crime in order to preserve capitalist slavery, which is perishing.

And a more striking example of this decay of the *entire* European bourgeoisie can scarcely be cited than the support it is lending to *reaction* in Asia on behalf of the selfish aims of the financial dealers and capitalist swindlers.

Everywhere in Asia a mighty democratic movement is growing, spreading and gaining in strength. There the bourgeoisie is *still* siding with the people against reaction.

1. From his *Selected Works,* in two volumes, Vol. I (London, 1947), pp. 550-551. Reprinted by permission of Lawrence and Wishart Ltd.

Hundreds of millions of people are awakening to life, light and liberty. What delight this world movement is arousing in the hearts of all class-conscious workers, who know that the path to collectivism lies through democracy! What sympathy all honest democrats cherish for young Asia!

And "advanced" Europe? It is plundering China and helping the foes of democracy, the foes of liberty in China!

Here is a simple but instructive little calculation. The new Chinese loan has been concluded *against* Chinese democracy: "Europe" is *for* Yuan Shih-kai, who is paving the way for a military dictatorship. Why is it for him? Because of a profitable little deal. The loan has been concluded for a sum of about 250,000,000 rubles, at the rate of 84 per 100. That means that the bourgeois of "Europe" will *pay* the Chinese 210,000,000 rubles, but will take from the public 225,000,000 rubles. There you have at one stroke a pure profit of *fifteen million rubles* in a few weeks! "*Pure*" profit, indeed, is it not?

But what if the Chinese people do not recognize the loan? China, after all, is a republic, and the majority in parliament are *against* the loan.

Oh, then "advanced" Europe will cry "civilization," "order," "culture" and "country"! Then it will set the *guns* in motion and crush the republic of "backward" Asia, in alliance with the adventurer, traitor and friend of reaction, Yuan Shih-kai!

All commanding Europe, all the European bourgeoisie is *in alliance* with all the forces of reaction and medievalism in China.

But on the other hand, all young Asia, that is, the hundreds of millions of toilers in Asia, have a reliable ally in the shape of the proletariat of all the civilized countries. No force on earth can prevent its victory, which will liberate both the peoples of Europe and the peoples of Asia.

NIKOLAI LENIN: *Imperialism:*
A Special Stage of Capitalism [2]

Imperialism emerged as the development and direct continuation of the fundamental attributes of capitalism in general. But capitalism only became capitalist imperialism

2. *Ibid.*, pp. 694-701. Reprinted by permission of Lawrence and Wishart Ltd.

at a definite and very high stage of its development, when certain of its fundamental attributes began to be transformed into their opposites, when the features of a period of transition from capitalism to a higher social and economic system began to take shape and reveal themselves all along the line. Economically, the main thing in this process is the substitution of capitalist monopolies for capitalist free competition. Free competition is the fundamental attribute of capitalism, and of commodity production generally. Monopoly is exactly the opposite of free competition; but we have seen the latter being transformed into monopoly before our eyes, creating large-scale industry and eliminating small industry, replacing large-scale industry by still larger-scale industry, finally leading to such a concentration of production and capital that monopoly has been and is the result: cartels, syndicates and trusts, and merging with them, the capital of a dozen or so banks manipulating thousands of millions. At the same time monopoly, which has grown out of free competition, does not abolish the latter, but exists over it and alongside of it, and thereby gives rise to a number of very acute, intense antagonisms, friction and conflicts. Monopoly is the transition from capitalism to a higher system.

If it were necessary to give the briefest possible definition of imperialism we should have to say that imperialism is the monopoly stage of capitalism. Such a definition would include what is most important, for, on the one hand, finance capital is the bank capital of a few big monopolist banks, merged with the capital of the monopolist combines of manufacturers; and, on the other hand, the division of the world is the transition from a colonial policy which has extended without hindrance to territories unoccupied by any capitalist power, to a colonial policy of monopolistic possession of the territory of the world which has been completely divided up.

But very brief definitions, although convenient, for they sum up the main points, are nevertheless inadequate, because very important features of the phenomenon that has to be defined have to be especially deduced. And so, without forgetting the conditional and relative value of all definitions, which can never include all the concatenations of a phenomenon in its complete development, we must give a definition of imperialism that will embrace the following five essential features:

1. The concentration of production and capital developed to such a high stage that it created monopolies which play a decisive role in economic life.

2. The merging of bank capital with industrial capital, and the creation, on the basis of this "finance capital," of a financial oligarchy.

3. The export of capital, which has become extremely important, as distinguished from the export of commodities.

4. The formation of international capitalist monopolies which share the world among themselves.

5. The territorial division of the whole world among the greatest capitalist powers is completed.

Imperialism is capitalism in that stage of development in which the dominance of monopolies and finance capital has established itself; in which the export of capital has acquired pronounced importance; in which the division of the world among the international trusts has begun; in which the division of all territories of the globe among the great capitalist powers has been completed.

We shall see later that imperialism can and must be defined differently if consideration is to be given, not only to the basic, purely economic factors—to which the above definition is limited—but also to the historical place of this stage of capitalism in relation to capitalism in general, or in the relations between imperialism and the two main trends in the working-class movement. The point to be noted just now is that imperialism, as interpreted above, undoubtedly represents a special stage in the development of capitalism. In order to enable the reader to obtain as well grounded an idea of imperialism as possible, we deliberately quoted largely from bourgeois economists who are obliged to admit the particularly incontrovertible facts regarding modern capitalist economy. With the same object in view, we have produced detailed statistics which reveal the extent to which bank capital, etc., has developed, showing how the transformation of quantity into quality, of developed capitalism into imperialism, has expressed itself. Needless to say, all boundaries in nature and in society are conditional and changeable, and, consequently, it would be absurd to discuss the exact year or the decade in which imperialism "definitely" became established.

In this matter of defining imperialism, however, we have to enter into controversy, primarily, with K. Kautsky, the principal Marxian theoretician of the epoch of the so-called Second International—that is, of the twenty-five years between 1889 and 1914.

Kautsky, in 1915 and even in November 1914, very emphatically attacked the fundamental ideas expressed in our definition of imperialism. Kautsky said that imperialism must not be regarded as a "phase" or stage of economy, but as a policy; a definite policy "preferred" by finance capital; that imperialism cannot be "identified" with "contemporary capitalism"; that if imperialism is to be understood to mean "all the phenomena of contemporary capitalism"—cartels, protection, the domination of the financiers and colonial policy—then the question as to whether imperialism is necessary to capitalism becomes reduced to the "flattest tautology"; because, in that case, "imperialism is naturally a vital necessity for capitalism," and so on. The best way to present Kautsky's ideas is to quote his own definition of imperialism, which is diametrically opposed to the substance of the ideas which we have set forth (for the objections coming from the camp of the German Marxists, who have been advocating such ideas for many years already, have been long known to Kautsky as the objections of a definite trend in Marxism).

Kautsky's definition is as follows:

"Imperialism is a product of highly developed industrial capitalism. It consists in the striving of every industrial capitalist nation to bring under its control or to annex increasingly big *agrarian*" (Kautsky's italics) "regions irrespective of what nations inhabit those regions."

This definition is utterly worthless because it one-sidedly, i.e., arbitrarily, brings out the national question alone (although this is extremely important in itself as well as in its relation to imperialism), it arbitrarily and *inaccurately* relates this question *only* to industrial capital in the countries which annex other nations, and in an equally arbitrary and inaccurate manner brings out the annexation of agrarian regions.

Imperialism is a striving for annexations—this is what the *political* part of Kautsky's definition amounts to. It is correct, but very incomplete, for politically, imperialism is, in general, a striving toward violence and reaction. For the moment, however, we are interested in the *economic* aspect of the question, which Kautsky *himself* introduced into his definition. The inaccuracy of Kautsky's definition is strikingly obvious. The characteristic feature of imperialism is *not* industrial capital, *but* finance capital. It is not an accident that in France it was precisely the extraordinarily rapid development of *finance* capital, and the weakening of industrial capital, that, from 1830 onward, gave rise to the extreme extension of annexationist (colonial) policy. The characteristic feature of imperialism is precisely that it strives to annex *not* only agricultural regions, but even highly industrialized regions (German appetite for Belgium; French appetite for Lorraine), because 1) the fact that the world is already divided up obliges those contemplating a *new* division to reach out for *any kind* of territory, and 2) because an essential feature of imperialism is the rivalry between a number of great powers in the striving for hegemony, i.e., for the conquest of territory, not so much directly for themselves as to weaken the adversary and undermine *his* hegemony. (Belgium is chiefly necessary to Germany as a base for operations against England; England needs Bagdad as a base for operations against Germany, etc.)

Kautsky refers especially—and repeatedly—to English writers who, he alleges, have given a purely political meaning to the word "imperialism" in the sense that Kautsky understands it. We take up the work by the Englishman Hobson, *Imperialism,* which appeared in 1902, and therein we read:

> "The new imperialism differs from the older, first, in substituting for the ambition of a single growing empire the theory and the practice of competing empires, each motivated by similar lusts of political aggrandisement and commercial gain; secondly, in the dominance of financial or investing over mercantile interests."

We see, therefore, that Kautsky is absolutely wrong in referring to English writers generally (unless he meant the vulgar English imperialist writers, or the avowed apologists for imperialism). We see that Kautsky, while claiming that he continues to defend Marxism, as a matter of fact takes a step backward compared with the *social-liberal* Hobson, who *more correctly* takes into account two "historically concrete" (Kautsky's definition is a mockery of historical concreteness) features of modern imperialism: 1) the competition between *several* imperialisms, and 2) the predominance of the financier over the merchant. If it were chiefly a question of the annexation of agrarian countries by industrial countries, the role of the merchant would be predominant.

Kautsky's definition is not only wrong and un-Marxian. It serves as a basis for a whole system of views which run counter to Marxian theory and Marxian practice all along the line. We shall refer to this again later. The argument about words which Kautsky raises as to whether the modern stage of capitalism should be called "imperialism" or "the stage of finance capital" is of no importance. Call it what you will, it matters little. The fact of the matter is that Kautsky detaches the politics of imperialism from its economics, speaks of annexations as being a policy "preferred" by finance capital, and opposes to it another bourgeois policy which, he alleges, is possible on this very basis of finance capital. According to his argument, monopolies in economics are compatible with non-monopolistic, non-violent, non-annexationist methods in politics. According to his argument, the territorial division of the world, which was completed precisely during the period of finance capital, and which constitutes the basis of the present peculiar forms of rivalry between the biggest capitalist states, is compatible with a non-imperialist policy. The result is a slurring-over and a blunting of the most profound contradictions of the latest stage of capitalism, instead of an exposure of their depth; the result is bourgeois reformism instead of Marxism.

Kautsky enters into controversy with the German apologist of imperialism and annexations, Cunow, who clumsily and cynically argues that imperialism is modern capitalism: the development of capitalism is inevitable and progressive; therefore imperialism is progressive; therefore, we should cringe before and eulogize it. This is something like the caricature of Russian Marxism which the Narodniks drew in 1894-95. They used to argue as follows: if the Marxists believe that capitalism is inevitable in Russia, that it is progressive, then they ought to open a public house and begin to implant capitalism! Kautsky's reply to Cunow is as follows: imperialism is not modern capitalism. It is only one of the forms of the policy of modern capitalism. This policy we can and should fight; we can and should fight against imperialism, annexations, etc.

The reply seems quite plausible, but in effect it is a more subtle and more disguised (and therefore more dangerous) propaganda of conciliation with imperialism; for unless it strikes at the economic basis of the trusts and banks, the "struggle" against the policy of the trusts and banks reduces itself to bourgeois reformism and pacifism, to an innocent and benevolent expression of pious hopes. Kautsky's theory means refraining from mentioning existing contradictions, forgetting the most important of them, instead of revealing them in their full depth; it is a theory that has nothing in common with Marxism. Naturally, such a "theory" can only serve the purpose of advocating unity with the Cunows.

Kautsky writes:

"from the purely economic point of view it is not impossible that capitalism will yet go through a new phase, that of the extension of the policy of the cartels to foreign policy, the phase of ultra-imperialism,"

i.e., of a super-imperialism, a union of world imperialism and not struggles among imperialisms; a phase when wars shall cease under capitalism, a phase of "the joint exploitation of the world by internationally combined finance capital."

We shall have to deal with this "theory of ultra-imperialism" later on in order to show in detail how definitely and utterly it departs from Marxism. In keeping with the plan of the present work, we shall examine the exact economic data on this question. Is "ultra-imperialism" possible "from the purely economic point of view" or is it ultra-nonsense?

If, by purely economic point of view a "pure" abstraction is meant, then all that can be said reduces itself to the following proposition: evolution is proceeding toward monopoly; therefore the trend is toward a single world monopoly, to a universal trust. This is indisputable, but it is also as completely meaningless as is the statement that "evolution is proceeding" toward the manufacture of foodstuffs in laboratories. In this sense the "theory" of ultra-imperialism is no less absùrd than a "theory of ultra-agriculture" would be.

If, on the other hand, we are discussing the "purely economic" conditions of the epoch of finance capital as a historically concrete epoch, which opened at the beginning of the twentieth century, then the best reply that one can make to the lifeless abstractions of "ultra-imperialism" (which serve an exclusively reactionary aim: that of diverting attention from the depth of *existing* antagonisms) is to contrast them with the concrete economic realities of present-day world economy. Kautsky's utterly meaningless talk about ultra-imperialism encourages, among other things, that profoundly mistaken idea which only brings grist to the mill of the apologists of imperialism, *viz.*, that the rule of finance capital *lessens* the unevenness and contradictions inherent in world economy, whereas in reality it *increases* them. . . .

We notice three areas of highly developed capitalism with a high development of means of transport, of trade and of industry: the Central European, the British and the American areas. Among these are three states which dominate the world: Germany, Great Britain, the United States. Imperialist rivalry and the struggle between these countries have become very keen because Germany has only a restricted area and few colonies (the creation of "Central Europe" is still a matter for the future; it is being born in the midst of desperate struggles). For the moment the distinctive feature of Europe is political disintegration. In the British and American areas, on the other hand, political concentration is very highly developed, but there is a tremendous disparity between the immense colonies of the one and the insignificant colonies of the other. In the colonies, capitalism is only beginning to develop. The struggle for South America is becoming more and more acute.

There are two areas where capitalism is not strongly developed: Russia and Eastern Asia. In the former, the density of population is very low, in the latter it is very high; in the former political concentration is very high, in the latter it does not exist. The partition of China is only beginning, and the struggle between Japan, U.S.A., etc., in connection therewith is continually gaining in intensity.

Compare this reality, the vast diversity of economic and

political conditions, the extreme disparity in the rate of development of the various countries, etc., and the violent struggles of the imperialist states, with Kautsky's silly little fable about "peaceful" ultra-imperialism. Is this not the reactionary attempt of a frightened philistine to hide from stern reality? Are not the international cartels which Kautsky imagines are the embryos of "ultra-imperialism" (with as much reason as one would have for describing the manufacture of tabloids in a laboratory as ultra-agriculture in embryo) an example of the division *and the redivision* of the world, the transition from peaceful division to non-peaceful division and vice versa? Is not American and other finance capital, which divided the whole world peacefully, with Germany's participation, for example, in the international rail syndicate, or in the international mercantile shipping trust, now engaged in *redividing* the world on the basis of a new relation of forces, which is being changed by methods *by no means* peaceful?

Finance capital and the trusts are increasing instead of diminishing the differences in the rate of development of the various parts of the world economy. When the relation of forces is changed, how else, *under capitalism,* can the solution of contradictions be found, except by resorting to *violence?*

NIKOLAI LENIN: *Main Trends of Monopoly Capitalism* [3]

We have seen that the economic quintessence of imperialism is monopoly capitalism. This very fact determines its place in history, for monopoly that grew up on the basis of free competition, and precisely out of free competition, is the transition from the capitalist system to a higher social-economic order. We must take special note of the four principal forms of monopoly, or the four principal manifestations of monopoly capitalism, which are characteristic of the epoch under review.

Firstly, monopoly arose out of the concentration of production at a very advanced stage of development. This refers to the monopolist capitalist combines, cartels, syndicates and trusts. We have seen the important part that these play in modern economic life. At the beginning of the

3. *Ibid.,* pp. 721-725. Reprinted by permission of Lawrence and Wishart Ltd.

twentieth century, monopolies acquired complete supremacy in the advanced countries. And although the first steps toward the formation of the cartels were first taken by countries enjoying the protection of high tariffs (Germany, America), Great Britain, with her system of free trade, was not far behind in revealing the same basic phenomenon, namely, the birth of monopoly out of the concentration of production.

Secondly, monopolies have accelerated the capture of the most important sources of raw materials, especially for the coal and iron industries, which are the basic and most highly cartelized industries in capitalist society. The monopoly of the most important sources of raw materials has enormously increased the power of big capital, and has sharpened the antagonism between cartelized and non-cartelized industry.

Thirdly, monopoly has sprung from the banks. The banks have developed from modest intermediary enterprises into the monopolists of finance capital. Some three or five of the biggest banks in each of the foremost capitalist countries have achieved the "personal union" of industrial and bank capital, and have concentrated in their hands the disposal of thousands upon thousands of millions which form the greater part of the capital and income of entire countries. A financial oligarchy, which throws a close net of relations of dependence over all the economic and political institutions of contemporary bourgeois society without exception—such is the most striking manifestation of this monopoly.

Fourthly, monopoly has grown out of colonial policy. To the numerous "old" motives of colonial policy, finance capital has added the struggle for the sources of raw materials, for the export of capital, for "spheres of influence," i.e., for spheres for profitable deals, concessions, monopolist profits and so on; in fine, for economic territory in general. When the colonies of the European powers in Africa, for instance, comprised only one-tenth of that territory (as was the case in 1876), colonial policy was able to develop by methods other than those of monopoly—by the "free grabbing" of territories, so to speak. But when nine-tenths of Africa had been seized (approximately by 1900), when the whole world had been divided up, there was inevitably ushered in a period of colonial monopoly and, consequently, a period of particularly intense struggle for the division and the redivision of the world.

The extent to which monopolist capital has intensified all the contradictions of capitalism is generally known. It is sufficient to mention the high cost of living and the oppression of the cartels. This intensification of contradictions constitutes the most powerful driving force of the transitional period of history, which began from the time of the definite victory of world finance capital.

Monopolies, oligarchy, the striving for domination instead of striving for liberty, the exploitation of an increasing number of small or weak nations by an extremely small group of the richest or most powerful nations—all these have given birth to those distinctive characteristics of imperialism which compel us to define it as parasitic or decaying capitalism. More and more prominently there emerges, as one of the tendencies of imperialism, the creation of the "bondholding" (rentier) state, the usurer state, in which the bourgeoisie lives on the proceeds of capital exports and by "clipping coupons." It would be a mistake to believe that this tendency to decay precludes the possibility of the rapid growth of capitalism. It does not. In the epoch of imperialism, certain branches of industry, certain strata of the bourgeoisie and certain countries betray, to a more or less degree, one or other of these tendencies. On the whole, capitalism is growing far more rapidly than before. But this growth is not only becoming more and more uneven in general; its unevenness also manifests itself, in particular, in the decay of the countries which are richest in capital (such as England).

In regard to the rapidity of Germany's economic development, Riesser, the author of the book on the big German banks states:

"The progress of the preceding period (1848-70), which had not been exactly slow, stood in about the same ratio to the rapidity with which the whole of Germany's national economy, and with it German banking, progressed during this period (1870-1905) as the mail coach of the Holy Roman Empire of the German nation stood to the speed of the present-day automobile . . . which in whizzing past, it must be said, often endangers not only innocent pedestrians in its path, but also the occupants of the car."

In its turn, this finance capital which has grown so rapidly is not unwilling (precisely because it has grown so quickly) to pass on to a more "tranquil" possession of colonies which have to be seized—and not only by peaceful methods—from richer nations. In the United States, economic development in the last decades has been even more rapid than in Germany, and *for this very reason,* the parasitic character of modern American capitalism has stood out with particular prominence. On the other hand, a comparison of, say, the republican American bourgeoisie with the monarchist Japanese or German bourgeoisie shows that the most pronounced political distinctions diminish to an extreme degree in the epoch of imperialism—not because they are unimportant in general, but because in all these cases we are discussing a bourgeoisie which has definite features of parasitism.

The receipt of high monopoly profits by the capitalists in one of the numerous branches of industry, in one of numerous countries, etc., makes it economically possible for them to corrupt certain sections of the working class, and for a time a fairly considerable minority, and win them to the side of the bourgeoisie of a given industry or nation against all the others. The intensification of antagonisms between imperialist nations for the division of the world increases this striving. And so there is created that bond between imperialism and opportunism, which revealed itself first and most clearly in England, owing to the fact that certain features of imperialist development were observable there much earlier than in other countries.

Some writers, L. Martov, for example, try to evade the fact that there is a connection between imperialism and opportunism in the labor movement—which is particularly striking at the present time—by resorting to "official optimistic" arguments (*à la* Kautsky and Huysmans) like the following: the cause of the opponents of capitalism would be hopeless if it were precisely progressive capitalism that led to the increase of opportunism, or, if it were precisely the best paid workers who were inclined toward opportunism, etc. We must have no illusion regarding "optimism" of this kind. It is optimism in regard to opportunism: it is optimism which serves to conceal opportunism. As a matter of fact the extraordinary rapidity and the particularly revolting character of the development of opportunism is by no means a guarantee that its victory will be durable: the rapid growth of a malignant abscess on a healthy body only causes it to burst more quickly and thus to relieve the body of it. The most dangerous people of all in this respect are those who do not wish to understand that the fight against imperialism is a sham and humbug unless it is inseparably bound up with the fight against opportunism.

From all that has been said in this book on the economic nature of imperialism, it follows that we must define it as capitalism in transition, or, more precisely, as moribund capitalism. It is very instructive in this respect to note that the bourgeois economists, in describing modern capitalism, frequently employ terms like "interlocking," "absence of isolation," etc.; "in conformity with their functions and course of development," banks are "not purely private business enterprises; they are more and more outgrowing the sphere of purely private business regulations." And this very Riesser, who uttered the words just quoted, declares with all seriousness that the "prophecy" of the Marxists concerning "socialization" has "not come true"!

What then does this word "interlocking" express? It merely expresses the most striking feature of the process going on before our eyes. It shows that the observer counts the separate trees, but cannot see the wood. It slavishly copies the superficial, the fortuitous, the chaotic. It reveals the observer as one who is overwhelmed by the mass of raw material and is utterly incapable of appreciating its meaning and importance. Ownership of shares and relations between owners of private property "interlock in a haphazard way." But the underlying factor of this interlocking, its very base, is the changing social relations of production. When a big enterprise assumes gigantic proportions, and, on the basis of exact computation of mass data, organizes according to plan the supply of primary raw materials to the extent of two-thirds, or three-fourths of all that is necessary for tens of millions of people; when the raw materials are transported to the most suitable place of production, sometimes hundreds or thousands of miles away, in a systematic and organized manner; when a single center directs all the successive stages of work right up to the manufacture of numerous varieties of finished articles; when these products are distributed according to a single plan among tens and hundreds of millions of consumers (as in the case of the distribution of oil in America and Germany by the

American "oil trust")—then it becomes evident that we have socialization of production, and not mere "interlocking"; that private economic relations and private property relations constitute a shell which is no longer suitable for its contents, a shell which must inevitably begin to decay if its destruction be delayed by artificial means; a shell which may continue in a state of decay for a fairly long period (particularly if the cure of the opportunist abscess is protracted), but which will inevitably be removed.

The enthusiastic admirer of German imperialism, Schulze-Gävernitz exclaims:

"Once the supreme management of the German banks has been entrusted to the hands of a dozen persons, their activity is even today more significant for the public good than that of the majority of the Ministers of State." (The "interlocking" of bankers, ministers, magnates of industry and rentiers, is here conveniently forgotten.) ... "If we conceive of the tendencies of development which we have noted as realized to the utmost: the money capital of the nation united in the banks; the banks themselves combined into cartels; the investment capital of the nation cast in the shape of securities, then the brilliant forecast of Saint-Simon will be fulfilled: 'The present anarchy of production caused by the fact that economic relations are developing without uniform regulation must make way for organization in production. Production will no longer be shaped by isolated manufacturers, independent of each other and ignorant of man's economic needs, but by a social institution. A central body of management, being able to survey the large fields of social economy from a more elevated point of view, will regulate it for the benefit of the whole of society, will be able to put the means of production into suitable hands, and above all will take care that there be constant harmony between production and consumption. Institutions already exist which have assumed as part of their task a certain organization of economic labor: the banks.' The fulfillment of the forecasts of Saint-Simon still lies in the future, but we are on the way to its fulfillment—Marxism, different from what Marx imagined, but different only in form."

A crushing "refutation" of Marx, indeed! It is a retreat from Marx's precise, scientific analysis to Saint-Simon's guesswork, the guesswork of a genius, but guesswork all the same.

NIKOLAI LENIN: *The State and Its Evolution* [4]

What is the state, how did it arise and what fundamentally should be the attitude to the state of the Party of the working class, which is fighting for the complete overthrow of capitalism—the Communist Party? . . .

To approach this question as scientifically as possible we must cast at least a fleeting glance back on the history of the rise and development of the state. The most reliable thing in a question of social science and one that is most necessary in order really to acquire the habit of approaching this question correctly and not allowing oneself to get lost in the mass of detail or in the immense variety of conflicting opinions—the most important thing in order to approach this question scientifically is not to forget the underlying historical connection, to examine every question from the standpoint of how the given phenomenon arose in history and what principal stages this phenomenon passed through in its development, and, from the standpoint of its development, to examine what the given thing has become today. . . . In connection with this question it should first of all be noted that the state has not always existed. There was a time when there was no state. It appears wherever and whenever a division of society into classes appears, whenever exploiters and exploited appear.

Before the first form of exploitation of man by man arose, the first form of division into classes—slaveowners and slaves—there existed the patriarchal family, or, as it is sometimes called, the clan family. Fairly definite traces of these primitive times have survived in the life of many primitive peoples; and if you take any work whatsoever on primitive culture, you will always come across more or less definite descriptions, indications and recollections of the fact that there was a time, more or less similar to primitive communism, when the division of society into slaveowners and slaves did not exist. And in those times there

4. From *The State*, a lecture of July, 1919 (New York, 1947), pp. 5-24. Reprinted by permission of New Century Publishers.

was no state, no special apparatus for the systematic application of force and the subjugation of people by force. Such an apparatus is called the state.

In primitive society, when people still lived in small tribes and were still at the lowest stages of their development, in a condition approximating to savagery—an epoch from which modern, civilized human society is separated by several thousands of years—there were yet no signs of the existence of a state. We find the predominance of custom, authority, respect, the power enjoyed by the elders' of the tribe; we find this power sometimes accorded to women— the position of women then was not like the unfranchised and oppressed condition of women today—but nowhere do we find a special category of people who are set apart to rule others and who, in the interests and with the purpose of rule, systematically and permanently command a certain apparatus of coercion, an apparatus of violence, such as is represented at the present time, as you all realize, by the armed detachments of troops, the prisons and the other means of subjugating the will of others by force—all that which constitutes the essence of the state.

If we abstract ourselves from the so-called religious teachings, subtleties, philosophical arguments and the various opinions advanced by bourgeois scholars, and try to get at the real essence of the matter, we shall find that the state really does amount to such an apparatus of rule separated out from human society. When there appears such a special group of men who are occupied with ruling and nothing else, and who in order to rule need a special apparatus of coercion and of subjugating the will of others by force —prisons, special detachments of men, armies, etc.—there appears the state.

But there was a time when there was no state, when general ties, society itself, discipline and the ordering of work were maintained by force of custom and tradition, or by the authority or the respect enjoyed by the elders of the tribe or by women—who in those times not only frequently enjoyed equal status with men, but not infrequently enjoyed even a higher status—and when there was no special category of persons, specialists in ruling. History shows that the state as a special apparatus for coercing people arose only wherever and whenever there appeared a division of society into classes, that is, a division into groups of people some of whom are permanently in a position to appropriate the labor of others, when some people exploit others.

And this division of society into classes must always be clearly borne in mind as a fundamental fact of history. The development of all human societies for thousands of years, in all countries without exception, reveals a general conformity to law, regularity and consistency in this development; so that at first we had a society without classes —the first patriarchal, primitive society, in which there were no aristocrats; then we had a society based on slavery— a slaveowning society. The whole of modern civilized Europe has passed through this stage—slavery ruled supreme two thousand years ago. The vast majority of the peoples of other parts of the world also passed through this stage. Among the less developed peoples traces of slavery survive to this day; you will find the institution of slavery in Africa, for example, at the present time. Slaveowners and slaves were the first important class divisions. The former group not only owned all the means of production—the land and tools, however primitive they may have been in those times—but also owned people. This group was known as slaveowners, while those who labored and supplied labor for others were known as slaves.

This form was followed in history by another—feudalism. In the great majority of countries slavery evolved into feudalism. The fundamental divisions of society were now the feudal landlords and the peasant serfs. The form of relations between people changed. The slaveowners had regarded the slaves as their property; the law had confirmed this view and regarded the slave as a chattel completely owned by the slaveowner. As far as the peasant serf was concerned, class oppression and dependence remained, but it was not considered that the feudal landlord owned the peasants as chattels, but that he was only entitled to their labor and to compel them to perform certain services. In practice, as you know, feudalism, especially in Russia, where it survived longest of all and assumed the grossest forms, in no way differed from slavery.

Further, with the development of trade, the appearance of the world market and the development of money circulation, a new class arose within feudal society—the capitalist class. From the commodity, the exchange of commodities and the rise of the power of money, there arose the power of capital. During the eighteenth century—or rather, from the end of the eighteenth century and during the nineteenth century—revolutions took place all over the world. Feudalism was eliminated in all the countries of Western Europe. This took place latest of all in Russia. In 1861 a radical change took place in Russia as well, as a consequence of which one form of society was replaced by another—feudalism was replaced by capitalism, under which division into classes remained as well as various traces and relics of feudalism, but in which the division into classes fundamentally assumed a new form.

The owners of capital, the owners of the land, the owners of the mills and factories in all capitalist countries constituted and still constitute an insignificant minority of the population who have complete command of the labor of the whole people, and who therefore command, oppress and exploit the whole mass of laborers, the majority of whom are proletarians, wageworkers, that procure their livelihood in the process of production only by the sale of their labor power. With the transition to capitalism, the peasants, who were already impoverished and downtrodden in feudal times, were converted partly (the majority) into proletarians, and partly (the minority) into wealthy peasants who themselves hired workers and who constituted a rural bourgeoisie.

This fundamental fact—the transition of society from primitive forms of slavery to feudalism and finally to capitalism—you must always bear in mind, for only by remembering this fundamental fact, only by inserting all political doctrines into this fundamental framework will you be able properly to appraise these doctrines and to understand what they refer to: for each of these great periods in the history of mankind—slaveowning, feudal and capitalist—embraces scores and hundreds of centuries and presents such a mass of political forms, such a variety of political doctrines, opinions and revolutions, that we can understand this extreme diversity and immense variety—especially in connection with the political, philosophical and other doctrines of bourgeois scholars and politicians—only if we firmly hold to the guiding thread, this division of society into classes and this change in the forms of class rule, and from this standpoint examine all social questions—economic, political, spiritual, religious, etc.

If you examine the state from the standpoint of this fundamental division, you will find that before the division of society into classes, as I have already said, no state existed. But as the social division into classes arose and took firm root, as class society arose, the state also arose and took firm root. The history of mankind knows scores and hundreds of countries that have passed through and are still passing through slavery, feudalism and capitalism. In each of these countries, despite the immense historical changes that have taken place, despite all the political vicissitudes and all the revolutions associated with this development of mankind, in the transition from slavery through feudalism to capitalism and to the present worldwide struggle against capitalism, you will always discern the rise of the state. It has always been a certain apparatus which separated out from society and consisted of a group of people engaged solely, or almost solely, or mainly, in ruling. People are divided into ruled and into specialists in ruling, those who rise above society and are called rulers, representatives of the state. This apparatus, this group of people who rule others, always takes command of a certain apparatus of coercion, of physical force, irrespective of whether this coercion of people is expressed in the primitive club, or—in the epoch of slavery—in more perfected types of weapons, or in the firearms which appeared in the Middle Ages, or, finally, in modern weapons, which in the twentieth century are marvels of technique and are entirely based on the latest achievements of modern technology. The methods of coercion changed, but whenever there was a state there existed in every society a group of persons who ruled, who commanded, who dominated and who in order to maintain their power possessed an apparatus of physical coercion, an apparatus of violence, with those weapons which corresponded to the technical level of the given epoch. And by examining these general phenomena, by asking ourselves why no state existed when there were no classes, when there were no exploiters and exploited, and why it arose when classes arose—only in this way shall we find a definite answer to the question of the essence of the state and its significance.

The state is a machine for maintaining the rule of one class over another. When there were no classes in society, when, before the epoch of slavery, people labored in primitive conditions of greater equality, in conditions when productivity of labor was still at its lowest, and when primitive man could barely procure the wherewithal for the crudest and most primitive existence, a special group of people especially separated off to rule and dominate over the rest of society had not yet arisen, and could not have arisen. Only when the first form of the division of society into classes appeared, only when slavery appeared, when a certain class of people, by concentrating on the crudest forms of agricultural labor, could produce a certain surplus, when this surplus was not absolutely essential for the most wretched existence of the slave and passed into the hands of the slaveowner, when in this way the existence of this class of slaveowners took firm root—then in order that it might take firm root it was essential a state should appear.

And this state did appear—the slaveowning state, an apparatus which gave the slaveowners power and enabled them to rule over the slaves. Both society and the state were then much smaller than they are now, they possessed an incomparably weaker apparatus of communication—the modern means of communication did not then exist. Mountains, rivers and seas were immeasurably greater obstacles than they are now, and the formation of the state was confined within far narrower geographical boundaries. A technically weak state apparatus served a state confined within relatively narrow boundaries and a narrow circle of action. Nevertheless, there did exist an apparatus which compelled the slaves to remain in slavery, which kept one part of society subjugated to and oppressed by another. It is impossible to compel the greater part of society to work systematically for the other part of society without a permanent apparatus of coercion. So long as there were no classes, there was no apparatus like this. When classes appeared, everywhere and always as this division grew and took firmer hold, there also appeared a special institution—the state. The forms of state were extremely varied. During the period of slavery we already find diverse forms of the state in the most advanced, cultured and most civilized countries according to the standards of the time, for example, in ancient Greece and Rome, which rested entirely on slavery. At that time the difference was already arising between the monarchy and the republic, between the aristocracy and the democracy. A monarchy is the power of a single person, a republic is the absence of any non-elected power; an aristocracy is the power of a relatively small minority, a democracy is the power of the people (democracy in Greek literally means the power of the people). All these differences arose in the epoch of slavery. Despite these differences, the state in slave times was a slave state, irrespective of whether it was a monarchy or a republic, aristocratic or democratic.

In every course on the history of ancient times, when hearing a lecture on the subject you will hear about the struggle which was waged between the monarchical and republican states. But the fundamental fact is that the slaves were not regarded as human beings—they were not only not regarded as citizens, but not even as human beings. Roman law regarded them as chattels. The law on murder, not to mention the other laws for the protection of the person, did not extend to slaves. It defended only the slaveowners, who were alone recognized as citizens with full rights. But whether a monarchy was instituted or a republic, it was a monarchy of the slaveowners or a republic of the slaveowners. All rights under them were enjoyed by the slaveowners, while the slave was a chattel in the eyes of the law; and not only could any sort of violence be perpetrated against a slave, but even the murder of a slave was not considered a crime. Slaveowning republics differed in their internal organization: there were aristocratic republics and democratic republics. In an aristocratic republic a small number of privileged persons took part in the elections; in a democratic republic everybody took part in the elections—but again only the slaveowners, everybody except the slaves. This fundamental fact must be borne in mind, because it throws more light than any other on the question of the state and clearly demonstrates the nature of the state.

The state is a machine for the oppression of one class by another, a machine for keeping in subjugation to one class other, subordinated classes. There are various forms of this machine. In the slaveowning state we had a monarchy, an aristocratic republic or even a democratic republic. In fact the forms of government varied extremely, but their essence was always the same: the slaves enjoyed no rights and constituted an oppressed class; they were not regarded as human beings. We find the same state of affairs in the feudal state.

The change in the form of exploitation transformed the slave state into the feudal state. This was of immense importance. In slave society the slave enjoys no rights whatever and is not regarded as a human being; in feudal society the peasant is tied to the soil. The chief feature of feudalism was that the peasants (and at that time the peasants constituted the majority; there was a very poorly developed urban population) were considered attached, or in fee, to the land—hence the term feudalism. The peasant might work a definite number of days for himself on the plot assigned to him by the landlord; on the other days the peasant serf worked for this lord. The essence of class society remained: society was based on class exploitation. Only the landlords could enjoy full rights; the peasants had no rights at all. In practice their condition differed very little from the condition of slaves in the slave state. Nevertheless a wider road was opened for their emancipation, for the emancipation of the peasants, since the peasant serf was not regarded as the direct property of the landlord. He could work part of his time on his own plot, could, so to speak, belong to himself to a certain extent; and with the wider opportunities for the development of exchange and trade relations the feudal system steadily disintegrated and the scope of emancipation of the peasantry steadily widened. Feudal society was always more complex than slave society. There was a greater element of the development of trade and industry, which even in those days led to capitalism. In the Middle Ages feudalism predominated. And here too the forms of state differed, here too we find both monarchies and republics, although much more weakly expressed. But always the feudal landlord was regarded as the only ruler. The peasant serfs were absolutely excluded from all political rights.

Both under slavery and under the feudal system the small minority of people could not dominate over the vast majority without coercion. History is full of the constant attempts of the oppressed classes to rid themselves of oppression. The history of slavery contains records of wars of emancipation from slavery which lasted for decades. Incidentally, the name "Spartacist" now adopted by the German Communists—the only German party which is really fighting the yoke of capitalism—was adopted by them because Spartacus was one of the most prominent heroes of one of the greatest revolts of slaves which took place about two thousand years ago. For many years the apparently omnipotent Roman Empire, which rested entirely on slavery, experienced the shocks and blows of a vast uprising of slaves who armed and united to form a vast army under the leadership of Spartacus. In the end they were defeated, captured and tortured by the slave-owners. Such civil wars mark the whole history of the existence of class society. I have just mentioned an example of the greatest of these civil wars in the epoch of slavery. The whole epoch of feudalism is likewise marked by constant uprisings of the peasants. For example, in Germany in the Middle Ages the struggle between the two classes—the landlords and the serfs—assumed wide dimensions and was transformed into a civil war of the peasants against the landlords. You are all familiar with similar examples of repeated uprisings of the peasants against the feudal landlords in Russia.

In order to maintain their rule and to preserve their power, the landlords had to have an apparatus by which they could subjugate a vast number of people and subordinate them to certain laws and regulations; and all these laws fundamentally amounted to one thing—the maintenance of the power of the landlords over the peasant serfs. And this was the feudal state, which in Russia, for example, or in extremely backward Asiatic countries, where feudalism prevails to this day—it differed in form—was either republican or monarchical. When the state was a monarchy, the rule of one person was recognized; when it was a republic, the participation in one degree or another of the elected representatives of landlord society was recognized —this was in feudal society. Feudal society represented a division of classes under which the vast majority—the peasant serfs—were completely subjected to an insignificant minority—the landlords, who owned the land.

The development of trade, the development of commodity exchange, led to the crystallization of a new class— the capitalists. Capital arose at the close of the Middle Ages, when, after the discovery of America, world trade developed enormously, when the quantity of precious metals increased, when silver and gold became the means of exchange, when money circulation made it possible for individuals to hold tremendous wealth. Silver and gold were recognized as wealth all over the world. The economic power of the landlord class declined and the power of the new class—the representatives of capital—developed. The reconstruction in society was such that all citizens supposedly became equal, the old division into slaveowners and slaves disappeared, all were regarded as equal before the law irrespective of what capital they owned; whether they owned land as private property, or were starvelings who owned nothing but their labor power—they were all equal before the law. The law protects everybody equally; it protects the property of those who have it from attack by the masses who, possessing no property, possessing nothing but their labor power, grow steadily impoverished and ruined and become converted into proletarians. Such is capitalist society.

... This society advanced against serfdom, against the old feudal system, under the slogan of liberty. But it was liberty for those who owned property. And when feudalism was shattered, which occurred at the end of the eighteenth century and the beginning of the nineteenth century—it occurred in Russia later than in other countries, in 1861—the feudal ·state. was superseded by the capitalist state, which proclaims liberty for the whole people as its slogan, which declares that it expresses the will of the whole people and denies that it is a class state. And here there developed a struggle between the Socialists, who are fighting for the liberty of the whole people, and the capitalist state —a struggle which has now led to the creation of the Soviet Socialist Republic and which embraces the whole world.

To understand the struggle that has been started against world capital, to understand the essence of the capitalist state, we must remember that when the capitalist state advanced against the feudal state it entered the fight under the slogan of liberty. The abolition of feudalism meant liberty for the representatives of the capitalist state and served their purpose, inasmuch as feudalism was breaking down and the peasants had acquired the opportunity of owning as their full property the land which they had purchased for compensation or in part by quit rent—this did not concern the state: it protected property no matter how it arose, since it rested on private property. The peasants became private owners in all the modern civilized states. Even when the landlord surrendered part of his land to the peasant, the state protected private property, rewarding the landlord by compensation, sale for money. The state as it were declared that it would fully preserve private property, and it accorded it every support and protection. The state recognized the property rights of every merchant, industrialist and manufacturer. And this society, based on private property, on the power of capital, on the complete subjection of the propertyless workers and laboring masses of the peasantry, proclaimed that its rule was based on liberty. Combating feudalism, it proclaimed freedom of property and was particularly proud of the fact that the state had supposedly ceased to be a class state.

Yet the state continued to be a machine which helped the capitalists to hold the poor peasants and the working class in subjection. But externally it was free. It proclaimed universal suffrage, and declared through its champions, preachers, scholars and philosophers that it was not a class state. Even now, when the Soviet Socialist Republics have begun to fight it, they accuse us of violating liberty, of building a state based on coercion, on the suppression of certain people by others, whereas they represent a popular, democratic state. And now, when the world Socialist revolution has begun, and just when the revolution has succeeded in certain countries, when the fight against world capital has grown particularly acute, this question of the state has acquired the greatest importance and has become, one might say, the most burning one, the focus of all political questions and of all political disputes of the present day.

Whatever party we take in Russia or in any of the more civilized countries, we find that nearly all political disputes, disagreements and opinions now center around the conception of the state. Is the state in a capitalist country, in a democratic republic—especially one like Switzerland or America—in the freest democratic republics, an expression of the popular will, the sum total of the general decision of the people, the expression of the national will, and so forth; or is the state a machine that enables the capitalists of the given country to maintain their power over the working class and the peasantry? That is the fundamental question around which all political disputes all over the world now center. . . .

I have already advised you to turn for help to Engels' book, *The Origin of the Family, Private Property and the State.* This book says that every state in which private property in land and in the means of production exists, in which capital prevails, however democratic it may be, is a capitalist state, a machine used by the capitalists to keep the working class and the poor peasants in subjection; while universal suffrage, a Constituent Assembly, parliament are merely a form, a sort of promissory note, which does not alter matters in any essential way.

The forms of domination of the state may vary: capital manifests its power in one way where one form exists, and in another way where another form exists—but essentially the power is in the hands of capital, whether there are voting qualifications or not, or whether the republic is a democratic one or not—in fact the more democratic it is the cruder and more cynical is the rule of capitalism. One of the most democratic republics in the world is the United States of America, yet nowhere (and those who were there after 1905 probably know it) is the power of capital, the power of a handful of billionaires over the whole of society, so crude and so openly corrupt as in America. Once capital exists, it dominates the whole of society, and no democratic republic, no form of franchise can alter the essence of the matter.

The democratic republic and universal suffrage were a great progressive advance on feudalism: they have enabled the proletariat to achieve its present unity and solidarity, to form those firm and disciplined ranks which are waging a systematic struggle against capital. There was nothing even approximately resembling this among the peasant serfs, not to speak of the slaves. The slaves as we know revolted, rioted, started civil wars, but they could never create a class-conscious majority and parties to lead the struggle, they could not clearly realize what they were aiming for, and even in the most revolutionary moments of history they were always pawns in the hands of the ruling classes. The bourgeois republic, parliament, universal suffrage all represent great progress from the standpoint of the world development of society. Mankind moved toward capitalism, and it was capitalism alone which, thanks to urban culture, enabled the oppressed class of proletarians to learn to know itself and to create the world working class movement, the millions of workers who are organized all over the world in parties—the Socialist parties which are consciously leading the struggle of the masses. Without parliamentarianism, without elections, this development of the working class would have been impossible. That is why all these things have acquired such great importance in the eyes of the broad masses of people. That is why a radical change seems to be so difficult.

It is not only the conscious hypocrites, scientists and priests that uphold and defend the bourgeois lie that the state is free and that it is its duty to defend the interests of all, but also a large number of people who sincerely adhere to the old prejudices and who cannot understand the transition from the old capitalist society to Socialism. It is not only people who are directly dependent on the bourgeoisie, not only those who are oppressed by the yoke of capital or who have been bribed by capital (there are a large number of all sorts of scientists, artists, priests, etc., in the service of capital), but even people who are simply under the sway of the prejudice of bourgeois liberty that have taken up arms against Bolshevism all over the world because of the fact that when it was founded the Soviet Republic rejected these bourgeois lies and openly declared: you say that your state is free, whereas in reality, as long as there is private property, your state, even if it is a democratic republic, is nothing but a machine used by the capitalists to suppress the workers, and the freer the state, the more clearly is this expressed. Examples of this are Switzerland in Europe and the United States in the Americas. Nowhere does capital rule so cynically and ruthlessly, and nowhere is this so apparent, as in these countries, although they are democratic republics, no matter how finely they are painted and notwithstanding all the talk about labor democracy and the equality of all citizens. The fact is that in Switzerland and America capital dominates, and every attempt of the workers to achieve the slightest real improvement in their condition is immediately met by civil war. There are fewer soldiers, a smaller standing army in these countries—Switzerland has a militia and every Swiss has a gun at home, while in America there was no standing army until quite recently—and so when there is a strike the bourgeoisie arms, hires soldiery and suppresses the strike; and nowhere is the suppression of the working class movement accompanied by such ruthless severity as in Switzerland and in America, and nowhere does the influence of capital in parliament manifest itself as powerfully as in these countries. The power of capital is everything, the stock exchange is everything, while parliament and elections are marionettes, puppets. . . . But the eyes of the workers are being opened more and more, and the idea of

Soviet government is spreading wider and wider, especially after the bloody carnage through which we have just passed. The necessity for a merciless war on the capitalists is becoming clearer and clearer to the working class.

Whatever forms a republic may assume, even the most democratic republic, if it is a bourgeois republic, if it retains private property in land, mills and factories, and if private capital keeps the whole of society in wage slavery, that is, if it does not carry out what is proclaimed in the program of our Party and in the Soviet Constitution, then this state is a machine for the suppression of certain people by others. And we shall place this machine in the hands of the class that is to overthrow the power of capital. We shall reject all the old prejudices about the state meaning universal equality. That is a fraud: as long as there is exploitation there cannot be equality. The landlord cannot be the equal of the worker, the hungry man the equal of the full man. The proletariat casts aside the machine which was called the state and before which people bowed in superstitious awe, believing the old tales that it means popular rule—the proletariat casts aside the machine and declares that it is a bourgeois lie. We have deprived the capitalists of this machine and have taken it over. With this machine, or bludgeon, we shall destroy all exploitation. And when the possibility of exploitation no longer exists anywhere in the world, when there are no longer owners of land and owners of factories, and when there is no longer a situation in which some gorge while others starve—only when the possibility of this no longer exists shall we consign this machine to the scrap heap. Then there will be no state and no exploitation. Such is the view of our Communist Party.

NIKOLAI LENIN: *Workers' Control of the State and the Economy* [5]

Democracy is of great importance to the working class in its struggle for emancipation from the capitalists. But democracy is by no means a boundary that must not be overstepped; it is only one of the stages on the road from

5. From "The State and Revolution," *Selected Works*, Vol. II, *op. cit.*, pp. 209-211. Reprinted by permission of Lawrence and Wishart Ltd.

feudalism to capitalism, and from capitalism to Communism.

Democracy means equality. The great significance of the proletariat's struggle for equality and the significance of equality as a slogan will be clear if we correctly interpret it as meaning the abolition of *classes*. But democracy means only *formal* equality. And as soon as equality is obtained for all members of society *in relation to* the ownership of the means of production, that is, equality of labor and equality of wages, humanity will inevitably be confronted with the question of going beyond formal equality to real equality, i.e., to applying the rule, "from each according to his ability, to each according to his needs." By what stages, by what practical measures humanity will proceed to this higher aim—we do not and cannot know. But it is important to realize how infinitely mendacious is the ordinary bourgeois conception of Socialism as something lifeless, petrified, fixed once for all, whereas in reality *only* under Socialism will a rapid, genuine, really mass forward movement, embracing first the *majority* and then the whole of the population, commence in all spheres of social and personal life.

Democracy is a form of state, one of its varieties. Consequently, it, like every state, on the one hand represents the organized, systematic application of force against persons; but on the other hand it signifies the formal recognition of the equality of all citizens, the equal right of all to determine the structure and administration of the state. This, in turn, is connected with the fact that, at a certain stage in the development of democracy, it first rallies the proletariat as the revolutionary class against capitalism, and enables it to crush, smash to atoms, wipe off the face of the earth the bourgeois, even the republican bourgeois, state machine, the standing army, the police and bureaucracy, and to substitute for them a *more* democratic state machine, but a state machine nevertheless, in the shape of the armed masses of workers who are being transformed into a universal people's militia.

Here "quantity is transformed into quality": *such* a degree of democracy implies overstepping the boundaries of bourgeois society, the beginning of its Socialist reconstruction. If, indeed, *all* take part in the administration of the state, capitalism cannot retain its hold. And the development of capitalism, in turn, itself creates the *premises* that really *enable* "all" to take part in the administration of the state. Some of the premises are: universal literacy, which is already achieved in a number of the most advanced capitalist countries, then the "training and disciplining" of millions of workers by the huge, complex, socialized apparatus of the postoffice, railways, big factories, large-scale commerce, banking, etc., etc.

Given these *economic* premises it is quite possible, after the overthrow of the capitalists and bureaucrats, to proceed immediately, overnight, to supersede them in the *control* of production and distribution, in the work of *keeping account* of labor and products by the armed workers, by the whole of the armed population. : . .

Accounting and control—that is the *main* thing required for the "setting up" and correct functioning of the *first phase* of Communist society. *All* citizens are transformed into the salaried employees of the state, which consists of the armed workers. *All* citizens become employees and workers of a *single* national state "syndicate." All that is required is that they should work equally—do their proper share of work—and get paid equally. The accounting and control necessary for this have been *simplified* by capitalism to an extreme and reduced to the extraordinarily simple operations—which any literate person can perform—of checking and recording, knowledge of the four rules of arithmetic, and issuing receipts.

When the *majority* of the people begin independently and everywhere to keep such accounts and maintain such control over the capitalists (now converted into employees) and over the intellectual gentry who preserve their capitalist habits, this control will really become universal, general, national; and there will be no way of getting away from it, there will be "nowhere to go."

The whole of society will have become a single office and a single factory, with equality of labor and equality of pay.

But this "factory" discipline, which the proletariat will extend to the whole of society after the defeat of the capitalists and the overthrow of the exploiters, is by no means our ideal, or our ultimate goal. It is but a necessary *step* for the purpose of thoroughly purging society of all the hideousness and foulness of capitalist exploitation, *and for further* progress.

From the moment all members of society, or even only

the vast majority, have learned to administer the state *themselves,* have taken this business into their own hands, have "set up" control over the insignificant minority of capitalists, over the gentry who wish to preserve their capitalist habits, and over the workers who have been profoundly corrupted by capitalism—from this moment the need for government begins to disappear altogether. The more complete democracy, the nearer the moment approaches when it becomes unnecessary. The more democratic the "state" which consists of the armed workers, and which is "no longer a state in the proper sense of the word," the more rapidly does *every* form of the state begin to wither away.

For when *all* have learned to administer and actually do administer social production independently, independently to keep accounts and exercise control over the idlers, the gentlefolk, the swindlers and similar "guardians of capitalist traditions," the escape from this national accounting and control will inevitably become so incredibly difficult, such a rare exception, and will probably be accompanied by such swift and severe punishment (for the armed workers are practical men and not sentimental intellectuals, and they will scarcely allow anyone to trifle with them), that very soon the *necessity* of observing the simple, fundamental rules of human intercourse will become a *habit.*

And then the door will be wide open for the transition from the first phase of Communist society to its higher phase, and with it to the complete withering away of the state.

NIKOLAI LENIN: *On Tactics in the 1917 Revolution* [6]

Marxism demands an extremely precise and objectively verifiable analysis of the interrelation of classes and of the concrete peculiarities of each historical moment. We Bolsheviks have always tried faithfully to fulfil this demand, since it is absolutely imperative for a scientific foundation of politics.

"Our teaching is not a dogma, but a guide to action," Marx and Engels used to say; and they ridiculed, and

6. From "Letters on Tactics" *Selected Works,* in 12 volumes, Vol. VI (New York, 1929), pp. 32-44. Reprinted by permission of International Publishers Co., Inc.

rightly ridiculed, the learning and repetition by rote of "formulas" which at best are capable of giving only an outline of *general* tasks that are necessarily liable to be modified by the *concrete* economic and political condition of each particular *phase* of the historical process.

What, then, are the clearly established objective *facts* that must guide the party of the revolutionary proletariat at present in defining the tasks and forms of its activity? ...

I define as the "specific feature of the present situation" in Russia the fact that it is a period of *transition* from the first stage of the revolution to the second. And I therefore considered the basic slogan, the "task of the day," at *that* moment to be: "Workers, you have displayed marvels of proletarian heroism, the heroism of the people, in the civil war against tsarism; you must display marvels of organization, organization of the proletariat and the people, in order to prepare for victory in the second stage of the revolution."

In what does the first stage consist?

In the transfer of the power of state to the bourgeoisie.

Before the February-March Revolution of 1917, the state power in Russia was in the hands of one old class, namely, the feudal landed nobility, headed by Nicholas Romanov.

Now, after that revolution, the state power is in the hands of *another* class, a new class, namely, the *bourgeoisie*.

The transfer of state power from one class to another *class* is the first, the principal, the basic sign of a *revolution*, both in the strictly scientific and in the practical political meaning of the term.

To this extent, the bourgeois, or the bourgeois-democratic, revolution in Russia *has been completed*.

At this point we hear the clamor of the objectors, of those who so readily call themselves "old Bolsheviks": Did we not always maintain, they say, that the bourgeois-democratic revolution is completed only by the "revolutionary-democratic dictatorship of the proletariat and peasantry"? Has the agrarian revolution, which is also a bourgeois-democratic revolution, ended? On the contrary, is it not a fact *that it has not even begun?*

My answer is: The Bolshevik slogans and ideas *in general* have been fully corroborated by history; but *concretely*, things have turned out *differently* than could have been anticipated (by anyone): they are more original, more specific, more variegated.

Had we ignored or forgotten this fact, we should have resembled those "old Bolsheviks" who have more than once played so sorry a part in the history of our Party by repeating a formula meaninglessly *learned by rote,* instead of *studying* the specific and new features of actual reality.

"The revolutionary-democratic dictatorship of the proletariat and peasantry" has *already* become a reality in the Russian revolution; for this "formula" envisages only the *interrelation of classes,* but does not envisage the *concrete political institution which gives effect* to this interrelation, to this co-operation. "The Soviet of Workers' and Soldiers' Deputies"—here we have the "revolutionary-democratic dictatorship of the proletariat and peasantry" already accomplished in reality.

This formula is already antiquated. Events have removed it from the realm of formulas into the realm of reality, clothed it in flesh and blood, lent it concrete form, and *by this very act* modified it.

A new and different task now faces us: to effect a split *within* this dictatorship between the proletarian elements (the anti-defensist, internationalist, "communist" elements, who stand for a transition to the commune) and the petty-proprietor or *petty-bourgeois* elements (Chkheidze, Tseretelli, Steklov, the Socialist-Revolutionaries and other revolutionary defensists, who are opposed to the movement toward the commune and who favor "supporting" the bourgeoisie and the bourgeois government).

Whoever speaks *now* of a "revolutionary-democratic dictatorship of the proletariat and peasantry" only is behind the times, has consequently in effect *gone over* to the side of the petty bourgeoisie and is against the proletarian class struggle. He deserves to be consigned to the archive of "Bolshevik" pre-revolutionary antiques (which might be called the archive of "old Bolsheviks").

The revolutionary-democratic dictatorship of the proletariat and peasantry has already been realized, but in an extremely original form, and with a number of highly important modifications. I will deal with them in one of my subsequent letters. For the present it is essential to realize the incontestable truth that a Marxist must take cognizance of actual events, of the precise facts of *reality,* and must not cling to a past theory, which, like all theories, at best only outlines the main and the general, and only *approximates* to an inclusive grasp of the complexities of living reality.

"Theory, my friend, is gray, but green is the eternal tree of life."

He who continues to regard the "completion" of the bourgeois revolution *in the old way* sacrifices living Marxism to the dead letter. According to the old conception, the rule of the proletariat and peasantry, their dictatorship, can and must come after the rule of the bourgeoisie.

But in actual fact, it has already turned out differently: an extremely original, novel and unprecedented *interlacing of the one with the other* has taken place. Side by side, existing together and simultaneously, we have both the rule of the bourgeoisie (the government of Lvov and Guchkov) and a revolutionary-democratic dictatorship of the proletariat and peasantry, the latter *voluntarily* ceding power to the bourgeoisie and voluntarily transforming itself into an appendage of the bourgeoisie.

For it must not be forgotten that in Petrograd the power is actually in the hands of the workers and soldiers: the new government does not and cannot use violence against them, for there is no police, no army separate from the people, no officialdom standing omnipotently above the people. This is a fact; and it is the kind of fact that is characteristic of a state of the type of the Paris Commune. This fact does not fit into the old schemes. One must know how to adapt schemes to facts, rather than repeat words regarding a "dictatorship of the proletariat and peasantry" *in general*, words which have become meaningless.

In order the better to illuminate the question, let us approach it from another angle.

A Marxist must not abandon the solid ground of analysis of class relations. The bourgeoisie is in power. But is not the mass of peasants *also* a bourgeoisie, only of a different stratum, a different kind, a different character? Whence does it follow that *this* stratum *cannot* come into power and thus "consummate" the bourgeois-democratic revolution? Why should this be impossible?

That is how the old Bolsheviks often argue.

My reply is that it is quite possible. But, when analyzing any given situation, a Marxist must proceed *not from the possible*, but from the actual.

And actuality reveals the *fact*—that the freely elected

soldiers' and peasants' deputies freely enter the second, the parallel government and freely supplement, develop and complete it. And, just as freely, they *surrender* their power to the bourgeoisie; which phenomenon does not in the least "undermine" the theory of Marxism, for, as we have always known and have repeatedly pointed out, the bourgeoisie maintains itself not only by virtue of force but also by virtue of the lack of class consciousness, the clinging to old habits, the timidity and lack of organization of the masses.

In view of this present-day actuality it is simply ridiculous to turn one's back on this fact and speak of "possibilities."

It is possible that the peasantry may seize all the land and the entire power. Far from forgetting this possibility, far from confining myself to the present moment only, I definitely and clearly formulate the agrarian program in accordance with the *new* phenomenon, viz., the profounder cleavage between the agricultural laborers and the poor peasants, on the one hand, and the peasant owners, on the other.

But there is another possibility; it is possible that the peasants will hearken to the advice of the petty-bourgeois party of Socialist-Revolutionaries, which has succumbed to the influence of the bourgeoisie, has gone over to defensism, and which advises waiting until the convocation of the Constituent Assembly, even though the date of its convocation has not yet been fixed. It is possible that the peasants will *preserve* and prolong their pact with the bourgeoisie, a pact which they have now concluded through the Soviets of Workers' and Soldiers' Deputies in both form and deed.

Many things are possible. It would be a profound mistake to forget the agrarian movement and the agrarian program. But it would be equally mistaken to forget *reality*, and reality reveals the fact that an *agreement*, or—to use a more exact, less legal, but more class-economic expression—that class *collaboration exists between the bourgeoisie* and the peasantry.

When this fact ceases to be a fact, when the peasantry severs itself from the bourgeoisie, when it seizes the land and power in spite of the bourgeoisie, that will be a new stage of the bourgeois-democratic revolution; and of that I will speak separately.

A Marxist who, in view of the possibility of such a stage in the future, were to forget his duties *at the present moment,* when the peasantry is *compromising* with the bourgeoisie, would become a petty bourgeois. For he would in practice be preaching to the proletariat *confidence* in the petty bourgeoisie ("the petty bourgeoisie, the peasantry, must separate itself from the bourgeoisie within the limits of the bourgeois-democratic revolution"). . . .

This hypothetical person would be a sugary Louis Blanc, a sugary Kautskian, but not a revolutionary Marxist. . . .

In the theses I definitely reduced the question to one of a *struggle for influence* within the Soviets of Workers', Agricultural Laborers', Soldiers' and Peasants' Deputies. In order to leave no trace of doubt in this respect, I *twice* emphasized in the theses the necessity for patient and persistent "explanatory" work "adapted to the *practical needs of the masses."*

Ignorant persons or renegades from Marxism, such as Mr. Plekhanov, may cry anarchism, Blanquism, and so forth. But those who really want to think and learn cannot fail to understand that Blanquism means the seizure of power by a minority, whereas the Soviets of Workers', Agricultural Laborers', Soldiers' and Peasants' Deputies are admittedly the direct and immediate organization of the *majority* of the people. Work confined to a struggle for influence *within* these Soviets cannot, absolutely *cannot,* blunder into the swamp of Blanquism. Nor can it blunder into the swamp of anarchism, for anarchism *denies the necessity for a state and for state power in the period of transition* from the rule of the bourgeoisie to the rule of the proletariat, whereas I, with a precision that excludes all possibility of misunderstanding, *insist* on the necessity for a state in this period, although, in accordance with Marx and the experience of the Paris Commune, not the usual parliamentary bourgeois state, but a state *without* a standing army, *without* a police opposed to the people, *without* an officialdom placed above the people. . . .

Let us now see how Comrade Kamenev in his article in No. 27 of *Pravda* formulates his "differences" with my theses and the views expressed above. It will help us to understand them more clearly.

"As regards Comrade Lenin's general scheme," writes

Comrade Kamenev, "it appears to us unacceptable, inasmuch as it proceeds from the assumption that the bourgeois-democratic revolution *has been completed*, and is calculated on the immediate transformation of that revolution into a socialist revolution."

Here we have two major errors.

The first is that the question of the "completeness" of the bourgeois-democratic revolution is wrongly *formulated*. It is formulated in an abstract, simplified, monochromatic way, if we may so express it, which *does not* correspond to objective reality. Those who formulate the question *thus*, those who *now* ask, "Is the bourgeois-democratic revolution completed?" *and nothing more*, deprive themselves of the possibility of understanding the real situation, which is extraordinarily complicated and, at least, "bichromatic." This—as regards theory. In practice, they impotently capitulate to *petty-bourgeois revolutionism*.

And, indeed, in reality we find *both* the transfer of power to the bourgeoisie (a "completed" bourgeois-democratic revolution of the ordinary type) *and* the existence, side by side with the actual government, of a parallel government, which represents a "revolutionary-democratic dictatorship of the proletariat and peasantry." This "also-government" has *voluntarily* ceded power to the bourgeoisie and has *voluntarily* chained itself to the bourgeois government.

Is this reality covered by the old-Bolshevik formula of Comrade Kamenev, which declares that "the bourgeois-democratic revolution is not completed"? No, that formula is antiquated. It is worthless. It is dead. And all attempts to revive it will be vain.

Secondly, a practical question. Who can say whether a special "revolutionary-democratic dictatorship of the proletariat and peasantry," *detached* from the bourgeois government, is now still possible in Russia? Marxist tactics must not be based on unknown factors.

But if it is still possible, then there is one, and only one way to obtain it, namely, the immediate, decisive and irrevocable severance of the proletarian communist elements from the petty-bourgeois elements. Why?

Because it is not by chance but by necessity that the whole petty bourgeoisie has turned toward chauvinism (defensism), toward "supporting" the bourgeoisie, that it has accepted dependence on the bourgeoisie and fears to do without the bourgeoisie.

How can the petty bourgeoisie be "pushed" into power, when the petty bourgeoisie could assume power now, but *does not wish to?*

Only the severance of the proletarian, Communist Party and only a proletarian class struggle exempt from the timidity of the petty bourgeois; only the consolidation of proletarians exempt from the influence of the petty bourgeoisie both in deed and in word, can make things so "hot" for the petty bourgeoisie that, under certain circumstances, it will be *obliged* to assume power. . . .

Those who at once, immediately and irrevocably, separate the proletarian elements of the Soviets (i.e., the proletarian, Communist Party) from the petty-bourgeois elements, will correctly express the interests of the movement in both eventualities: *both* in the eventuality that Russia will still pass through a special "dictatorship of the proletariat and peasantry," not subordinated to the bourgeoisie, *and* in the eventuality that the petty bourgeoisie will not be able to sever itself from the bourgeoisie and will forever (that is, until socialism is established) waver between us and it.

Those who in their activities are guided by the simple formula, "The bourgeois-democratic revolution is not completed," give, as it were, a certain guarantee that the petty bourgeoisie is capable of becoming independent of the bourgeoisie; and by that very fact they hopelessly surrender themselves to the tender mercies of the petty bourgeoisie.

Incidentally, on the subject of the "formula," the dictatorship of the proletariat and the peasantry, it would not be amiss to recall that in my article "Two Tactics" (July 1905) I particularly pointed out that:

"Like everything else in the world, the revolutionary-democratic dictatorship of the proletariat and the peasantry has a past and a future. Its past is autocracy, serfdom, monarchy and privileges. . . . Its future is the struggle against private property, the struggle of the wageworker against his master, the struggle for socialism. . . ."

The mistake made by Comrade Kamenev is that even now, in 1917, he sees only the *past* of the revolutionary-democratic dictatorship of the proletariat and peasantry, when, as a matter of fact, its *future* has already begun, for the interests and policies of the wage earner and the master have already become sundered *in fact,* and, moreover, on such an important question as "defensism," the attitude toward the imperialist war.

And this brings me to the second mistake in the remarks of Comrade Kamenev quoted above. He reproaches me with the fact that my scheme "is calculated on the immediate transformation of that [bourgeois-democratic] revolution into a socialist revolution."

That is not true. Far from "calculating" on the "immediate transformation" of our revolution into a *socialist* revolution, I actually caution against it, and in Thesis No. 8 plainly state: "Our *immediate* task" is *not* the "introduction of socialism. . . ."

Is it not obvious that if one calculates on the immediate transformation of our revolution into a socialist revolution one cannot be opposed to the introduction of socialism as an immediate task?

Moreover, it is not possible to establish even a "commune state" (i.e., a state organized on the type of the Paris Commune) in Russia "immediately," since that would require that the *majority* of the deputies in all (or in most of) the Soviets should clearly recognize the utter erroneousness and perniciousness of the tactics and policy of the Socialist-Revolutionaries, Chkheidze, Tseretelli, Steklov, etc. And I explicitly declared that in this respect I calculate only on "patient" explanation (is it necessary to be patient in order to bring about a change which can be realized "immediately"?).

Comrade Kamenev rather "impatiently" let himself go and repeated the bourgeois prejudice regarding the Paris Commune, namely, that it wanted to introduce socialism "immediately." That is not so. The Commune, unfortunately, was far too slow in introducing socialism. The real essence of the Commune lies not where the bourgeois usually looks for it, but in the creation of a particular type of *state.* A state of this type has already been born in Russia: it is the Soviets of Workers' and Soldiers' Deputies.

Comrade Kamenev has not pondered over the fact and the significance of the *existing* Soviets, their identity as to type and social and political character with the state of the Commune; and instead of studying a *fact,* he talks of what I allegedly calculated on as a thing of the "immediate" future. The result is, unfortunately, a repetition of the trick practiced by many bourgeois: attention is diverted from the question of the *nature* of the Soviets of Workers' and Soldiers' Deputies, of whether they are a type superior to the parliamentary republic, whether they are more *beneficial* to the people, more *democratic* and more *adapted,* for instance, to the struggle for bread—attention is diverted from this essential, immediate question, rendered urgent by the force of events, to the frivolous, pseudo-scientific, but in reality hollow and professorially lifeless question of "calculations on an immediate transformation."

A frivolous question falsely stated. I "calculate" *solely* and *exclusively* on the workers, soldiers and peasants being able to tackle better than the officials, better than the police, the *practical* and difficult problems of increasing the production of foodstuffs and their better distribution, the better provisioning of the soldiers, etc., etc.

I am profoundly convinced that the Soviets of Workers' and Soldiers' Deputies will develop the independent activity of the *masses* of the people far more quickly and far more effectively than a parliamentary republic. They will decide more effectively, more practically, and more correctly what steps can be taken toward socialism, and how. Control over a bank, amalgamation of all banks into one, is not *yet* socialism, but it is a *step* toward socialism. Today such steps are being taken in Germany by the *Junkers* and the bourgeoisie against the interests of the people. Tomorrow, if the entire power of the state is in its hands, the Soviet of Workers' and Soldiers' Deputies will more effectively take these steps to the advantage of the people.

And what renders these steps *essential?*

Famine. Economic disorganization. Impending collapse. The horrors of war. The horror of the wounds being inflicted on mankind by the war.

Comrade Kamenev concludes his article with the statement that "in a broad discussion he hopes to carry his point of view, the only possible point of view from the revolutionary Social-Democratic Party, if it wishes, as it must, to remain to the end the party of the revolutionary masses of the proletariat, and not to become transformed into a group of Communist propagandists."

It seems to me that these words betray a completely

erroneous estimate of the situation. Comrade Kamenev contrasts a "party of the masses" and a "group of propagandists." But just now the "masses" have yielded to the intoxication of "revolutionary" defensism. Is it not more worthy of internationalists at this moment to be able to resist "mass" intoxication than to "wish to remain" with the masses, i.e., to succumb to the general epidemic? Have we not seen how the chauvinists in all the belligerent countries of Europe justified themselves by the wish to "remain with the masses"? Is is not essential to be able for a while to remain in a minority as against the "mass" intoxication? Is it not the work of the propagandists which at the present moment is the main factor in *clearing* the proletarian line of defensist and petty-bourgeois "mass" intoxication? It was just this fusion of the masses, proletarian and nonproletarian, without distinction of class differences among those masses, that formed one of the conditions for the defensist epidemic. To speak with contempt of a "group of propagandists" advocating a *proletarian* line is, we think, not altogether becoming.

NIKOLAI LENIN: *Prospects of Revolution in Russia and in Europe* [7]

We must say a few words regarding our understanding of the tasks of the Russian revolution. We deem this all the more necessary since, through the medium of the Swiss workers, we can and should address the German, French, and Italian workers, who speak the same languages as the population of Switzerland, which still enjoys the advantages of peace and of the greatest relative amount of political freedom. . . . •

To the Russian proletariat has fallen the great honor of *initiating* the series of revolutions which are arising from the imperialist war with objective inevitability. But the idea that the Russian proletariat is a chosen revolutionary proletariat among the workers of the world is absolutely alien to us. We know full well that the proletariat of Russia is *less* organized, less prepared, and less class conscious than the proletariat of other countries. It is not any partic-

7. From "Farewell Letter to the Swiss Workers," *ibid.*, pp. 14, 17-20. Reprinted by permission of International Publishers Co., Inc.

ular virtues it possessed, but rather the specific historical circumstances, that have made the proletariat of Russia for a certain, *perhaps very brief,* period the skirmishers of the world revolutionary proletariat.

Russia is a peasant country, one of the most backward of European countries. Socialism *cannot triumph there directly at once.* But the peasant character of the country, coupled with the vast land possessions of the noble landlords, *may,* to judge by the experience of 1905, give tremendous scope to the bourgeois-democratic revolution in Russia, and make our revolution a *prelude* to and a *step* toward the world socialist revolution.

It is in the struggle for these ideas, which have been fully confirmed by the experience of 1905 and the spring of 1917, that our Party was formed and waged an implacable fight against all other parties. For these ideas we shall continue to fight.

Socialism cannot triumph directly and immediately in Russia. But the peasant masses *may* carry the inevitable and already mature agrarian revolution to the point of *confiscating* the immense estates of the landlords. This has always been our slogan, and it is now being advocated in Petrograd by the Central Committee of our Party, as well as by our Party newspaper, *Pravda.* The proletariat will fight for this slogan, while not closing its eyes to the inevitability of obdurate class conflicts between the agricultural wageworkers and the improverished peasants closely associated with them, on the one hand, and the prosperous peasants, whose position was strengthened by the Stolypin agrarian "reform" (1907-14), on the other. One must not forget that 104 peasant deputies in the First (1906) and Second (1907) Dumas proposed a revolutionary agrarian bill demanding the nationalism of all lands and their disposal through local committees elected on a completely democratic basis.

Such a revolution would not in itself be a socialist revolution. But it would give a great impetus to the world labor movement. It would greatly strengthen the position of the socialist proletariat in Russia and its influence on the agricultural workers and the poor peasants. It would, on the strength of this influence, enable the urban proletariat to develop such revolutionary organizations as the "Soviets of Workers' Deputies," to substitute them for the old instruments of oppression of the bourgeois states, the army, the police, and the bureaucracy, and to effect, under the pressure of the intolerable burden of the imperialist war and its consequences, a series of revolutionary measures establishing control over the production and distribution of goods.

The Russian proletariat single-handed cannot successfully *complete* the socialist revolution. But it can lend such a sweep to the Russian revolution as would create the most favorable conditions for a socialist revolution, and, in a sense, *start that revolution.* It can render more favorable the conditions under which its *most important,* most trustworthy and most reliable coadjutor, the *European* and the American *socialist* proletariat, will undertake its decisive battles. . . .

The objective conditions of the imperialist war make it certain that the revolution will not be limited to the *first stage* of the Russian revolution, that the revolution will *not* be limited to Russia. . . . The transformation of the imperialist war into civil war is *becoming* a fact.

Long live the proletarian revolution *which is beginning* in Europe!

NIKOLAI LENIN: *Co-operatives under Socialism* [8]

I think that inadequate attention is being paid to the co-operative movement in this country. Not everyone understands that now, since the October Revolution, and quite apart from the New Economy Policy (on the contrary, in this connection we must say, precisely because of the NEP), our co-operative movement assumes really exceptional importance. Many of the dreams of the old co-operators were fantastic. Sometimes they were ridiculously fantastic. But why were they fantastic? Because these old co-operators did not understand the fundamental, root significance of the political struggle of the working class for the overthrow of the rule of the exploiters. We have overthrown the rule of the exploiters, and much that was fantastic, even romantic and banal in the dreams of the old co-operators is now becoming the most unvarnished reality.

Indeed, since state power is in the hands of the working class, since this state power owns all the means of production, the only task that really remains for us to perform is

8. From "On Co-operation," *Selected Works,* Vol. II, *op. cit.,* pp. 830-835. Reprinted by permission of Lawrence and Wishart Ltd.

to organize the population in co-operative societies. When the population is organized in co-operative societies to the utmost, the Socialism which in the past was legitimately treated with ridicule, scorn and contempt by those who were justly convinced that it was necessary to wage the class struggle, the struggle for political power, etc., automatically achieves its aims. But not all comrades understand how vastly, how infinitely important it is now to organize the population of Russia in co-operative societies. By adopting the NEP we made a concession to the peasant as a trader, to the principle of private trade; it is precisely for this reason that (contrary to what some people think) the co-operative movement assumes such importance. As a matter of fact, all that we need under the NEP is to organize the population of Russia in co-operative societies on a sufficiently wide scale, for now we have found that degree of the combination of private interest, trading interest, with state supervision and control of this interest, that degree of its subordination to the common interests that was formerly the stumbling block for very many Socialists. As a matter of fact, the power of state over all large-scale means of production, the power of state in the hands of the proletariat, the alliance of this proletariat with the many millions of small and very small peasants, the assured leadership of the peasantry by the proletariat, etc.—is not this all that is necessary in order to build a complete Socialist society from the co-operatives, from the co-operatives alone, which we formerly treated as huckstering and which from a certain aspect we have the right to treat as such now, under NEP? Is this not all that is necessary for the purpose of building a complete Socialist society? This is not yet the building of Socialist society, but it is all that is necessary and sufficient for this building.

This is what many of our practical workers underrate. They look down upon our co-operative societies with contempt and fail to appreciate their exceptional importance, first, from the standpoint of principle (the means of production are owned by the state) and second, from the standpoint of the transition to the new order by means that will be *simplest, easiest and most intelligible for the peasantry*.

But this again is the most important thing. It is one thing to draw up fantastic plans for building Socialism by means of all sorts of 'workers' associations; but it is quite another thing to learn to build it practically, in such a way that *every* small peasant may take part in the work of construction. This is the stage we have reached now. And there is no doubt that, having reached it, we take too little advantage of it.

We went too far in introducing the NEP not in that we attached too much importance to the principle of free industry and trade; we went too far in introducing the NEP in that we lost sight of the co-operatives, in that we now underrate the co-operatives, in that we are already beginning to forget the vast importance of the co-operatives from the two standpoints mentioned above.

I now propose to discuss with the reader what can and should at once be done practically on the basis of this "co-operative" principle. By what means can we and should we start at once to develop this "co-operative" principle so that its Socialist meaning may be clear to all?

Politically, we must place the co-operatives in the position of always enjoying not only privileges in general, but privileges of a purely material character (bank rate, etc.). The co-operatives must be granted state loans which should exceed, even if not much, the loans we grant to the private enterprises, even as large as those granted to heavy industry, etc.

Every social system arises only with the financial assistance of a definite class. There is no need to mention the hundreds and hundreds of millions of rubles that the birth of "free" capitalism cost. Now we must realize, and apply in our practical work, the fact that the social system which we must now assist more than usual is the co-operative system. But it must be assisted in the real sense of the word, i.e., it will not be enough to interpret assistance to mean assistance for any kind of co-operative trade; by assistance we mean assistance for co-operative trade, in which *really large masses of the population really take part*. It is certainly a correct form of assistance to give a bonus to peasants who take part in co-operative trade; but the whole point is to verify the nature of this participation, to verify the intelligence behind it, to verify its quality. Strictly speaking, when a co-operator goes to a village and opens a co-operative store, the people take no part in this whatever; but at the same time, guided by their own interests, the people will hasten to try to take part in it.

There is another aspect to this question. We have not very much more to do from the point of view of the "civilized" (primarily, literate) European to induce absolutely everyone to take not a passive, but an active part in co-operative operations. Strictly speaking, there is *"only"* one more thing we have to do, and that is, to make our people so "civilized" as to understand all the advantages of having them all take part in the work of the co-operatives, and to organize this participation. *"Only"* this. We need no other cunning devices to enable us to pass to Socialism. But to achieve this "only," a complete revolution is needed; the entire people must go through a whole period of cultural development. Therefore, our rule must be: as little philosophizing and as few acrobatics as possible. In this respect the NEP is an advance, in that it is suited to the level of the ordinary peasant, in that it does not demand anything higher of him. But it will take a whole historical epoch to get the whole population to take part in the work of the co-operatives through the NEP. At best we can achieve this in one or two decades. Nevertheless, this will be a special historical epoch, and without this historical epoch, without universal literacy, without a proper degree of efficiency, without sufficiently training the population to acquire the habit of reading books, and without the material basis for this, without certain safeguards against, say, bad harvests, famine, etc., we shall fail to achieve our object. The whole thing now is to learn to combine the wide revolutionary range of action, the revolutionary enthusiasm which we have displayed sufficiently and crowned with complete success—to learn, to combine this with (I am almost ready to say) the ability to be an efficient and capable merchant, which is sufficient to be a good co-operator. By ability to be a merchant I mean the ability to be a cultured merchant. Let those Russians, or plain peasants, who imagine that *since* they trade they can be good merchants, get this well into their heads. It does not follow at all. They trade, but this is far from being cultured merchants. They are now trading in an Asiatic manner; but to be a merchant one must be able to trade in a European manner. A whole epoch separates them from that position.

In conclusion: a number of economic, financial and banking privileges must be granted to the co-operatives—this is the way our Socialist state must promote the new principle on which the population must be organized. But this is only the general outline of the task; it does not define, depict in detail the entire content of the practical tasks, i.e., we must ascertain what form of "bonus" we should give for organizing the co-operatives (and the terms on which we should give it), the form of bonus by which we shall sufficiently assist the co-operatives, the form of bonus by means of which we shall obtain the civilized co-operator. And a system of civilized co-operators under the social ownership of the means of production, with the class victory of the proletariat over the bourgeoisie, is Socialism.

Whenever I wrote about the New Economic Policy I always quoted the article on state capitalism which I wrote in 1918. More than once this has aroused doubts in the minds of certain young comrades. But their doubts arose mainly in connection with abstract political questions.

It seemed to them that the term state capitalism cannot be applied to the system under which the means of production are owned by the working class, and in which the working class holds political power. They failed to observe, however, that I used the term "state capitalism," *first,* in order to establish the historical connection between our present position and the position I held in my controversy with the so-called Left Communists; and already at that time I argued that state capitalism would be superior to the existing system of economy. It was important for me to show the continuity between ordinary state capitalism and the unusual, even very unusual, state capitalism to which I referred in introducing the reader to the new economic policy. *Secondly,* I always attached importance to the practical aim. And the practical aim of our new economic policy was to grant concessions. Undoubtedly, under the conditions prevailing in our country, concessions would have been a pure type of state capitalism. That is how I conceived the argument about state capitalism.

But there is another aspect of the matter for which we may need state capitalism, or at least, something in juxtaposition with it. This raises the question of co-operation.

There is no doubt that under the capitalist state the co-operatives are collective capitalist institutions. Nor is there any doubt that under our present economic conditions, when we combine private capitalist enterprises—but situated on public land and controlled by the state power which is in the hands of the working class—with enterprises of a consistently Socialist type (the means of production, the land on which the enterprises are situated, and the enterprises as a whole, belonging to the state), the question of a third type of enterprise arises, which formerly was not regarded as an independent type differing in principle from the others, *viz.*, co-operative enterprises. Under private capitalism, co-operative enterprises differ from capitalist enterprises as collective enterprises differ from private enterprises. Under state capitalism, co-operative enterprises differ from state capitalist enterprises, firstly, in that they are private enterprises, and secondly, in that they are collective enterprises. Under our present system, co-operative enterprises differ from private capitalist enterprises because they are collective enterprises, but they do not differ from Socialist enterprises if the land on which they are situated and the means of production belong to the state, i. e., the working class.

This circumstance is not taken into consideration sufficiently when co-operation is discussed. It is forgotten that owing to the special features of our state system, our co-operatives acquire an altogether exceptional significance. If we exclude concessions, which, incidentally, we have not granted on any considerable scale, co-operation, under our conditions, very often entirely coincides with Socialism.

I shall explain my idea. Why were the plans of the old co-operators, from Robert Owen onward, fantastic? Because they dreamt of peacefully transforming present-day society into Socialism without taking into account fundamental questions like that of the class struggle, of the working class capturing political power, of overthrowing the rule of the exploiting class. That is why we are right in regarding this "co-operative" Socialism as being entirely fantastic, and the dream of being able to transform the class enemies into class colleagues and the class struggle into class peace (so-called civil peace), merely by organizing the population in co-operative societies, as something romantic and even banal.

Undoubtedly we were right from the point of view of the fundamental task of the present day, for Socialism cannot be established without the class struggle for political power in the state.

But see how things have changed now that political power is in the hands of the working class, now that the political power of the exploiters is overthrown, and all the means of production (except those which the workers' state voluntarily loans to the exploiters for a certain time and on definite terms in the form of concessions) are owned by the working class.

Now we are right in saying that for us, the mere growth of co-operation (with the "slight" exception mentioned above) is identical with the growth of Socialism, and at the same time we must admit that a radical change has taken place in our point of view concerning Socialism. This radical change lies in that formerly we placed, and had to place, the main weight of emphasis on the political struggle, on revolution, on winning power, etc. Now we have to shift the weight of emphasis to peaceful, organizational, "cultural" work. I would be prepared to say that the weight of emphasis should be placed on educational work were it not for our international relations, were it not for the fact that we have to fight for our position on a world scale. If we leave that aside, however, and confine ourselves entirely to internal economic relations, the weight of emphasis in our work is certainly shifted to educational work.

Two main tasks confront us which constitute the epoch: the first is to reorganize our machinery of state, which is utterly useless, and which we took over in its entirety from the preceding epoch; during the past five years of struggle we did not, and could not, make any serious changes in it. The second is to conduct educational work among the peasants. And the economic object of this educational work among the peasants is to organize them in co-operative societies. If the whole of the peasantry were organized in co-operatives, we would be standing firmly with both feet on the soil of Socialism. But the organization of the entire peasantry in co-operative societies presupposes such a standard of culture among the peasants (precisely among the peasants as the overwhelming majority of the population) that this cannot be achieved without a complete cultural revolution.

Our opponents have told us more than once that we are undertaking the rash task of implanting Socialism in an insufficiently cultured country. But they were misled by the fact that we did not start from the end that was assumed by theory (the theory that all sorts of pedants subscribe to), and that in our country the political and social revolution preceded the cultural revolution, the cultural revolution which now confronts us.

This cultural revolution would be sufficient to transform

this country into a completely Socialist country; but it bristles with immense difficulties of a purely educational (for we are illiterate) and material character (for to be cultured we must achieve a certain level in the development of the material means of production, we must have some material base).

NIKOLAI LENIN:
Workers' Councils and the People's Militia [9]

... the March revolution was only the *first stage* of the revolution. Russia is going through a unique historical period of *transition* from the first to the next stage of the revolution, or, as Skobelev expresses it, to "a second revolution."

If we want to be Marxists and to learn from the experience of the revolutions the world over, we must try to understand just wherein lies the *uniqueness* of this transition period, and what are the tactics that follow from its objective peculiarities.

The uniqueness of the situation lies in the fact that the Guchkov-Miliukov government has won the first victory with unusual ease because of the three following main circumstances: 1. The help received from Anglo-French finance capital and its agents; 2. The help received from the upper layers of the army; 3. The fact that the entire Russian bourgeoisie had been organized in zemstvo and city institutions, in the Imperial Duma, in the war industries committees, etc.

The Guchkov government finds itself between the upper and nether millstones. Bound by capitalist interests, it is compelled to strive to prolong the predatory war for plunder, to protect the monstrous profits of the capitalists and the landlords, to restore the monarchy. Bound by its revolutionary origin and the necessity of an abrupt change from tsarism to democracy, finding itself under the pressure of the hungry masses that clamor for peace, the government is forced to lie, to shift about, to procrastinate, to make as many "declarations" and promises as possible (promises are the only things that are very cheap even in an epoch of insanely high prices), and to carry out as few of them as

9. From *Letters from Afar* (New York, 1932), pp. 25-34. Reprinted by permission of International Publishers Co., Inc.

possible, to make concessions with one hand, and to withdraw them with the other.

Under certain conditions, if circumstances are most favorable to it, the new government, relying on the organizing abilities of the entire Russian bourgeoisie and the bourgeois intelligentsia, may temporarily avert the final crash. But even under such conditions it cannot escape the crash altogether, for it is *impossible* to escape the claws of that terrible monster, begotten by world-capitalism—the imperialist war and famine—without abandoning the whole basis of bourgeois relations, without resorting to revolutionary measures, without appealing to the greatest historical heroism of the Russian and the world proletariat.

Hence the conclusion: We shall not be able to overthrow the new government with one stroke, or, should we be able to do so (in revolutionary times the limits of the possible are increased a thousandfold), we could not retain power, *unless we met* the splendid organization of the entire Russian bourgeoisie and the entire bourgeois intelligentsia with an *organization of the proletariat* just as splendid, leading the vast mass of the city and country poor, the semi-proletarians and the petty proprietors.

It matters little whether the "second revolution" has already broken out in Petrograd (I have stated that it would be absurd to attempt to estimate from abroad the actual tempo of its growth), whether it has been postponed for a time, or whether it has begun in isolated localities in Russia (there are some indications that this is the case)—*in any* case the slogan of the hour right now, on the eve of the revolution, during the revolution, and on the day after the revolution, must be—*proletarian organization*.

Comrade-workers! Yesterday you displayed wonders of proletarian heroism when you overthrew the tsarist monarchy. Sooner or later (perhaps even now, while I am writing these lines) you will inevitably be called upon again to display wonders of similar heroism in overthrowing the power of the landowners and the capitalists who are waging the imperialist war. But you will not be able to win a *permanent victory* in this forthcoming "true" revolution, unless you display *wonders of proletarian organization!*

The slogan of the hour is organization. But organization in itself does not mean much, because, on the one hand, organization is always necessary, and, hence, the mere insistence on "the organization of the masses" does not yet clarify anything, and because, on the other hand, he who contents himself with organization only is merely echoing the views of the liberals; for the liberals, to strengthen their rule, desire nothing better than to have the workers refuse to go *beyond the usual "legal"* forms of organization (from the point of view of "normal" bourgeois society), i. e., to have them *merely* become members of their party, their trade union, their co-operative society, etc., etc.

The workers, guided by their class instinct, have realized that in revolutionary times they need an entirely different organization, of a type above the ordinary. They have taken the right attitude suggested by the experience of our revolution of 1905 and by the Paris Commune of 1871: they have created a *Soviet of Workers' Deputies*, they have set out to develop it, widen and strengthen it, by attracting to it representatives of the soldiers and no doubt of the hired agricultural workers, as well as (in one form or another) of the entire poor section of the peasantry.

To create similar organizations in all the localities of Russia without exception, for all the trades and layers of the proletarian and semi-proletarian population without exception, i.e., for all the toilers and the exploited (to use an expression that is less exact from the point of view of economics but more popular), is our most important and most urgent task. I will note right here that to the peasant masses our party (whose specific role in the proletarian organizations of the new type I shall have occasion to discuss in one of the forthcoming letters) must recommend with special emphasis the organization of Soviets of hired workers and petty agriculturists, such as do not sell their grain, those Soviets *to have no connection* with the prosperous peasants—otherwise it will be impossible to pursue a true proletarian policy, in a general sense,* nor will it be possible correctly to approach the most important practical question involving the life and death of millions of people, i. e., the question of an equitable assessment of food deliveries, of increasing its production, etc.

The question, then, is: What is to be the work of the

---

* There will now develop in the village a struggle for the petty, and partly the middle, peasantry. The landowners, basing themselves on the well-to-do peasants, will lead them to submission to the bourgeoisie. We, basing ourselves on the hired agricultural workers and poor peasants, must lead them to the closest possible alliance with the proletariat of the cities.

Soviets of Workers' Deputies? We repeat what we once said in No. 47 of the Geneva *Social-Democrat* (October 13, 1915): "They must be regarded as organs of insurrection, as organs of revolutionary power."

This theoretical formula, derived from the experience of the Commune of 1871 and of the Russian Revolution of 1905, must be elucidated and concretely developed on the basis of the practical experience gained at this very stage of this very revolution in Russia.

We need revolutionary *power,* we need (for a certain period of transition) the *state.* Therein we differ from the Anarchists. The difference between revolutionary Marxists and Anarchists lies not only in the fact that the former stand for huge, centralized, communist production, while the latter are for decentralized, small-scale production. No, the difference as to government authority and the state consists in this, that we stand *for* the revolutionary utilization of revolutionary forms of the state in our struggle for Socialism, while the Anarchists are *against* it.

We need the state. But we need none of those types of state varying from a constitutional monarchy to the most democratic republic which the bourgeoisie has established everywhere. And herein lies the difference between us and the opportunists and Kautskians of the old, decaying Socialist parties who have distorted or forgotten the lessons of the Paris Commune and the analysis of these lessons by Marx and Engels.

We need the state, but not the kind needed by the bourgeoisie, with organs of power in the form of police, army, bureaucracy, distinct from and opposed to the people. All bourgeois revolutions have merely perfected this government apparatus, have merely transferred it from one party to another.

The proletariat, however, if it wants to preserve the gains of the present revolution and to proceed further to win peace, bread, and freedom, must *"destroy,"* to use Marx's word, this "ready-made" state machinery, and must replace it by another one, *merging* the police, the army, and the bureaucracy *with the universally armed people.* Advancing along the road indicated by the experience of the Paris Commune of 1871 and the Russian Revolution of 1905, the proletariat must organize and arm *all* the poorest and most exploited sections of the population, so that they *themselves* may take into their own hands all the organs of state power, that they *themselves* may constitute these organs.

The workers of Russia have already, with the very first stage of the first revolution, March, 1917, *entered* on this course. The whole problem now is to understand clearly the nature of this new course and courageously, firmly, and persistently, to continue on it.

The Anglo-French and the Russian capitalists wanted "only" to displace, or merely to "scare," Nicholas II, leaving the old machinery of the state—the police, the army, the bureaucracy—intact.

The workers have gone further; they have smashed it. And now not only the Anglo-French, but even the German capitalists howl with rage and horror when they see Russian soldiers shooting their officers, some of whom were even supporters of Guchkov and Miliukov, as Admiral Nepenin, for example.

I have said that the workers have smashed the old state machinery. To be more precise. They *have begun* to smash it.

Let us take a concrete example.

The police of Petrograd and many other places have been partly killed off, and partly removed. The Guchkov-Miliukov government will not be able to restore the monarchy, or even to retain power, unless it re-establishes the police as an organization of armed men separated from and opposed to the people and under the command of the bourgeoisie. This is as clear as the clearest day.

On the other hand, the new government must reckon with the revolutionary masses, must humor them with half-concessions and promises, trying to gain time. Hence it agrees to half-measures: it institutes a "people's militia" with elected officers (this sounds terribly imposing, terribly democratic, revolutionary, and beautiful!). But . . . but . . . first of all, it places the militia under the control of the local zemstvo and city organs of self-government, i. e., under the control of landowners and capitalists elected under the laws of Nicholas the Bloody and Stolypin the Hangman!! Secondly, though it calls it the "people's" militia to throw dust into the eyes of the "people," it does not, as a matter of fact call the people for *universal* service in this militia, nor does it compel the bosses and the capitalists to *pay* their employees the usual wage for the hours and the days they devote to public service, i. e., to the militia.

There is where the main trick is. That is how the landowner and capitalist government of the Guchkovs and Miliukovs achieves its aim of keeping the "people's militia" on paper, while in reality it is quietly and step by step organizing a bourgeois militia hostile to the people, first of "8,000 students and professors" (as the foreign press describes the present militia in Petrograd)—which is obviously a mere toy!—then, gradually, of the old and the new police.

Do not permit the re-establishment of the police! Do not let go the local government organs! Create a really universal militia, led by the proletariat! This is the task of the day, this is the slogan of the present hour, equally in accord with the correctly understood requirements of the further development of the class struggle, the further course of the revolution, and with the democratic instinct of every worker, every peasant, every toiler, every one who is exploited, who cannot but hate the police, the constables, the command of landowners and capitalists over armed men who wield power over the people.

What kind of police do *they* need, these Guchkovs and Miliukovs, these landowners and capitalists? The same kind that existed during the tsarist monarchy. Following very brief revolutionary periods, *all* the bourgeois and bourgeois-democratic republics of the world organized or re-established precisely that kind of police—a special organization of armed men, separated from and opposed to the people, and in one way or another subordinated to the bourgeoisie.

What kind of militia do we need, we, the proletariat, all the toilers? A real people's militia, i. e., first of all, one that consists of the entire population, of all the adult citizens of both sexes; secondly, one that combines the functions of a people's army with those of the police, and with the functions of the main and fundamental organ of the state system and the state administration.

To give more concreteness to these propositions, let us try a schematic example. Needless to say, the idea of laying out any "plan" for a proletarian militia would be absurd: when the workers, and all the people as a real mass, take up this task in a practical way, they will work it out and secure it a hundred times better than any theoretician can propose. I am not offering a plan—all I want is to illustrate my thought.

Petrograd has a population of about two million, more

than half of which is between the ages of 15 and 65. Let us take a half—one million. Let us deduct one-fourth to allow for the sick or other instances where people cannot be engaged in public service for a valid reason. There still remain 750,000 persons, who, working in the militia one day out of every fifteen (continuing to receive payment from their employers for this time), would make up an army of 50,000 people.

This is the type of "state" that we need!

This is the kind of militia that would be, in deed, and not only in name, a "people's militia."

This is the road we must follow if we wish to make impossible the re-establishment of a special police, or a special army, separated from the people.

Such a militia would, in ninety-five cases out of a hundred, be composed of workers and peasants, and would express the real intelligence and the will, the strength and the authority of the overwhelming majority of the people. Such a militia would actually arm and give military training to the people at large, thus making sure, in a manner not employed by Guchkov, nor Miliukov, against all attempts to re-establish reaction, against all efforts of the tsarist agents. Such a militia would be the executive organ of the "Soviets of Workers' and Soldiers' Deputies," it would enjoy the *full* respect and confidence of the population, because it would, itself, be an organization of the entire population. Such a militia would change democracy from a pretty signboard, hiding the enslavement and deception of the people by the capitalists, into a real means for *educating the masses* so that they might be able to take part in *all* the affairs of the state. Such a militia would draw the youngsters into political life, training them not only by word, but by deed and *work*. Such a militia would develop those functions which belong, to use learned terms, to the welfare police, sanitary supervision, etc., by drawing into such activities all the adult women without exception. Without drawing the women into social service, into the militia, into political life, without tearing the women away from the stupefying domestic and kitchen atmosphere it is impossible to secure real freedom, it is impossible to build a democracy, let alone Socialism.

Such a militia would be a proletarian militia, because the industrial and the city workers would just as naturally and inevitably assume in it the leadership of the masses of the poor, as naturally and inevitably as they took the leading position in all the revolutionary struggles of the people in the years 1905-1907, and in 1917.

Such a militia would guarantee absolute order and a comradely discipline practiced with enthusiasm. At the same time, it would afford a means of struggling in a real democratic manner against the crisis through which all the warring nations are now passing; it would make possible the regular and prompt assessment of food and other supply levies, the establishment of "universal labor duty" which the French now call "civil mobilization" and the Germans —"obligatory civil service," and without which, as has been demonstrated, it is impossible to heal the wounds that were and are being inflicted by this predatory and horrible war.

Has the proletariat of Russia shed its blood only to receive luxurious promises of mere political democratic reforms? Will it not demand and make sure that every toiler should see and feel a certain improvement in his life right now? That every family should have sufficient bread? That every child should have a bottle of good milk, and that no adult in a rich family should dare take extra milk until all the children are supplied? That the palaces and luxurious homes left by the Tsar and the aristocracy should not stand idle but should provide shelter to the homeless and the destitute? What other organization except a universal people's militia with women participating on a par with the men can effect these measures?

Such measures *do not yet* constitute Socialism. They deal with distribution of consumption, not with the reorganization of industry. They do not yet constitute the "dictatorship of the proletariat," but merely a "revolutionary-democratic dictatorship of the proletariat and the poorest peasantry." Theoretical classification doesn't matter now. It would indeed be a grave error if we tried now to fit the complex, urgent, rapidly unfolding practical tasks of the revolution into the Procrustean bed of a narrowly conceived "theory," instead of regarding theory first of all and above all as a *guide to action*.

Will the mass of Russian workers have sufficient class-consciousness, self-discipline and heroism to show "wonders of proletarian organization" after they have displayed wonders of courage, initiative and self-sacrifice in direct revolutionary struggle? This we do not know, and to make conjectures about it would be idle, for such questions are answered *only* by life itself.

What we do know definitely and what we must as a party explain to the masses is that we have on hand a historic motive power of tremendous force that causes an unheard-of crisis, hunger and countless miseries. This motive is the war which the capitalists of *both* warring camps are waging for predatory purposes. This "motive power" has brought a number of the richest, freest, and most enlightened nations to the brink of an abyss. It *forces* nations to strain all their strength to the breaking point, it places them in an insufferable position, it makes imperative the putting into effect not of "theories" (that is out of the question, and Marx had repeatedly warned Socialists against this illusion), but of most extreme yet practical measures, because *without* these extreme measures there is death, immediate and indubitable death for millions of people through hunger.

That revolutionary enthusiasm on the part of the most advanced class can accomplish much when objective conditions demand extreme measures from the entire people, need not be argued. *This* aspect of the case is clearly seen and felt by everyone in Russia.

It is important to understand that in revolutionary times the objective situation changes as rapidly and as suddenly as life itself. We should be able to adjust our tactics and our immediate objectives to the peculiarities of every given situation. Up to March, 1917, our task was to conduct a bold revolutionary-internationalist propaganda, to awaken and call the masses to struggle. In the March days there was required the courage of heroic struggle to crush tsarism —the most immediate foe. We are now going through a transition from the first stage of the revolution to the second, from a "grapple" with tsarism to a "grapple" with the imperialism of Guchkov-Miliukov, of the capitalists and the landowners. Our immediate problem is organization, not in the sense of effecting ordinary organization by ordinary methods, but in the sense of drawing large masses of the oppressed classes in unheard-of numbers into the organization, and of embodying in this organization military, state, and national economic problems.

The proletariat has approched this unique task and will approach it in a variety of ways. In some localities of Russia the March revolution has given the proletariat almost full power—in others, the proletariat will begin to build up and strengthen the proletarian militia perhaps by "usurpation"; in still others, it will, probably, work for immediate elections, on the basis of universal suffrage, to the city councils and zemstvos, in order to turn them into revolutionary centers, etc., until the growth of proletarian organization, the rapprochement of soldiers and workers, the stirring within the peasantry, the disillusionment of very many about the competence of the militarist-imperialist government of Guchkov and Miliukov shall have brought nearer the hour when that government will give place to the "government" of the Soviets of Workers' Deputies.

Nor must we forget that right near Petrograd there is one of the most advanced, actually republican, countries —Finland—a country which from 1905 up to 1917, shielded by the revolutionary struggles in Russia, has developed a democracy by comparatively peaceful means, and has won the majority of its population over to Socialism. The Russian proletariat will insure the freedom of the Finnish republic, even to the point of separation (there is hardly a Social-Democrat who would hesitate on this score now, when the Cadet Rodichev is so shamefully haggling in Helsingfors over bits of privileges for the Great Russians), and thus gain the full confidence and comradely aid of the Finnish workers for the all-Russian proletarian cause. In a difficult and great cause errors are unavoidable, nor shall we avoid them; the Finnish workers are better organizers, they will help us in this and, *in their own way*, bring nearer the establishment of a Socialist republic.

Revolutionary victories in Russia itself—quiet organizational successes in Finland shielded by the above victories —the Russian workers taking up revolutionary-organizational tasks on a new scale—conquest of power by the proletariat and the poorest strata of the population—encouraging and developing the Socialist revolution in the West— this is the path that will lead us to peace and Socialism.

NIKOLAI LENIN: *National Liberation Movements and the Socialist Revolution* [10]

The social revolution cannot be the united action of the proletarians of *all* countries, for the simple reason that the majority of the countries and the majority of the inhabitants of the globe have not even reached the capitalist stage of development, or are only at the beginning of that stage. . . . Socialism will be achieved by the united action of the proletarians, not of all countries, but of a minority of countries, namely, of the countries that have reached the stage of development of *advanced* capitalism. P. Kievsky's failure to understand this point is the cause of his error. In *those* advanced countries (England, France, Germany, etc.), the national problem was solved long ago; national unity has long outlived its purpose; *objectively,* there are no "national tasks" to be fulfilled. Hence, only in those countries is it possible *now* to "blow up" national unity, and establish class unity.

In the undeveloped countries, in the whole of Eastern Europe and all the colonial and semi-colonial countries, the situation is entirely different. In those countries as a general rule, we *still have* oppressed and capitalistically undeveloped nations. Objectively, these nations still have national tasks to fulfil, namely, *democratic* tasks, the tasks of *throwing off foreign oppression.*

As an example of precisely such nations, Engels quoted India, and said that she may make a revolution against victorious socialism, for Engels was remote from that ridiculous *"Imperialist economism"* which imagines that the proletariat, having achieved victory in the advanced countries, will "automatically" without definite *democratic* measures, abolish national oppression everywhere. The victorious proletariat will recognize the countries in which it has achieved victory. This cannot be done all at once; nor indeed is it possible to "vanquish" the bourgeoisie all at once.

The undeveloped and oppressed nations are not waiting, they are not ceasing to live, they are not disappearing, while

10. From "A Caricature of Marxism," *Selected Works,* Vol. 19 (New York, 1942), pp. 245-247. Reprinted by permission of International Publishers Co., Inc.

the proletariat of the advanced countries is overthrowing the bourgeoisie and repelling its attempts at counter-revolution. If, to rise in rebellion, they (the colonies, Ireland), take advantage of an imperialist bourgeois crisis like the war of 1915-16, which is only a minor crisis compared with social revolution, we can be quite sure that they, all the more so, will take advantage of the great crises of civil war in the advanced countries.

The social revolution cannot come about except in the form of an epoch of proletarian civil war against the bourgeoisie in the advanced countries combined with a *whole series* of democratic and revolutionary movements, including movements for national liberation, in the undeveloped, backward and oppressed nations.

Why? Because capitalism develops unevenly, and objective reality gives us highly developed capitalist nations side by side with a number of nations only slightly developed economically, or totally undeveloped.

LEON TROTSKY: *The Law of Uneven and Combined Development in Russian History* [11]

A backward country assimilates the material and intellectual conquests of the advanced countries. But this does not mean that it follows them slavishly, reproduces all the stages of their past. The theory of the repetition of historic cycles—Vico and his more recent followers—rests upon an observation of the orbits of old pre-capitalistic cultures, and in part upon the first experiments of capitalist development. A certain repetition of cultural stages in ever new settlements was in fact bound up with the provincial and episodic character of that whole process. Capitalism means, however, an overcoming of those conditions. It prepares and in a certain sense realizes the universality and permanence of man's development. By this a repetition of the forms of development by different nations is ruled out. Although compelled to follow after the advanced countries, a backward country does not take things in the same order. The privilege of historic backwardness—and such a privilege exists—permits, or rather compels, the adoption of whatever is ready in advance of any specified date, skipping a

11. From *The History of the Russian Revolution*, Vol. I, translated by Max Eastman (New York, 1932), pp. 4-9. Copyright, 1932, by Simon and Schuster, Inc. Copyright renewed, 1959, by Max Eastman.

whole series of intermediate stages. Savages throw away their bows and arrows for rifles all at once, without traveling the road which lay between those two weapons in the past. The European colonists in America did not begin history all over again from the beginning. The fact that Germany and the United States have now economically outstripped England was made possible by the very backwardness of their capitalist development. On the other hand, the conservative anarchy in the British coal industry —as also in the heads of MacDonald and his friends—is a paying-up for the past when England played too long the role of capitalist pathfinder. The development of historically backward nations leads necessarily to a peculiar combination of different stages in the historic process. Their development as a whole acquires a planless, complex, combined character.

The possibility of skipping over intermediate steps is of course by no means absolute. Its degree is determined in the long run by the economic and cultural capacities of the country. The backward nation, moreover, not infrequently debases the achievements borrowed from outside in the process of adapting them to its own more primitive culture. In this the very process of assimilation acquires a self-contradictory character. Thus the introduction of certain elements of Western technique and training, above all military and industrial, under Peter I, led to a strengthening of serfdom as the fundamental form of labor organization. European armament and European loans—both indubitable products of a higher culture—led to a strengthening of tsarism, which delayed in its turn the development of the country.

The laws of history have nothing in common with a pedantic schematism. Unevenness, the most general law of the historic process, reveals itself most sharply and complexly in the destiny of the backward countries. Under the whip of external necessity their backward culture is compelled to make leaps. From the universal law of unevenness thus derives another law which, for the lack of a better name, we may call the law of *combined development*—by which we mean a drawing together of the different stages of the journey, a combining of separate steps, an amalgam of archaic with more contemporary forms. Without this law, to be taken of course in its whole material content, it is impossible to understand the history of Russia, and indeed of any country of the second, third or tenth cultural class.

Under pressure from richer Europe the Russian State swallowed up a far greater relative part of the people's wealth than in the West, and thereby not only condemned the people to a twofold poverty, but also weakened the foundations of the possessing classes. Being at the same time in need of support from the latter, it forced and regimented their growth. As a result the bureaucratized privileged classes never rose to their full height, and the Russian state thus still more approached an Asiatic despotism. The Byzantine autocratism,' officially adopted by the Muscovite tsars at the beginning of the sixteenth century, subdued the feudal Boyars with the help of the nobility, and then gained the subjection of the nobility by making the peasantry their slaves, and upon this foundation created the St. Petersburg imperial absolutism. The backwardness of the whole process is sufficiently indicated in the fact that serfdom, born at the end of the sixteenth century, took form in the seventeenth, flowered in the eighteenth, and was juridically annulled only in 1861.

The clergy, following after the nobility, played no small role in the formation of the tsarist autocracy, but nevertheless a servile role. The church never rose in Russia to that commanding height which it attained in the Catholic West; it was satisfied with the role of spiritual servant of the autocracy, and counted this a recompense for its humility. The bishops and metropolitans enjoyed authority merely as deputies of the temporal power. The patriarchs were changed along with the tsars. In the Petersburg period the dependence of the church upon the state became still more servile. Two hundred thousand priests and monks were in all essentials a part of the bureaucracy, a sort of police of the gospel. In return for this the monopoly of the orthodox clergy in matters of faith, land and income was defended by a more regular kind of police. . . .

The meagerness not only of Russian feudalism, but of all the old Russian history, finds its most depressing expression in the absence of real medieval cities as centers of commerce and craft. Handicraft did not succeed in Russia in separating itself from agriculture, but preserved its character of home industry. The old Russian cities were commercial, administrative, military and manorial—centers of consumption, consequently, not of production. Even Novgorod, similar to Hansa and not subdued by the Tartars, was only a commercial, and not an industrial city. True, the distribution of the peasant industries over various districts created a demand for trade mediation on a large scale. But nomad traders could not possibly occupy that place in social life which belonged in the West to the craft-guild and merchant-industry petty and middle bourgeoisie, inseparably bound up with its peasant environment. The chief roads of Russian trade, moreover, led across the border, thus from time immemorial giving the leadership to foreign commercial capital, and imparting a semi-colonial character to the whole process, in which the Russian trader was a mediator between the Western cities and the Russian villages. This kind of economic relation developed further during the epoch of Russian capitalism and found its extreme expression in the imperialistic war.

The insignificance of the Russian cities, which more than anything else promoted the development of an Asiatic state, also made impossible a Reformation—that is, a replacement of the feudal-bureaucratic orthodoxy by some sort of modernized kind of Christianity adapted to the demands of a bourgeois society. The struggle against the state church did not go farther than the creation of peasant sects, the faction of the Old Believers being the most powerful among them.

Fifteen years before the great French revolution there developed in Russia a movement of the Cossacks, peasants and worker-serfs of the Urals, known as the Pugachev Rebellion. What was lacking to this menacing popular uprising in order to convert it into a revolution? A Third Estate. Without the industrial democracy of the cities a peasant war could not develop into a revolution, just as the peasant sects could not rise to the height of a Reformation. The result of the Pugachev Rebellion was just the opposite —a strengthening of bureaucratic absolutism as the guardian of the interests of the nobility, a guardian which had again justified itself in the hour of danger.

The Europeanization of the country, formally begun in the time of Peter, became during the following century more and more a demand of the ruling class itself, the nobility. In 1825 the aristocratic intelligentsia, generalizing this demand politically, went to the point of a military conspiracy to limit the powers of autocracy. Thus, under pressure from the European bourgeois development, the progressive nobility attempted to take the place of the lacking Third Estate. But nevertheless they wished to combine their liberal regime with the security of their own caste domination, and therefore feared most of all to arouse the peasantry. It is thus not surprising that the conspiracy remained a mere attempt on the part of a brilliant but isolated officer caste which gave up the sponge almost without a struggle. Such was the significance of the Dekabrist uprising.

The landlords who owned factories were the first among their caste to favor replacing serfdom by wage labor. The growing export of Russian grain gave an impulse in the same direction. In 1861 the noble bureaucracy, relying upon the liberal landlords, carried out its peasant reform. The impotent bourgeois liberalism during this operation played the role of humble chorus. It is needless to remark that tsarism solved the fundamental problem of Russia, the agarian problem, in a more niggardly and thieving fashion than that in which the Prussian monarchy during the next decade was to solve the fundamental problem of Germany, its national consolidation. The solution of the problems of one class by another is one of those combined methods natural to backward countries.

The law of combined development reveals itself most indubitably, however, in the history and character of Russian industry. Arising late, Russian industry did not repeat the development of the advanced countries, but inserted itself into this development, adapting their latest achievements to its own backwardness. Just as the economic evolution of Russia as a whole skipped over the epoch of craft-guilds and manufacture, so also the separate branches of industry made a series of special leaps over technical productive stages that had been measured in the West by decades. Thanks to this, Russian industry developed at certain periods with extraordinary speed. Between the first revolution and the war, industrial production in Russia approximately doubled. This has seemed to certain Russian historians a sufficient basis for concluding that "we must abandon the legend of backwardness and slow growth." In reality the possibility of this swift growth was determined by that very backwardness which, alas, continued not only up to the moment of liquidation of the old Russia, but as her legacy up to the present day.

LEON TROTSKY: *How to Make an Insurrection* [12]

People do not make revolution eagerly any more than they do war. There is this difference, however, that in war compulsion plays the decisive role, in revolution there is no compulsion except that of circumstances. A revolution takes place only when there is no other way out. And the insurrection, which rises above a revolution like a peak in the mountain chain of its events, can no more be evoked at will than the revolution as a whole. The masses advance and retreat several times before they make up their minds to the final assault.

Conspiracy is ordinarily contrasted to insurrection as the deliberate undertaking of a minority to a spontaneous movement of the majority. And it is true that a victorious insurrection, which can only be the act of a class called to stand at the head of the nation, is widely separated both in method and historic significance from a governmental overturn accomplished by conspirators acting in concealment from the masses.

In every class society there are enough contradictions so that a conspiracy can take root in its cracks. Historic experience proves, however, that a certain degree of social disease is necessary—as in Spain, for instance, or Portugal, or South America—to supply continual nourishment for a regime of conspiracies. A pure conspiracy even when victorious can only replace one clique of the same ruling class by another—or still less, merely alter the governmental personages. Only mass insurrection has ever brought the victory of one social regime over another. Periodical conspiracies are commonly an expression of social stagnation and decay, but popular insurrections on the contrary come usually as a result of some swift growth which has broken down the old equilibrium of the nation. The chronic "revolutions" of the South American republics have nothing in common with the Permanent Revolution; they are in a sense the very opposite thing.

This does not mean, however, that popular insurrection and conspiracy are in all circumstances mutually exclusive. An element of conspiracy almost always enters to some de-

12. From "The Art of Insurrection," *ibid.*, Vol. III, pp. 167-174. Reprinted by arrangement with the University of Michigan Press. Copyright, 1933, by Simon and Schuster, Inc. Copyright renewed, 1961, by Max Eastman.

gree into any insurrection. Being historically conditioned by a certain stage in the growth of a revolution, a mass insurrection is never purely spontaneous. Even when it flashes out unexpectedly to a majority of its own participants, it has been fertilized by those ideas in which the insurrectionaries see a way out of the difficulties of existence. But a mass insurrection can be foreseen and prepared. It can be organized in advance. In this case the conspiracy is subordinate to the insurrection, serves it, smooths its path, hastens its victory. The higher the political level of a revolutionary movement and the more serious its leadership, the greater will be the place occupied by conspiracy in a popular insurrection.

It is very necessary to understand the relations between insurrection and conspiracy, both as they oppose and as they supplement each other. It is especially so, because the very use of the word conspiracy, even in Marxian literature, contains a superficial contradiction due to the fact that it sometimes implies an independent undertaking initiated by the minority, at others a preparation by the minority of a majority insurrection.

History testifies, to be sure, that in certain conditions a popular insurrection can be victorious even without a conspiracy. Arising "spontaneously" out of the universal indignation, the scattered protests, demonstrations, strikes, street fights, an insurrection can draw in a part of the army, paralyze the forces of the enemy, and overthrow the old power. To a certain degree this is what happened in February 1917 in Russia. Approximately the same picture is presented by the development of the German and Austro-Hungarian revolutions of the autumn of 1918. Since in these events there was no party at the head of the insurrectionaries imbued through and through with the interests and aims of the insurrection, its victory had inevitably to transfer the power to those parties which up to the last moment had been opposing it.

To overthrow the old power is one thing; to take the power in one's own hands is another. The bourgeoisie may win the power in a revolution not because it is revolutionary, but because it is bourgeois. It has in its possession property, education, the press, a network of strategic positions, a hierarchy of institutions. Quite otherwise with the proletariat. Deprived in the nature of things of all social advantages, an insurrectionary proletariat can count only on its numbers, its solidarity, its cadres, its official staff.

Just as a blacksmith cannot seize the red hot iron in his naked hand, so the proletariat cannot directly seize the power; it has to have an organization accommodated to this task. The co-ordination of the mass insurrection with the conspiracy, the subordination of the conspiracy to the insurrection, the organization of the insurrection through the conspiracy, constitutes that complex and responsible department of revolutionary politics which Marx and Engels called "the art of insurrection." It presupposes a correct general leadership of the masses, a flexible orientation in changing conditions, a thought-out plan of attack, cautiousness in technical preparation, and a daring blow.

Historians and politicians usually give the name of *spontaneous insurrection* to a movement of the masses united by a common hostility against the old regime, but not having a clear aim, deliberate methods of struggle, or a leadership consciously showing the way to victory. This spontaneous insurrection is condescendingly recognized by official historians—at least those of democratic temper—as a necessary evil the responsibility for which falls upon the old regime. The real reason for their attitude of indulgence is that "spontaneous" insurrection cannot transcend the framework of the bourgeois regime.

The social democrats take a similar position. They do not reject revolution at large as a social catastrophe, any more than they reject earthquakes, volcanic eruptions, eclipses and epidemics of the plague. What they do reject—calling it "Blanquism," or still worse, Bolshevism—is the conscious preparation of an overturn, the plan, the conspiracy. In other words, the social democrats are ready to sanction—and that only *ex post facto*—those overturns which hand the power to the bourgeoisie, but they implacably condemn those methods which might alone bring the power to the proletariat. Under this pretended objectivism they conceal a policy of defense of the capitalist society.

From his observations and reflections upon the failure of the many insurrections he witnessed or took part in, Auguste Blanqui derived a number of tactical rules which if violated will make the victory of any insurrection extremely difficult, if not impossible. Blanqui demanded these things: a timely creation of correct revolutionary detachments, their centralized command and adequate equipment, a well calculated placement of barricades, their definite construction, and a systematic, not a mere episodic, defense of them. All these rules, deriving from the military problems of the insurrection, must of course change with social conditions and military technique, but in themselves they are not by any means "Blanquism" in the sense that this word approaches the German "putschism," or revolutionary adventurism.

Insurrection is an art, and like all arts it has its laws. The rules of Blanqui were the demands of a military revolutionary realism. Blanqui's mistake lay not in his direct but his inverse theorem. From the fact that tactical weakness condemns an insurrection to defeat, Blanqui inferred that an observance of the rules of insurrectionary tactics would itself guarantee the victory. Only from this point on is it legitimate to contrast Blanquism with Marxism. Conspiracy does not take the place of insurrection. An active minority of the proletariat, no matter how well organized, cannot seize the power regardless of the general conditions of the country. In this point history has condemned Blanquism. But only in this. His affirmative theorem retains all its force. In order to conquer the power, the proletariat needs more than a spontaneous insurrection. It needs a suitable organization, it needs a plan; it needs a conspiracy. Such is the Leninist view of this question.

Engels' criticism of the fetishism of the barricade was based upon the evolution of military technique and of technique in general. The insurrectionary tactic of Blanquism corresponded to the character of the old Paris, the semi-handicraft proletariat, the narrow streets and the military system of Louis Philippe. Blanqui's mistake in principle was to identify revolution with insurrection. His technical mistake was to identify insurrection with the barricade. The Marxian criticism has been directed against both mistakes. Although at one with Blanquism in regarding insurrection as an art, Engels discovered not only the subordinate place occupied by insurrection in a revolution, but also the declining role of the barricade in an insurrection. Engels' criticism had nothing in common with a renunciation of the revolutionary methods in favor of pure parliamentarism, as the philistines of the German Social Democracy, in cooperation with the Hohenzollern censorship, attempted in their day to pretend. For Engels the question about barricades remained a question about one of the technical elements of an uprising. The reformists have attempted to infer from his rejection of the decisive importance of the barricade a rejection of revolutionary violence in general. That is about the same as to infer the destruction of militarism from considerations of the probable decline in importance of trenches in future warfare.

The organization by means of which the proletariat can both overthrow the old power and replace it, is the soviets. This afterward became a matter of historic experience, but was up to the October revolution a theoretical prognosis—resting, to be sure, upon the preliminary experience of 1905. The soviets are organs of preparation of the masses for insurrection, organs of insurrection, and after the victory organs of government.

However, the soviets by themselves do not settle the question. They may serve different goals according to the program and leadership. The soviets receive their program from the party. Whereas the soviets in revolutionary conditions—and apart from revolution they are impossible—comprise the whole class with the exception of its altogether backward, inert or demoralized strata, the revolutionary party represents the brain of the class. The problem of conquering the power can be solved only by a definite combination of party with soviets—or with other mass organizations more or less equivalent to soviets.

When headed by a revolutionary party the soviet consciously and in good season strives toward a conquest of power. Accommodating itself to changes in the political situation and the mood of the masses, it gets ready the military bases of the insurrection, unites the shock troops upon a single scheme of action, works out a plan for the offensive and for the final assault. And this means bringing organized conspiracy into mass insurrection.

The Bolsheviks were compelled more than once, and long before the October revolution, to refute accusations of conspiratism and Blanquism directed against them by their enemies. Moreover, nobody waged a more implacable struggle against the system of pure conspiracy than Lenin. The opportunists of the international social democracy more than once defended the old Social Revolutionary tactic of individual terror directed against the agents of tsarism, when this tactic was ruthlessly criticized by the Bolsheviks with their insistence upon mass insurrection as opposed to the individual adventurism of the intelligentsia. But in refuting all varieties of Blanquism and anarchism, Lenin did not for one moment bow down to any "sacred" spontaneousness of the masses. He thought out before anybody else, and more deeply, the correlation between the objective and subjective factors in a revolution, between the spontaneous movement and the policy of the party, between the popular masses and the progressive class, between the proletariat and its vanguard, between the soviets and the party, between insurrection and conspiracy.

But if it is true that an insurrection cannot be evoked at will, and that nevertheless in order to win it must be organized in advance, then the revolutionary leaders are presented with a task of correct diagnosis. They must feel out the growing insurrection in good season and supplement it with a conspiracy. The interference of the midwife in labor pains—however this image may have been abused—remains the clearest illustration of this conscious intrusion into an elemental process. Herzen once accused his friend Bakunin of invariably in all his revolutionary enterprises taking the second month of pregnancy for the ninth. Herzen himself was rather inclined to deny even in the ninth that pregnancy existed. In February the question of determining the date of birth hardly arose at all, since the insurrection flared up unexpectedly without centralized leadership. But exactly for this reason the power did not go to those who had accomplished the insurrection, but to those who had applied the brakes. It was quite otherwise with the second insurrection. This was consciously prepared by the Bolshevik party. The problem of correctly seizing the moment to give the signal for the attack was thus laid upon the Bolshevik staff.

Moment here is not to be taken too literally as meaning a definite day and hour. Physical births also present a considerable period of uncertainty—their limits interesting not only to the art of the midwife, but also to the casuistics of the Surrogate's Court. Between the moment when an attempt to summon an insurrection must inevitably prove premature and lead to a revolutionary miscarriage, and the moment when a favorable situation must be considered hopelessly missed, there exists a certain period—it may be measured in weeks, and sometimes in a few months—in the course of which an insurrection may be carried out with more or less chance of success. To discriminate this comparatively short period and then choose the definite moment—now in the more accurate sense of the very day and hour—for the last blow, constitutes the most responsible task of the revolutionary leaders. It can with full justice be called the key problem, for it unites the policy of revolution with the technique of insurrection—and it is needless to add that insurrection, like war, is a continuation of politics with other instruments.

Intuition and experience are necessary for revolutionary leadership, just as for all other kinds of creative activity. But much more than that is needed. The art of the magician can also successfully rely upon intuition and experience. Political magic is adequate, however, only for epochs and periods in which routine predominates. An epoch of mighty historic upheavals has no use for witchdoctors. Here experience, even illumined by intuition, is not enough. Here you must have a synthetic doctrine comprehending the interactions of the chief historic forces. Here you must have a materialistic method permitting you to discover, behind the moving shadows of program and slogan, the actual movement of social bodies.

The fundamental premise of a revolution is that the existing social structure has become incapable of solving the urgent problems of development of the nation. A revolution becomes possible, however, only in case the society contains a new class capable of taking the lead in solving the problems presented by history. The process of preparing a revolution consists of making the objective problems involved in the contradictions of industry and of classes find their way into the consciousness of living human masses, change this consciousness and create new correlations of human forces.

LEON TROTSKY: *Theory of the Permanent Revolution* [13]

The permanent revolution, in the sense which Marx attached to the conception, means a revolution which makes no compromise with any form of class rule, which does not stop at the democratic stage, which goes over to socialist measures and to war against the reaction from without, that is, a revolution whose every next stage is an-

13. From *The Permanent Revolution*, translated by Max Shachtman (New York, 1931), pp. 22-27. Reprinted by permission of Pioneer Publishers.

chored in the preceding one and which can only end in the complete liquidation of all class society.

To dispel the chaos that has been created around the theory of the permanent revolution, it is necessary to distinguish three lines of thought that are united in this theory.

First, it embraces the problem of the transition of the democratic revolution into the socialist. This is really the historical origin of the theory.

The conception of the permanent revolution was set up by the great Communists of the middle of the nineteenth century, by Marx and his adherents, in opposition to that democratic ideology which, as is known, presumed that all questions should be settled peacefully, in a reformist or evolutionary way, by the erection of the "rational" or democratic state. Marx regarded the bourgeois revolution of '48 as the direct introduction in the proletarian revolution. Marx "erred." Yet his error has a factual and not a methodological character. The revolution of 1848 did not turn into the socialist revolution. But that is just why it also did not achieve democracy. As to the German revolution of 1918, it is no democratic completion of the bourgeois revolution: it is a proletarian revolution decapitated by the social democracy; more correctly, it is the bourgeois *counter-revolution*, which is compelled to preserve pseudo-democratic forms after the victory over the proletariat.

Vulgar "Marxism" has worked out a schema of historical development, according to which every bourgeois society sooner or later secures a democratic regime, and after which it gradually organizes and raises the proletariat, under the conditions of democracy, to socialism. As to the transition to socialism itself, there have been various notions: the avowed reformists imagined this transition as the reformist cramming of democracy with a socialist content (Jaurès). The formal revolutionists acknowledged the inevitability of applying revolutionary violence in the transition to socialism (Guesde). But both of them regarded democracy and socialism with regard to all peoples and countries as two not only entirely separated stages in the development of society, but also lying at great distances from each other. This view was predominant also among those Russian Marxists who, in the period of 1905, belonged to the Left Wing of the Second International. Plekhanov, the brilliant progenitor of Russian Marxism, considered the idea of the dictatorship of the proletariat a delusion in contemporary Russia. The same standpoint was defended not only by the Mensheviks, but also by the overwhelming majority of the leading Bolsheviks, among them all the present party leaders without exception, who at that time were resolute revolutionary democrats, for whom the problem of the socialist revolution, not only in 1905 but also on the eve of 1917, still signified the vague music of a distant future.

These ideas and moods declared war upon the theory of the permanent revolution, risen anew in 1905. It pointed out that the democratic tasks of the backward bourgeois nations in our epoch led to the dictatorship of the proletariat and that the dictatorship of the proletariat puts the socialist tasks on the order of the day. In that lay the central idea of the theory. If the traditional view was that the road to the dictatorship of the proletariat led through a long period of democracy, the theory of the permanent revolution established the fact that for backward countries the road to democracy passed through the dictatorship of the proletariat. By that alone, democracy does not become a regime anchored within itself for decades, but rather a direct introduction to the socialist revolution. Each is bound to the other by an unbroken chain. In this way, there arises between the democratic revolution and the socialist transformation of society a permanency of revolutionary development.

The second aspect of the "permanent" theory already characterizes the socialist revolution as such. For an indefinitely long time and in constant internal struggle, all social relations are transformed. The process necessarily retains a political character, that is, it develops through collisions of various groups of society in transformation. Outbreaks of civil war and foreign wars alternate with periods of "peaceful" reforms. Revolutions in economy, technique, science, the family, morals and usages develop in complicated reciprocal action and do not allow society to reach equilibrium. Therein lies the permanent character of the socialist revolution as such.

The international character of the socialist revolution, which constitutes the third aspect of the theory of the permanent revolution, results from the present state of economy and the social structure of humanity. Internationalism is no abstract principle, but a theoretical and political reflection of the character of world economy, of the world development of productive forces, and the world scale of the class struggle. The socialist revolution begins on national grounds. But it cannot be completed on these grounds. The maintenance of the proletarian revolution within a national framework can only be a provisional state of affairs, even though, as the experience of the Soviet Union shows, one of long duration. In an isolated proletarian dictatorship, the internal and external contradictions grow inevitably together with the growing successes. Remaining isolated, the proletarian state must finally become a victim of these contradictions. The way out for it lies only in the victory of the proletariat of the advanced countries. Viewed from this standpoint, a national revolution is not a self-sufficient whole: it is only a link in the international chain. The international revolution presents a permanent process, in spite of all fleeting rises and falls.

The struggle of the epigones is directed, even if not always with the same distinctness, against all three aspects of the theory of the permanent revolution. And how could it be otherwise when it is a question of three inseparably connected parts of a whole. The epigones mechanically separate the *democratic* and the *socialist* dictatorships. They separate the *national* socialist revolution from the *international*. The conquest of power within national limits is considered by them in essence not as the initial act but as the final act of the revolution: after that follows the *period of reforms* which leads to the national socialist society. In 1905, they did not even grant the idea that the proletariat could conquer power in Russia earlier than in Western Europe. In 1917, they preached the self-sufficing democratic revolution in Russia and spurned the dictatorship of the proletariat. In 1925-1927, they steered a course toward the national revolution in China under the leadership of the bourgeoisie. Subsequently, they raised the slogan for China of the democratic dictatorship of the workers and peasants—in opposition to the dictatorship of the proletariat. They proclaimed the possibility of the construction of an isolated and self-sufficient socialist society in the Soviet Union. The world revolution became for them, instead of an indispensable precondition for victory, only a favourable circumstance. This profound breach with Marxism was reached by the epigones in the process of the permanent struggle against the theory of the permanent revolution.

The struggle, which began with an artificial revival of historical reminiscences and the falsification of the distant past, led to the complete transformation of the world outlook of the ruling stratum of the revolution. We have already repeatedly set forth that this transvaluation of values was accomplished under the influence of the social requirements of the Soviet bureaucracy, which became ever more conservative, strove for national order, and demanded that the already achieved revolution, which insured the privileged positions to the bureaucracy, now be considered adequate for the peaceful construction of socialism. We do not wish to return to this theme here. Let it simply be observed that the bureaucracy is deeply conscious of the connection of its material and ideological positions with the theory of national socialism. This is being expressed most crassly right now, in spite of or rather because of the fact that the Stalinist apparatus, under the pressure of contradictions which it did not foresee, is driving to the Left with all its might and inflicting quite severe blows upon its Right wing inspirers of yesterday. The hostility of the bureaucrats toward the Marxist Opposition, whose slogans and arguments they have borrowed in great haste, does not, as is known, diminish in the least. The condemnation of the theory of the permanent revolution above all, and an acknowledgment, even if only indirect, of the theory of socialism in one country, is demanded of the Oppositionists who raise the question of their readmission into the party for the purpose of supporting the course toward industrialization, and so forth. By this, the Stalinist bureaucracy reveals the purely *tactical* character of its swing to the Left with the retention of the national reformist *strategical* foundations. It is superfluous to explain what this means; in politics as in the military affairs, tactics are subordinated in the long run, to strategy.

The question has long ago grown out of the specific sphere of the struggle against "Trotskyism." Gradually extending itself, it has today literally embraced all the problems of the revolutionary world outlook. Permanent revolution *or* socialism in one country—this alternative embraces at the same time the internal problems of the Soviet Union, the perspectives of the revolution in the East, and finally, the fate of the whole Communist International.

LEON TROTSKY: *Fourteen Propositions on the Permanent Revolution* [14]

I hope that the reader will not object if . . . I attempt to formulate briefly the most fundamental conclusions.

1. The theory of the permanent revolution now demands the greatest attention of every Marxist, for the course of the ideological and class struggle has finally and conclusively raised this question from the realm of reminiscences over the old differences of opinion among Russian Marxists and converted it into a question of the character, the inner coherence and the methods of the international revolution in general.

2. With regard to the countries with a belated bourgeois development, especially the colonial and semi-colonial countries, the theory of the permanent revolution signifies that the complete and genuine solution of their tasks, *democratic and national emancipation,* is conceivable only through the dictatorship of the proletariat as the leader of the subjugated nation, above all of its peasant masses.

3. Not only the agrarian, but also the national question, assigns to the peasantry, the overwhelming majority of the population of the backward countries, an important place in the democratic revolution. Without an alliance of the proletariat with the peasantry, the tasks of the democratic revolution cannot be solved, nor even seriously posed. But the alliance of these two classes can be realized in no other way than through an intransigent struggle against the influence of the national liberal bourgeoisie.

4. No matter how the first episodic stages of the revolution may be in the individual countries, the realization of the revolutionary alliance between the proletariat and the peasantry is conceivable only under the political direction of the proletarian vanguard, organized in the Communist party. This in turn means that the victory of the democratic revolution is conceivable only through the dictatorship of the proletariat which bases itself upon the alliance with the peasantry and first solves the problems of the democratic revolution.

5. The old slogan of Bolshevism—"the democratic dictatorship of the proletariat and peasantry"—expresses pre-

14. *Ibid.,* pp. 166-171. Reprinted by permission of Pioneer Publishers.

cisely the above characterized relationship of the proletariat, the peasantry and the liberal bourgeoisie. This has been confirmed by the experience of October. But the old formula of Lenin does not settle in advance the problem of what the mutual relations between the proletariat and the peasantry inside of the revolutionary bloc will be. In other words, the formula has unknown algebraic quantities which have to make way for precise arithmetical quantities in the process of historical experience. The latter showed, and under circumstances that exclude every other interpretation, that no matter how great the revolutionary role of the peasantry may be, it can nevertheless not be an independent role and even less a leading one. The peasant follows either the worker or the bourgeois. This means that the "democratic dictatorship of the proletariat and peasantry" is only conceivable as a *dictatorship of the proletariat that leads the peasant masses behind it.*

6. A democratic dictatorship of the proletariat and peasantry, as a regime that is distinguished from the dictatorship of the proletariat by its class content, might be realized only in case an independent revolutionary party could be constituted which expresses the interests of the peasants and in general of petty-bourgeois democracy—a party that is capable of conquering power with this or that aid of the proletariat and of determining its revolutionary program. As modern history teaches—especially the history of Russia in the last twenty-five years—an insurmountable obstacle on the road to the creation of a peasants' party is the economic and political dependence of the petty bourgeoisie and its deep internal differentiation, thanks to which the upper sections of the petty bourgeoisie (the peasantry) go with the big bourgeoisie in all decisive cases, especially in war and in revolution, and the lower sections—with the proletariat, while the intermediate section has the choice between the two extreme poles. Between the Kerenskiad and the Bolshevik power, between the Kuomintang and the dictatorship of the proletariat there cannot and does not lie any intermediate stage, that is, no democratic dictatorship of the workers and peasants.

7. The endeavor of the Comintern to foist upon the Eastern countries the slogan of the democratic dictatorship of the proletariat and peasantry, finally and long ago exhausted by history, can have only a reactionary effect. In so far as this slogan is counter-posed to the slogan of the

dictatorship of the proletariat, it contributes to the dissolution of the proletariat into the petty-bourgeois masses and in this manner creates better conditions for the hegemony of the national bourgeoisie and consequently for the collapse of the democratic revolution. The introduction of this slogan into the program of the Comintern is a direct betrayal of Marxism and of the October traditions of Bolshevism.

8. The dictatorship of the proletariat which has risen to power as the leader of the democratic revolution is inevitably and very quickly placed before tasks that are bound up with deep inroads into the rights of bourgeois property. The democratic revolution grows over immediately into the socialist, and thereby becomes a *permanent* revolution.

9. The conquest of power by the proletariat does not terminate the revolution, but only opens it. Socialist construction is conceivable only on the foundation of the class struggle, on a national and international scale. This struggle, under the conditions of an overwhelming predominance of capitalist relationships in the world arena, will inevitably lead to explosions, that is, internally to civil wars, and externally to revolutionary wars. Therein lies the permanent character of the socialist revolution as such, regardless of whether it is a backward country that is involved, which only yesterday accomplished its democratic revolution, or an old capitalist country, which already has behind it a long epoch of democracy and parliamentarianism.

10. The completion of the socialist revolution within national limits is unthinkable. One of the basic reasons for the crisis in bourgeois society is the fact that the productive forces created by it conflict with the framework of the national state. From this follow, on the one hand, imperialist wars, and on the other, the utopia of the bourgeois United States of Europe. The socialist revolution commences on the national arena, is developed further on the inter-state and finally on the world arena. Thus, the socialist revolution becomes a permanent revolution in a newer and broader sense of the word; it attains completion only in the final victory of the new society on our entire planet.

11. The above outlined schema of the development of the world revolution eliminates the question of the coun-

tries that are "mature" or "immature" for socialism in the spirit of that pedantic, lifeless classification given by the present program of the Comintern. In so far as capitalism has created the world market, the division of labor and productive forces throughout the world, it has also prepared world economy for socialist transformation.

The various countries will go through this process at different tempos. Backward countries, under certain conditions, can arrive at the dictatorship of the proletariat sooner than the advanced countries, but they come later than the latter to socialism.

A backward colonial or semi-colonial country, whose proletariat is insufficiently prepared to unite the peasantry and seize power, is thereby incapable of bringing the democratic revolution to its conclusion. On the contrary, in a country where the proletariat has power in its hands as the result of the democratic revolution, the subsequent fate of the dictatorship and socialism is not only and not so much dependent in the final analysis upon the national productive forces, as it is upon the development of the international socialist revolution.

12. The theory of socialism in one country which rose on the yeast of the reaction against October is the only theory that consistently, and to the very end, opposes the theory of the permanent revolution.

The attempt of the epigones, under the blows of our criticism, to confine the application of the theory of socialism in one country exclusively to Russia, because of its specific characteristics (its extensiveness and its natural resources) does not improve matters but only makes them worse. The break with the international position always leads to a national messianism, that is, to attribute special prerogatives and peculiarities to one's own country, which would permit it to play a role that other countries cannot attain.

The world division of labor, the dependence of Soviet industry upon foreign technique, the dependence of the productive forces of the advanced countries of Europe upon Asiatic raw materials, etc., etc., make the construction of a socialist society in any single country impossible.

13. The theory of Stalin-Bucharin not only contrasts the democratic revolution quite mechanically to the socialist revolution, but also tears the national revolution from the international path.

This theory sets the revolution in the backward countries the task of establishing an unrealizable regime of the democratic dictatorship, it contrasts this regime to the dictatorship of the proletariat, thus introducing illusion and fiction into politics, paralyzing the struggle for power of the proletariat in the East, and hampering the victory of the colonial revolution.

The very seizure of power by the proletariat signifies, from the standpoint of the theory of the epigones, the completion of the revolution (to "nine-tenths," according to Stalin's formula) and the opening of the epoch of national reform. The theory of the kulak growing into socialism and the theory of the "neutralization" of the world bourgeoisie are consequently inseparable from the theory of socialism in one country. They stand and fall together.

By the theory of national socialism, the Communist International is degraded to a weapon useful only for the struggle against military intervention. The present policy of the Comintern, its regime, and the selection of its leading personnel, correspond entirely to the debasement of the Communist International to an auxiliary corps which is not destined to solve independent tasks.

14. The program of the Comintern created by Bucharin is thoroughly eclectic. It makes the hopeless attempt to reconcile the theory of socialism in one country with Marxian internationalism, which is, however, inseparable from the permanent character of the world revolution. The struggle of the Communist Left Opposition for a correct policy and a healthy regime in the Communist International is inseparably combined with a struggle for a Marxian program. The question of the program in turn is inseparable from the question of the two mutually exclusive theories: the theory of permanent revolution and the theory of socialism in one country. The problem of the permanent revolution has long ago outgrown the episodic differences of opinion between Lenin and Trotsky, which were completely exhausted by history. The struggle is between the basic ideas of Marx and Lenin on the one side and the eclectics of the Centrists on the other.

LEON TROTSKY: *Life in the Socialist Future* [15]

There is no doubt that, in the future—and the farther we go, the more true it will be—such monumental tasks as the planning of city gardens, of model houses, of railroads, and of ports, will interest vitally not only engineering architects, participators in competitions, but the large popular masses as well. The imperceptible, ant-like piling up of quarters and streets, brick by brick, from generation to generation will give way to titanic constructions of city-villages, with map and compass in hand. Around this compass will be formed true peoples' parties, the parties of the future for special technology and construction, which will agitate passionately, hold meetings and vote. In this struggle, architecture will again be filled with the spirit of mass feelings and moods, only on a much higher plane, and mankind will educate itself plastically, it will become accustomed to look at the world as submissive clay for sculpting the most perfect forms of life. The wall between art and industry will come down. The great style of the future will be formative, not ornamental. Here the Futurists are right. But it would be wrong to look at this as a liquidating of art, as a voluntary giving way to technique.

Take the penknife as an example. The combination of art and technique can proceed along two fundamental lines; either art embellishes the knife and pictures an elephant, a prize beauty, or the Eiffel Tower on its handle; or art helps technique to find an "ideal" form for the knife, that is, such a form which will correspond most adequately to the material of a knife and its purpose. To think that this task can be solved by purely technical means is incorrect, because purpose and material allow for an innumerable number of variations. To make an "ideal" knife, one must have, besides the knowledge of the properties of the material and the methods of its use, both imagination and taste. In accord with the entire tendency of industrial culture, we think that the artistic imagination in creating material objects will be directed toward working out the ideal form of a thing, as a thing, and not toward the embellishment of the thing as an esthetic premium to

15. From *Literature and Revolution* (New York, 1957), pp. 249-256.

itself. If this is true for penknives, it will be truer still for wearing apparel, furniture, theaters and cities. This does not mean the doing away with "machine-made" art, not even in the most distant future. But it seems that the direct co-operation between art and all branches of technique will become of paramount importance.

Does this mean that industry will absorb art, or that art will lift industry up to itself on Olympus? This question can be answered either way, depending on whether the problem is approached from the side of industry, or from the side of art. But in the object attained, there is no difference between either answer. Both answers signify a gigantic expansion of the scope and artistic quality of industry, and we understand here, under industry, the entire field without excepting the industrial activity of man; mechanical and electrified agriculture will also become part of industry.

The wall will fall not only between art and industry, but simultaneously between art and nature also. This is not meant in the sense of Jean Jacques Rousseau, that art will come nearer to a state of nature, but that nature will become more "artificial." The present distribution of mountains and rivers, of fields, of meadows, of steppes, of forests and of seashores, cannot be considered final. Man has already made changes in the map of nature that are not few nor insignificant. But they are mere pupils' practice in comparison with what is coming. Faith merely promises to move mountains; but technology, which takes nothing "on faith," is actually able to cut down mountains and move them. Up to now this was done for industrial purposes (mines) or for railways (tunnels); in the future this will be done on an immeasurably larger scale, according to a general industrial and artistic plan. Man will occupy himself with re-registering mountains and rivers, and will earnestly and repeatedly make improvements in nature. In the end, he will have rebuilt the earth, if not in his own image, at least according to his own taste. We have not the slightest fear that this taste will be bad. . . .

The new man, who is only now beginning to plan and to realize himself, will not contrast a barn-floor for grouse and a drag-net for sturgeons with a crane and a steam-hammer, as does Kliuev and Razumnik after him. Through the machine, man in Socialist society will command nature in its entirety, with its grouse and its sturgeons. He will point out places for mountains and for passes. He will change the course of the rivers, and he will lay down rules for the oceans. The idealist simpletons may say that this will be a bore, but that is why they are simpletons. Of course this does not mean that the entire globe will be marked off into boxes, that the forests will be turned into parks and gardens. Most likely, thickets and forests and grouse and tigers will remain, but only where man commands them to remain. And man will do it so well that the tiger won't even notice the machine, or feel the change, but will live as he lived in primeval times. The machine is not in opposition to the earth. The machine is the instrument of modern man in every field of life. The present-day city is transient. But it will not be dissolved back again into the old village. On the contrary, the village will rise in fundamentals to the plane of the city. Here lies the principal task. The city is transient, but it points to the future, and indicates the road. The present village is entirely of the past. That is why its esthetics seem archaic, as if they were taken from a museum of folk art.

Mankind will come out of the period of civil wars much poorer from terrific destructions, even without the earthquakes of the kind that occurred in Japan. The effort to conquer poverty, hunger, want in all its forms, that is, to conquer nature, will be the dominant tendency for decades to come. The passion for mechanical improvements, as in America, will accompany the first stage of every new Socialist society. The passive enjoyment of nature will disappear from art. Technique will become a more powerful inspiration for artistic work, and later on the contradiction itself between technique and nature will be solved in a higher synthesis.

The personal dreams of a few enthusiasts today for making life more dramatic and for educating man himself rhythmically, find a proper and real place in this outlook. Having rationalized his economic system, that is, having saturated it with consciousness and planfulness, man will not leave a trace of the present stagnant and worm-eaten domestic life. The care for food and education, which lies like a millstone on the present-day family, will be removed, and will become the subject of social intiative and of an endless collective creativeness. Woman will at last free herself from her semi-servile condition. Side by side with technique, education, in the broad sense of the psycho-physical molding of new generations, will take its place as the crown of social thinking. Powerful "parties" will form themselves around pedagogic systems. Experiments in social education and an emulation of different methods will take place to a degree which has not been dreamed of before. Communist life will not be formed blindly, like coral islands, but will be built consciously, will be tested by thought, will be directed and corrected. Life will cease to be elemental, and for this reason stagnant. Man, who will learn how to move rivers and mountains, how to build peoples' palaces on the peaks of Mont Blanc and at the bottom of the Atlantic, will not only be able to add to his own life richness, brilliancy and intensity, but also a dynamic quality of the highest degree. The shell of life will hardly have time to form before it will burst open again under the pressure of new technical and cultural inventions and achievements. Life in the future will not be monotonous.

More than that. Man at last will begin to harmonize himself in earnest. He will make it his business to achieve beauty by giving the movement of his own limbs the utmost precision, purposefulness and economy in his work, his walk and his play. He will try to master first the semiconscious and then the subconscious processes in his own organism, such as breathing, the circulation of the blood, digestion, reproduction, and, within necessary limits, he will try to subordinate them to the control of reason and will. Even purely physiologic life will become subject to collective experiments. The human species, the coagulated *homo sapiens*, will once more enter into a state of radical transformation, and, in his own hands, will become an object of the most complicated methods of artificial selection and psycho-physical training. This is entirely in accord with evolution. Man first drove the dark elements out of industry and ideology, by displacing barbarian routine by scientific technique, and religion by science. Afterward he drove the unconscious out of politics, by overthrowing monarchy and class with democracy and rationalist parliamentarianism and then with the clear and open Soviet dictatorship. The blind elements have settled most heavily in economic relations, but man is driving them out from there also, by means of Socialist organization of economic life. This makes it possible to reconstruct fundamentally the traditional family life. Finally, the nature of man himself is hidden in the deepest and darkest corner of the unconscious, of the elemental, of the subsoil. Is it not self-evident that the greatest efforts of investigative thought and of creative initiative will be in that direction? The human race will not have ceased to crawl on all fours before God, kings and capital, in order later to submit humbly before the dark laws of heredity and a blind sexual selection! Emancipated man will want to attain a greater equilibrium in the work of his organs and a more proportional developing and wearing out of his tissues, in order to reduce the fear of death to a rational reaction of the organism toward danger. There can be no doubt that man's extreme anatomical and physiological disharmony, that is, the extreme disproportion in the growth and wearing out of organs and tissues, give the life instinct the form of a pinched, morbid and hysterical fear of death, which darkens reason and which feeds the stupid and humiliating fantasies about life after death.

Man will make it his purpose to master his own feelings, to raise his instincts to the heights of consciousness, to make them transparent, to extend the wires of his will into hidden recesses, and thereby to raise himself to a new plane, to create a higher social biologic type, or, if you please, a superman.

It is difficult to predict the extent of self-government which the man of the future may reach or the heights to which he may carry his technique. Social construction and psycho-physical self-education will become two aspects of one and the same process. All the arts—literature, drama, painting, music and architecture will lend this process beautiful form. More correctly, the shell in which the cultural construction and self-education of Communist man will be enclosed, will develop all the vital elements of contemporary art to the highest point. Man will become immeasurably stronger, wiser and subtler; his body will become more harmonized, his movements more rhythmic, his voice more musical. The forms of life will become dynamically dramatic. The average human type will rise to the heights of an Aristotle, a Goethe, or a Marx. And above this ridge new peaks will rise.

10. The Stalinist Consolidation

JOSEPH STALIN: *Foundations of Leninism*[1]

The idea of "permanent" revolution is not new. It was propounded for the first time by Marx at the end of the forties in his well-known *Address to the Communist League* (1850). This document is the source from which our "permanentists" derived the idea of uninterrupted revolution. It should be noted, however, that, in taking it from Marx, our "permanentists" slightly altered it and in altering it "spoiled" it and made it unfit for practical use. The skillful hand of Lenin was needed to correct this error, to bring out Marx's idea of uninterrupted revolution in its pure form and make it a cornerstone of his theory of the revolution.

This is what Marx says in regard to uninterrupted revolution in his *Address*. After enumerating a number of the revolutionary-democratic demands which he called upon the Communists to win, he says:

> While the democratic petty bourgeois wish to bring the revolution to a conclusion as quick as possible, and with the achievement, at most, of the above demands, it is our interest and our task to make the revolution permanent, until all more or less possessing classes have been displaced from domination, until the proletariat has conquered state power and the association of proletarians, not only in one country but in all the dominant countries of the world, has advanced so far that completion among the proletarians of these countries has ceased and that at least the decisive productive forces are concentrated in the hands of the proletarians.

1. This is the 1924 speech in which Stalin defines what he is going to mean by "Leninism." From *Leninism* (New York, 1933), pp. 38-41, 44-49, 96-97. Reprinted by permission of International Publishers Co., Inc.

In other words:

a. The plan of our "permanentists" *notwithstanding*, Marx did not at all propose to *begin* the revolution in the Germany of the fifties with the direct establishment of the proletarian power.

b. Marx proposed the establishment of proletarian state power merely as the *crowning* event of the revolution, after hurling step by step one section of the bourgeoisie after another from its height of power, in order to ignite the torch of revolution in every country after the proletariat had come to power. Now this is *perfectly consistent* with all that Lenin taught, with all that he did in the course of our revolution in pursuit of his theory of the proletarian revolution in an imperalist environment.

It turns out that our Russian "permanentists" have not only underestimated the role of the peasantry in the Russian revolution and the importance of the conception of the hegemony of the proletariat, but have modified (for the worse) the Marxian idea of "permanent" revolution and deprived it of all practical value.

That is why Lenin ridiculed their theory, ironically calling it "original" and "splendid," and accused them of refusing to "think why life, during a whole decade, has passed by this beautiful theory."

That is why he thought this theory was semi-Menshevik and said that it takes from the Bolsheviks their call for the decisive revolutionary struggle of the proletariat and for the conquest of political power by it; from the Mensheviks it takes the "negation" of the role of the peasantry.

This then, is how Lenin conceived the growth of the bourgeois-democratic revolution into the proletarian revolution and the utilization of the bourgeois revolution for the "immediate" transition to the proletarian revolution.

Let us continue. Formerly, the victory of the revolution in a single country was considered impossible, on the assumption that the combined action of the proletarians of all, or at least of a majority, of the advanced countries was necessary in order to achieve victory over the bourgeoisie. This point of view no longer corresponds with reality. Now we must start out from the possibility of such a victory, because the uneven and spasmodic character of the development of the various capitalist countries in the conditions of imperialism, the development of catastrophic contradictions within imperialism, leading inevitably to wars, the growth of the revolutionary movement in all countries of the world—all these lead, not only to the possibility, but also to the necessity of the victory of the proletariat in individual countries. The history of the Russian revolution is definite proof of that. In this connection it need only be borne in mind that the overthrow of the bourgeoisie can be successfully accomplished only when there are certain indispensable prerequisites, in the absence of which the proletariat cannot even dream of seizing power.

This is what Lenin says of these prerequisites in his pamphlet, *"Left-Wing" Communism, etc.*:

The fundamental law of revolution, confirmed by all three Russian revolutions of the twentieth century, is as follows: It is not sufficient for revolution that the exploited and oppressed masses understand the impossibility of living in the old way and demand changes; for revolution, it is necessary that the exploiters should not be able to live and rule in the old way. Only when the "lower classes" *do not want the old,* and when the "upper classes" *cannot continue in the old way,* then only can revolution succeed. This truth may be expressed in other words: *Revolution is impossible without a national crisis, affecting both the exploited and the exploiters.** It follows that for revolution it is essential, first, that a majority of the workers (or at least a majority of the class conscious, thinking, politically active workers) should fully understand the necessity for revolution, and be ready to sacrifice their lives for it; secondly, that the ruling classes be in a state of governmental crisis, which draws even the most backward masses into politics ... weakens the government and makes it possible for the revolutionaries to overthrow it rapidly.

But overthrowing the power of the bourgeoisie and establishing the power of the proletariat in a single country does not yet guarantee the complete victory of socialism. After consolidating its power and leading the peasantry after it, the proletariat of the victorious country can and must build up socialist society. But does that mean that in this way the proletariat will secure a complete and final victory for socialism, i. e., does it mean that with the

* My italics—J.S.

forces of a single country it can finally consolidate socialism and fully guarantee that country against intervention, which means against restoration? Certainly not. That requires victory for the revolution in at least several countries. It is therefore the essential task of the victorious revolution in one country to develop and support the revolution in others. So the revolution in a victorious country ought not to consider itself as a self-contained unit, but as an auxiliary and a means of hastening the victory of the proletariat in other countries.

Lenin has tersely expressed this thought by saying that the task of the victorious revolution is to do the "utmost possible in one country *for* the development, support and stirring up of the revolution *in all countries.*"

These in general are the characteristic features of Lenin's theory of proletarian revolution.

The Dictatorship of the Proletariat

From this theme I will take three main questions. . . .
1. *The Dictatorship of the Proletariat as the Instrument of the Proletarian Revolution*
The question of the proletarian dictatorship is above all a question of the basic content of the proletarian revolution. The proletarian revolution, its movement, its sweep and its achievements acquire flesh and blood only through the dictatorship of the proletariat. The dictatorship of the proletariat is the weapon of the proletarian revolution, its organ, its most important stronghold which is called into being, first, to crush the resistance of the overthrown exploiters and to consolidate its achievements; secondly, to lead the proletarian revolution to its completion, to lead the revolution onward to the complete victory of socialism. Victory over the bourgeoisie and the overthrow of its power may be gained by revolution even without the dictatorship of the proletariat. But the revolution will not be in a position to crush the resistance of the bourgeoisie, maintain its victory and move on to the decisive victory for socialism, unless at a certain stage of its development it creates a special organ in the form of the dictatorship of the proletariat as its principal bulwark. . . .

2. *The Dictatorship of the Proletariat as the Domination of the Proletariat over the Bourgeoisie*

. . . The dictatorship of the proletariat does not arise on the basis of the bourgeois order; it arises while this order is being torn down, after the overthrow of the bourgeoisie, in the process of the expropriation of the landlords and capitalists, during the process of socialization of the principal instruments and means of production, in the process of violent proletarian revolution. The dictatorship of the proletariat is a revolutionary power based on violence against the bourgeoisie.

The state is an instrument in the hands of the ruling class for suppressing the resistance of its class enemies. *In this respect* the dictatorship of the proletariat in no way differs, in essence, from the dictatorship of any other class, for the proletarian state is an instrument for the suppression of the bourgeoisie. Nevertheless, there is an *essential* difference between the two, which is, that all class states that have existed heretofore have been dictatorships of an exploiting minority over the exploited majority, whereas the dictatorship of the proletariat is the dictatorship of the exploited majority over an exploiting minority.

To put it briefly: *the dictatorship of the proletariat is the domination of the proletariat over the bourgeoisie, untrammeled by law and based on violence and enjoying the sympathy and support of the toiling and exploited masses.*

From this two fundamental deductions may be drawn.

First deduction: the dictatorship of the proletariat cannot be "complete" democracy, a democracy for *all,* for rich and poor alike; the dictatorship of the proletariat "must be a state that is democratic in *a new way—for** the proletariat and the poor in general—and dictatorial in *a new way—against** the bourgeoisie. . . ." The talk of Kautsky and Co. about universal equality, about "pure" democracy, about "perfect" democracy and the like, are but bourgeois screens to conceal the indubitable fact that equality between exploited and exploiters is impossible. The theory of "pure" democracy is the theory of the upper stratum of the working class which is tamed and fed by the imperialist plunderers. It was invented to hide the sores of capitalism, to camouflage imperialism and lend it moral strength in its struggle against the exploited masses. Under the capitalist system there is no true "freedom" for the exploited, nor can there be, if for no other reason than that the buildings, printing plants, paper supplies, etc., indispensable for the

* My italics—J.S.

actual enjoyment of this "freedom," are the privilege of the exploiters. Under the capitalist system the exploited masses do not, nor can they, really participate in the administration of the country, if for no other reason than that even with the most democratic system under capitalism, the governments are set up not by the people, but by the Rothschilds and Stinneses, the Morgans and Rockefellers. Democracy under the capitalist system is *capitalist* democracy, the democracy of an exploiting minority based upon the restriction of the rights of the exploited majority and directed against this majority. Only under the dictatorship of the proletariat is real "freedom" for the exploited and real participation in the administration of the country by the proletarians and peasants possible. Under the dictatorship of the proletariat, democracy is *proletarian* democracy —the democracy of the exploited majority based upon the restriction of the rights of the exploiting minority and directed against this minority.

Second deduction: the dictatorship of the proletariat cannot come about as a result of the peaceful development of bourgeois society and of bourgeois democracy; it can come only as the result of the destruction of the bourgeois state machine, of the bourgeois army, of the bourgeois civil administration and of the bourgeois police. . . .

Of course, in the remote future, if the proletariat is victorious in the most important capitalist countries and if the present capitalist encirclement gives way to a socialist encirclement, a "peaceful" course of development is quite possible for some of the capitalist countries whose capitalists, in view of the "unfavorable" international situation, will consider it advisable "voluntarily" to make substantial concessions to the proletariat. But this supposition deals only with the remote and possible future; it has no bearing whatever on the immediate future.

Lenin is therefore right in saying: "The proletarian revolution is impossible without the violent destruction of the bourgeois state machine and its replacement by a *new one.*"

3. The Soviet Power as the State Form of the Dictatorship of the Proletariat

The victory of the dictatorship of the proletariat signifies the suppression of the bourgeoisie, the break-up of the bourgeois state machine and the replacement of bourgeois democracy by proletarian democracy. That is clear. But what organizations are to be employed in order to carry out this colossal work? There can hardly be any doubt that the old forms of organization of the proletariat which grew up with bourgeois parliamentarianism as their base, are not equal to this task. What are the new forms of organization of the proletariat that can serve as the grave-digger of the bourgeois state machine, that are capable not only of breaking this machine, not only of replacing bourgeois democracy by proletarian democracy, but also of serving as the foundation of the state power of the proletariat?

This new form of organization of the proletariat is the soviets.

In what lies the strength of the soviets as compared with the old forms of organization?

In that the soviets are the most *all-embracing* mass organization of the proletariat, for they and they alone embrace all workers without exception. . . .

The Role of the Party

The proletariat needs the Party *for* the purpose of achieving and maintaining the dictatorship. The Party is the instrument of the dictatorship of the proletariat. From this it follows that when classes disappear and the dictatorship of the proletariat dies out, the Party will also die out.

The achievement and maintenance of the dictatorship of the proletariat are impossible without a party strong in its cohesion and iron discipline. But iron discipline in the Party is impossible without unity of will and without absolute and complete unity of action on the part of all members of the Party. This does not mean of course that the possibility of a conflict of opinion within the Party is thus excluded. On the contrary, iron discipline does not preclude but presupposes criticism and conflicts of opinion within the Party. Least of all does it mean that this discipline must be "blind" discipline. On the contrary, iron discipline does not preclude but presupposes conscious and voluntary submission, for only conscious discipline can be truly iron discipline. But after a discussion has been closed, after criticism has run its course and a decision has been made, unity of will and unity of action of all Party members become indispensable conditions without which Party unity and iron discipline in the Party are inconceivable.

In the present epoch of intensified civil war—says Lenin—the Communist Party can discharge its duty only if it is organized with the highest degree of centralization, ruled by iron discipline bordering on military discipline, and if its Party center proves to be a potent authoritative body invested with broad powers and enjoying the general confidence of the Party members.

This is the position in regard to discipline in the Party in the period of struggle preceding the establishment of the dictatorship.

The same thing applies, but to a greater degree, to discipline in the Party after the establishment of the dictatorship.

In this connection, Lenin said: "Whoever in the least weakens the iron discipline of the party of the proletariat (especially during its dictatorship) actually aids the bourgeoisie against the proletariat."

It follows that the existence of factions is incompatible with Party unity and with its iron discipline. It need hardly be emphasized that the existence of factions leads to the creation of a number of centers, and the existence of a number of centers connotes the absence of a common center in the Party, a breach in the unity of will, the weakening and disintegration of discipline, the weakening and disintegration of the dictatorship. It is true that the parties of the Second International, which are fighting against the dictatorship of the proletariat and have no desire to lead the proletariat to power, can permit themselves the luxury of such liberalism as freedom for factions, for they have no need whatever of iron discipline. But the parties of the Communist International, which organize their activities on the basis of the task of achieving and strengthening the dictatorship of the proletariat, cannot afford to be "liberal" or to permit the formation of factions. The Party is synonymous with unity of will, which leaves no room for any factionalism or division of authority in the Party.

JOSEPH STALIN: *The October Revolution and Tactics* [2]

Formerly it was commonly thought that the revolution would develop through the even "ripening" of the elements of socialism, especially in the more developed, the more "advanced" countries. At the present time this view must be considerably modified.

The system of international relationships—says Lenin —has now become such that in Europe one state, namely, Germany, has been enslaved by the victorious states. Next, a number of states including the oldest states of the West have proved, as a result of their victory, to be in a position to take advantage of this victory to make a number of unimportant concessions to their oppressed classes, concessions which nevertheless delay the revolutionary movement in those countries and create some semblance of "social peace."

At the same time a whole series of countries, the Orient, India, China, etc., by reason of the last imperialist war, have proved to be completely thrown out of their orbits. Their development has once and for all been directed along the general European and capitalist path. The general European ferment has begun to work in them. And it is now clear to the entire world that they have been drawn into a line of development which cannot but lead to the crisis of world capitalism.

In view of this fact and in connection with it:

The West European capitalist countries are completing their development toward socialism . . . not as we formerly expected, not by the even "maturing" of socialism in these countries, but through the exploitation of some states by others, through the exploitation of the first state that was defeated in the imperialist war in conjunction with the exploitation of the entire East. The East, on the other hand, has definitely entered the revolutionary movement as a result of this first imperialist

2. *Ibid.*, pp. 134-137. Reprinted by permission of International Publishers Co., Inc.

war; it has definitely been drawn into the common whirl-pool of the world revolutionary movement.

If we add to this the fact that not only the defeated countries and colonies are being exploited by the victorious countries, but that some of the victorious countries have fallen into the orbit of financial exploitation by the more powerful of the victorious powers, America and England; that the contradictions among all these countries form a very important factor in the decay of world capitalism; that, in addition to these contradictions very profound contradictions exist and are developing within each one of these countries; that all these contradictions are growing in profundity and acuteness because of the existence, alongside these countries, of the republic of Soviets—if all this is taken into consideration, then the picture of the peculiar nature of the international situation becomes more or less complete.

Most probably, the world revolution will develop along the line of a series of new countries dropping out of the system of the imperialist countries as a result of revolution, while the proletarians of these countries will be supported by the proletariat of the imperialist states. We see that the first country to break away, the first country to win is already supported by the workers and toiling masses of other countries. Without this support it could not maintain itself. Beyond a doubt, this support will grow and become stronger and stronger. But it is likewise beyond a doubt that the very development of the world revolution, the very process of the breaking away of a number of new countries from imperialism will be more rapid and more thorough, the more thoroughly socialism fortifies itself in the first victorious country, the faster this country is transformed into the basis for the further unfolding of the world revolution, into the lever for the further disintegration of imperialism.

If the postulate that the *final* victory of socialism in the first country to emancipate itself is impossible without the combined efforts of the proletarians of several countries is true, then it is equally true that the more effective the assistance rendered by the first socialist country to the workers and toiling masses of all other countries, the more rapid and thorough will be the development of the world revolution.

By what should this assistance be expressed?

It should be expressed, first, by the victorious country achieving the "utmost possible in one country *for* the development, support and stirring up of the revolution *in all countries.*"

Second, it should be expressed in that the "victorious proletariat" of one country, "having expropriated the capitalists and organized its own socialist production, would rise . . . against the rest of the capitalist world, attract to itself the oppressed classes of other countries, raise revolts among them against the capitalists, and in the event of necessity, come out even with armed force against the exploiting classes and their states."

The characteristic feature of the assistance given by the victorious country is that it not only hastens the victory of the proletarians of other countries, but likewise guarantees, by facilitating this victory, the *final* victory of socialism in the first victorious country.

The most probable thing is that, side by side with the centers of imperialism in separate capitalist countries and the systems of these countries throughout the world, centers of socialism will be created, in the course of the world revolution, in separate Soviet countries and systems of these centers throughout the world, and the struggle between these two systems will constitute the history of the development of the revolution: "For"—says Lenin—"the free federation of nations in socialism is impossible without a more or less prolonged and stubborn struggle by the socialist republics against the backward states."

The world significance of the October Revolution lies not only in its constituting a great start made by one country in the work of breaking through the system of imperialism and the creation of the first land of socialism in the ocean of imperialist countries, but likewise in its constituting the first stage in the world revolution and a mighty basis for its further development.

Therefore, those who, forgetting the international character of the October Revolution, declare the victory of socialism in one country to be purely national, and only a national phenomenon, are wrong. And those too, who, although bearing in mind the international character of the October Revolution, are inclined to regard this revolution as something passive, merely destined to accept help from without, are equally wrong. As a matter of fact not only does the October Revolution need support from the revolutionary movement of other countries, but revolution in those countries needs the support of the October Revolution in order to accelerate and advance the cause of overthrowing world imperialism.

JOSEPH STALIN: *Bases and Superstructure* [3]

The superstructure is a product of the [economic] base; but this does not mean that it merely reflects the base, that it is passive, neutral, indifferent to the fate of its base, to the fate of the classes, to the character of the system. On the contrary, no sooner does it arise than it becomes an exceedingly active force, actively assisting its base to take shape and consolidate itself, and doing everything it can to help the new system finish off and eliminate the old base and the old classes.

It cannot be otherwise. The base creates the superstructure precisely in order that it may serve it, that it may actively help it to take shape and consolidate itself, that it may actively strive for the elimination of the old, moribund base and its old superstructure. The superstructure has only to renounce its role of auxiliary, it has only to pass from a position of active defense of its base to one of indifference toward it, to adopt the same attitude to all classes, and it loses its virtue and ceases to be a superstructure.

* * *

Marxism holds that the transition of a language from an old quality to a new does not take place by way of an explosion, by the destruction of an existing language and the creation of a new one, but by the gradual accumulation of the elements of the new quality, and, hence, by the gradual dying away of the elements of the old quality.

It should be said in general for the benefit of comrades who have an infatuation for such explosions that the law of transition from an old quality to a new by means of an explosion is inapplicable not only to the history of the development of languages; it is not always applicable to some other social phenomena of a basal or superstructural char-

3. From *Marxism and Linguistics* (New York, 1951), pp. 10, 27-28. Reprinted by permission of International Publishers Co., Inc.

acter. It is compulsory for a society divided into hostile classes. But it is not at all compulsory for a society which has no hostile classes. In a period of eight to ten years we effected a transition in the agriculture of our country from the bourgeois individual-peasant system to the socialist, collective-farm system. This was a revolution which eliminated the old bourgeois economic system in the countryside and created a new, socialist system. But this revolution did not take place by means of an explosion, that is, by the overthrow of the existing power and the creation of a new power, but by a gradual transition from the old bourgeois system of the countryside to a new system. And we succeeded in doing this because it was a revolution from above, because the revolution was accomplished on the initiative of the existing power with the support of the overwhelming mass of the peasantry.

JOSEPH STALIN: *Inevitability of Wars Between Capitalist Countries* [4]

Some comrades hold that, owing to the development of new international conditions since the Second World War, wars between capitalist countries have ceased to be inevitable. They consider that the contradictions between the socialist camp and the capitalist camp are more acute than the contradictions among the capitalist countries; that the U.S.A. has brought the other capitalist countries sufficiently under its sway to be able to prevent them going to war among themselves and weakening one another; that the foremost capitalist minds have been sufficiently taught by the two world wars and the severe damage they caused to the whole capitalist world, not to venture to involve the capitalist countries in war with one another again—and that, because of all this, wars between capitalist countries are no longer inevitable.

These comrades are mistaken. They see the outward phenomena that come and go on the surface, but they do not see those profound forces which, although they are so far operating imperceptibly, will nevertheless determine the course of developments.

Outwardly, everything would seem to be "going well":

4. From *Economic Problems of Socialism in the USSR* (New York, 1952), pp. 27-30. Reprinted by permission of International Publishers Co., Inc.

the U.S.A. has put Western Europe, Japan and the other capitalist countries on rations; Germany (Western), Britain, France, Italy and Japan have fallen into the clutches of the U.S.A. and are meekly obeying its commands. But it would be mistaken to think that things can continue to "go well" for "all eternity," that these countries will tolerate the domination and oppression of the United States endlessly, that they will not endeavor to tear loose from American bondage and take the path of independent development.

Take, first of all, Britain and France. Undoubtedly, they are imperialist countries. Undoubtedly, cheap raw materials and secure markets are of paramount importance to them. Can it be assumed that they will endlessly tolerate the present situation, in which, under the guise of "Marshall plan aid," Americans are penetrating into the economies of Britain and France and trying to convert them into adjuncts of the United States economy, and American capital is seizing raw materials and markets in the British and French colonies and thereby plotting disaster for the high profits of the British and French capitalists? Would it not be truer to say that capitalist Britain, and, after her, capitalist France, will be compelled in the end to break from the embrace of the U.S.A. and enter into conflict with it in order to secure an independent position and, of course, high profits?

Let us pass to the major vanquished countries, Germany (Western) and Japan. These countries are now languishing in misery under the jackboot of American imperialism. Their industry and agriculture, their trade, their foreign and home policies, and their whole life are fettered by the American occupation "regime." Yet only yesterday these countries were great imperialist powers and were shaking the foundations of the domination of Britain, the U.S.A. and France in Europe and Asia. To think that these countries will not try to get on their feet again, will not try to smash U.S. domination and force their way to independent development, is to believe in miracles.

It is said that the contradictions between capitalism and socialism are stronger than the contradictions among the capitalist countries. Theoretically, of course, that is true. It is not only true now, today; it was true before the Second World War. And it was more or less realized by the leaders of the capitalist countries. Yet the Second World

War began not as a war with the U.S.S.R., but as a war between capitalist countries. Why? Firstly, because war with the U.S.S.R., as a socialist land, is more dangerous to capitalism than war between capitalist countries; for whereas war between capitalist countries puts in question only the supremacy of certain capitalist countries over others, war with the U.S.S.R. must certainly put in question the existence of capitalism itself. Secondly, because the capitalists, although they clamor, for "propaganda" purposes, about the aggressiveness of the Soviet Union, do not themselves believe that it is aggressive, because they are aware of the Soviet Union's peaceful policy and know that it will not itself attack capitalist countries.

After the First World War it was similarly believed that Germany had been definitely put out of action, just as certain comrades now believe that Japan and Germany have been definitely put out of action. Then, too, it was said and clamored in the press that the United States had put Europe on rations; that Germany would never rise to her feet again, and that there would be no more wars between capitalist countries. In spite of this, Germany rose to her feet again as a great power within the space of some fifteen or twenty years after her defeat, having broken out of bondage and taken the path of independent development. And it is significant that it was none other than Britain and the United States that helped Germany to recover economically and to enhance her economic war potential. Of course, when the United States and Britain assisted Germany's economic recovery, they did so with a view to setting a recovered Germany against the Soviet Union, to utilizing her against the land of socialism. But Germany directed her forces in the first place against the Anglo-French-American bloc. And when Hitler Germany declared war on the Soviet Union, the Anglo-French-American bloc, far from joining with Hitler Germany, was compelled to enter into a coalition with the U.S.S.R. against Hitler Germany.

Consequently, the struggle of the capitalist countries for markets and their desire to crush their competitors proved in practice to be stronger than the contradictions between the capitalist camp and the socialist camp.

What guarantee is there, then, that Germany and Japan will not rise to their feet again, will not attempt to break out of American bondage and live their own independent lives? I think there is no such guarantee.

But it follows from this that the inevitability of wars between capitalist countries remains in force.

It is said that Lenin's thesis that imperialism inevitably generates war must now be regarded as obsolete, since powerful popular forces have come forward today in defense of peace and against another world war. That is not true.

The object of the present-day peace movement is to rouse the masses of the people to fight for the preservation of peace and for the prevention of another world war. Consequently, the aim of this movement is not to overthrow capitalism and establish socialism—it confines itself to the democratic aim of preserving peace. In this respect, the present-day peace movement differs from the movement of the time of the First World War for the conversion of the imperialist war into civil war, since the latter movement went farther and pursued socialist aims.

It is possible that in a definite conjuncture of circumstances, the fight for peace will develop here or there into a fight for socialism. But then it will no longer be the present-day peace movement; it will be a movement for the overthrow of capitalism.

What is most likely, is that the present-day peace movement, as a movement for the preservation of peace, will, if it succeeds, result in preventing a *particular* war, in its temporary postponement, in the temporary preservation of a *particular* peace, in the resignation of a bellicose government and its supersession by another that is prepared temporarily to keep the peace. That, of course, will be good. Even very good. But, all the same, it will not be enough to eliminate the inevitability of wars between capitalist countries generally. It will not be enough, because, for all the successes of the peace movement, imperialism will remain, continue in force—and, consequently, the inevitability of wars will also continue in force.

To eliminate the inevitability of war, it is necessary to abolish imperialism.

11. Critics of Stalinism

ROSA LUXEMBURG: *Democracy and Dictatorship* [1]

The basic error of the Lenin-Trotsky theory is that they too, just like Kautsky, oppose dictatorship to democracy. "Dictatorship *or* democracy" is the way the question is put by Bolsheviks and Kautsky alike. The latter naturally decides in favor of "democracy," that is, of bourgeois democracy, precisely because he opposes it to the alternative of the socialist revolution. Lenin and Trotsky, on the other hand, decide in favor of dictatorship in contradistinction to democracy, and thereby, in favor of the dictatorship of a handful of persons, that is, in favor of dictatorship on the bourgeois model. They are two opposite poles, both alike being far removed from a genuine socialist policy. The proletariat, when it seizes power, can never follow the good advice of Kautsky, given on the pretext of the "unripeness of the country," the advice being to renounce the socialist revolution and devote itself to democracy. It cannot follow this advice without betraying thereby itself, the International, and the revolution. It should and must at once undertake socialist measures in the most energetic, unyielding and unhesitant fashion, in other words, exercise a dictatorship, but a dictatorship of the *class*, not of a party or of a clique—dictatorship of the class, that means in the broadest public form on the basis of the most active, unlimited participation of the mass of the people, of unlimited democracy.

"As Marxists," writes Trotsky, "we have never been idol worshipers of formal democracy." Surely, we have never been idol worshipers of formal democracy. Nor have we ever been idol worshipers of socialism or Marxism either. Does it follow from this that we may also throw socialism on the scrap-heap, à la Cunow, Lensch, and Par-

1. From *The Russian Revolution* (New York, 1940), pp. 52-56.

vus, if it becomes uncomfortable for us? Trotsky and Lenin are the living refutation of this answer.

"We have never been idol-worshipers of formal democracy." All that that really means is: We have always distinguished the social kernel from the political form of *bourgeois* democracy; we have always revealed the hard kernel of social inequality and lack of freedom hidden under the sweet shell of formal equality and freedom—not in order to reject the latter but to spur the working class into not being satisfied with the shell, but rather, by conquering political power, to create a socialist democracy to replace bourgeois democracy—not to eliminate democracy altogether.

But socialist democracy is not something which begins only in the promised land after the foundations of socialist economy are created; it does not come as some sort of Christmas present for the worthy people who, in the interim, have loyally supported a handful of socialist dictators. Socialist democracy begins simultaneously with the beginnings of the destruction of class rule and of the construction of socialism. It begins at the very moment of the seizure of power by the socialist party. It is the same thing as the dictatorship of the proletariat.

Yes, dictatorship! But his dictatorship consists in the *manner of applying democracy*, not in its *elimination*, in energetic, resolute attacks upon the well-entrenched rights and economic relationships of bourgeois society, without which a socialist transformation cannot be accomplished. But this dictatorship must be the work of the *class* and not of a little leading minority in the name of the class—that is, it must proceed step by step out of the active participation of the masses; it must be under their direct influence, subjected to the control of complete public activity; it must arise out of the growing political training of the mass of the people.

Doubtless the Bolsheviks would have proceeded in this very way were it not that they suffered under the frightful compulsion of the world war, the German occupation and all the abnormal difficulties connected therewith, things which were inevitably bound to distort any socialist policy, however imbued it might be with the best intentions and the finest principles.

A crude proof of this is provided by the use of terror to so wide an extent by the Soviet government, especially in the most recent period just before the collapse of German imperialism, and just after the attempt on the life of the German ambassador. The commonplace to the effect that revolutions are not pink teas is in itself pretty inadequate.

Everything that happens in Russia is comprehensible and represents an inevitable chain of causes and effects, the starting point and end term of which are: the failure of the German proletariat and the occupation of Russia by German imperialism. It would be demanding something superhuman from Lenin and his comrades if we should expect of them that under such circumstances they should conjure forth the finest democracy, the most exemplary dictatorship of the proletariat and a flourishing socialist economy. By their determined revolutionary stand, their exemplary strength in action, and their unbreakable loyalty to international socialism, they have contributed whatever could possibly be contributed under such devilishly hard conditions. The danger begins only when they make a virtue of necessity and want to freeze into a complete theoretical system all the tactics forced upon them by these fatal circumstances, and want to recommend them to the international proletariat as a model of socialist tactics. When they get in their own light in this way, and hide their genuine, unquestionable historical service under the bushel of false steps forced upon them by necessity, they render a poor service to international socialism for the sake of which they have fought and suffered; for they want to place in its storehouse as new discoveries all the distortions prescribed in Russia by necessity and compulsion— in the last analysis only by-products of the bankruptcy of international socialism in the present world war.

Let the German Government Socialists cry that the rule of the Bolsheviks in Russia is a distorted expression of the dictatorship of the proletariat. If it was or is such, that is only because it is a product of the behavior of the German proletariat, in itself a distorted expression of the socialist class struggle. All of us are subject to the laws of history, and it is only internationally that the socialist order of society can be realized. The Bolsheviks have shown that they are capable of everything that a genuine revolutionary party can contribute within the limits of the historical possibilities. They are not supposed to perform miracles. For a model and faultless proletarian revolution in an isolated land, exhausted by world war, strangled by imperialism, betrayed by the international proletariat, would be a miracle.

What is in order is to distinguish the essential from the non-essential, the kernel from the accidental excrescences in the policies of the Bolsheviks. In the present period, when we face decisive final struggles in all the world, the most important problem of socialism was and is the burning question of our time. It is not a matter of this or that secondary question of tactics, but of the capacity for action of the proletariat, the strength to act, the will to power of socialism as such. In this, Lenin and Trotsky and their friends were the *first*, those who went ahead as an example to the proletariat of the world; they are still the *only ones* up to now who can cry with Hutten: "I have dared!"

This is the essential and *enduring* in Bolshevik policy. In *this* sense theirs is the immortal historical service of having marched at the head of the international proletariat with the conquest of political power and the practical placing of the problem of the realization of socialism, and of having advanced mightily the settlement of the score between capital and labor in the entire world. In Russia the problem could only be posed. It could not be solved in Russia. And in *this* sense, the future everywhere belongs to "Bolshevism."

LEON TROTSKY: *The Rise of Soviet Bureaucracy* [2]

The historian of the Soviet Union cannot fail to conclude that the policy of the ruling bureaucracy upon great questions has been a series of contradictory zigzags. The attempt to explain or justify them by "changing circumstances" obviously won't hold water. To guide means at least in some degree to exercise foresight. The Stalin faction have not in the slightest degree foreseen the inevitable results of the development; they have been caught napping every time. They have reacted with mere administrative reflexes. The theory of each successive turn has been created after the fact, and with small regard for what they were teaching yesterday. On the basis of the

2. From *The Revolution Betrayed* (New York, 1945), pp. 86-114, 248-256. Reprinted by permission of Pioneer Publishers.

same irrefutable facts and documents, the historian will be compelled to conclude that the so-called "Left Opposition" offered an immeasurably more correct analysis of the processes taking place in the country, and far more truly foresaw their further development.

This assertion is contradicted at first glance by the simple fact that the faction which could not see ahead was steadily victorious, while the more penetrating group suffered defeat after defeat. That kind of objection, which comes automatically to mind, is convincing, however, only for those who think rationalistically, and see in politics a logical argument or a chess match. A political struggle is in its essence a struggle of interests and forces, not of arguments. The quality of the leadership is, of course, far from a matter of indifference for the outcome of the conflict, but it is not the only factor, and in the last analysis is not decisive. Each of the struggling camps moreover demands leaders in its own image.

The February revolution raised Kerensky and Tseretelli to power, not because they were "cleverer" or "more astute" than the ruling tsarist clique, but because they represented, at least temporarily, the revolutionary masses of the people in their revolt against the old regime. Kerensky was able to drive Lenin underground and imprison other Bolshevik leaders, not because he excelled them in personal qualification, but because the majority of the workers and soldiers in those days were still following the patriotic petty bourgeoisie. The personal "superiority" of Kerensky, if it is suitable to employ such a word in this connection, consisted in the fact that he did not see farther than the overwhelming majority. The Bolsheviks in their turn conquered the petty bourgeois democrats, not through the personal superiority of their leaders, but through a new correlation of social forces. The proletariat had succeeded at last in leading the discontented peasantry against the bourgeoisie.

The consecutive stages of the great French Revolution, during its rise and fall alike, demonstrate no less convincingly that the strength of the "leaders" and "heroes" that replaced each other consisted primarily in their correspondence to the character of those classes and strata which supported them. Only this correspondence and not any irrelevant superiorities whatever, permitted each of them to place

the impress of his personality upon a certain historic
period. . . .

It is sufficiently well known that every revolution up to
this time has been followed by a reaction, or even a counter-revolution. This, to be sure, has never thrown the nation all the way back to its starting point, but it has always taken from the people the lion's share of their conquests. The victims of the first reactionary wave have
been, as a general rule, those pioneers, initiators, and in-
stigators who stood at the head of the masses in the period
of the revolutionary offensive. In their stead people of
the second line, in league with the former enemies of the
revolution, have been advanced to the front. Beneath this
dramatic duel of "coryphées" on the open political scene,
shifts have taken place in the relations between classes,
and, no less important, profound changes in the psychology
of the recently revolutionary masses.

Answering the bewildered questions of many comrades
as to what has become of the activity of the Bolshevik party
and the working class—where is its revolutionary initiative,
its spirit of self-sacrifice and plebeian pride—why, in place
of all this, has appeared so much vileness, cowardice, pusillanimity and careerism—Rakovsky referred to the life
story of the French revolution of the eighteenth century,
and offered the example of Babeuf, who on emerging from
the Abbaye prison likewise wondered what had become of
the heroic people of the Parisian suburbs. A revolution is a
mighty devourer of human energy, both individual and
collective. The nerves give way. Consciousness is shaken
and characters are worn out. Events unfold too swiftly for
the flow of fresh forces to replace the loss. Hunger, unemployment, the death of the revolutionary cadres, the
removal of the masses from administration, all this led
to such a physical and moral impoverishment of the Parisian suburbs that they required three decades before they
were ready for a new insurrection.

The axiomlike assertions of the Soviet literature, to the
effect that the laws of bourgeois revolutions are "inapplicable" to a proletarian revolution, have no scientific content whatever. The proletarian character of the October
revolution was determined by the world situation and by
a special correlation of internal forces. But the classes
themselves were formed in the barbarous circumstances

of tsarism and backward capitalism, and were anything but made to order for the demands of a socialist revolution. The exact opposite is true. It is for the very reason that a proletariat still backward in many respects achieved in the space of a few months the unprecedented leap from a semifeudal monarchy to a socialist dictatorship, that the reaction in its ranks was inevitable. This reaction has developed in a series of consecutive waves. External conditions and events have vied with each other in nourishing it. Intervention followed intervention. The revolution got no direct help from the west. Instead of the expected prosperity of the country an ominous destitution reigned for long. Moreover, the outstanding representatives of the working class either died in the civil war, or rose a few steps higher and broke away from the masses. And thus after an unexampled tension of forces, hopes and illusions, there came a long period of weariness, decline and sheer disappointment in the results of the revolution. The ebb of the "plebeian pride" made room for a flood of pusillanimity and careerism. The new commanding caste rose to its place upon this wave.

The demobilization of the Red Army of five million played no small role in the formation of the bureaucracy. The victorious commanders assumed leading posts in the local Soviets, in economy, in education, and they persistently introduced everywhere that regime which had insured success in the civil war. Thus on all sides the masses were pushed away gradually from actual participation in the leadership of the country.

The reaction within the proletariat caused an extraordinary flush of hope and confidence in the petty bourgeois strata of town and country, aroused as they were to new life by the NEP, and growing bolder and bolder. The young bureaucracy, which had arisen at first as an agent of the proletariat, began now to feel itself a court of arbitration between the classes. Its independence increased from month to month.

The international situation was pushing with mighty forces in the same direction. The Soviet bureaucracy became more self-confident, the heavier the blows dealt to the world working class. Between these two facts there was not only a chronological, but a causal connection, and one which worked in two directions. The leaders of the bureaucracy promoted the proletarian defeats; the defeats promoted the rise of the bureaucracy. The crushing of the Bulgarian insurrection and the inglorious retreat of the German workers' party in 1923, the collapse of the Esthonian attempt at insurrection in 1924, the treacherous liquidation of the General Strike in England and the unworthy conduct of the Polish workers' party at the installation of Pilsudski in 1926, the terrible massacre of the Chinese revolution in 1927, and, finally, the still more ominous recent defeats in Germany and Austria—these are the historic catastrophes which killed the faith of the Soviet masses in world revolution, and permitted the bureaucracy to rise higher and higher as the sole light of salvation.

As to the causes of the defeat of the world proletariat during the last thirteen years, the author must refer to his other works, where he has tried to expose the ruinous part played by the leadership in the Kremlin, isolated from the masses and profoundly conservative as it is, in the revolutionary movement of all countries. Here we are concerned primarily with the irrefutable and instructive fact that the continual defeats of the revolution in Europe and Asia, while weakening the international position of the Soviet Union, have vastly strengthened the Soviet bureaucracy.

Two dates are especially significant in this historic series. In the second half of 1923, the attention of the Soviet workers was passionately fixed upon Germany, where the proletariat, it seemed, had stretched out its hand to power. The panicky retreat of the German Communist Party was the heaviest possible disappointment to the working masses of the Soviet Union. The Soviet bureaucracy straightway opened a campaign against the theory of "permanent revolution," and dealt the Left Opposition its first cruel blow. During the years 1926 and 1927 the population of the Soviet Union experienced a new tide of hope. All eyes were now directed to the East where the drama of the Chinese revolution was unfolding. The Left Opposition had recovered from the previous blows and was recruiting a phalanx of new adherents. At the end of 1927 the Chinese revolution was massacred by the hangman, Chiang Kai-shek, into whose hands the Communist International had literally betrayed the Chinese workers and peasants. A cold wave of disappointment swept over the masses of the Soviet Union. After an unbridled baiting in the press and at meetings, the bureaucracy finally, in 1928, ventured upon mass arrests among the Left Opposition.

To be sure, tens of thousands of revolutionary fighters gathered around the banner of the Bolshevik-Leninists. The advanced workers were indubitably sympathetic to the Opposition, but that sympathy remained passive. The masses lacked faith that the situation could be seriously changed by a new struggle. Meantime the bureaucracy asserted: "For the sake of an international revolution, the Opposition proposes to drag us into a revolutionary war. Enough of shake-ups! We have earned the right to rest. We will build the socialist society at home. Rely upon us, your leaders!" This gospel of repose firmly consolidated the *apparatchiki* and the military and state officials and indubitably found an echo among the weary workers, and still more the peasant masses. Can it be, they asked themselves, that the Opposition is actually ready to sacrifice the interests of the Soviet Union for the idea of "permanent revolution"? In reality, the struggle had been about the life interests of the Soviet state. The false policy of the International in Germany resulted ten years later in the victory of Hitler—that is, in a threatening war danger from the West. And the no less false policy in China reinforced Japanese imperialism and brought very much nearer the danger in the East. But periods of reaction are characterized above all by a lack of courageous thinking.

The Opposition was isolated. The bureaucracy struck while the iron was hot, exploiting the bewilderment and passivity of the workers, setting their more backward strata against the advanced, and relying more and more boldly upon the kulak and the petty bourgeois ally in general. In the course of a few years, the bureaucracy thus shattered the revolutionary vanguard of the proletariat.

It would be naïve to imagine that Stalin, previously unknown to the masses, suddenly issued from the wings full armed with a complete strategical plan. No indeed. Before he felt out his own course, the bureaucracy felt out Stalin himself. He brought it all the necessary guarantees: the prestige of an old Bolshevik, a strong character, narrow vision, and close bonds with the political machine as the sole source of his influence. The success which fell upon him was a surprise at first to Stalin himself. It was the friendly welcome of the new ruling group, trying to free itself from the old principles and from the control of the masses, and having need of a reliable arbiter in its inner affairs. A secondary figure before the masses and in the events of the revolution, Stalin revealed himself as the indubitable leader of the Thermidorian bureaucracy, as first in its midst.

The new ruling caste soon revealed its own ideas, feelings and, more important, its interests. The overwhelming majority of the older generation of the present bureaucracy had stood on the other side of the barricades during the October revolution. . . . Or at best they had stood aside from the struggle. Those of the present bureaucrats who were in the Bolshevik camp in the October days played in the majority of cases no considerable role. As for the young bureaucrats, they have been chosen and educated by the elders, frequently from among their own offspring. These people could not have achieved the October revolution, but they were perfectly suited to exploit it.

Personal incidents in the interval between these two historic chapters were not, of course, without influence. Thus the sickness and death of Lenin undoubtedly hastened the denouement. Had Lenin lived longer, the pressure of bureaucratic power would have developed, at least during the first years, more slowly. But as early as 1926 Krupskaya said, in a circle of Left Oppositionists: "If Ilych were alive, he would probably already be in prison." The fears and alarming prophecies of Lenin himself were then still fresh in her memory, and she cherished no illusions as to his personal omnipotence against opposing historic winds and currents.

The bureaucracy conquered something more than the Left Opposition. It conquered the Bolshevik party. It defeated the program of Lenin, who had seen the chief danger in the conversion of the organs of the state "from servants of society to lords over society." It defeated all these enemies, the Opposition, the party and Lenin, not with ideas and arguments, but with its own social weight. The leaden rump of the bureaucracy outweighed the head of the revolution. That is the secret of the Soviet's Thermidor.

The Bolshevik party prepared and insured the October victory. It also created the Soviet state, supplying it with a sturdy skeleton. The degeneration of the party became both cause and consequence of the bureaucratization of the state. It is necessary to show at least briefly how this happened.

The inner regime of the Bolshevik party was character-ized by the method of *democratic centralism*. The com-bination of these two concepts, democracy and centralism, is not in the least contradictory. The party took watchful care not only that its boundaries should always be strictly defined, but also that all those who entered these bound-aries should enjoy the actual right to define the direction of the party policy. Freedom of criticism and intellectual struggle was an irrevocable content of the party democ-racy. The present doctrine that Bolshevism does not toler-ate factions is a myth of the epoch of decline. In reality the history of Bolshevism is a history of the struggle of factions. And, indeed, how could a genuinely revolutionary organization, setting itself the task of overthrowing the world and uniting under its banner the most audacious iconoclasts, fighters and insurgents, live and develop with-out intellectual conflicts, without groupings and temporary factional formations? The farsightedness of the Bolshevik leadership often made it possible to soften conflicts and shorten the duration of factional struggle, but no more than that. The Central Committee relied upon this seething democratic support. From this it derived the audacity to make decisions and give orders. The obvious correctness of the leadership at all critical stages gave it that high au-thority which is the priceless moral capital of centralism.

The regime of the Bolshevik party, especially before it came to power, stood thus in complete contradiction to the regime of the present sections of the Communist Inter-national, with their "leaders" appointed from above, mak-ing complete changes of policy at a word of command, with their uncontrolled apparatus, haughty in its attitude to the rank and file, servile in its attitude to the Kremlin. But in the first years after the conquest of power also, even when the administrative rust was already visible on the party, every Bolshevik, not excluding Stalin, would have de-nounced as a malicious slanderer anyone who should have shown him on a screen the image of the party ten or fifteen years later.

The very center of Lenin's attention and that of his colleagues was occupied by a continual concern to pro-tect the Bolshevik ranks from the vices of those in power. However, the extraordinary closeness and at times actual merging of the party with the state apparatus had already in those first years done indubitable harm to the freedom and elasticity of the party regime. Democracy had been narrowed in proportion as difficulties increased. In the beginning, the party had wished and hoped to preserve freedom of political struggle within the framework of the Soviets. The civil war introduced stern amendments into this calculation. The opposition parties were forbidden one after the other. This measure, obviously in conflict with the spirit of Soviet democracy, the leaders of Bolshevism regarded not as a principle, but as an episodic act of self-defense.

The swift growth of the ruling party, with the novelty and immensity of its tasks, inevitably gave rise to inner disagreements. The underground oppositional currents in the country exerted a pressure through various channels upon the sole legal political organization, increasing the acuteness of the factional struggle. At the moment of completion of the civil war, this struggle took such sharp forms as to threaten to unsettle the state power. In March 1921, in the days of the Kronstadt revolt, which attracted into its ranks no small number of Bolsheviks, the tenth congress of the party thought it necessary to resort to a prohibition of factions—that is, to transfer the political regime prevailing in the state to the inner life of the ruling party. This forbidding of factions was again regarded as an exceptional measure to be abandoned at the first serious improvement in the situation. At the same time, the Central Committee was extremely cautious in applying the new law, concerning itself most of all lest it lead to a strangling of the inner life of the party.

However, what was in its original design merely a necessary concession to a difficult situation, proved perfectly suited to the taste of the bureaucracy, which had then begun to approach the inner life of the party exclusively from the viewpoint of convenience in administration. Already in 1922, during a brief improvement in his health, Lenin, horrified at the threatening growth of bureaucratism, was preparing a struggle against the faction of Stalin, which had made itself the axis of the party machine as a first step toward capturing the machinery of state. A second stroke and then death prevented him from measuring forces with this internal reaction.

The entire effort of Stalin, with whom at that time Zinoviev and Kamenev were working hand in hand, was thenceforth directed to freeing the party machine from the control of the rank-and-file members of the party. In this struggle for "stability" of the Central Committee, Stalin proved the most consistent and reliable among his colleagues. He had no need to tear himself away from international problems; he had never been concerned with them. The petty bourgeois outlook of the new ruling stratum was his own outlook. He profoundly believed that the task of creating socialism was national and administrative in its nature. He looked upon the Communist International as a necessary evil which should be used so far as possible for the purposes of foreign policy. His own party kept a value in his eyes merely as a submissive support for the machine.

Together with the theory of socialism in one country, there was put into circulation by the bureaucracy a theory that in Bolshevism the Central Committee is everything and the party nothing. This second theory was in any case realized with more success than the first. Availing itself of the death of Lenin, the ruling group announced a "Leninist levy." The gates of the party, always carefully guarded, were now thrown wide open. Workers, clerks, petty officials, flocked through in crowds. The political aim of this maneuver was to dissolve the revolutionary vanguard in raw human material, without experience, without independence, and yet with the old habit of submitting to the authorities. The scheme was successful. By freeing the bureaucracy from the control of the proletarian vanguard, the "Leninist levy" dealt a death blow to the party of Lenin. The machine had won the necessary independence. Democratic centralism gave place to bureaucratic centralism. In the party apparatus itself there now took place a radical reshuffling of personnel from top to bottom. The chief merit of a Bolshevik was declared to be obedience. Under the guise of a struggle with the Opposition, there occurred a sweeping replacement of revolutionists with *chinovniks*.* The history of the Bolshevik party became a history of its rapid degeneration.

The political meaning of the developing struggle was darkened for many by the circumstance that the leaders of all three groupings, Left, Center and Right, belonged to one and the same staff in the Kremlin, the Politburo. To superficial minds it seemed to be a mere matter of personal rivalry, a struggle for the "heritage" of Lenin. But

* Professional governmental functionaries.

in the conditions of iron dictatorship social antagonisms could not show themselves at first except through the institutions of the ruling party. . . .

Of the Politburo of Lenin's epoch there now remains only Stalin. Two of its members, Zinoviev and Kamenev, collaborators of Lenin throughout many years as émigrés, are enduring ten-year prison terms for a crime which they did not commit. Three other members, Rykov, Bukharin and Tomsky, are completely removed from the leadership, but as a reward for submission occupy secondary posts. And, finally, the author of these lines is in exile. The widow of Lenin, Krupskaya, is also under the ban, having proved unable with all her efforts to adjust herself completely to the Thermidor.

The members of the present Politburo occupied secondary posts throughout the history of the Bolshevik party. If anybody in the first years of the revolution had predicted their future elevation, they would have been the first in surprise, and there would have been no false modesty in their surprise. For this very reason, the rule is more stern at present that the Politburo is always right, and in any case that no man can be right against the Politburo. But, moreover, the Politburo cannot be right against Stalin, who is unable to make mistakes and consequently cannot be right against himself.

Demands for party democracy were through all this time the slogans of all the oppositional groups, as insistent as they were hopeless. The above-mentioned platform of the Left Opposition demanded in 1927 that a special law be written into the Criminal Code "punishing as a serious state crime every direct or indirect persecution of a worker for criticism." Instead of this, there was introduced into the Criminal Code an article against the Left Opposition itself.

Of party democracy there remained only recollections in the memory of the older generation. And together with it had disappeared the democracy of the soviets, the trade unions, the co-operatives, the cultural and athletic organizations. Above each and every one of them there reigns an unlimited hierarchy of party secretaries. The regime had become "totalitarian" in character several years before this word arrived from Germany. "By means of demoralizing methods, which convert thinking communists into machines, destroying will, character and human dignity," wrote Rakovsky in 1928, "the ruling circles have succeeded in converting themselves into an unremovable and inviolate oligarchy, which replaces the class and the party." Since those indignant lines were written, the degeneration of the regime has gone immeasurably farther. The G.P.U. has become the decisive factor in the inner life of the party. If Molotov in March 1936 was able to boast to a French journalist that the ruling party no longer contains any factional struggle, it is only because disagreements are now settled by the automatic intervention of the political police. The old Bolshevik party is dead, and no force will resurrect it.

Parallel with the political degeneration of the party, there occurred a moral decay of the uncontrolled apparatus. . . .

The conquest of power changes not only the relations of the proletariat to other classes, but also its own inner structure. The wielding of power becomes the specialty of a definite social group, which is the more impatient to solve its own "social problem," the higher its opinion of its own mission. "In a proletarian state, where capitalist accumulation is forbidden to the members of the ruling party, the differentiation is at first functional, but afterward becomes social. I do not say it becomes a class differentiation, but a social one . . ." Rakovsky further explains: "The social situation of the communist who has at his disposition an automobile, a good apartment, regular vacations, and receives the party maximum of salary, differs from the situation of the communist who works in the coal mines, where he receives from fifty to sixty rubles a month."

* * *

We are far from intending to contrast the abstraction of dictatorship with the abstraction of democracy, and weigh their merits on the scales of pure reason. Everything is relative in this world, where change alone endures. The dictatorship of the Bolshevik party proved one of the most powerful instruments of progress in history. But here too, in the words of the poet, "Reason becomes unreason, kindness a pest." The prohibition of oppositional parties brought after it the prohibition of factions. The prohibition of factions ended in a prohibition to think otherwise than the infallible leaders. The police-manufactured monolith-ism of the party resulted in a bureaucratic impunity which has become the source of all kinds of wantonness and cor-ruption.

We have defined the Soviet Thermidor as a triumph of the bureaucracy over the masses. We have tried to disclose the historic conditions of this triumph. The revolutionary vanguard of the proletariat was in part devoured by the administrative apparatus and gradually demoralized, in part annihilated in the civil war, and in part thrown out and crushed. The tired and disappointed masses were indiffer-ent to what was happening on the summits. These condi-tions, however, important as they may have been in them-selves, are inadequate to explain why the bureaucracy suc-ceeded in raising itself above society and getting its fate firmly into its own hands. Its own will to this would in any case be inadequate; the arising of a new ruling stratum must have deep social causes.

The victory of the Thermidorians over the Jacobins in the eighteenth century was also aided by the weariness of the masses and the demoralization of the leading cadres, but beneath these essentially incidental phenomena a deep organic process was taking place. The Jacobins rested upon the lower petty bourgeoisie lifted by the great wave. The revolution of the eighteenth century, however, corre-sponding to the course of development of the productive forces, could not but bring the great bourgeoisie to politi-cal ascendancy in the long run. The Thermidor was only one of the stages in this inevitable process. What similar social necessity found expression in the Soviet Thermidor? . . . . Let us again compare theoretic prophecy with reality. "It is still necessary to suppress the bourgeoisie and its re-sistance," wrote Lenin in 1917, speaking of the period which should begin immediately after the conquest of power, "but the organ of suppression here is now the ma-jority of the population, and not the minority as has here-tofore always been the case. . . . In that sense the state *is beginning to die away*." In what does this dying away ex-press itself? Primarily in the fact that "in place of special institutions of a privileged minority (privileged officials, commanders of a standing army), the majority itself can directly carry out" the functions of suppression. Lenin follows this with a statement axiomatic and unanswerable:

"The more universal becomes the very fulfillment of the functions of the state power, the less need is there of this power." The annulment of private property in the means of production removes the principal task of the historic state—defense of the proprietary privileges of the minority against the overwhelming majority.

The dying away of the state begins, then, according to Lenin, on the very day after the expropriation of the expropriators—that is, before the new regime has had time to take up its economic and cultural problems. Every success in the solution of these problems means a further step in the liquidation of the state, its dissolution in the socialist society. The degree of this dissolution is the best index of the depth and efficacy of the socialist structure. We may lay down approximately this sociological theorem: The strength of the compulsion exercised by the masses in a workers' state is directly proportional to the strength of the exploitive tendencies, or the danger of a restoration of capitalism, and inversely proportional to the strength of the social solidarity and the general loyalty to the new regime. Thus the bureaucracy—that is, the "privileged officials and commanders of a standing army"—represents a special kind of compulsion which the masses cannot or do not wish to exercise, and which, one way or another, is directed against the masses themselves.

If the democratic soviets had preserved to this day their original strength and independence, and yet were compelled to resort to repressions and compulsions on the scale of the first years, this circumstance might of itself give rise to serious anxiety. How much greater must be the alarm in view of the fact that the mass soviets have entirely disappeared from the scene, having turned over the function of compulsion to Stalin, Yagoda, and company. And what forms of compulsion! First of all we must ask ourselves: What social cause stands behind this stubborn virility of the state and especially behind its policification? The importance of this question is obvious. In dependence upon the answer, we must either radically revise our traditional views of the socialist society in general, or as radically reject the official estimates of the Soviet Union.

Let us now take from the latest number of a Moscow newspaper a stereotyped characterization of the present Soviet regime, one of those which are repeated throughout the country from day to day and which school children learn by heart: "In the Soviet Union the parasitical classes of capitalists, landlords and kulaks are completely liquidated, and thus is forever ended the exploitation of man by man. The whole national economy has become socialistic, and the growing Stakhanov movement is preparing the conditions for a transition from socialism to communism." (*Pravda*, April 4, 1936.) The world press of the Communist International, it goes without saying, has no other thing to say on this subject. But if exploitation is "ended forever," if the country is really now on the road from socialism, that is, the lowest stage of communism, to its higher stage, then there remains nothing for society to do but to throw off at last the straitjacket of the state. In place of this—it is hard even to grasp this contrast with the mind!—the Soviet state has acquired a totalitarian-bureaucratic character.

The same fatal contradiction finds illustration in the fate of the party. Here the problem may be formulated approximately thus: Why, from 1917 to 1921, when the old ruling classes were still fighting with weapons in their hands, when they were actively supported by the imperialists of the whole world, when the kulaks in arms were sabotaging the army and food supplies of the country—why was it possible to dispute openly and fearlessly in the party about the most critical questions of policy? Why now, after the cessation of intervention, after the shattering of the exploiting classes, after the indubitable successes of industrialization, after the collectivization of the overwhelming majority of the peasants, is it impossible to permit the slightest word of criticism of the unremovable leaders? Why is it that any Bolshevik who should demand a calling of the congress of the party in accordance with its constitution would be immediately expelled, any citizen who expressed out loud a doubt of the infallibility of Stalin would be tried and convicted almost as though a participant in a terrorist plot? Whence this terrible, monstrous and unbearable intensity of repression and of the police apparatus?

Theory is not a note which you can present at any moment to reality for payment. If a theory proves mistaken we must revise it or fill out its gaps. We must find out those real social forces which have given rise to the contrast between Soviet reality and the traditional Marxian conception. In any case we must not wander in the dark, repeating ritual phrases, useful for the prestige of the leaders, but which nevertheless slap the living reality in the face. We shall now see a convincing example of this.

In a speech at a session of the Central Executive Committee in January 1936, Molotov, the president of the Council of People's Commissars, declared: "The national economy of the country has become socialistic (applause). In that sense we have solved the problem of the liquidation of classes (applause)." However, there still remain from the past "elements in their nature hostile to us," fragments of the former ruling classes. Moreover, among the collectivized farmers, state employees and sometimes also the workers, "petty speculators" are discovered, "grafters in relation to the collective and state wealth, anti-Soviet gossips, etc." And hence results the necessity of a further reinforcement of the dictatorship. In opposition to Engels, the workers' state must not "fall asleep," but on the contrary become more and more vigilant.

The picture drawn by the head of the Soviet government would be reassuring in the highest degree, were it not murderously self-contradictory. Socialism completely reigns in the country: "In that sense" classes are abolished. (If they are abolished in that sense, then they are in every other.) To be sure, the social harmony is broken here and there by fragments and remnants of the past, but it is impossible to think that scattered dreamers of a restoration of capitalism, deprived of power and property, together with "petty speculators" (not even *speculators!*) and "gossips" are capable of overthrowing the classless society. Everything is getting along, it seems, the very best you can imagine. But what is the use then of the iron dictatorship of the bureaucracy?

Those reactionary dreamers, we must believe, will gradually die out. The "petty speculators" and "gossips" might be disposed of with a laugh by the super-democratic Soviets. "We are not Utopians," responded Lenin in 1917 to the bourgeois and reformist theoreticians of the bureaucratic state, and "by no means deny the possibility and inevitability of excesses on the part of *individual persons,* and likewise the necessity for suppressing *such* excesses. But . . . for this there is no need of a special machine, a special apparatus of repression. This will be done by the armed people themselves, with the same simplicity and ease with which any crowd of civilized people even in contemporary society separate a couple of fighters or stop an act of violence against a woman." Those words sound as though the author had especially foreseen the remarks of one of his successors at the head of the government. Lenin is taught in the public schools of the Soviet Union, but apparently not in the Council of People's Commissars. Otherwise it would be impossible to explain Molotov's daring to resort without reflection to the very construction against which Lenin directed his well-sharpened weapons. The flagrant contradiction between the founder and his epigones is before us! Whereas Lenin judged that even the liquidation of the exploiting classes might be accomplished without a bureaucratic apparatus, Molotov, in explaining why *after* the liquidation of classes the bureaucratic machine has strangled the independence of the people, finds no better pretext than a reference to the "remnants" of the liquidated classes.

To live on these "remnants" becomes, however, rather difficult since, according to the confession of authoritative representatives of the bureaucracy itself, yesterday's class enemies are being successfully assimilated by the Soviet society. Thus Postyshev, one of the secretaries of the Central Committee of the party, said in April 1936, at a congress of the League of Communist Youth: "Many of the sabotagers . . . have sincerely repented and joined the ranks of the Soviet people." In view of the successful carrying out of collectivization, "the children of kulaks are not to be held responsible for their parents." And yet more: "The kulak himself now hardly believes in the possibility of a return to his former position of exploiter in the village." Not without reason did the government annul the limitations connected with social origin! But if Postyshev's assertion, wholly agreed to by Molotov, makes any sense it is only this: Not only has the bureaucracy become a monstrous anachronism, but state compulsion in general has nothing whatever to do in the land of the Soviets. However, neither Molotov nor Postyshev agrees with that immutable inference. They prefer to hold the power even at the price of self-contradiction.

In reality, too, they cannot reject the power. Or, to translate this into objective language: The present Soviet society cannot get along without a state, nor even—within limits—without a bureaucracy. But the cause of this is by no means the pitiful remnants of the past, but the mighty forces and tendencies of the present. The justification for the existence of a Soviet state as an apparatus of compulsion lies in the fact that the present transitional structure is still full of social contradictions, which in the sphere of *consumption*—most close and sensitively felt by all—are extremely tense, and forever threaten to break over into the sphere of production. The triumph of socialism cannot be called either final or irrevocable.

The basis of bureaucratic rule is the poverty of society in objects of consumption, with the resulting struggle of each against all. When there is enough goods in a store, the purchasers can come whenever they want to. When there is little goods, the purchasers are compelled to stand in line. When the lines are very long, it is necessary to appoint a policeman to keep order. Such is the starting point of the power of the Soviet bureaucracy. It "knows" who is to get something and who has to wait.

A raising of the material and cultural level ought, at first glance, to lessen the necessity of privileges, narrow the sphere of application of "bourgeois law," and thereby undermine the standing ground of its defenders, the bureaucracy. In reality the opposite thing has happened: the growth of the productive forces has been so far accompanied by an extreme development of all forms of inequality, privilege and advantage, and therewith of bureaucratism. That too is not accidental.

In its first period, the Soviet regime was undoubtedly far more equalitarian and less bureaucratic than now. But that was equality of general poverty. The resources of the country were so scant that there was no opportunity to separate out from the masses of the population any broad privileged strata. At the same time the "equalizing" character of wages, destroying personal interestedness, became a brake upon the development of the productive forces. Soviet economy had to lift itself from its poverty to a somewhat higher level before fat deposits of privilege became possible. The present state of production is still far from guaranteeing all necessities to everybody. But it is already adequate to give significant privileges to a minority, and convert inequality into a whip for the spurring on of the majority. That is the first reason why the growth of production has so far strengthened not the socialist, but the bourgeois features of the state.

But that is not the sole reason. Alongside the economic factor dictating capitalistic methods of payment at the present stage, there operates a parallel political factor in the person of the bureaucracy itself. In its very essence it is the planter and protector of inequality. It arose in the beginning as the bourgeois organ of a workers' state. In establishing and defending the advantages of a minority, it of course draws off the cream for its own use. Nobody who has wealth to distribute ever omits himself. Thus out of a social necessity there has developed an organ which had far outgrown its socially necessary function, and become an independent factor and therewith the source of great danger for the whole social organism.

The social meaning of the Soviet Thermidor now begins to take form before us. The poverty and cultural backwardness of the masses has again become incarnate in the malignant figure of the ruler with a great club in his hand. The deposed and abused bureaucracy, from being a servant of society, has again become its lord. On this road it has attained such a degree of social and moral alienation from the popular masses, that it cannot now permit any control over either its activities or its income.

The bureaucracy's seemingly mystic fear of "petty speculator's, grafters, and gossips" thus finds a wholly natural explanation. Not yet able to satisfy the elementary needs of the population, the Soviet economy creates and resurrects at every step tendencies to graft and speculation. On the other side, the privileges of the new aristocracy awaken in the masses of the population a tendency to listen to anti-Soviet "gossips"—that is, to anyone who, albeit in a whisper, criticizes the greedy and capricious bosses. It is a question, therefore, not of specters of the past, not of the remnants of what no longer exists, not, in short, of the snows of yesteryear, but of new, mighty and continually reborn tendencies to personal accumulation. The first still very meager wave of prosperity in the country, just because of its meagerness, has not weakened, but strengthened, these centrifugal tendencies. On the other hand, there has developed simultaneously a desire of the unprivileged to slap the grasping hands of the new gentry. The social struggle again grows sharp. Such are the sources of the power of the bureaucracy. But from those same sources comes also a threat to its power.

Classes are characterized by their position in the social system of economy, and primarily by their relation to the means of production. In civilized societies, property relations are validated by laws. The nationalization of the land, the means of industrial production, transport and exchange, together with the monopoly of foreign trade, constitute the basis of the Soviet social structure. Through these relations, established by the proletarian revolution, the nature of the Soviet Union as a proletarian state is for us basically defined.

In its intermediary and regulating function, its concern to maintain social ranks, and its exploitation of the state apparatus for personal goals, the Soviet bureaucracy is similar to every other bureaucracy, especially the fascist. But it is also in a vast way different. In no other regime has a bureaucracy ever achieved such a degree of independence from the dominating class. In bourgeois society, the bureaucracy represents the interests of a possessing and educated class, which has at its disposal innumerable means of everyday control over its administration of affairs. The Soviet bureaucracy has risen above a class which is hardly emerging from destitution and darkness, and has no tradition of dominion or command. Whereas the fascists, when they find themselves in power, are united with the big bourgeoisie by bonds of common interest, friendship, marriage, etc., the Soviet bureaucracy takes on bourgeois customs without having beside it a national bourgeoisie. In this sense we cannot deny that it is something more than a bureaucracy. It is in the full sense of the word the sole privileged and commanding stratum in the Soviet society.

Another difference is no less important. The Soviet bureaucracy has expropriated the proletariat politically in order by methods of *its own* to defend the social conquests. But the very fact of its appropriation of political power in a country where the principal means of production are in the hands of the state, creates a new and hitherto unknown relation between the bureaucracy and the riches of the nation. The means of production belong to the state. But the state, so to speak, "belongs" to the bureaucracy. If these as yet wholly new relations should solidify, become the norm and be legalized, whether with or without resistance from the workers, they would, in the long run, lead to a complete liquidation of the social conquests of the proletarian revolution. But to speak of that now is at least premature. The proletariat has not yet said its last word. The bureaucracy has not yet created social supports for its dominion in the form of special types of property. It is compelled to defend state property as the source of its power and its income. In this aspect of its activity it still remains a weapon of proletarian dictatorship.

The attempt to represent the Soviet bureaucracy as a class of "state capitalists" will obviously not withstand criticism. The bureaucracy has neither stocks nor bonds. It is recruited, supplemented and renewed in the manner of an administrative hierarchy, independently of any special property relations of its own. The individual bureaucrat cannot transmit to his heirs his rights in the exploitation of the state apparatus. The bureaucracy enjoys its privileges under the form of an abuse of power. It conceals its income; it pretends that as a special social group it does not even exist. Its appropriation of a vast share of the national income has the character of social parasitism. All this makes the position of the commanding Soviet stratum in the highest degree contradictory, equivocal and undignified, not withstanding the completeness of its power and the smoke screen of flattery that conceals it.

Bourgeois society has in the course of its history displaced many political regimes and bureaucratic castes, without changing its social foundations. It has preserved itself against the restoration of feudal and guild relations by the superiority of its productive methods. The state power has been able either to co-operate with capitalist development, or put brakes on it. But in general the productive forces, upon a basis of private property and competition, have been working out their own destiny. In contrast to this, the property relations which issued from the socialist revolution are indivisibly bound up with the new state as their repository. The predominance of socialist over petty bourgeois tendencies is guaranteed, not by the automatism of the economy—we are still far from that—but by political measures taken by the dictatorship. The character of the economy as a whole thus depends upon the character of the state power.

A collapse of the Soviet regime would lead inevitably to the collapse of the planned economy, and thus to the abolition of state property. The bond of compulsion between the trusts and the factories within them would fall away. The more successful enterprises would succeed in coming out on the road of independence. They might convert themselves into stock companies, or they might find some other transitional form of property—one, for example, in which the workers should participate in the profits. The collective farms would disintegrate at the same time, and far more easily. The fall of the present bureaucratic dictatorship, if it were not replaced by a new socialist power, would thus mean a return to capitalist relations with a catastrophic decline of industry and culture.

But if a socialist government is still absolutely necessary for the preservation and development of the planned economy, the question is all the more important, upon whom the present Soviet government relies, and in what measure the socialist character of its policy is guaranteed. At the 11th Party Congress in March 1922, Lenin, in practically bidding farewell to the party, addressed these words to the commanding group: "History knows transformations of all sorts. To rely upon conviction, devotion and other excellent spiritual qualities—that is not to be taken seriously in politics." Being determines consciousness. During the last fifteen years, the government has changed its social composition even more deeply than its ideas. Since of all the strata of Soviet society the bureaucracy has best solved its own social problem, and is fully content with the existing situation, it has ceased to offer any subjective guarantee whatever of the socialist direction of its policy. It continues to preserve state property only to the extent that it fears the proletariat. This saving fear is nourished and supported by the illegal party of Bolshevik-Leninists, which is the most conscious expression of the socialist tendencies opposing that bourgeois reaction with which the Thermidorian bureaucracy is completely saturated. As a conscious political force the bureaucracy has betrayed the revolution. But a victorious revolution is fortunately not only a program and a banner, not only political institutions, but also a system of social relations. To betray it is not enough. You have to overthrow it. The October revolution has been betrayed by the ruling stratum, but not yet overthrown. It has a great power of resistance, coinciding with the established property relations, with the living force of the proletariat, the consciousness of its best elements, the impasse of world capitalism, and the inevitability of world revolution.

In order better to understand the character of the present

Soviet Union, let us make two different hypotheses about its future. Let us assume first that the Soviet bureaucracy is overthrown by a revolutionary party having all the attributes of the old Bolshevism, enriched moreover by the world experience of the recent period. Such a party would begin with the restoration of democracy in the trade unions and the Soviets. It would be able to, and would have to, restore freedom of Soviet parties. Together with the masses, and at their head, it would carry out a ruthless purgation of the state apparatus. It would abolish ranks and decorations, all kind of privileges, and would limit inequality in the payment of labor to the life necessities of the economy and the state apparatus. It would give the youth free opportunity to think independently, learn, criticize and grow. It would introduce profound changes in the distribution of the national income in correspondence with the interests and will of the worker and peasant masses. But so far as concerns property relations, the new power would not have to resort to revolutionary measures. It would retain and further develop the experiment of planned economy. After the political revolution—that is, the deposing of the bureaucracy—the proletariat would have to introduce in the economy a series of very important reforms, but not another social revolution.

If—to adopt a second hypothesis—a bourgeois party were to overthrow the ruling Soviet caste, it would find no small number of ready servants among the present bureaucrats, administrators, technicians, directors, party secretaries and privileged upper circles in general. A purgation of the state apparatus would, of course, be necessary in this case too. But a bourgeois restoration would probably have to clean out fewer people than a revolutionary party. The chief task of the new power would be to restore private property in the means of production. First of all, it would be necessary to create conditions for the development of strong farmers from the weak collective farms, and for converting the strong collectives into producers' cooperatives of the bourgeois type—into agricultural stock companies. In the sphere of industry, denationalization would begin with the light industries and those producing food. The planning principle would be converted for the transitional period into a series of compromises between state power and individual "corporations"—potential proprietors, that is, among the Soviet captains of industry, the émigré former proprietors and foreign capitalists. Notwithstanding that the Soviet bureaucracy has gone far toward preparing a bourgeois restoration, the new regime would have to introduce in the matter of forms of property and methods of industry not a reform, but a social revolution.

Let us assume—to take a third variant—that neither a revolutionary nor a counter-revolutionary party seizes power. The bureaucracy continues at the head of the state. Even under these conditions social relations will not jell. We cannot count upon the bureaucracy's peacefully and voluntarily renouncing itself in behalf of socialist equality. If at the present time, notwithstanding the too obvious inconveniences of such an operation, it has considered it possible to introduce ranks and decorations, it must inevitably in future stages seek supports for itself in property relations. One may argue that the big bureaucrat cares little what are the prevailing forms of property, provided only they guarantee him the necessary income. This argument ignores not only the instability of the bureaucrat's own rights, but also the question of his descendants. The new cult of the family has not fallen out of the clouds. Privileges have only half their worth, if they cannot be transmitted to one's children. But the right of testament is inseparable from the right of property. It is not enough to be the director of a trust; it is necessary to be a stockholder. The victory of the bureaucracy in this decisive sphere would mean its conversion into a new possessing class. On the other hand, the victory of the proletariat over the bureaucracy would insure a revival of the socialist revolution. The third variant consequently brings us back to the two first, with which, in the interests of clarity and simplicity, we set out.

To define the Soviet regime as transitional, or intermediate, means to abandon such finished social categories as *capitalism* (and therewith "state capitalism") and also *socialism*. But besides being completely inadequate in itself, such a definition is capable of producing the mistaken idea that from the present Soviet regime *only* a transition to socialism is possible. In reality a backslide to capitalism is wholly possible. A more complete definition will of necessity be complicated and ponderous.

The Soviet Union is a contradictory society halfway

between capitalism and socialism, in which: (a) the productive forces are still far from adequate to give the state property a socialist character; (b) the tendency toward primitive accumulation created by want breaks out through innumerable pores of the planned economy; (c) norms of distribution preserving a bourgeois character lie at the basis of a new differentiation of society; (d) the economic growth, while slowly bettering the situation of the toilers, promotes a swift formation of privileged strata; (e) exploiting the social antagonisms, a bureaucracy has converted itself into an uncontrolled caste alien to socialism; (f) the social revolution, betrayed by the ruling party, still exists in property relations and in the consciousness of the toiling masses; (g) a further development of the accumulating contradictions can as well lead to socialism as back to capitalism; (h) on the road to capitalism the counter-revolution would have to break the resistance of the workers; (i) on the road to socialism the workers would have to overthrow the bureaucracy. In the last analysis, the question will be decided by a struggle of living social forces, both on the national and the world arena.

Doctrinaires will doubtless not be satisfied with this hypothetical definition. They would like categorical formulae: yes—yes, and no—no. Sociological problems would certainly be simpler, if social phenomena had always a finished character. There is nothing more dangerous, however, than to throw out of reality, for the sake of logical completeness, elements which today violate your scheme and tomorrow may wholly overturn it. In our analysis, we have above all avoided doing violence to dynamic social formations which have had no precedent and have no analogies. The scientific task, as well as the political, is not to give a finished definition to an unfinished process, but to follow all its stages, separate its progressive from its reactionary tendencies, expose their mutual relations, foresee possible variants of development, and find in this foresight a basis for action.

RUDOLF HILFERDING: *State Capitalism or Totalitarian State Economy* [3]

The concept of "state capitalism" can scarcely pass the test of serious economic analysis. Once the state becomes the exclusive owner of all means of production, the functioning of a capitalist economy is rendered impossible by destruction of the mechanism which keeps the life-blood of such a system circulating. A capitalist economy is a market economy. Prices, which result from competition among capitalist owners (it is this competition that "in the last instance" gives rise to the law of value), determine what and how much is produced, what fraction of the profit is accumulated, and in what particular branches of production this accumulation occurs. They also determine how in an economy, which has to overcome crises again and again, proportionate relations among the various branches of production are re-established whether in the case of simple or expanded reproduction.

A capitalist economy is governed by the laws of the market (analyzed by Marx) and the autonomy of these laws constitutes the decisive symptom of the capitalist system of production. A state economy, however, eliminates precisely the autonomy of economic laws. It represents not a market but a consumers' economy. It is no longer price but rather a state planning commission that now determines what is produced and how. Formally, prices and wages still exist, but their function is no longer the same; they no longer determine the process of production which is now controlled by a central power that fixes prices and wages. Prices and wages become means of distribution which determine the share that the individual receives out of the sum total of products that the central power places at the disposal of society. They now constitute a technical form of distribution which is simpler than direct individual allotment of products which no longer can be classed as merchandise. Prices have become symbols of distribution and no longer comprise a regulating factor in the economy. While maintaining the form, a complete transformation of function has occurred.

3. A 1940 Social Democratic view of Stalin's Russia. From *The Modern Review*, June, 1947, pp. 266-271.

Both the "stimulating fire of competition" and the passionate striving for profit, which provide the basic incentive of capitalist production, die out. Profit means individual appropriation of surplus products and is therefore possible only on the basis of private ownership. But, objects Mr. Worrall, did Marx not consider accumulation as an essential ear-mark of capitalism and does not accumulation play a decisive role in the Russian economy? Is that not state capitalism?

Mr. Worrall has overlooked one slight detail; namely, that Marx refers to the accumulation of *capital,* of an ever-increasing amount of the means of production which produce profit and the appropriation of which supplies the driving force to capitalist production. In other words, he refers to the accumulation of value which creates surplus value; i. e., a specifically *capitalist* process of expanding economic activity.

On the other hand, the accumulation of means of production and of products is so far from being a specific feature of capitalism that it plays a decisive part in all economic systems, except perhaps in the most primitive collecting of food. In a consumer economy, in an economy organized by the state, there is not accumulation of values but of consumers' goods—products that the central power wants in order to satisfy consumers' need. The mere fact that the Russian state economy accumulates does not make it a capitalist economy, for it is not capital that is being accumulated. Mr. Worrall's argument is based on a gross confusion between value and use value. And he really believes that a socialist economy could do without accumulation!

But what then (and here we come to the basic question) is that central power that rules over the Russian economy? Trotsky and Worrall reply: "Bureaucracy." But while Trotsky refuses to consider the bureaucracy as a class (according to Marx a class is characterized by the place it occupies in the process of production), Worrall makes an amazing discovery. Soviet bureaucracy in its structure (which unfortunately he does not analyze) differs "basically" from any other bourgeoisie, but its function remains the same—the accumulation of capital. The fact that, despite great structural differences, the function can remain unchanged is, of course, a miracle that cannot occur in nature but seems (according to Worrall) possible in human society.

In any case, Worrall accepts this as evidence that Russia is dominated by a bourgeois class and thus by state capitalism. He clings obstinately to his confusion of capital and the means of production and seems unable to conceive of any form of accumulation other than capitalist accumulation. He fails to understand that accumulation (i. e. the expansion of production) in any economic system is the task of the managers of production; that even in an ideal socialist system this accumulation can result only from the surplus product (which only under capitalism takes the form of surplus value), and that the fact of accumulation in itself does not prove the capitalist nature of an economy.

But does the "bureaucracy" really "rule" the economy and consequently the people? Bureaucracy everywhere, and particularly in the Soviet Union, is composed of a conglomeration of the most varied elements. To it belong not only government officials in the narrow sense of the word (i. e. from minor employees up to the generals and even Stalin himself) but also the directors of all branches of industry and such functionaries as, for example, the postal and railway employees. How could this variegated lot possibly achieve a unified rule? Who are its representatives? How does it adopt decisions? What organs are at its disposal?

In reality, the "bureaucracy" is not an independent bearer of power. In accordance with its structure as well as function, it is only an instrument in the hands of the real rulers. It is organized as an hierarchy and subordinated to the commanding power. It receives but does not give orders. Any functionary, as Trotsky justly puts it, "can be sacrificed by his superior in the hierarchical system in order to decrease any kind of dissatisfaction." And these are the new masters of production, the substitute for capitalists! Stalin thoroughly exploded this myth when, during the last purges, he ordered shot, among others, thousands of industrial managers.

It is not the bureaucracy that rules, but he who gives orders to the bureaucracy. And it is Stalin who gives orders to the Russian bureaucracy. Lenin and Trotsky with a select group of followers who were never able to come to independent decisions as a party but always remained an instrument in the hands of the leaders (the same was true later with the fascist and national-socialist parties) seized power at a time when the old state apparatus was collapsing. They changed the state apparatus to suit their needs as rulers, eliminating democracy and establishing their own dictatorship which in their ideology, but by no means in practice, was identified with the "dictatorship of the proletariat." Thus they created the first *totalitarian state* —even before the name was invented. Stalin carried on with the job, removing his rivals through the instrument of the state apparatus and establishing an unlimited personal dictatorship.

This is the reality which should not be obscured by construing alleged domination by a "bureaucracy" which is in fact subordinate to the government to the same extent as are the rest of the people. This is true even though some modest crumbs from the master's table may be doled out to it—without, of course, a guarantee that other crumbs are to follow and at the price of constant danger to their very lives. Their material share does not constitute any important portion of the social product. Nevertheless, the psychological effect of such a differentiation may be quite considerable.

Important economic consequences flow from this fact. It is the essence of a totalitarian state that it subjects the economy to its aims. The economy is deprived of its own laws, it becomes a controlled economy. Once this control is effected, it transforms the market economy into a consumers' economy. The character and extent of needs are then determined by the state. The German and Italian economies provide evidence of the fact that such control, once initiated in a totalitarian state, spreads rapidly and tends to become all-embracing as was the case in Russia from the very beginning. Despite great differences in their points of departure, the economic system of totalitarian states are drawing close to each other. In Germany, too, the state, striving to maintain and strengthen its power, determines the character of production and accumulation. Prices lose their regulating function and become merely means of distribution. The economy, and with it the exponents of economic activity, are more or less subjected to the state, becoming its subordinates. The economy loses the primacy which it held under bourgeois society. This does not mean, however, that economic circles do not have great influence on the ruling power in Germany as well as in Russia. But their influence is conditional, has limits and is not decisive in relation to the essence of policy. Policy is actually determined by a small circle of those who are in power. It is their interests, their ideas as to what is required to maintain, exploit, and strengthen their own power that determines the policy which they impose as law upon the subordinated economy. This is why the subjective factor, the "unforeseeable," "irrational" character of political development has gained such importance in politics.

The faithful believe only in heaven and hell as determining forces; the Marxist sectarian only in capitalism and socialism, in classes—bourgeoisie and proletariat. The Marxist sectarian cannot grasp the idea that present-day state power, having achieved independence, is unfolding its enormous strength according to its own laws, subjecting social forces and compelling them to serve its ends for a short or long period of time.

Therefore neither the Russian nor the totalitarian system in general is determined by the character of the economy. On the contrary, it is the economy that is determined by the policy of the ruling power and subjected to the aims and purposes of this power. The totalitarian power lives by the economy, but not for the economy or even for the class ruling the economy—as is the case of the bourgeois state, though the latter (as any student of foreign policy can demonstrate) may occasionally pursue aims of its own. An analogy to the totalitarian state may be found in the era of the late Roman Empire, in the regime of the Praetorians and their emperors.

Of course, from a social democratic viewpoint the Bolshevik economy can hardly be called "socialist," for to us socialism is indissolubly linked to democracy. According to our concept, socialization of the means of production implies freeing the economy from the rule of one class and vesting it in society as a whole—a society which is democratically self-governed. We never imagined that the political form of that "managed economy" which was to replace capitalist production for a free market could be unrestricted absolutism. The correlation between the economic basis and the political structure seemed to us a very definite one: namely, that the socialist society would inaugurate the highest realization of democracy. Even those among us who believed that the strictest application of centralized power would be necessary or inevitable for the period of transition, considered this period only temporary and bound to end after the suppression of the propertied classes. Together with the disappearance of classes, class rule was also to vanish—that class rule which we considered the only possible form of political rule in general. "The state is withering away . . ."

But history, this "best of all Marxists," has taught us differently. It has taught us that "administering of things," despite Engels' expectations, may turn into unlimited "administering of people," and thus not only lead to the emancipation of the state from the economy but even to the subjection of the economy to the state.

Once subjected to the state, the economy secures the continued existence of this form of government. The fact that such a result flows from a unique situation primarily brought about by war does not exclude a Marxist analysis, but it alters somewhat our rather simplified and schematic conception of the correlation between economy and state and between economy and politics which developed in a completely different period. The emergence of the state as an independent power greatly complicates the economic characterization of a society in which politics (i. e. the state) plays a determining and decisive role.

For this reason the controversy as to whether the economic system of the Soviet Union is "capitalist" or "socialist" seems to me rather pointless. It is neither. It represents a *totalitarian state economy*, i. e. a system to which the economics of Germany and Italy are drawing closer and closer.

FRANZ BORKENAU: *Communism as an International Movement.* [4]

The history of the Communist International, as it has unfolded itself between 1919 and the present day, is certainly a puzzling phenomenon. It is difficult to find a central point in the story around which to group the whole. There is no climax. The events seem to pass one after another, without any very close link between them. The history of the Comintern can be summed up as a series of hopes

4. The major criticism of stalinist parties outside Russia. From *World Communism* (New York, 1939), pp. 413-429. Reprinted by arrangement with Faber & Faber Ltd.

and disappointments. Ever and again Russia and the communist parties abroad imagined that in this or that country revolution was approaching, victory near. The front of the bourgeoisie would be broken, and through the gap world revolution would make its way. Then, instead of success, there was always failure. Progress made by the various communist parties during difficult years of struggle, won at the price of heavy sacrifices, vanished into nothing within a few days, as in Germany in 1923, in England in 1926, in China in 1927. The communists hunted a phantom which deceived them continually: the vain phantom of social revolution such as Marx had seen it. [The history of the Comintern contains many ups and downs. It contains no steady progress, not a single lasting success.]

But against this disappointing reality there stand the firm hopes of the communists. They are convinced, every single time they enter on a new policy, an attack on a new country, that this time it will be different from what it was before, that now they have found the true method, that this time advance will not end in a complete rout. The basic conviction of communism is that it needs only a truly "Bolshevist" party, applying the appropriate tactics, in order to win. Therefore every defeat—and the history of the Comintern consists of defeats—brings about a change both of leadership and of policy. One day the Comintern tries a policy to the "right"; then the importance of democracy is emphasized, collaboration is sought with the other sections of the labor movement, care is taken to participate in the day-to-day struggles of the workers and of the lower classes in general, the communist parties grow, both in membership and in influence. Everything seems to be smooth going till the decisive moment when an attempt is made to leap out of the preparatory stage into revolutionary action. Then, suddenly, the parties feel somehow unable to make the jump and break down. The communists are convinced that the failure was only due to wrong ideology. In taking account of the pacifist and constitutional "prejudices" of the masses the communists have imbued themselves with them, have themselves become "opportunists"; that is the view of the orthodox.

A turn to the left is effected. Often armed insurrection, which was not undertaken at the height of communist mass influence, is launched when the decisive moment is over and the party has lost all influence or at least every chance of victory: thus in Bulgaria in 1923, and in China in 1927, to mention only two outstanding examples. But even when no sudden rising takes place the turn to the left implies a wholesale change of policy. Suddenly the communists refuse to acknowledge any difference between democracy on the one hand and autocracy and Fascism on the other. All contracts with the democratic mass parties are broken off. Attempts are made to split the trade unions. Bona fide participation in the day-to-day struggles of the masses is decried as "opportunism." Propaganda of revolution takes the place of every other sort of propaganda. And the parties are rigidly purged of all "opportunist" elements. But if the policy of the "right" wing has led to defeat at the decisive moment that of the "left" wing reduces the party to the exiguity and the lack of influence of a sect, until the decline is patent and the policy of the "right" is given a new trial. And so forth in endless rotation.

The movements of communism proceed with an increasing momentum. At first the "right" and the "left" wing policies are not clearly distinguishable. Only after the end of the revolutionary period is this distinction established. And then every turn to the left or to the right exceeds the previous one in vehemence. The communist parties seem to be driven to avoid the repetition of the failures of the preceding period by trying something still more extreme. On the whole six phases of Comintern policy, three of a "left" and three of a "right" character, can be distinguished. Taking the "left" turns first it is interesting to note that, in 1920 and 1921, the social-democrats are simply "social-patriots." "social-traitors," and the like. During the left period of 1924–5 they are already regarded as a bourgeois party, the "third party of the bourgeoisie." But during the extreme rages of the left tack of the 1929–34 they have been promoted to the rank of "social-Fascists," and both the German and French communists unite in practice with the real Fascists of their respective countries in order to defeat "social-Fascism."

Taking the swings to the right, the first one, that of 1922–3, limits itself to a thorough use of the tactics of the united front, with a tendency to assimilate the language of the party to that of the democratic working-class parties. The next swing to the right, that of 1925–6, however, implies already a partial liquidation of the basic notion of the task of a communist party. Zinoviev himself states that in Britain revolution may come, not through the door of the Communist Party but through that of the trade unions. Similar hopes are cherished as to the American farmer-labor movement and to the Croat peasants, and, in China, the Communist Party is ordered not to oppose, in any respect, the Kuomintang of Chiang Kai-shek. We need not enlarge upon the extension of these tendencies during the present, third swing to the right, which implies attempts at merging with the socialists, denial of all revolutionary intentions, opposition to all sections of the labor movement in Spain as too advanced, etc.

Only one thing the communists seem unable to acquire through all the shiftings of their policy: a sense of the adequacy of means and ends. During the rapid swings from right to left and from left to right there is generally one short moment when communist policy moves along a middle line: as when, lately, in 1934, the communists veered round to defend democracy together with all other democratic forces. But those are only points of transition between opposite extremes.

From a description of this basic law of the evolution of the Comintern evolves at once one important result: it would be a grave mistake to overestimate the role of Russia, or, more correctly to regard the basic character of the communist parties simply as a result of "orders from Moscow." Moscow's influence upon world communism, rooted both in its prestige and its financial power, of late even in the control the Russian G.P.U. exerts over all communist parties, is strong indeed. But this domination of Moscow over the Comintern is much more the result than the cause of the evolution of communism outside Russia. As long as there were relatively strong revolutionary movements outside Russia, these movements, in spite of all the prestige of the Russian revolution, did not accept orders from Moscow. Kun in 1919 flatly refused to sever the organic links with the social-democrats during the Hungarian dictatorship, in spite of Lenin's advice. Rosa Luxemburg and Levi, while leading the Spartakusbund, saw to it that the Russians were treated as allies but not as masters. No other section of the Comintern has ever had so much independence as the Chinese Soviets, and only when their vigor was broken by Chiang Kai-shek's "annihilation drives" did they become simple instruments of Russian foreign policy, which during the last year decided to dissolve them altogether. When the Comintern was founded, during the year 1919, at the height of the post-war revolutionary crisis, it ought to have had tremendous authority. In reality, precisely during that year 1919, it was quite an insignificant force because the revolutionary movements of other countries did not care to take orders from Moscow.

The Comintern as an organization under the sway of Moscow is itself a product of defeat. When in 1920 it became clear that the post-war revolutionary wave was ebbing away, the star of Moscow rose. The ideas of Bolshevism, the dogma that the labor movement must be purged thoroughly of all unorthodox elements before being able to win, was only now accepted by the defeated left wing of the Continental socialist parties, and the split inaugurated by the second world-congress of the Comintern started from that assumption. Only this split led to the formation of communist mass parties. The new communist parties, believing that with the creation of a communist party the chief condition of success was fulfilled, threw themselves into battle, only to learn in the German disaster of March 1921 that they had been entirely mistaken and that the existence of a communist mass party could not make up for the lack of revolutionary impetus in the masses. When the Comintern was born the revolution in the West was already at an end.

The coincidence of these two events was not a matter of chance. Before the war, no revolutionary socialist had conceived the idea that the proletariat could win in a state of disunion. Yet already the outbreak of the war had brought about precisely such a state. The majority of the labor parties all over the world had buried the ideals of the class-struggle precisely at the moment when these ideals, for the first time for many decades, would have had practical revolutionary implications. The revolutionary minority, which stood firm to its convictions, cried treason. But this is a moral point of view and its acceptance depends on the conviction that it is the duty of a decent man to be a revolutionary. The majority of the workers and their leaders, however, had thought at that moment that it was their duty to defend home and country. The national allegiance had proved to be much stronger than the social one. It was a long time before the revolutionaries accepted this verdict of history. Even in 1919 Lenin and Zinoviev imagined that it was sufficient to raise the banner of the new, revolutionary International for the workers to gather swiftly round it. But this was not the case and so the split, with its twenty-one points, grew from an incident to a lasting reality. Twenty-one points, with their stipulations about repeated purges, started from the implicit assumption that a large section of the labor movement, not to mention the other sections of the lower classes, would always remain reformist, as long as the capitalist regime existed. But if this was so, how was a proletarian revolution to succeed? By the very act of its creation as a mass organization, by the perpetuation of the split which it implied, the Comintern signed the death warrant for the proletarian revolution to which it was pledged and which had never had many chances.

What followed was again natural enough. In matters of organization and finance the communist parties, who had only a relatively small following of their own, had to rely on help from Moscow, on which they became thus dependent. But more important still was the ideological dependence on Russia. The further real chances of revolution recede into the background the more the adoration of the accomplished revolution in Russia takes their place. Every defeat of revolution in the West and in the East is accompanied by an increase of admiration for Russia. During the first years of the Comintern there is still a very serious concern for the possible chances of revolution abroad. There are constant attempts to square these interests with the interests of Russia as a state, but these attempts gradually change in character. On the one hand, Russia leaves its own revolution ever further behind. Precisely because revolution in Russia is an established fact, the revolutionary impetus of Russia abroad fades out. At the same time, revolution recedes further into the background everywhere, at least that sort of revolution which the Russians regard as desirable.

The defeat of the Chinese revolution is the turning-point in this respect. During the year 1925 the dissensions in Russia had begun to influence the Comintern considerably. Now the chances of the left wing of the Chinese revolutionaries are really spoilt by Moscow. In all other cases the revolutionary chances existed only in the heads of the communists. In Germany in 1921 and 1923, in Britain in

1926, there could not have been a revolution. But the Chinese revolution was in fact ruined by the interference of Moscow, which tried to square its interests with the interests of the revolutionaries, which proved to be impossible. The defeat of the Chinese revolution destroys the last serious chance of the Comintern in all the world. Henceforth the Comintern, which has no longer a serious task of its own, becomes a plaything in the hands of the ruling group at Moscow. The left extremism of 1929–34 is largely a maneuver of Stalin in his factional fight against the right of Bukharin and Rykov in Russia.

The situation changes once more with the advent of Hitler. Moscow for the first time since 1921 feels itself seriously menaced and feels its revolutionary past as a handicap in its defense. The Comintern must stop its extremist talk, which might hamper Russia's attempts at finding suitable alliances, and by doing so becomes automatically an instrument of Russian foreign policy, which it had not before primarily been.

Thus, three periods can be clearly distinguished. During the first period the Comintern is mainly an instrument to bring about revolution. During the second period it is mainly an instrument in the Russian factional struggles. During the third period it is mainly an instrument of Russian foreign policy. The boundary lines between these three periods are naturally not rigid. But one thing remains clear: for the true communist this whole evolution can only be the result of an immense betrayal. Leon Trotsky fills the world with his accusations that the German, the French, the Spanish, the Belgian, and what not revolution had been possible, had only Stalin not betrayed. In reality it is the other way round. The evolution of the Comintern and partly even that of Russia are due to the fact that that international proletarian revolution after which the Bolsheviks originally hunted was a phantom. After many disappointments they had indirectly to acknowledge it by their deeds, and take things as they were. This change of the function of the Comintern is the real trend of its evolution behind the welter of shifts to the right and to the left which constitute its surface.

This change could not possibly remain without effect on the structure of the communist parties themselves. This structure did not from the beginning correspond at all to the ideas which the communists held about their own party.

In Russia the Bolshevik party had really been, to a great extent, what Lenin wanted it to be: a select community, a sort of religious order of professional revolutionaries, crusaders of a materialistic faith, a selection of the most self-sacrificing, the most decided and active among the revolutionary intelligentsia. But the structure of the communist parties of the West and the East never corresponded to this idea. They consisted essentially of shifting elements, which came and went. This character of the membership explains to a great extent the rapid changes of policy. Such contradictory policies as those followed by the various communist parties could not have been carried out one after another by the same men.

The complete lack of tradition has the same source. Russian Bolshevism was conscious of having its roots in the deeds of the revolutionaries of a century before, and the membership kept a close memory of the history of the party, until Stalin ordered the reading of a revolutionary history entirely of his own invention. The membership in the Western and Eastern parties, however, is a new one every five years and ready to believe anything the newest version of official communism tells it about the past of the party. Serious studies of party history are not encouraged.

But this lack of consistency and of tradition has one still more important consequence: with the shifting of the membership the social character of the communist parties shifts too. There was a moment, after the second world-congress, in 1921, when the more important communist parties were really working-class parties. But this has changed long since. With the shifting of the membership the communist parties tended to attract, more and more, *déclassé* elements: young intellectuals with Bohemian leanings on the one hand, unemployed on the other. During the period of left extremism between 1929 and 1934 most communist parties consisted primarily of these elements. Today an even more radical change announces itself. In China the Communist Party is a party of the peasants and the Red Army, in Spain it is a party of all classes except the urban proletariat, in Britain and U.S.A. it is mostly a party of young intellectuals; among the refugees of many countries communism is enormously popular, but the majority of these refugees have also been bourgeois intellectuals. Only in France and, to a certain extent, in Czechoslovakia, can the communists still be regarded as a real working-class party with real influence on the proletarian masses.

In this slow transformation of the social structure of the Communist International we strike again one of the roots of its history. The proletarian revolution, in which Marx and Lenin believed, seems to be incompatible with the real labor movement as it is. Certain elements of Marx's and Lenin's revolutionary predictions have proved only too true. It is true that the "capitalist" society of private ownership and private initiative is unable to cope with the problems of our period. It is true, as Marx has predicted, that at a certain stage of its development it enters on a cycle of gigantic economic crises for which, as most experts are agreed today, there is no remedy but state control, state interference, and planning. It is true, moreover, that economic crises bring with them tremendous social dislocations and political convulsions. Only one thing is certainly not true: the idea that, at the height of such a crisis, the proletariat will rise and, throwing all the propertied classes into the dust, will take the lead of society, abolish private property in the means of production, and create a regime where there are no more classes. This leading role of the proletariat in the upheavals of our time has proved to be the Utopian element of Marxism. In Russia, not the proletariat, but a quasi-religious order of professional revolutionaries of the intelligentsia took the lead, with the help of the peasants, the peasant soldiers, and the workers. In the West, where there was neither such an order nor masses willing to follow it, the idea of a proletarian revolution proved to be a complete illusion.

There are many reasons for this, reasons which have little or nothing to do with a betrayal. Had all the socialist leaders sided with the revolutionaries the majority of the proletariat would simply have left them for some more moderate party. For the idea of the proletariat opposing, victoriously, all other classes of a complex modern society is a fantastic one. In the West there are no revolutionary peasants such as in Russia. Moreover, in Russia there existed that absolute cleavage between the people and the ruling classes which is completely absent in the West. The old civilization of the West has given its seal, not only to an alleged workers' aristocracy, but to all strata of the working classes, who all have something to lose, who all share with the upper classes their chief loyalties and beliefs. If somebody wants to express this in Marxist terms he may say that in the most developed modern countries all classes and groups are much too "bourgeois" to make a proletarian revolution a practical proposition.

Therefore, in the West only two solutions for the crisis of the existing social regime remained: in some countries a revolutionary party coming from all classes and taking a stand above them all has curbed the class struggle with iron hand and subordinated all group antagonisms within the nation to the violent struggle for domination of their own nation over all others. Such is Fascism. In other countries, and this is the second possibility, all classes, by a tradition of co-operation and compromise, have hitherto managed to hold the inevitable social antagonisms within bounds and co-operate in the gradual bringing about of a new type of society: this is typical of a progressive and evolutionary democracy. There is no third solution in the conditions of highly developed modern industrial countries. Industrially backward countries such as Russia, Spain, South America, China, are a different matter.

The labor movement of the West, moreover, knows very well why, by instinct and conviction, it holds to democracy. The achievements of the dictatorships may be ever so brilliant; but not from the end of the crisis in Germany, nor from the colonial expansion of Italy, nor from the Five-Year Plan of Russia, have the masses had more than the slightest advantages. Liberty of movement for the working-class organizations, notably the trade unions, is the primary condition for the workers to share in the fruits of the economic and political successes of their nation. But the liberty of the trade unions depends on liberty as a basic principle of the political regime. To this liberal and constitutional spirit of the Western labor movement the communists could only either submit, and then the Comintern would have dissolved itself, or they could fight the bulk of the labor movement, which they did. But in doing so they gradually severed their ties with the real proletariat. The possibility of such a severance was contained in Lenin's basic assumption when he formed the Bolshevik Party: the revolutionary party must not be an agent of the proletariat, but a separate group, only knitted with it by its convictions. The Western labor parties are the labor movement itself, are identical with it. The communist parties were only linked with it. But what is linked can be severed.

The communists wanted to lead the proletariat along their road. But their own rule, the dictatorship of the Communist Party, was their primary aim from the beginning. When the Western proletariat proved not to be responsive it was only natural for the communists to seek support elsewhere. The fight for the power of the party and the International was and remained the central point. It was not a result of any betrayal, therefore, but the most logical result of their basic assumptions that, in due course of time, the communists became a classless party, held together by the worship of their totalitarian state—Russia—and their *voshd,* their Führer, the leader-superman, Stalin. In this transformation the communist parties had only followed the evolution of other mass movements in those countries which were ridden by revolution. Everywhere, in eastern and central Europe in 1919, parties of proletarian revolution had been in the forefront, had failed, and then the revolutionary trends had been taken up, in a different manner, by classless, Führer-worshiping parties, in one word by Fascist parties. In this development, inevitable unless countries are successfully managed by way of democratic compromise, the Comintern simply participated.

But it did so in a paradoxical way. Much of what the Comintern does today is conscious and intentional imitation of Fascism: the Führer-worship of the leader of every communist party, the nationalism, the appeal to youth, the military atmosphere. But: "Si duo idem faciunt non est idem." The Germans worship Hitler, who is a German. The French workers cannot worship Stalin, who is a Russian. German Fascism is sincerely nationalist and aggressive for its own nation. But a Fascism aggressive on behalf of a foreign nation is a preposterous idea. . . . A movement whose loyalty is split between its home country and a foreign country can never have the convincing force which the genuine Fascist movements have had in their respective countries. It was impossible for Russia to transfer its revolution abroad. It will prove equally impossible for it to spread its totalitarian regime. . . .

In the West communism hardly ever was more than a big nuisance for the police. And Trotskyism, which still keeps to the principles of 1917, is not even that and could hardly ever be. But if communism as a revolutionary force was something infinitely more futile than its fervent adversaries would be ready to admit, the same thing need not apply to

present-day non-revolutionary communism with its narrower aims. . . .

The appeal of present-day non-revolutionary communism
is a strange psychological phenomenon. It is not due to a
revolutionary program, because the communists are no
longer revolutionary; it is not due to a moderate program,
because there is no lack of moderate parties of old standing. It is due, however, to the strange merging of an utterly
unrevolutionary and anti-revolutionary policy with the belief in the myth that paradise on earth has already been
achieved over "one-sixth of the earth's inhabited surface."
At home the masses which vote communist would never
fight against democracy, for revolution. It is only the more
gratifying, therefore, to adore the dictatorship in Russia
and to indulge, in its service, in all those impulses of violence, of vilification and extermination of one's adversaries,
which cannot be satisfied at home. Present-day communism
is essentially the belief in a savior abroad; for this very
reason it is a serious symptom of the decay of liberalism
and democracy. For the essence of both is a belief in the
capacity to manage politics without a savior, by the forces
of the politically emancipated people themselves. The communists may perorate about the defense of democracy and
liberty; in fact, the basic impulses upon which their appeal
relies are diametrically opposed to both. Nor can this
strange combination of moderation at home and worship
of violence and horror abroad continue indefinitely. At
present, in most countries, the real "toilers" are hardly
touched by communist propaganda. If these real "toilers"
at any time should lose their faith in liberty and democracy
under some very severe stress and look out for a savior, the
happy smile on the photos of Stalin would give them no
consolation. They would then turn to a savior, not abroad
but at home, as they did in Germany. And, again as in
Germany, many thousands who have been communists
would then become Fascists. In those countries where
Fascism has not yet had any opportunity, communism, in
its present form, supplies that belief in a savior which is
essential to Fascism; but its savior is more remote, as is suitable, in a situation less tense, for social groups far away
from practical possibilities of action. Yet the effect, the
slow sapping of the democratic and liberal spirit, is there.
As the constant interference of communist forces in the
foreign policy of their respective countries sometimes con-

stitutes a serious nuisance in matters of international policy, so communist ideals represent a constant menace to the basic forces of the European polity. It is not that the communists want to overthrow the polity at present; on the contrary, few men are so intensely interested in the strength and fighting power of the democratic countries as is Stalin, though this interest will change to the contrary the very day that Russia finds it suitable to change her foreign policy. Whether Stalin wants an alliance with the democratic countries or not is immaterial, however. The effect of communist ideals is to menace liberty and democracy; and in the end, in all likelihood, the effect of communist propaganda will have been to strengthen Fascism.

From the point of view of the democratic powers the question naturally arises whether there exist means to check these effects of communist activities. . . . Democratic powers cannot use the means of repression which are customary in Italy, Germany, and Russia, and it would obviously be very bad policy to evolve a system of pin-pricks, which would only be apt to create exasperation without being efficient. But the question remains, whether, from the point of view of Moscow, the Comintern is so valuable an asset as appears at first sight.

There can be little doubt, in fact, that the superficial advantages derived from the existence of communist parties abroad are balanced by very heavy liabilities for Russian foreign policy. With all its efforts to be a great military power, and with all the pains taken to drown its revolutionary past in a sea of blood, Russia, up to now, has not won a single reliable ally. . . . One of the chief reasons for this reluctance on the part of all powers to combine with Russia is the existence of the Comintern. At the same time, the Comintern provides the Fascist powers with their best pretext of aggression, and it is the existence of the Comintern which is invoked by those parties of the right which, in democratic countries, favor co-operation with Germany in preference to co-operation with Russia. The dubious and limited influence Russia exerts in the political game of various democratic countries through its communist parties is certainly not worth the price paid for it. There is every chance that, in case of a large-scale international conflict, the Comintern will prove almost powerless, but will contribute to the isolation of Russia and to the grouping against it of many forces which might have remained neutral. To allay these consequences it will not be sufficient to cut off as many heads of ancient communists as are available. The very existence of the Comintern, in public opinion at large, rouses anxieties deriving from the aims it originally pursued. And there is no saying that, in a final emergency, the Comintern may not return in fact to its original methods. As long as the Comintern exists the average citizen and even the average politician in the West will judge Russia more after the revolution of 1917 than after the execution of Zinoview and Bucharin. It would therefore be in the interest of Russia itself to dissolve the Comintern and to prove, by scrupulous abstention from interference abroad, that it can be treated on an equal footing with those democratic powers whose ideals it professes to share. Closer cooperation between the great democratic powers and Russia would become a practical proposition as the result, and the mere possibility of such closer co-operation would be a powerful contribution to the maintenance of peace and the prevention of aggression.

Whether such a solution will come about will mainly depend on the psychology of the leaders at Moscow. Unfortunately, precisely the attitude of Stalin and his staff is one of the sorest spots of international politics. Comprehension of the West, its views, impulses, and driving forces has never been the strong point of Russian Bolshevism, and this has led already to more than one miserable failure. Moreover, a naïve sort of Machiavellism has been adopted in Russia, with metaphysical thoroughness. Lenin and the original Bolsheviks were already actuated by the conviction that all capitalist promises are deceptions and all ideals cheats. Under Stalin this view has evolved into a real all-round belief in human wickedness. Both in Russian home politics and in the activities of the Comintern double-dealing has been carried to such a degree as to defeat, very often, its own ends. Stalin, the man who could not allow a single one of his old companions to live, is the last man to believe in the possibility of sincere collaboration in the international field. A man such as Stalin cannot be brought to reason by argument. There is, however, just a small chance that events will teach him, and that when finally given the choice of complete isolation or a genuine dissolution of the Comintern, he will choose the latter. It would be highly desirable from the angle of those ideals to which he and his Comintern are paying continual lip-service; to the causes of liberty, democracy, peace, and the integrity and greatness of the Russian people.

ISAAC DEUTSCHER: *The Ex-Communist's Conscience* [5]

Ignazio Silone relates that he once said jokingly to Togliatti, the Italian Communist leader: "The final struggle will be between the communists and the ex-communists." There is a bitter drop of truth in the joke. In the propaganda skirmishes against the U.S.R.R. and communism, the ex-Communist or the ex-fellow traveler is the most active sharpshooter. With the peevishness that distinguishes him from Silone, Arthur Koestler makes a similar point: "It's the same with all you comfortable, insular, Anglo-Saxon anti-communists. You hate our Cassandra cries and resent us as allies—but, when all is said, we ex-communists are the only people on your side who know what it's all about." . . . Now six writers—Koestler, Silone, André Gide, Louis Fischer, Richard Wright, and Stephen Spender—get together to expose and destroy *The God That Failed*.

The "legion" of ex-Communists does not march in close formation. It is scattered far and wide. Its members resemble one another very much, but they also differ. They have common traits and individual features. All have left an army and a camp—some as conscientious objectors, some as deserters, and others as marauders. A few stick quietly to their conscientious objections, while others vociferously claim commissions in an army which they had bitterly opposed. All wear threadbare bits and pieces of the old uniform, supplemented by the quaintest new rags. And all carry with them their common resentments and individual reminiscences.

Some joined the party at one time, others at another; the date of joining is relevant to their further experiences. Those, for instance, who joined in the 1920's went into a movement in which there was plenty of scope for revolutionary idealism. The structure of the party was still fluid; it had not yet gone into the totalitarian mold. Intellectual integrity was still valued in a Communist; it had not yet been surrendered for good to Moscow's *raison d'état*. Those who

5. A review of "The God That Failed," from *Russia In Transition*. Copyright © 1957 by Hamish Hamilton, Ltd., pp. 223-236. Reprinted by arrangement with Coward-McCann, Inc., New York.

joined the party in the 1930's began their experience on a much lower level. Right from the beginning they were manipulated like recruits on the party's barrack squares by the party's sergeant majors.

This difference bears upon the quality of the ex-Communist's reminiscences. Silone, who joined the party in 1921, recalls with real warmth his first contact with it; he conveys fully the intellectual excitement and moral enthusiasm with which communism pulsated in those early days. The reminiscences of Koestler and Spender, who joined in the 1930's, reveal the utter moral and intellectual sterility of the party's first impact on them. Silone and his comrades were intensely concerned with fundamental ideas before and after they became absorbed in the drudgery of day-to-day duty. In Koestler's story, his party "assignment," right from the first moment, overshadows all matters of personal conviction and ideal. The Communist of the early drafts was a revolutionary before he became, or was expected to become, a puppet. The Communist of the later drafts hardly got the chance to breathe the genuine air of revolution.

Nevertheless, the original motives for joining were similar, if not identical, in almost every case: experience of social injustice or degradation; a sense of insecurity bred by slumps and social crises; and the craving for a great ideal or purpose, or for a reliable intellectual guide through the shaky labyrinth of modern society. The newcomer felt the miseries of the old capitalist order to be unbearable; and the glowing light of the Russian revolution illumined those miseries with extraordinary sharpness.

Socialism, classless society, the withering away of the State—all seemed around the corner. Few of the newcomers had any premonition of the blood and sweat and tears to come. To himself, the intellectual convert to communism seemed a new Prometheus—except that he would not be pinned to the rock by Zeus's wrath. "Nothing henceforth [so Koestler now recalls his own mood in those days] can disturb the convert's inner peace and serenity—except the occasional fear of losing faith again. . . ."

Our ex-Communist now bitterly denounces the betrayal of his hopes. This appears to him to have had almost no precedent. Yet as he eloquently describes his early expectations and illusions, we detect a strangely familiar tone. Exactly so did the disillusioned Wordsworth and his contemporaries look back upon their first youthful enthusiasm for the French revolution: "Bliss was in that dawn to be alive, But to be young was very heaven!"

The intellectual Communist who breaks away emotionally from his party can claim some noble ancestry. Beethoven tore to pieces the title page of his *Eroica*, on which he had dedicated the symphony to Napoleon, as soon as he learned that the First Consul was about to ascend a throne. Wordsworth called the crowning of Napoleon "a sad reverse for all mankind." All over Europe the enthusiasts of the French revolution were stunned by their discovery that the Corsican liberator of the peoples and enemy of tyrants was himself a tyrant and an oppressor.

In the same way the Wordsworths of our days were shocked at the sight of Stalin fraternizing with Hitler and Ribbentrop. If no new *Eroicas* have been created in our days, at least the dedicatory pages of unwritten symphonies have been torn with great flourishes.

In *The God That Failed*, Louis Fischer tries to explain somewhat remorsefully and not quite convincingly why he adhered to the Stalin cult for so long. He analyzes the variety of motives, some working slowly and some rapidly, which determine the moment at which people recover from the infatuation with Stalinism. The force of the European disillusionment with Napoleon was almost equally uneven and capricious. A great Italian poet, Ugo Foscolo, who had been Napoleon's soldier and composed an *Ode to Bonaparte the Liberator*, turned against his idol after the Peace of Campoformio—this must have stunned a "Jacobin" from Venice as the Nazis-Soviet Pact stunned a Polish Communist. But a man like Beethoven remained under the spell of Bonaparte for seven years more, until he saw the despot drop his republican mask. This was an "eye-opener" comparable to Stalin's purge trials of the 1930's.

There can be no greater tragedy than that of a great revolution's succumbing to the mailed fist that was to defend it from its enemies. There can be no spectacle as disgusting as that of a post-revolutionary tyranny dressed up in the banners of liberty. The ex-Communist is morally as justified as was the ex-Jacobin in revealing and revolting against that spectacle.

But is it true, as Koestler claims, that "ex-communists are the only people . . . who know what it's all about"? One may risk the assertion that the exact opposite is true:

Of all people, the ex-Communists know least what it is all about.

At any rate, the pedagogical pretensions of ex-Communist men of letters seem grossly exaggerated. Most of them (Silone is a notable exception) have never been inside the real Communist movement, in the thick of its clandestine or open organization. As a rule, they moved on the literary or journalistic fringe of the party. Their notions of Communist doctrine and ideology usually spring from their own literary intuition, which is sometimes acute but often misleading.

Worse still is the ex-Communist's characteristic incapacity for detachment. His emotional reaction against his former environment keeps him in its deadly grip and prevents him from understanding the drama in which he was involved or half-involved. The picture of communism and Stalinism he draws is that of a gigantic chamber of intellectual and moral horrors. Viewing it, the uninitiated are transferred from politics to pure demonology. Sometimes the artistic effect may be strong—horrors and demons do enter into many a poetic masterpiece; but it is politically unreliable and even dangerous. Of course, the story of Stalinism abounds in horror. But this is only one of its elements; and even this, the demonic, has to be translated into terms of human motives and interests. The ex-Communist does not even attempt the translation.

In a rare flash of genuine self-criticism, Koestler makes this admission:

"As a rule, our memories romanticize the past. But when one has renounced a creed or been betrayed by a friend, the opposite mechanism sets to work. In the light of that later knowledge, the original experience loses its innocence, becomes tainted and rancid in recollection. I have tried in these pages to recapture the mood in which the experiences [in the Communist Party] related were originally lived— and I know that I have failed. Irony, anger, and shame kept intruding; the passions of that time seem transformed into perversions, its inner certitude into the closed universe of the drug addict; the shadow of barbed wire lies across the condemned playground of memory. Those who were caught by the great illusion of our time, and have lived through its moral and intellectual debauch, either give themselves up to a new addition of the opposite type, or are condemned to pay with a lifelong hangover."

This need not be true of all ex-Communists. Some may still feel that their experience has been free from the morbid overtones described by Koestler. Nevertheless, Koestler has given here a truthful and honest characterization of the type of ex-Communist to which he himself belongs. But it is difficult to square this self-portrait with his other claim that the confraternity for which he speaks "are the only people . . . who know what it's all about." With equal right a sufferer from traumatic shock might claim that he is the only one who really understands wounds and surgery. The most that the intellectual ex-Communist knows, or rather feels, is his own sickness; but he is ignorant of the nature of the external violence that has produced it, let alone the cure.

This irrational emotionalism dominates the evolution of many an ex-Communist. "The logic of opposition at all cost," says Silone, "has carried many ex-communists far from their starting-points, in some cases as far as fascism." What were those starting-points? Nearly every ex-Communist broke with his party in the name of communism. Nearly every one set out to defend the ideal of socialism from the abuses of bureaucracy subservient to Moscow. Nearly every one began by throwing out the dirty water of the Russian revolution to protect the baby bathing in it.

Sooner or later these intentions are forgotten or abandoned. Having broken with a party bureaucracy in the name of communism, the heretic goes on to break with communism itself. He claims to have made the discovery that the root of the evil goes far deeper than he at first imagined, even though his digging for that "root" may have been very lazy and very shallow. He no longer defends socialism from unscrupulous abuse; he now defends mankind from the fallacy of socialism. He no longer throws out the dirty water of the Russian revolution to protect the baby; he discovers that the baby is a monster which must be strangled. The heretic becomes a renegade.

How far he departed from his starting-point, whether, as Silone says, he becomes a fascist or not, depends on his inclinations and tastes—and stupid Stalinist heresy-hunting often drives the ex-Communist to extremes. But, whatever the shades of individual attitudes, as a rule the intellectual ex-Communist ceases to oppose capitalism. Often he rallies to its defense, and he brings to this job the lack of scruple, the narrow-mindedness, the disregard for truth, and the in-

tense hatred with which Stalinism has imbued him. He remains a sectarian. He is an inverted Stalinist. He continues
to see the world in white and black, but now the colors are
differently distributed. As a Communist he saw no difference between fascists and social democrats. As an anti-
Communist he sees no difference between nazism and communism. Once, he accepted the party's claim to infallibility;
now he believes himself to be infallible. Having once been
caught by the "greatest illusion," he is now obsessed by the
greatest disillusionment of our time.

His former illusion at least implied a positive ideal. His
disillusionment it utterly negative. His role is therefore intellectually and politically barren. In this, too, he resembles
the embittered ex-Jacobin of the Napoleonic era. Wordsworth and Coleridge were fatally obsessed with the
"Jacobin danger"; their fear dimmed even their poetic
genius. It was Coleridge who denounced in the House of
Commons a bill for the prevention of cruelty to animals as
the "strongest instance of legislative Jacobinism." The ex-
Jacobin became the prompter of the anti-Jacobin reaction
in England. Directly or indirectly, his influence was behind
the Bills Against Seditious Writings and Traitorous Correspondence, the Treasonable Practices Bill, and Seditious
Meetings Bill (1792-1794), the defeats of parliamentary
reform, the suspension of the Habeas Corpus Act, and the
postponement of the emancipation of England's religious
minorities for the lifetime of a generation. Since the conflict
with revolutionary France was "not a time to make hazard-
ous experiments," the slave trade, too, obtained a lease on
life—in the name of liberty.

In quite the same way our ex-Communist, for the best of
reasons, does the most vicious things. He advances bravely
in the front rank of every witch hunt. His blind hatred of
his former ideal is leaven to contemporary conservatism.
Not rarely he denounces even the mildest brand of the "welfare State" as "legislative Bolshevism." He contributes
heavily to the moral climate in which a modern counterpart to the English anti-Jacobin reaction is hatched. His
grotesque performance reflects the impasse in which he
finds himself. The impasse is not merely his—it is part of
a blind alley in which an entire generation leads an inco-
herent and absent-minded life.

The historical parallel drawn here extends to the wider
background of two epochs. The world is split between

Stalinism and an anti-Stalinist alliance in much the same way it was split between Napoleonic France and the Holy Alliance. It is a split between a "degenerated" revolution exploited by a despot and a grouping of predominantly, although not exclusively, conservative interests. In terms of practical politics the choice seems to be now, as it was then, confined to these alternatives. Yet the rights and the wrongs of this controversy are so hopelessly confused that whichever the choice, and whatever its practical motives, it is almost certain to be wrong in the long run and in the broadest historical sense.

An honest and critically minded man could reconcile himself to Napoleon as little as he can now to Stalin. But despite Napoleon's violence and frauds, the message of the French revolution survived to echo powerfully throughout the nineteenth century. The Holy Alliance freed Europe from Napoleon's oppression; and for a moment its victory was hailed by most Europeans. Yet what Castlereagh and Metternich and Alexander I had to offer to "liberated" Europe was merely the preservation of an old, decomposing order. Thus the abuses and the aggressiveness of an empire bred by the revolution gave a new lease on life to European feudalism. This was the ex-Jacobin's most unexpected triumph. But the price he paid for it was that presently he himself, and his anti-Jacobin cause, looked like vicious, ridiculous anachronisms. In the year of Napoleon's defeat, Shelley wrote to Wordsworth:

> In honored poverty thy voice did weave
> Songs consecrate to truth and liberty—
> Deserting these, thou leavest me to grieve,
> Thus having been, that thou shouldst cease to be.

If our ex-Communist had any historical sense, he would ponder this lesson. . . .

"Far, far more abject is thy enemy" might have been the text for *The God That Failed,* and for the philosophy of the lesser evil expounded in its pages. The ardor with which the writers of this book defend the West against Russia and communism is sometimes chilled by uncertainty or residual ideological inhibition. The uncertainty appears between the lines of their confessions, or in curious asides.

Silone, for instance, still describes the pre-Mussolini Italy, against which, as a Communist, he had rebelled, as "pseudo-democratic." He hardly believes that post-Mussolini Italy is any better, but he sees its Stalinist enemy to be "far, far more abject." More than the other co-authors of this book, Silone is surely aware of the price that Europeans of his generation have already paid for the acceptance of lesser-evil philosophies. Louis Fischer advocates the "double rejection" of communism and capitalism, but his rejection of the latter sounds like a feeble face-saving formula; and his newly found cult of Gandhiism impresses one as merely an awkward escapism. But it is Koestler who, occasionally, in the midst of all his affectation and anti-Communist frenzy, reveals a few curious mental reservations: ". . . if we survey history [he says] and compare the lofty aims, in the name of which revolutions were started, and the sorry end to which they came, we see again and again how a *polluted civilization pollutes its own revolutionary offspring*" (my italics) . . . If the "revolutionary offspring," communism, has really been "polluted" by the civilization against which it has rebelled, then no matter how repulsive the offspring may be, the source of the evil is not in it but in that civilization. And this will be so regardless of how zealously Koestler himself may act as the advocate of the "defenders" of civilization *à la* [Whitaker] Chambers.

Even more startling is another thought . . . with which Koestler unexpectedly ends his confession:

"I served the Communist Party for seven years—the same length of time as Jacob tended Laban's sheep to win Rachel his daughter. When the time was up, the bride was led into his dark tent; only the next morning did he discover that his ardors had been spent not on the lovely Rachel but on the ugly Leah. I wonder whether he ever recovered from the shock of having slept with an illusion. I wonder whether afterward he believed that he had ever believed in it. I wonder whether the happy end of the legend will be repeated; for at the price of another seven years of labor, Jacob was given Rachel too, and the illusion became flesh. And the seven years seemed unto him but a few days, for the love he had for her."

One might think that Jacob-Koestler reflects uneasily whether he has not too hastily ceased tending Laban-Stalin's sheep, instead of waiting patiently till his "illusion became flesh."

The words are not meant to blame, let alone to castigate, anybody. Their purpose, let this be repeated, is to throw into relief a confusion of ideas, from which the ex-Communist intellectual is not the only sufferer.

In one of his recent articles, Koestler vented his irritation at those good old liberals who were shocked by the excess of anti-Communist zeal in the former Communist, and viewed him with the disgust with which ordinary people look at "a defrocked priest taking out a girl to a dance."

Well, the good old liberals may be right, after all: this peculiar type of anti-Communist may appear to them like a defrocked priest "taking out," not just a girl, but a harlot. The ex-Communist's utter confusion of intellect and emotion makes him ill-suited for any political activity. He is haunted by a vague sense that he has betrayed either his former ideals or the ideals of bourgeois society; like Koestler, he may even have an ambivalent notion that he has betrayed both. He then tries to suppress his sense of guilt and uncertainty, or to camouflage it by a show of extraordinary certitude and frantic aggressiveness. He insists that the world should recognize his uneasy conscience as the clearest conscience of all. He may no longer be concerned with any cause except one—self-justification. And this is the most dangerous motive for any political activity.

It seems that the only dignified attitude the intellectual ex-Communist can take is to rise *au-dessus de la mêlée*. He cannot join the Stalinist camp or the anti-Stalinist Holy Alliance without doing violence to his better self. So let him stay outside any camp. Let him try to regain critical sense and intellectual detachment. Let him overcome the cheap ambition to have a finger in the political pie. Let him be at peace with his own self at least, if the price he has to pay for phony peace with the world is self-renunciation and self-denunciation. This is not to say that the ex-Communist man of letters, or intellectual at large, should retire into the ivory tower. (His contempt for the ivory tower lingers in him from his past.) But he may withdraw into a *watchtower* instead. To watch with detachment and alertness this heaving chaos of a world, to be on a sharp lookout for what is going to emerge from it, and to interpret it *sine ira et studio*—this is now the only honorable service the ex-Communist intellectual can render to a generation in which scrupulous observation and honest interpretation have become so sadly rare. (Is it not striking how little observation and interpretation, and how much philosophizing and sermonizing, one finds in the books of the gifted pleiad of ex-Communist writers?)

But can the intellectual really now be a detached observer of this world? Even if taking sides makes him identify himself with causes that, in truth, are not his, must he not take sides all the same? Well, we can recall some great "intellectuals" who, in a similar situation in the past, refused to identify themselves with any established Cause. Their attitude seemed incomprehensible to many of their contemporaries: but history has proved their judgment to have been superior to the phobias and hatreds of their age. Three names may be mentioned here: Jefferson, Goethe, and Shelley. All three, each in a different way, were confronted with the choice between the Napoleonic idea and the Holy Alliance. All three, again each in a different manner, refused to choose.

Jefferson was the stanchest friend of the French revolution in its early heroic period. He was willing to forgive even the Terror, but he turned away in disgust from Napoleon's "military despotism." Yet he had no truck with Bonaparte's enemies, Europe's "hypocritical deliverers," as he called them. His detachment was not merely suited to the diplomatic interest of a young and neutral republic; it resulted naturally from his republican conviction and democratic passion.

Unlike Jefferson, Goethe lived right inside the storm center. Napoleon's troops and Alexander's soldiers, in turn, took up quarters in his Weimar. As the Minister of his Prince, Goethe opportunistically bowed to every invader. But as a thinker and man, he remained noncommittal and aloof. He was aware of the grandeur of the French revolution and was shocked by its horrors. He greeted the sound of French guns at Valmy as the opening of a new and better epoch, and he saw through Napoleon's follies. He acclaimed the liberation of Germany from Napoleon, and he was acutely aware of the misery of that "liberation." His aloofness, in these as in other matters, gained him the reputation of "the Olympian"; and the label was not always meant to be flattering. But his Olympian appearance was due least of all to an inner indifference to the fate of his contemporaries. It veiled his drama: his incapacity and reluctance to identify himself with causes, each an inextricable tangle of right and wrong.

Finally, Shelley watched the clash of the two worlds with

all the burning passion, anger, and hope of which his great
young soul was capable: he surely was no Olympian. Yet,
not for a single moment did he accept the self-righteous
claims and pretensions of any of the belligerents. Unlike
the ex-Jacobins, who were older than he, he was true to the
Jacobin republican idea. It was as a republican, and not as
a patriot of the England of George III, that he greeted the
fall of Napoleon, that "most unambitious slave" who did
"dance and revel on the grave of Liberty." But as a republican he knew also that "virtue owns a more eternal foe"
than Bonapartist force and fraud—"Old Custom, legal
Crime, and bloody Faith" embodied in the Holy Alliance.

All three—Jefferson, Goethe, and Shelley—were in a
sense outsiders to the great conflict of their time, and because of this they interpreted their time with more truthfulness and penetration than did the fearful—the hate-
ridden partisans on either side.

What a pity and what a shame it is that most ex-Com-
munist intellectuals are inclined to follow the tradition of
Wordsworth and Coleridge rather than that of Goethe and
Shelley.

12. Soviet Marxism and the New Revisionists

NIKITA KHRUSHCHEV: *Speech before the 20th Congress, February 25, 1956* [1]

In speaking about the events of the October Revolution and about the Civil War, the impression was created that Stalin always played the main role, as if everywhere and always Stalin had suggested to Lenin what to do and how to do it. However, this is slander of Lenin.

I will probably not sin against the truth when I say that 99% of the persons present here heard and knew very little about Stalin before the year 1924, while Lenin was known to all; he was known to the whole Party, to the whole nation, from the children up to the graybeards.

All this has to be thoroughly revised, so that history, literature, and the fine arts properly reflect V. I. Lenin's role and the great deeds of our Communist Party and of the Soviet people—the creative people.

Comrades! The cult of the individual has caused the employment of faulty principles in Party work and in economic activity; it brought about rude violation of internal Party and Soviet democracy, sterile administration, deviations of all sorts, covering up of shortcomings and varnishing of reality. Our nation gave birth to many flatterers and specialists in false optimism and deceit.

We should also not forget that due to the numerous arrests of Party, Soviet and economic leaders, many workers began to work uncertainly, showed over-cautiousness, feared all which was new, feared their own shadows and began to show less initiative in their work.

Take, for instance, Party and Soviet resolutions. They were prepared in a routine manner often without consid-

1. From *The Anti-Stalin Campaign and International Communism,* edited by the Russian Institute, Columbia University (New York, 1956), pp. 75-89. Reprinted by permission of Columbia University Press.

ering the concrete situation. This went so far that Party workers, even during the smallest sessions, read their speeches. All this produced the danger of formalizing the Party and Soviet work and of bureaucratizing the whole apparatus.

Stalin's reluctance to consider life's realities and the fact that he was not aware of the real state of affairs in the provinces can be illustrated by his direction of agriculture.

All those who interested themselves even a little in the national situation saw the difficult situation in agriculture, but Stalin never even noted it. Did we tell Stalin about this? Yes, we told him, but he did not support us. Why? Because Stalin never traveled anywhere, did not meet city and kolkhoz workers; he did not know the actual situation in the provinces.

He knew the country and agriculture only from films. And these films had dressed up and beautified the existing situation in agriculture.

Many films so pictured kolkhoz life that the tables were bending from the weight of turkeys and geese. Evidently Stalin thought that it was actually so.

Vladimir Ilyich Lenin looked at life differently; he was always close to the people; he used to receive peasant delegates, and often spoke at factory gatherings; he used to visit villages and talk with the peasants.

Stalin separated himself from the people and never went anywhere. This lasted tens of years. The last time he visited a village was in January 1928 when he visited Siberia in connection with grain deliveries. How then could he have known the situation in the provinces?

And when he was once told during a discussion that our situation on the land was a difficult one and that the situation of cattle breeding and meat production was especially bad, a commission was formed which was charged with the preparation of a resolution called, "Means toward further development of animal breeding in kolkhozes and sovkhozes." We worked out this project.

Of course, our propositions of that time did not contain all possibilities, but we did charter ways in which animal breeding on the kolkhozes and sovkhozes would be raised. We had proposed then to raise the prices of such products in order to create material incentives for the kolkhoz, MTS and sovkhoz workers in the development of cattle breeding. But our project was not accepted and in February 1953 was laid aside entirely.

What is more, while reviewing this project Stalin proposed that the taxes paid by the kolkhozes and by the kolkhoz workers should be raised by 40 billion rubles; according to him the peasants are well-off and the kolkhoz worker would need to sell only one more chicken to pay his tax in full.

Imagine what this meant. Certainly 40 billion rubles is a sum which the kolkhoz workers did not realize for all the products which they sold to the government. In 1952, for instance, the kolkhozes and the kolkhoz workers received 26,280 million rubles for all their products delivered and sold to the government.

Did Stalin's position then rest on data of any sort whatever? Of course not.

In such cases facts and figures did not interest him. If Stalin said anything, it meant it was so—after all, he was a "genius" and a genius does not need to count, he only needs to look and can immediately tell how it should be. When he expresses his opinion, everyone has to repeat it and to admire his wisdom.

But how much wisdom was contained in the proposal to raise the agricultural tax by 40 billion rubles? None, absolutely none, because the proposal was not based on an actual assessment of the situation but on the fantastic ideas of a person divorced from reality. We are currently beginning slowly to work our way out of a difficult agricultural situation. The speeches of the delegates to the XXth Congress please us all; we are glad that many delegates deliver speeches, that there are conditions for the fulfillment of the Sixth Five-Year Plan for animal husbandry, not during the period of five years, but within two to three years. We are certain that the commitments of the new Five-Year Plan will be accomplished successfully.

Comrades! If we sharply criticize today the cult of the individual which was so widespread during Stalin's life and if we speak about the many negative phenomena generated by this cult which is so alien to the spirit of Marxism-Leninism, various persons may ask: How could it be? Stalin headed the Party and the country for 30 years and many victories were gained during his lifetime. Can we deny this? In my opinion, the question can be asked in this manner only by those who are blinded and hopelessly hypnotized by the cult of the individual, only by those who do not understand the essence of the revolution and of the Soviet state, only by those who do not understand, in a Leninist manner, the role of the Party and of the nation in the development of the Soviet society.

The socialist revolution was attained by the working class and by the poor peasantry with the partial support of middle-class peasants. It was attained by the people under the leadership of the Bolshevik Party. Lenin's great service consisted of the fact that he created a militant Party of the working class, but he was armed with Marxist understanding of the laws of social development and with the science of proletarian victory in the fight with capitalism, and he steeled this Party in the crucible of revolutionary struggle of the masses of the people. During this fight the Party consistently defended the interests of the people, became its experienced leader, and led the working masses to power, to the creation of the first socialist state.

You remember well the wise words of Lenin that the Soviet state is strong because of the awareness of the masses that history is created by the millions and tens of millions of people.

Our historical victories were attained thanks to the organizational work of the Party, to the many provincial organizations, and to the self-sacrificing work of our great nation. These victories are the result of the great drive and activity of the nation and of the Party as a whole; they are not at all the fruit of the leadership of Stalin, as the situation was pictured during the period of the cult of the individual.

If we are to consider this matter as Marxists and as Leninists, then we have to state unequivocally that the leadership practice which came into being during the last years of Stalin's life became a serious obstacle in the path of Soviet social development.

Stalin often failed for months to take up some unusually important problems concerning the life of the Party and of the state whose solution could not be postponed. During Stalin's leadership our peaceful relations with other nations were often threatened, because one-man decisions could cause and often did cause great complications.

In the last years, when we managed to free ourselves of the harmful practice of the cult of the individual and took several proper steps in the sphere of internal and external policies, everyone saw how activity grew before their very eyes, how the creative activity of the broad working masses developed, how favorably all this acted upon the development of economy and of culture.

Some comrades may ask us: Where were the members of the Political Bureau of the Central Committee? Why did they not assert themselves against the cult of the individual in time? And why is this being done only now?

First of all we have to consider the fact that the members of the Political Bureau viewed these matters in a different way at different times. Initially, many of them backed Stalin actively because Stalin was one of the strongest Marxists and his logic, his strength and his will greatly influenced the cadres and Party work.

It is known that Stalin, after Lenin's death, especially during the first years, actively fought for Leninism against the enemies of Leninist theory and against those who deviated. Beginning with Leninist theory, the Party, with its Central Committee at the head, started on a great scale the work of socialist industrialization of the country, agricultural collectivization and the cultural revolution. At that time Stalin gained great popularity, sympathy and support. The Party had to fight those who attempted to lead the country away from the correct Leninist path; it had to fight Trotskyites, Zinovievites and rightists, and the bourgeois nationalists. This fight was indispensable. Later, however, Stalin, abusing his power more and more, began to fight eminent Party and government leaders and to use terroristic methods against honest Soviet people. As we have already shown, Stalin thus handled such eminent Party and government leaders as Kossior, Rudzutak, Eikhe, Postyshev and many others.

Attempts to oppose groundless suspicions and charges resulted in the opponent falling victim of the repression. This characterized the fall of Comrade Postyshev.

In one of his speeches Stalin expressed his dissatisfaction with Postyshev and asked him, "What are you actually?"

Postyshev answered clearly, "I am a Bolshevik, Comrade Stalin, a Bolshevik."

This assertion was at first considered to show a lack of respect for Stalin; later it was considered a harmful act and consequently resulted in Postyshev's annihilation and branding without any reason as a "people's enemy."

In the situation which then prevailed I have talked often with Nikolai Alexandrovich Bulganin; once when we two were traveling in a car, he said, "It has happened sometimes that a man goes to Stalin on his invitation as a friend. And when he sits with Stalin, he does not know where he will be sent next, home or to jail."

It is clear that such conditions put every member of the Political Bureau in a very difficult situation. And when we also consider the fact that in the last years the Central Committee plenary sessions were not convened and that the sessions of the Political Bureau occurred only occasionally, from time to time, then we will understand how difficult it was for any member of the Political Bureau to take a stand against one or another injust or improper procedure, against serious errors and shortcomings in the practices of leadership.

As we have already shown, many decisions were taken either by one person or in a roundabout way, without collective discussions. The sad fate of Political Bureau member, Comrade Voznesensky, who fell victim to Stalin's repressions, is known to all. It is a characteristic thing that the decision to remove him from the Political Bureau was never discussed but was reached in a devious fashion. In the same way came the decision concerning the removal of Kuznetsov and Rodionov from their posts.

The importance of the Central Committee's Political Bureau was reduced and its work was disorganized by the creation within the Political Bureau of various commissions—the so-called "quintets," "sextets," "septets" and "novenaries." Here is, for instance, a resolution of the Political Bureau of October 3, 1946.

Stalin's Proposal:

1. The Political Bureau Commission for Foreign Affairs ("Sextet") is to concern itself in the future, in addition to foreign affairs, also with matters of internal construction and domestic policy.

2. The Sextet is to add to its roster the Chairman of the State Commission of Economic Planning of the USSR, Comrade Voznesensky, and is to be known as a Septet.

Signed: Secretary of the Central Committee, J. Stalin.

What a terminology of a card player! It is clear that the

creation within the Political Bureau of this type of commission—"quintets," "sextets," "septets," and "novenaries"—was against the principle of collective leadership. The result of this was that some members of the Political Bureau were in this way kept away from participation in reaching the most important state matters.

One of the oldest members of our Party, Kliment Yefremovich Voroshilov, found himself in an almost impossible situation. For several years he was actually deprived of the right of participation in Political Bureau sessions. Stalin forbade him to attend the Political Bureau sessions and to receive documents. When the Political Bureau was in session and Comrade Voroshilov heard about it, he telephoned each time and asked whether he would be allowed to attend. Sometimes Stalin permitted it, but always showed his dissatisfaction. Because of his extreme suspicion, Stalin toyed also with the absurd and ridiculous suspicion that Voroshilov was an English agent. It's true—an English agent. A special tapping device was installed in his home to listen to what was said there. . . .

Let us consider the first Central Committee Plenum after the XIXth Party Congress when Stalin, in his talk at the Plenum, characterized Vyacheslav Mikhailovich Molotov and Anastas Ivanovich Mikoyan and suggested that these old workers of our Party were guilty of some baseless charges. It is not excluded that had Stalin remained at the helm for another several months, Comrades Molotov and Mikoyan would probably have not delivered any speeches at this Congress.

Stalin evidently had plans to finish off the old members of the Political Bureau. He often stated that Political Bureau members should be replaced by new ones.

His proposal, after the XIXth Congress concerning the selection of 25 persons to the Central Committee Presidium, was aimed at the removal of the old Political Bureau members and the bringing in of less experienced persons so that these would extol him in all sorts of ways.

We can assume that this was also a design for the future annihilation of the old Political Bureau members and in this way a cover for all shameful acts of Stalin, acts which we are now considering.

Comrades! In order not to repeat errors of the past, the Central Committee has declared itself resolutely against the cult of the individual. We consider that Stalin was excessively extolled. However, in the past Stalin doubtlessly performed great services to the Party, to the working class, and to the international workers' movement.

This question is complicated by the fact that all this which we have just discussed was done during Stalin's life under his leadership and with his concurrence; here Stalin was convinced that this was necessary for the defense of the interests of the working classes against the plotting of the enemies and against the attack of the imperialist camp. He saw this from the position of the interest of the working class, of the interest of the laboring people, of the interest of the victory of socialism and Communism. We cannot say that these were the deeds of a giddy despot. He considered that this should be done in the interest of the Party; of the working masses, in the name of the defense of the revolution's gains. In this lies the whole tragedy!

Comrades! Lenin had often stressed that modesty is an absolutely integral part of a real Bolshevik. Lenin himself was the living personification of the greatest modesty. We cannot say that we have been following this Leninist example in all respects. It is enough to point out that many towns, factories and industrial enterprises, kolkhozes and sovkhozes, Soviet institutions and cultural institutions have been referred to by us with a title—if I may express it so— of private property of the names of these or those government or Party leaders who were still active and in good health. Many of us participated in the action of assigning our names to various towns, rayons, undertakings and kolkhozes. We must correct this.

But this should be done calmly and slowly. The Central Committee will discuss this matter and consider it carefully in order to prevent errors and excesses. I can remember how the Ukraine learned about Kossior's arrest. The Kiev radio used to start its programs thus: "This is radio Kossior." When one day the programs began without naming Kossior, everyone was quite certain that something had happened to Kossior, that he probably had been arrested.

Thus, if today we begin to remove the signs everywhere and to change names, people will think, that these comrades in whose honor the given enterprises, kolkhozes or cities are named, also met some bad fate and that they have also been arrested.

How is the authority and the importance of this or that leader judged? On the basis of how many towns, industrial enterprises and factories, kolkhozes and sovkhozes carry his name. Is it not about time that we eliminate this "private property" and "nationalize" the factories, the industrial enterprises, the kolkhozes and the sovkhozes? This will benefit our cause. After all the cult of the individual is manifested also in this way.

We should in all seriousness consider the question of the cult of the individual. We cannot let this matter get out of the Party, especially not to the press. It is for this reason that we are considering it here at a closed Congress session. We should know the limits; we should not give ammunition to the enemy; we should not wash our dirty linen before their eyes. I think that the delegates to the Congress will understand and assess properly all these proposals.

Comrades: We must abolish the cult of the individual decisively, once and for all; we must draw the proper conclusions concerning both ideological-theoretical and practical work.

It is necessary for this purpose:

First, in a Bolshevik manner to condemn and to eradicate the cult of the individual as alien to Marxism-Leninism and not consonant with the principles of Party leadership and the norms of Party life, and to fight inexorably all attempts at bringing back this practice in one form or another.

To return to and actually practice in all our ideological work the most important theses of Marxist-Leninist science about the people as the creator of history and as the creator of all material and spiritual good of humanity, about the decisive role of the Marxist Party in the revolutionary fight for the transformation of society, about the victory of Communism.

In this connection we will be forced to do much work in order to examine critically from the Marxist-Leninist viewpoint and to correct the widely spread erroneous views connected with the cult of the individual in the sphere of history, philosophy, economy and of other sciences, as well as in literature and the fine arts. It is especially necessary that in the immediate future we compile a serious textbook of the history of our Party which will be edited in accordance with scientific Marxist objectivism, a textbook of the history of Soviet society, a book pertaining to the events of the civil war and the Great Patriotic War.

Secondly, to continue systematically and consistently the work done by the Party's Central Committee during the last years, a work characterized by minute observation in all Party organizations, from the bottom to the top, of the Leninist principles of Party leadership, characterized, above all, by the main principle of collective leadership, characterized by the observation of the norms of Party life described in the Statutes of our Party, and finally, characterized by the wide practice of criticism and self-criticism.

Thirdly, to restore completely the Leninist principles of Soviet socialist democracy, expressed in the Constitution of the Soviet Union, to fight willfulness of individuals abusing their power. The evil caused by acts violating revolutionary socialist legality which have accumulated during a long time as a result of the negative influence of the cult of the individual has to be completely corrected.

Comrades! The XXth Congress of the Communist Party of the Soviet Union has manifested with a new strength the unshakable unity of our Party, its cohesiveness around the Central Committee, its resolute will to accomplish the great task of building Communism. And the fact that we present in all their ramifications the basic problems of overcoming the cult of the individual which is alien to Marxism-Leninism, as well as the problem of liquidating its burdensome consequences, is an evidence of the great moral and political strength of our Party.

We are absolutely certain that our Party, armed with the historical resolutions of the XXth Congress, will lead the Soviet people along the Leninist path to new successes, to new victories.

Long live the victorious banner of our Party—Leninism!

PALMIRO TOGLIATTI: *Answers to Nine Questions about Stalinism, June 16, 1956* [2]

1. *In your opinion, what is the meaning of the condemnation of the personality cult in the USSR? What are its internal, external, political, social, economic, psychological, and historical causes?*

2. *Ibid.*, pp. 98, 102-126, 129-130, 132-136, 139. Reprinted by arrangement with Columbia University Press.

In my opinion, the condemnation of the personality cult made by the Communists in the Soviet Union and the criticisms leveled against Stalin's work mean exactly what has been said and is being repeated by the Soviet Communist leaders: neither more nor less than that ...

It is necessary to accustom oneself to thinking that the criticisms against Stalin and the cult of his person mean to our Soviet comrades exactly what they have said up to now. And what is that, precisely? That as a result of Stalin's errors and the cult of his person, negative elements had accumulated and unfavorable, even positively bad, situations had developed in different sectors of the life of Soviet society and in different sectors of the activity of the Party and of the state. It is not a simple matter, however, to reduce all these negative points to a single general concept, because even in such a case, one runs the risk of excessive, arbitrary, and false generalizations, i. e., the risk of judging as bad, rejecting, and criticizing the entire Soviet economic, social and cultural reality, which would be a return to the usual reactionary idiocies.

The least arbitrary of the generalizations is the one which sees in Stalin's errors a progressive encroachment by personal power on the collective entities of a democratic origin and nature and, as a result of this, the pile-up of phenomena of bureaucracy, of violation of legality, of stagnation, and, also, partially, of degeneration at different points of the social organism. However, it must be said at once that this encroachment was partial and probably had its most serious manifestations at the summit of the leading organs of the state and Party. This was the origin of a tendency to restrict democratic life, initiative, and dynamic thought and action in numerous fields (technical and economic development, cultural activity, literature, art, etc.), but it cannot be stated categorically that there has arisen from this the destruction of those fundamental features of Soviet society from which it derives its democratic and socialist character and which make this society superior in quality to the modern capitalist societies. Soviet society could not fall into such errors, while, on the other hand, the bourgeois capitalist regimes fall into errors and situations which are much more serious. Those errors could not become a permanent and general part of its civil, economic, and political life. If they had lasted longer, perhaps the breaking point might have been reached, although even this hypothesis should be taken with caution, because a break would certainly have brought more harm than good to the masses and to the entire socialist movement; this danger was known not only to those men who could have engineered this break but also to wide strata of society.

I do not mean to say by this that the consequences of Stalin's errors were not extremely serious. They were very serious; they touched many fields, and I do not think it will be easy to overcome them, nor to do so quickly. In substance, it may be said that a large part of the leading cadres of Soviet society (Party, state, economy, culture, etc.) had become torpid in the cult of Stalin, losing or lessening its critical and creative ability in thought and action. For this reason it was absolutely necessary that Stalin's errors be denounced, and that it be done in such a way as to jolt them and to reactivate the entire life of the organisms on which the complex system of socialist society rests. Thus there will be a new democratic progress of this society, and that will be a powerful contribution to a better understanding among all peoples, to an international detente, to the advance of socialism, and to peace.

2. *Do you believe that criticism of the personality cult in the USSR will lead to institutional changes?*

3. *The legitimacy of power is the great problem of public law, and modern political thought tends to indicate that the people's will is the wellspring of legitimacy. Parliamentary democracies of the Western type believe that the people's will must have a plurality of parties to express itself. Do you believe that power is legitimate in a single-party system with elections offering no choice between government and opposition?*

I may be mistaken, but in my opinion there are not to be foreseen today any institutional changes in the Soviet Union, nor do the criticisms formulated openly at the XXth Congress imply the necessity for such changes. This does not mean that very profound modifications ought not to occur, some of which, incidentally, are already in progress.

First of all, what is meant by institutional changes? I believe that individuals who speak of them mean changes in the political structure which would usher Soviet society into at least some of the forms of political organization intrinsic in the so-called Western regimes, or would place a new emphasis on some of the institutions intrinsic in these regimes. If the problem is posed thus, my answer is negative.

Let us, if we must, begin by examining the legitimacy of power and of its source, but let us try to free ourselves from the hypocritical formalism with which this problem is treated by the apologists for Western civilization. We have read *State and Revolution* and, fortunately for us, we have not forgotten the substance of that teaching. Criticism of Stalin's errors will not make us forget it. The truth of the matter is that in the so-called Western civilizations, the source of legitimate power is not at all the will of the people. The people's will is at best only one of the contributing factors, periodically expressing itself in elections, in determining some government policies. However, elections (Italy is a typical example for some aspects) are marked by a complex system of pressure, intimidation, coercion, falsification, and legal and illegal subterfuges, which seriously limit and falsify the expression of the people's will. And this system works not only to the advantage of and in the hands of those in power at the moment, but also for whoever holds the real power in society, afforded by wealth, ownership of the means of production and trade, and by the end products, beginning with the actual direction of political life and going to the unfailing protection of the religious authorities and of all the other nerve centers of power which exist in a capitalist society. We maintain that today, because of the developments and the present strength of the democratic and socialist movement, very large rents can be torn in this system which hinders the free expression of the people's will, and, therefore, an increasingly wider breach can be opened to the expression of this will. For this reason we move on democratic grounds, and without leaving these grounds we believe that new developments are always possible. This does not mean, however, that we do not see things as they are, and that we should make a fetish, the universal and absolute model of democracy, out of the way democratic life is lived in the Western World (it is bad enough without going so far as to end up in Spain, or Turkey, or Latin America, or Portugal, or come upon the discriminatory electoral system of the U.S.A.)! As a matter of fact, we still believe that a democracy of the Western type is a limited and imperfect democracy which is false in many ways and needs to be developed and perfected through a series of economic and political reforms. Therefore, even if we should reach the conclusion that the XXth Congress opens a new process of democratic development in the Soviet Union, we are far from thinking, and believe that it is wrong to think, that this development can or must be made by a return to institutions of the "Western" type. . . .

Is it possible that there was in the operation of the Soviet system a halt, an obstacle by which Soviet democracy was limited? It is not only possible; it was openly admitted at the XXth Congress. Soviet democratic life was limited, partly suffocated, by the ascendancy of a bureaucratic and authoritarian method of leadership, and by violations of the legality of the regime. In theory such a thing is possible because a socialist regime is not in itself free of errors and danger. Whoever thinks this would be falling into a naïve infantilism. Socialist society is not only a society composed of men, but also a developing society in which there exist objective and subjective contrasts, and it is subject to the tides of history. In practice, we shall attempt to see how and why a limitation of Soviet democratic life could have come about, but whatever the answer to this question, there is for us no doubt that we will never need to return to the forms of organization of the capitalist societies.

The multi-party or single-party system may not in itself be considered a distinguishing element between bourgeois and socialist societies, just as in itself it does not mark the difference between a democratic and a non-democratic society. . . . The very notion of a party in the Soviet Union is something different from what we mean by this term. The party works and struggles to realize and develop socialism, but its work is essentially of a positive and constructive nature, not argumentative against a hypothetical domestic political opponent. The "opponent" against whom it fights is the objective difficulty to be overcome, the difference to be resolved by working, the reality to be mastered, the remnants of the old to be destroyed for the progress of the new, and so forth. The dialectic of conflict, which is essential for the development of society, is no longer expressed by the contests between various parties, either of the government or of the opposition, because there is no longer an objective basis (for things) or a subjective basis (in the spirit of men) for this kind of contest.

It is expressed within the unitarian system which comprises a whole series of co-ordinated organizations (party, soviets, trade unions, etc.). Stalin is criticized for having hindered this expression within the system. The correction consists in restoring it to normal, not in denying the system or in demolishing it. . . .

A judge must have an independent position, and the Soviet Constitution guarantees it to him, as do many other constitutions. But the violation of this standard always happens as a matter of fact rather than law. Moreover, a judge is not and cannot be a citizen who lives outside of society, of its conflicts, and of the currents which permeate and dominate it. Ten years ago no judge would have dreamed of sentencing a heroic partisan leader to life imprisonment—to life imprisonment!—for having killed, under war conditions, someone reported to him as a spy. This has been done. Can we call these judges "independent"? They are probably formally independent of direct ministerial injunction, but not independent of the campaign which DeGasperi and all the others conducted for ten years to smear the partisan movement, put it under indictment, and have its members convicted. Judges are part of the ruling class and influenced by currents of opinion in it, whether these be just or unjust. They tell us now that in the USSR, in Stalin's time, there were trials which ended in illegal and unjust sentences. The judges who decided those sentences were very probably not citizens who betrayed their own consciences. They were citizens who were convinced that the mistaken doctrines of Stalin, which had spread among the people and concerned the presence of "enemies of the people" everywhere to be destroyed, were just. Therefore, even though theoretically independent, they judged in that manner. The only true guarantee lies in the justice of the political policies of the Party and government, and this can be assured by a proper democratic life both in the Party and in the State, and by permanent and close contact with the popular masses in all walks of public life. The judge also will be that much more just, the more he is in close contact with the people.

4. *It has already been remarked that there is no common political language between the East and the West. Personality cult is known as tyranny in the West; the errors which lead to purges, trials and convictions are called crimes.*

Conversely, the East calls opposition treason; discussion is called deviation, and so on. A different language always means substantial differences. To what do you attribute this diversity of language?

This assertion about diversity of political language between West and East, if you will allow me, is pure reactionary foolishness. . . . It is not that two different languages are spoken in different parts of the world, but that the social groups, incapable of approving or even understanding the radical social and political changes which are taking place and to which they are hostile, would like to create abysses of misunderstanding between the various parts of the world, to the detriment of the progressive part. But they are not succeeding.

Political terminology in use in the West and East is absolutely the same. Tyranny has the same meaning here and there. In specific periods of the Stalin regime there were instances of tyranny, and criminal acts were perpetrated by the government which were morally repugnant. No one denies this. Democracy means, here as well as there, government by the people, in the interest of the people, equality for all the people, and so on. In their first constitutions, when the Russian Communists established a marked difference in the importance of the workers' and the peasants' vote, they were well aware that this was not strictly a democratic practice. But they adopted it because they desired that the leadership function, obtained through the revolution, be formally and legally guaranteed for the working class, saving the country from the foreign invasion and catastrophe, and creating the initial condition necessary to pave the way for socialism. Once these first steps were accomplished, this practice was abolished. And always this point was clearly made. It was openly stated that once the inequality and differentiation in the vote was removed, democracy was restored. Here in this wonderful West, I am waiting for someone to clarify for me what relationship there is between democracy and the political discrimination between citizens which a government coalition of Christian Democrats and Social Democrats sought to make a part of all government activity, and which today is the general rule of conduct of most state governing bodies, of land and factory owners, of welfare agencies, labor offices, and so forth.

It is completely untrue that in the "East," the term op-

position is synonymous with treason, discussion with deviation, etc. In a discussion views can be expressed which
do not agree with the existing political line, and this can
be called deviation because it is that. Here [in Italy] the
expressing of political views contrary to those of the ruling
parties instead is termed "ideological terrorism." I have
already spoken of the term opposition, and it cannot be
classed as treason. Undoubtedly there have been cases, and
times, when opposition took forms which could be considered treason, or which could have led to treason. . . .
The grave error committed by Stalin was to have illicitly
extended this system (worsening it, in fact, because respect for revolutionary legality had always been demanded
by Lenin, initially, even if then this legality was limited by
force of circumstances) to subsequent situations, when it
was no longer required and therefore became only the
basis for personal power. And the mistake of his collaborators was in not seeing this in time, in having allowed
him to go on until correction was no longer possible without damage to all concerned.

5. *Do you believe that the personal dictatorship of
Stalin came about contrary to, and outside, Russian historical and political traditions, or that instead it was a development of these traditions?*

6. *Stalin's personal dictatorship, to maintain and advance itself, made use of a series of coercive measures
which in the West, since the French Revolution, has been
called "terror." Do you feel that this "terror" was necessary?*

. . . The removal of Stalin from power when the seriousness of the mistakes that he was committing became apparent, while "legally possible," in practice was impossible
because, if the question had been aired, a conflict would
have ensued which probably would have compromised
the future of the revolution and of the state, against which
the weapons of all parts of the world were pointed. It
would suffice to have had even superficial contact with
Soviet public opinion, in the years Stalin was ruling the
country, and to have followed the international situation
of those years to realize that this point is very true. Today,
for example, the Soviet leaders denounce specific errors,
and a moment of lack of confidence by Stalin at the outset
of the war. But who in the Soviet Union at that time would
have understood and accepted, I won't say the removal of

Stalin but only a diminution of his authority? There would have been a collapse if this had been seen or even suspected. And the same holds true for other times. The observation made by Khrushchev explains, it is true, the difficulty confronting those individuals who would have wished to correct the situation, but at the same time Khrushchev's explanation complicates the over-all picture and increases its seriousness. We are forced to admit that either the mistakes Stalin made were unknown to the great mass of the leading cadres of the nation, and therefore to the people—and this does not seem likely—or else they were not regarded as errors by this mass of cadres, and therefore by the public opinion which they [the cadres] guided and led. As you see, I rule out the explanation that a change was impossible solely because of the presence of a military, police, terror apparatus which controlled the situation with its means. The same apparatus consisted of, and was led by, men who in a serious moment of stress, for example such as Hitler's attack, would have likewise been subject to elemental reactions if a crisis had developed. To me it seems much fairer to recognize that Stalin, in spite of the errors which he was committing, continued to command the solidarity of the overwhelming majority of the nation, and above all had the support of his leading cadres and also of the masses. Was this because Stalin not only erred, but also did good, "he did a great deal for the Soviet Union," "he was the most convinced of Marxists, and had the strongest faith in the people"? . . .

Here we must admit openly and without hesitation that while the XXth Congress greatly aided the proper understanding and solution of many serious and new problems confronting the democratic and socialist movement, and while it marks a most important milestone in the evolution of Soviet society, it is not possible, however, to consider satisfactory the position which was taken at the Congress and which today is being fully developed in the Soviet press regarding the errors of Stalin and the causes and conditions which made them possible. . . .

It is true that today they criticize themselves, and this is to their great credit, but in this criticism they are losing without doubt a little of their own prestige. But aside from this, as long as we confine ourselves, in substance, to denouncing the personal faults of Stalin as the cause of everything we remain within the realm of the "personality cult." First, all that was good was attributed to the super-human, positive qualities of one man: now all that is evil is attributed to his equally exceptional and even astonishing faults. In the one case, as well as in the other, we are outside the criterion of judgment intrinsic in Marxism. The true problems are evaded, which are why and how Soviet society could reach and did reach certain forms alien to the democratic way and to the legality which it had set for itself, even to the point of degeneration. This study must be made following the various stages of development of this society, and it is our Soviet comrades above all others who have to do it because they know the situation better than we, who might err because of partial or erroneous knowledge of the facts.

We are reminded, first of all, that Lenin, in his last speeches and writings, stressed the danger of bureaucracy which threatened the new society. It seems to us that undoubtedly Stalin's errors were tied in with an excessive increase in the bureaucratic apparatus in Soviet economic and political life, and perhaps, above all, in Party life. And here it is extremely difficult to distinguish between cause and effect. The one gradually became the expression of the other. Is this excessive bureaucratic burden also a traditional outgrowth of political and organizational forms and customs of Old Russia? . . . We then are not so much interested in evaluating the residue of the old, as we are in the fact that a new type of bureaucratic leadership was growing from the new leadership class when this class was assuming entirely new tasks. . . .

Perhaps we are not in error in asserting that the damaging restrictions placed on the democratic regime, and the gradual emergence of bureaucratic organizational forms stemmed from the Party.

More important it seems to me should be a close examination of that which followed, when the first Five-Year Plan was carried out, and agricultural collectivization was realized. Here we are dealing with fundamental questions. The successes attained were great, in fact, superlative. A large socialist industrial system was created without foreign assistance or loans, through commitment and development of the internal forces of the new society. . . .

It is an error of principle to believe that once the first great successes are achieved socialist construction goes ahead by itself and not through the interplay of contradictions of a new type, which must be solved within the framework of the new society by the action of the masses and of the party which leads them.

Two main consequences arose from this, I believe. The first was the stagnation of activity of the masses in the various places and organizations (Party, labor unions, factory, soviets) where the new and real difficulties of the situation should have been faced, and where, instead, writings and speeches full of pompous statements, of ready-made slogans, etc. began to become widespread. These were cold and ineffective because they had lost touch with life. True creative debate began to disappear little by little and at the same time the very activity of the masses diminished, directed more by orders from above than by its own stimulus. But the second consequence was still more serious. When reality came into play and difficulties came to light as the result of the imbalance and contrasts which still existed everywhere, there occurred little by little, until at last it was the main force, the tendency to consider that, always and in every case, every evil, every obstacle in the application of the plan, every difficulty in supplying provisions, in delivering raw materials, in the development of the various sectors of industry or agriculture, etc.—all was due to sabotage, to the work of class enemies, counter-revolutionary groups operating clandestinely, etc. It is not that these things did not exist; they did indeed exist. The Soviet Union was surrounded by merciless enemies who were ready to resort to any means to damage and to check its rise. But this erroneous trend in judging the objective situation caused a loss of the sense of limits, made them lose the idea of the borderline between good and evil, friend and enemy, incapacity or weakness and conscious hostility and betrayal, contrasts and difficulties which come from things and from the hostile action of one who has sworn to ruin you. Stalin gave a pseudo-scientific formulation to this fearful confusion through his erroneous thesis of the inherent increase in enemies and in the sharpening of the class struggle with the progress of building socialism. This made permanent and aggravated the confusion itself and was the origin of the unheard-of violations of socialist legality which have been denounced publicly today. It is necessary, however, to search more deeply in order to understand how these positions could be accepted and become popular. . . . Stalin was at the same

time the expression and the maker of a situation, because
he had shown himself the most expert organizer and leader
of a bureaucratic-type apparatus at the time when this got
the better of the democratic forms of life, as well as because he provided a doctrinal justification of what was in
reality an erroneous line and on which later was based his
personal power, to the point of taking on degenerate forms.
All this explains the consensus [solidarity] which surrounded him, which lasted until his demise, and which still
perhaps has retained some effectiveness. . . .

7. *To what do you attribute the fact that the Communists of the entire world believed the official Stalinist version of the trials and the plots?*

The Communists of the entire world always had limitless
faith in the Soviet Communist Party and in its leaders. It
is more than obvious what was the source of this faith.
The position of the Soviet Communists was correct in the
decisive moments of history and on the decisive questions
pertaining to the workers' movement and international
policy. The 1917 Revolution, in which they came to power,
aroused enthusiasm. The correctness of the policy advanced, defended, and followed after the Revolution was
based on facts. The superhuman difficulties which they
faced and finally overcame were known. The entire world
was against them, attacked them with every possible means,
abused them. The ruling classes of all nations were united
against them. In the opposition parties and even in the
workers' movement, there were few persons who expressed
at least understanding, if not approbation, of the gigantic
task that was being carried out in the Soviet Union. Today
all except the most extreme reactionaries are in agreement
in recognizing that the creation of the Soviet Union is
the greatest event in contemporary history; but, for the
most part, it was only, or almost only, the Communists who
followed this creation step by step, made it understood, defended it, and defended its authors. It was natural and
proper, under these conditions, that a relationship of trust
and of profound, complete solidarity should be established
between the workers' vanguards in the entire world and
that Communist Party, which truly stood in the van of the
entire political and social movement. It is necessary to
consider also that in almost every case those who had
begun by criticizing this or that aspect of the Communist
policy of the Soviet Union soon ended by joining the

ranks of the official denouncers of the entire Communist movement and eventually became open or undercover agents of the most reactionary political forces. Every Communist party, to a greater or lesser degree, did undergo this same experience. There was created, then, in addition to a relation of faith and complete solidarity with the Soviet Communists, the firm conviction that this solidarity was the distinctive trait of a truly revolutionary proletarian movement. And this was fundamentally true. None of us has to repent for this relationship of faith and solidarity. It is this which has permitted us, each fighting and working under the conditions of his own country, to express and to give a political and organizational form to the new revolutionary impulse which the October Revolution had awakened in the working class, which the progress made in the building of a socialist society in the Soviet Union supported, intensified, and gradually made more aware of itself. . . .

The trials, to which the question refers, I believe are placed (I shall explain later the significance of this limitation) in this period when there was a struggle in France for a popular front, in Spain with weapons, and the international policy of the Soviet Union was turning effectively to the defense of democracy and of peace. The Communist leaders had no factor which would permit them to doubt the legality of the judgments, particularly because they knew that, defeated politically and among the masses, the leaders of the old opposition groups (Trotskyites and rightists) were not averse to continuing the struggle by terrorist means, and that this was also going on outside the Soviet Union. (At Paris, in 1934, one of our best militants, Camillo Montanari from Reggio Emilia, was killed in cold blood by a Trotskyite. There were similar cases elsewhere.)

The fact that all the accused confessed caused, without doubt, surprise and discussion even among us, but nothing more. Besides, it is still not clear, to us, whether the current denunciations of the violation of legality and application of illegitimate and morally repugnant prosecuting methods extend to the entire period of the trials, or only to a given period, more recent than that to which I have referred. . . .

I repeat, with respect to the initial trials—which we were able to consider, the later trials for the most part not being public—my opinion today is that there existed simultaneously two elements: the conspiratorial attempts of the opponents against the regime to commit terrorist acts; and the application of illegal prosecuting methods, censurable on a moral basis. The first, naturally, does not minimize the gravity of the second.

8. *The criticism of the personality cult has been formulated from above without previous consultation of the people by the authorities. Do you consider that this is a proof that Stalinism is not dead, as many assert?*

The judgments which I give and which I have substantially explained bring me to deem it inevitable that the correction and criticism of Stalin's errors should come from above. The very restriction of democratic life in the Party and in the State, a part of and a consequence of these errors, and the solidarity with which Stalin had been surrounded, worked in such a way that criticism from below could have come about only slowly and would have been developed in a confused manner, not without dangerous ruptures. The thing may appear unpleasant, but it is a result of what has happened previously. . . . To re-educate for a normal democratic life on the model that Lenin established during the first years of the revolution; that is, to re-educate to take the initiative in the field of ideas and in practice, to be inquisitive, to engage in lively debate, to attain the degree of tolerance of errors that is indispensable for discovering truth, to attain full independence of judgment and of character, etc., etc., to re-educate thus a party framework of hundreds of thousands of men and women, through them the entire Party, and through the Party an enormous country where living conditions still differ greatly from region to region, is an enormous task which is not to be completed by three years of work nor by a congress. . . . It seems to me that the errors of Stalin must be corrected, through this broad development, by a method vastly different from that which Stalin himself followed in that period of his life when he abandoned the proper forms of party and State operation. . . .

9. *Do you believe that the criticism of the personality cult will bring a change in relations between the USSR and the People's Democracies, between the Russian Communist Party and the Communist parties of the other countries, and, in general, between the USSR and the international workers' movement?*

I hope that there is no longer anyone, at least in Italy,

who still believes the foolish myth that the Communist parties receive, step by step, instructions, directives, and orders from Moscow. If such a person still exists, there is no use writing for him because it is evident that his head is too hard and that he is absolutely incapable even of coming close to understanding the problems of the present workers' movement. Therefore, let us write for the others.

In the first years following the First World War, when the Communist International was formed, there is no doubt that the main questions pertaining to the political line of the workers' movement and later of the Communist movement in the individual countries were fully debated at the center, at Moscow, at congresses and other international meetings, out of which precise lines arose. During this period, it can be said that there was a centralized leadership of the Communist movement, and the main responsibility for this fell upon our Russian comrades, assisted by comrades from other countries. Very soon, however, the movement began to go ahead by itself, particularly where it had good leaders. . . . If the Communists advanced in the great wake of the international policy of the Soviet Union, it is because they were convinced that the policy was correct, and in reality it was.

The Information Bureau, formed in 1947 with tasks quite different from those of the International, essentially did two things: the first was good; the second, bad. The first was to guide properly the entire workers' movement in its resistance to, and struggle against, the war plans of imperialism. The second was the unfortunate intervention against the Yugoslav Communists. . . .

One general problem, common to the entire movement, has arisen from the criticisms of Stalin—the problem of the perils of bureaucratic degeneration, of stifling democratic life, of the confusion between the constructive revolutionary force and the destruction of revolutionary legality, of separation of the economic and political leadership from the life, criticism, and creative activity of the masses. We shall welcome a contest among the Communist parties in power to find the best way to avoid this peril once and for all. It will be up to us to work out our own method and life in order that we, too, may be protected against the evils of stagnation and bureaucratization, in order that we may learn to solve together the problems of freedom for the working masses and of social justice, and hence gain for ourselves ever-increasing prestige and membership among the masses.

MAO TSE-TUNG: *"Let a Hundred Flowers Bloom"* [3]

Led by the working class and the Communist party, and united as one, our 600,000,000 people are engaged in the great work of building socialism.

Unification of the country, unity of the people and unity among our various nationalities, these are the basic guarantees for the sure triumphs of our cause. However, this does not mean that there are no longer any contradictions in our society. It would be naïve to imagine that there are no more contradictions. To do so would be to fly in the face of objective reality. We are confronted by two types of social contradictions; contradictions between ourselves and the enemy and contradictions among the people. These two types of contradictions are totally different in nature.

If we are to have a correct understanding of these two different types of contradictions, we must first of all make clear what is meant by "the people" and what is meant by "the enemy."

The term "the people" has different meanings in different countries, and in different historical periods in each country. Take our country for example. During the Japanese aggression, all those classes, strata and social groups that opposed Japanese aggression belonged to the category of the people, while the Japanese imperialists, Chinese traitors and the pro-Japanese elements belonged to the category of enemies of the people.

During the war of liberation, the United States imperialists and their henchmen, the bureaucrat-capitalists and landlord class, and the Kuomintang reactionaries, who represented these two classes, were the enemies of the people, while all other classes, strata and social groups that opposed these enemies, belonged to the category of the people.

At this stage of building socialism, all classes, strata and social groups that approve, support and work for the cause

3. From *On the Correct Handling of Contradictions Among the People* (New York, 1957), pp. 3-5, 7-12, 22-26. Reprinted by permission of New Century Publishers.

of Socialist construction belong to the category of the
people, while those social forces and groups that resist the
Socialist revolution, and are hostile to and try to wreck
Socialist construction, are enemies of the people.

The contradictions between ourselves and our enemies
are antagonistic ones. Within the ranks of the people, contradictions among the working people are nonantagonistic,
while those between the exploiters and the exploited classes
have, apart from their antagonistic aspect, a nonantagonistic aspect. Contradictions among the people have always
existed, but their content differs in each period of the revolution and during the building of socialism. In the conditions existing in China today what we call contradictions
among the people include the following:

Contradictions within the working class, contradictions
within the peasantry, contradictions within the intelligentsia,
contradictions between the working class and the peasantry, on the one hand, and the intelligentsia on the other,
between the working class and other sections of the working people, on the one hand, and the national bourgeoisie,
on the other; contradictions within the national bourgeoisie,
and so forth.

Our people's Government is a Government that truly
represents the interests of the people and serves the people,
yet certain contradictions do exist between the Government and the masses. These include contradictions between
the interests of the state, collective interests and individual
interests; between democracy and centralism; between those
in positions of leadership and the led, and contradictions
arising from the bureaucratic practices of certain state
functionaries in their relations with the masses. All these
are contradictions among the people. Generally speaking,
underlying the contradictions among the people is the basic
identity of the interests of the people.

In our country, the contradiction between the working
class and the national bourgeoisie is a contradiction among
the people. The class struggle waged between the two is, by
and large, a class struggle within the ranks of the people.
This is because of the dual character of the national bourgeoisie in our country.

In the years of the bourgeois-democratic revolution,
there was a revolutionary side to their character; there was
also a tendency to compromise with the enemy; this was
the other side. In the period of the socialist revolution,

exploitation of the working class to make profits is one side, while support of the constitution and willingness to accept Socialist transformation is the other.

The national bourgeoisie differs from the imperialists, the landlords and the bureaucrat-capitalists. The contradiction between exploiter and exploited, which exists between the national bourgeoisie and the working class, is an antagonistic one. But, in the concrete conditions existing in China, such an antagonistic contradiction, if properly handled, can be transformed into a nonantagonistic one and resolved in a peaceful way. But if it is not properly handled, if, say, we do not follow a policy of uniting, criticizing and educating the national bourgeoisie, or if the national bourgeoisie does not accept this policy, then the contradictions between the working class and the national bourgeoisie can turn into an antagonistic contradiction as between ourselves and the enemy.

Since the contradictions between ourselves and the enemy and those among the people differ in nature, they must be solved in different ways. To put it briefly, the former is a matter of drawing a line between us and our enemies, while the latter is a matter of distinguishing between right and wrong. It is, of course, true that drawing a line between ourselves and our enemies is also a question of distinguishing between right and wrong. For example, the question as to who is right, we or the reactionaries at home and abroad, that is, the imperialists, the feudalists and bureaucrat-capitalists, is also a question of distinguishing between right and wrong, but it is different in nature from questions of right and wrong among the people. . . .

While we stand for freedom with leadership and democracy under centralized guidance, in no sense do we mean that coercive measures should be taken to settle ideological matters and questions involving the distinction between right and wrong among the people. Any attempt to deal with ideological matters or questions involving the right and wrong by administrative orders or coercive measures will not only be ineffective but harmful. We cannot abolish religion by administrative orders; nor can we force people not to believe in it. We cannot compel people to give up idealism, any more than we can force them to believe in Marxism.

In settling matters of an ideological nature or controversial issues among the people, we can only use democratic methods, methods of discussion, of criticism or persuasion and education, not coercive, high-handed methods. In order to carry on their production and studies effectively and to order their lives properly, the people want their Government, the leaders of productive work and of educational and cultural bodies to issue suitable orders of an obligatory nature. It is common sense that the maintenance of law and order would be impossible without administrative orders. Administrative orders and the methods of persuasion and education complement each other in solving contradictions among the people. Administrative orders issued for the maintenance of social order must be accompanied by persuasion and education, for in many cases administrative orders alone will not work. . . .

Under ordinary circumstances, contradictions among the people are not antagonistic. But if they are not dealt with properly or if we relax vigilance and lower our guard, antagonism may arise. In a Socialist country, such a development is usually only of a localized and temporary nature. This is because there the exploitation of man by man has been abolished and the interests of the people are basically the same. Such antagonistic actions on a fairly wide scale as took place during the Hungarian events are accounted for by the fact that domestic and foreign counter-revolutionary elements were at work. These actions were also of a temporary, though special, nature. In cases like this, the reactionaries in a Socialist country, in league with the imperialists, take advantage of contradictions among the people to foment disunity and dissension and fan the flames of disorder in an attempt to achieve their conspiratorial aims. This lesson of the Hungarian events deserves our attention.

Many people seem to think that the proposal to use democratic methods to resolve contradictions among the people raises a new question, but actually that is not so. Marxists have always held that the cause of the proletariat can only be promoted by relying on the masses of the people; that Communists must use democratic methods of persuasion and education when working among the working people and must on no account resort to commandism or coercion. The Chinese Communist party faithfully adheres to this Marxist-Leninist principle. We have always maintained that, under the people's democratic dictatorship, two different methods, dictatorial and democratic, should be used to resolve the two different kinds of contradictions, those between ourselves and the enemy and those among the people. This idea has been explained again and again in our party documents and in speeches by many responsible party leaders. . . .

We have spoken on this question of using democratic methods to resolve contradictions among the people on many occasions in the past, and, furthermore, we have in the main acted on this principle, a principle of which many cadres and many people have a practical understanding. Why then do some people now feel that this is a new issue? The reason is that in the past, an acute struggle raged between ourselves and our enemies both within and without, and contradictions among the people did not attract as much attention as they do today.

Quite a few people fail to make a clear distinction between these two different types of contradictions, those between ourselves and the enemy and those among the people, and are prone to confuse the two. It must be admitted that it is sometimes easy to confuse them. We had instances of such confusion in our past work. In the suppression of the counter-revolution, good people were sometimes mistaken for bad. Such things have happened before, and still happen today. We have been able to keep our mistakes within bounds because it has been our policy to draw a sharp line between our own people and our enemies and, where mistakes have been made, to take suitable measures of rehabilitation.

Marxist philosophy holds that the law of the unity of opposites is a fundamental law of the universe. This law operates everywhere in the natural world, in human society, and in man's thinking. Opposites in contradiction unite as well as struggle with each other, and thus impel all things to move and change. Contradictions exist everywhere, but as things differ in nature, so do contradictions; in any given phenomenon or thing, the unity of opposites is conditional, temporary and transitory, and hence relative, whereas struggle between opposites is absolute.

Lenin gave a very clear exposition of this law. In our country a growing number of people have come to understand it. For many people, however, acceptance of this law is one thing, and its application in examining and dealing with problems is quite another. Many dare not acknowledge openly that there still exist contradictions among the people, which are the very forces that move our society forward. Many people refuse to admit that contradictions still exist in a Socialist society, with the result that when confronted with social contradictions they become timid and helpless. They do not understand that Socialist society grows more united and consolidated precisely through the ceaseless process of correctly dealing with and resolving contradictions. For this reason, we need to explain things to our people, our cadres in the first place, to help them understand contradictions in a Socialist society and learn how to deal with such contradictions in a correct way.

Contradictions in a Socialist society are fundamentally different from contradictions in old societies, such as capitalist society. There they find expression in acute antagonisms and conflicts, in sharp class struggle, which cannot be resolved by the capitalist system itself and can only be resolved by Socialist revolution. Contradictions in Socialist society are, on the contrary, not antagonistic and can be resolved one after the other by the Socialist system itself.

The basic contradictions in Socialist society are still those between the relations of production and the productive forces and between the superstructure and the economic base. These contradictions, however, are fundamentally different in character and have different features from contradictions between the relations of production and the productive forces and between the superstructure and the economic base in the old societies. The present social system of our country is far superior to that of the old days. If this were not so, the old system would not have been overthrown and the new system could not have been set up.

When we say that Socialist relations of production are better suited than the old relations of production to the development of the productive forces, we mean that the former permits the productive forces to develop at a speed unparalleled in the old society, so that production can expand steadily and the constantly growing needs of the people can be met step by step. Under the rule of imperialism, feudalism and bureaucrat-capitalism, production in old China developed very slowly.

For more than fifty years before liberation, China produced only a few score thousand tons of steel a year, not counting the output of the northeastern provinces. If we include these provinces, the peak annual output of steel of our country was only something over 900,000 tons. In 1949, the country's output of steel was only something over 100,000 tons. Now, only seven years after liberation of the country, our steel output already exceeds 4,000,000 tons. In the old China, there was hardly any engineering industry to speak of; motorcar and aircraft industries were non-existent; now, we have them.

When the rule of imperialism, feudalism and bureaucrat-capitalism was overthrown by the people, many were not clear as to where China was headed, to capitalism or to socialism. Facts give the answer: Only socialism can save China. The Socialist system has promoted the rapid development of the productive forces of our country. This is a fact that even our enemies abroad have had to acknowledge.

But our Socialist system has just been set up; it is not yet fully established, nor yet fully consolidated. In joint state-private industrial and commercial enterprises, capitalists still receive a fixed rate of interest on their capital, that is to say, exploitation still exists. So far as ownership is concerned, these enterprises are not yet completely Socialist in character. Some of our agricultural and handicraft producer co-operatives are still semi-Socialist, while even in the fully Socialist co-operatives certain problems about ownership remain to be solved. Relationships in production and exchange are still being gradually established along Socialist lines in various sectors of our economy and more and more appropriate forms are being sought.

It is a complicated problem to settle on a proper ratio between accumulation and consumption within that sector of Socialist economy in which the means of production are owned by the whole people and that sector in which the means of production are collectively owned, as well as between these two sectors. It is not easy to work out a perfectly rational solution to this problem all at once.

To sum up, Socialist relations of production have been established; they are suited to the development of the productive forces, but they are still far from perfect, and their imperfect aspects stand in contradiction to the development of the productive forces. There is conformity as well as contradiction between the relations of production and the development of the productive forces; similarly, there is conformity as well as contradiction between the super-structure and the economic base.

The superstructure, our state institutions of people's democratic dictatorship and its laws, and Socialist ideology under the guidance of Marxism-Leninism, has played a positive role in facilitating the victory of Socialist trans-formation and establishment of a Socialist organization of labor; it is suited to the Socialist economic base, that is, Socialist relations of production. But survivals of bourgeois ideology, bureaucratic ways of doing things in our state organs, and flaws in certain links of our state in-stitutions stand in contradiction of the economic base of socialism. We must continue to resolve such contradictions in the light of specific conditions.

Of course, as these contradictions are resolved, new problems and new contradictions will emerge and call for solution. For instance, a constant process of readjustment through state planning is needed to deal with the contradic-tion between production and the needs of society, which will of course long remain with us.

Every year our country draws up an economic plan in an effort to establish a proper ratio between accumulation and consumption and achieve a balance between produc-tion and the needs of society. By "balance" we mean a temporary, relative unity of opposites. By the end of each year, such a balance, taken as a whole, is upset by the struggle of opposites, the unity achieved undergoes a change, balance becomes imbalance, unity becomes dis-unity, and once again it is necessary to work out a balance and unity for the next year. This is the superior quality of our planned economy. As a matter of fact, this bal-ance and unity is partly upset every month and every quarter, and partial readjustments are called for. Some-times, because our arrangements do not correspond to ob-jective reality, contradictions arise and the balance is upset; this is what we call making a mistake. Contradictions arise continually and are continually resolved; this is the dialec-tical law of the development of things.

This is how things stand today! The turbulent class strug-gles waged by the masses on a large scale characteristic of the revolutionary periods have, in the main, concluded, but the class struggle is not entirely over. While the broad masses of the people welcome the new system, they are not yet quite accustomed to it. Government workers are not sufficiently experienced, and should continue to examine and explore ways of dealing with questions relating to specific policies.

In other words, time is needed for our Socialist system to grow and consolidate itself, for the masses to get accustomed to the new system, and the Government workers to study and acquire experience. It is imperative that at this juncture we raise the question of distinguishing contradictions among the people from contradictions between ourselves and the enemy, as well as the question of the proper handling of contradictions among the people, so as to rally the people of all nationalities in our country to wage a new battle, the battle against nature, to develop our economy and culture, enable all our people to go through this transition period in a fairly smooth way, make our new system secure, and build up our new state.

* * *

"Let a Hundred Flowers Blossom," and "Let a Hundred Schools of Thought Contend," "Long-Term Co-existence and Mutual Supervision," how did these slogans come to be put forward?

They were put forward in the light of the specific conditions existing in China, on the basis of the recognition that various kinds of contradictions still exist in a Socialist society, and in response to the country's urgent need to speed up its economic and cultural development.

The policy of letting a hundred flowers blossom and a hundred schools of thought contend is designed to promote the flourishing of the arts and the progress of science; it is designed to enable a Socialist culture to thrive in our land. Different forms and styles in art can develop freely and different schools in science can contend freely. We think that it is harmful to the growth of art and science if administrative measures are used to impose one particular style of art or school of thought and to ban another.

Questions of right and wrong in the arts and sciences should be settled through free discussion in artistic and scientific circles and in the course of practical work in the arts and sciences. They should not be settled in summary fashion. A period of trial is often needed to determine whether something is right or wrong. In the past, new and correct things often failed at the outset to win recognition from the majority of people and had to develop by twists and turns in struggle.

Correct and good things have often at first been looked upon not as fragrant flowers but as poisonous weeds. The Copernicus theory of the solar system and Darwin's theory of evolution were once dismissed as erroneous and had to win through over bitter opposition. Chinese history offers many similar examples. In Socialist society, conditions for the growth of new things are radically different from and far superior to those in the old society. Nevertheless, it still often happens that new, rising forces are held back and reasonable suggestions smothered.

The growth of new things can also be hindered, not because of deliberate suppression, but because of lack of discernment. That is why we should take a cautious attitude in regard to questions of right and wrong in the arts and sciences, encourage free discussion, and avoid hasty conclusions. We believe that this attitude will facilitate the growth of the arts and sciences.

Marxism has also developed through struggle. At the beginning, Marxism was subjected to all kinds of attacks and regarded as a poisonous weed. It is still being attacked and regarded as a poison weed in many parts of the world. However, it enjoys a different position in the Socialist countries. But even in these countries, there are non-Marxist as well as anti-Marxist ideologies. It is true that in China, Socialist transformation, so far as a change in the system of ownership is concerned, has in the main been completed, and the turbulent, large-scale class struggles characteristic of the revolutionary periods have in the main been concluded.

But remnants of the overthrown landlord and comprador classes still exist, the bourgeoisie still exists, and the petty bourgeoisie has only just begun to remold itself. Class struggle is not yet over. The class struggle between the proletariat and the bourgeoisie, the class struggle between various political forces, and the class struggle in the ideological field between the proletariat and the bourgeoisie will still be long and devious and at times may even become very acute.

The proletariat seeks to transform the world according to its own world outlook, so does the bourgeoisie. In this respect, the question whether socialism or capitalism will win is still not really settled. Marxists are still a minority of the entire population as well as of the intellectuals. Marxism therefore must still develop through struggle. Marxism can only develop through struggle. This is true not only in the past and present, it is necessarily true in the future also. What is correct always develops in the course of struggle with what is wrong. The true, the good and the beautiful always exist in comparison with the false, the evil and the ugly, and grow in struggle with the latter. As mankind in general rejects an untruth and accepts a truth, a new truth will begin struggling with new erroneous ideas. Such struggles will never end. This is the law of development of truth and it is certainly also the law of development of Marxism.

It will take a considerable time to decide the issue in the ideological struggle between socialism and capitalism in our country. This is because the influence of the bourgeoisie and of the intellectuals who come from the old society will remain in our country as the ideology of a class for a long time to come. Failure to grasp it, or still worse, failure to understand it at all, can lead to the gravest mistakes, to ignoring the necessity of waging the struggle in the ideological field.

Ideological struggle is not like other forms of struggle. Crude, coercive methods should not be used in this struggle, but only the method of painstaking reasoning. Today, socialism enjoys favorable conditions in the ideological struggle. The main power of the state is in the hands of the working people led by the proletariat. The Communist Party is strong and its prestige stands high.

Although there are defects and mistakes in our work, every fair-minded person can see that we are loyal to the people, that we are both determined and able to build up our country together with the people, and that we have achieved great successes and will achieve still greater ones. The vast majority of the bourgeoisie and intellectuals who come from the old society are patriotic; they are willing to serve their flourishing Socialist motherland, and they know that if they turn away from the Socialist cause and the working people, led by the Communist Party, they will have no one to rely on and no bright future to look forward to.

People may ask: Since Marxism is accepted by the majority of the people in our country as the guiding ideology, can it be criticized? Certainly it can. As a scientific truth, Marxism fears no criticism. If it did, and could be defeated in argument, it would be worthless. In fact, are not the idealists criticizing Marxism every day and in all sorts of ways? As for those who harbor bourgeois ideas and do not wish to change, are not they also criticizing Marxism in all sorts of ways?

Marxists should not be afraid of criticism from any quarter. Quite the contrary, they need to steel and improve themselves and win new positions in the teeth of criticism and the storm and stress of struggle. Fighting against wrong ideas is like being vaccinated: a man develops greater immunity from disease after the vaccine takes effect. Plants raised in hothouses are not likely to be robust. Carrying out the policy of letting a hundred flowers blossom and a hundred schools of thought contend will not weaken but strengthen the leading position of Marxism in the ideological field.

What should our policy be toward non-Marxist ideas? As far as unmistakable counter-revolutionaries and wreckers of the socialist cause are concerned, the matter is easy; we simply deprive them of their freedom of speech. But it is quite a different matter when we are faced with incorrect ideas among the people. Will it do to ban such ideas and give them no opportunity to express themselves? Certainly not.

It is not only futile but very harmful to use crude and summary methods to deal with ideological questions among the people, with questions relating to the spiritual life of man. You may ban the expression of wrong ideas, but the ideas will still be there. On the other hand, correct ideas, if pampered in hothouses without being exposed to the elements or immunized from disease, will not win out against wrong ones. That is why it is only by employing methods of discussion, criticism and reasoning that we can really foster correct ideas, overcome wrong ideas, and really settle issues.

The bourgeoisie and petty bourgeoisie are bound to give expression to their ideologies. It is inevitable that they should stubbornly persist in expressing themselves in every way possible on political and ideological questions. You cannot expect them not to do so. We should not use methods of suppression to prevent them from expressing themselves, but should allow them to do so and at the same time argue with them and direct well-considered criticism at them.

There can be no doubt that we should criticize all kinds of wrong ideas. It certainly would not do to refrain from criticism and look on while wrong ideas spread unchecked and acquire their market. Mistakes should be criticized and poisonous weeds fought against wherever they crop up. But such criticism should not be doctrinaire. We should not use the metaphysical method, but strive to employ the dialectical method. What is needed is scientific analysis and fully convincing arguments. Doctrinaire criticism settles nothing. We do not want any kind of poisonous weeds, but we should carefully distinguish between what is really a poisonous weed and what is really a fragrant flower. We must learn together with the masses of the people how to make this careful distinction and use the correct methods to fight poisonous weeds.

While criticizing doctrinairism, we should at the same time direct our attention to criticizing revisionism. Revisionism, or Rightist opportunism, is a bourgeois trend of thought which is even more dangerous than doctrinairism. The revisionists, or Right-opportunists, pay lip-service to Marxism and also attack doctrinairism. But the real target of their attack is actually the most fundamental elements of Marxism. They oppose or distort materialism and dialectics, oppose or try to weaken the people's democratic dictatorship and the leading role of the Communist Party, oppose or try to weaken Socialist transformation and Socialist construction. Even after the basic victory of the Socialist revolution in our country, there are still a number of people who vainly hope for a restoration of the capitalist system. They wage a struggle against the working class on every front, including the ideological front. In this struggle, their right-hand men are the revisionists.

On the surface, these two slogans "Let a hundred flowers blossom and a hundred schools of thought contend" have no class character; the proletariat can turn them to account, so can the bourgeoisie and other people.

But different classes, strata and social groups each have their own views on what are fragrant flowers and what are poisonous weeds. So what, from the point of view of the broad masses of the people should be a criterion today for distinguishing between fragrant flowers and poisonous weeds?

In the political life of our country, how are our people to determine what is right and what is wrong in our words and actions? Basing ourselves on the principles of our Constitution, the will of the overwhelming majority of our people and the political programs jointly proclaimed on various occasions by our political parties and groups, we believe that, broadly speaking, words and actions can be judged right if they:

1. Help to unite the people of our various nationalities, and do not divide them;

2. Are beneficial, not harmful, to Socialist transformation and Socialist construction;

3. Help to consolidate, not undermine or weaken, the people's democratic dictatorship;

4. Help to consolidate, not undermine or weaken, democratic centralism;

5. Tend to strengthen, not to cast off or weaken, the leadership of the Communist Party;

6. Are beneficial, not harmful, to international Socialist solidarity and the solidarity of the peace-loving peoples of the world.

Of these six criteria, the most important are the Socialist path and the leadership of the Party. These criteria are put forward in order to foster and not hinder, the free discussion of various questions among the people.

Those who do not approve of these criteria can still put forward their own views and argue their cases. When the majority of the people have clear-cut criteria to go by, criticism and self-criticism can be conducted along proper lines, and these criteria can be applied to people's words and actions to determine whether they are fragrant flowers or poisonous weeds. These are political criteria.

Naturally, in judging the truthfulness of scientific theories or assessing the esthetic value of works of art, other pertinent criteria are needed, but these six political criteria are also applicable to all activities in the arts or sciences. In a Socialist country like ours, can there possibly be any useful scientific or artistic activity which runs counter to these political criteria?

All that is set out above stems from the specific historical conditions in our country. Since conditions vary in different Socialist countries and with different Communist Parties, we do not think that other countries and parties must or need to follow the Chinese way.

APPEAL TO THE PEOPLES OF THE WORLD
by 81 Marxist-Leninist Parties [4]

We, the representatives of the Communist and Workers' Parties of the five continents, gathered in Moscow for the 43rd anniversary of the Great October Socialist Revolution, imbued with a sense of responsibility for the future of mankind, call on you to wage *a world-wide struggle in defense of peace, against the threat of a new world war.*

Three years ago the Communist and Workers' Parties issued a Peace Manifesto to the people of all the world.

Since then, the peace forces have won notable victories in the struggle against the warmongers.

With still greater confidence in the victory of the cause of peace are we today able to oppose the war danger that menaces millions of men, women and children. Never before in the history of mankind have there been such real opportunities to realize the age-old aspirations of the peoples—to live in peace and freedom.

In face of the threat of a military catastrophe which would cause vast sacrifice, the loss of hundreds of millions of lives and would lay in ruins the key centers of world civilization, the question of preserving peace agitates all mankind more deeply than ever before.

We Communists are fighting for peace, for universal security, for conditions in which all men and all peoples will enjoy peace and freedom.

The goal of every socialist country and of the socialist community as a whole is to assure lasting peace for all peoples.

Socialism does not need war. The historic debate between the old and the new system, between socialism and capitalism, should be settled, not by a world war, but in peaceful competition, in a competition as to which social system achieves the higher level of economy, technology and culture, and provides the people with the best living conditions.

We Communists consider it our sacred duty to do every-

4. From *Political Affairs*, January, 1961, pp. 32-36. Reprinted by permission of New Century Publishers.

thing in our power to deliver mankind from the horrors of a modern war.

Acting upon the teachings of the great Lenin, all the socialist countries have made the principle of the *peaceful coexistence* of countries with different social systems the cornerstone of their foreign policy.

In our epoch the peoples and states have but one choice: peaceful coexistence and competition of socialism and capitalism, or nuclear war of extermination. There is no other way. . . .

Today as in the past, it is the reactionary, monopoly and military groups in the imperialist countries that organize and instigate aggressive wars. Peace is menaced by the policy of the governments of the imperialist powers, which, contrary to the will of their own peoples, impose upon nations a disastrous arms race, fan the cold war against the socialist and other peace-loving countries, and suppress the peoples' aspiration for freedom.

The peoples welcomed the proposals for universal, complete and controlled disarmament made by the Soviet Union and enthusiastically supported by all the socialist countries. Who opposes the implementation of these proposals? It is the governments of the imperialist countries headed by the United States of America, which, instead of controlled disarmament, propose control over armaments, and try to turn disarmament negotiations into empty talk.

The peoples rejoice that for two years now three great powers have made no tests of nuclear weapons. Who obstructs a new step forward and a decision to ban the deadly tests for all time? It is the governments of the imperialist powers, which constantly declare that they intend to resume atomic weapons tests, and continuously threaten to wreck the test-ban negotiations they were compelled to enter into under the pressure of the peoples.

The peoples do not want foreign military bases to remain in their sovereign territories. They oppose aggressive military pacts, which curtail the independence of their countries and endanger them.

Who wants the policy of aggressive pacts and bases? It is the governments of the Atlantic bloc countries, which furnish war bases on foreign soil to the West-German militarists and revenge-seekers, put weapons of mass annihilation in their hands and speed up the atomic arming of NATO troops.

It is the ruling circles of the United States of America which have imposed aggressive military pacts upon Jordan, Pakistan and other countries in the Middle and Far East, which incite them against the peace-loving countries, which have occupied South Korea and made it their bridgehead and which are reviving Japanese militarism. It is they who are interfering in the internal affairs of Laos and South Vietnam, backing the Dutch imperialists in West Irian, the Belgian imperialists in the Congo, the Portuguese in Goa and other colonialists, preparing an armed intervention against the Cuban revolution, and involving Latin-American countries in military pacts.

It is the United States that has occupied the Chinese island of Taiwan, that keeps on sending military aircraft into the air space of the People's Republic of China, and rejects the latter's legitimate right to have its representatives in the United Nations.

Combat-ready rocket installations, depots stocked with nuclear weapons, airborn H-bomb patrols, combat-ready warships and submarines cruising the seas and oceans, and a web of military bases on foreign soil—such are the present-day practices of imperialism. In such a situation, any country on earth, big or small, may suddenly be enveloped by the flames of a nuclear war.

Imperialism is pushing the world to the brink of war for the sake of the selfish interests of a handful of big monopolies and colonialists.

The enemies of peace spread falsehoods about an alleged threat of "Communist aggression." They need these falsehoods to camouflage their true goals, to paralyze the will of the peoples and justify the arms race.

There is no task more pressing for mankind today than the struggle against the menace of a nuclear-missile war, for general and complete disarmament, for the maintenance of peace. There is no duty more lofty today than participation in that struggle. . . .

War is not inevitable, war can be prevented, peace can be preserved and made secure.

This conviction of ours is prompted not only by our will for peace and hatred of the warmongers. The possibility of averting war follows from the actual facts of the new world situation.

The world socialist system is becoming an increasingly decisive factor of our time. Embracing more than one-third of mankind, the socialist system with the Soviet Union as its main force uses its steadily growing economic, scientific and technical might to curb the actions of imperialism and handcuff the advocates of military gambles.

The international working-class movement, which holds high the banner of struggle for peace, heightens the vigilance of the peoples and inspires them actively to combat the aggressive policies of the imperialists.

The peoples of Asia, Africa and Latin America, many millions strong who have won their freedom and political independence, and peoples fighting for national emancipation, are becoming increasingly active champions of peace and natural allies of the peace policy of the socialist countries.

The neutral countries, which disagree with the aggressive policy of the imperialists, work for peace and peaceful coexistence. . . .

By rallying to a resolute struggle, all these forces of peace can foil the criminal plans of war, safeguard peace and reinforce international friendship.

Peace does not come of itself. It can be defended and consolidated only through joint struggle by all the forces of peace.

We Communists appeal to all working people, to the peoples of all continents;

Fight for an easing of international tension and for peaceful coexistence, against cold war, against the arms race! If used for peaceful purposes, the vast resources squandered on armaments would make it possible to improve the condition of the people, to reduce unemployment, to raise wages and living standards, to expand housing construction and to enhance social insurance.

Prevent the further stockpiling of nuclear weapons and the arming of the German and Japanese militarists with weapons of mass annihilation!

Demand the conclusion of a peace treaty with the two German states and the conversion of West Berlin into a demilitarized free city!

Combat attempts by the governments of the imperialist powers to involve new countries in the cold war, to draw them into the orbit of war preparations!

Demand the abolition of foreign military bases, the

withdrawal of foreign troops from other countries, and prohibition of the establishment of new bases. Fight for the liberation of your countries from the aggressive military pacts imposed upon them! Work for agreements on nuclear-free zones!

Do not let the U.S. monopolies rob the heroic Cuban people of their freedom by economic blockade or armed intervention!

We Communists, who are fighting for the cause of the working class and the peoples, hold out our hand to the Social-Democrats and members of other parties and organizations fighting for peace, to all members of trade unions, to all patriots: Work in concert with us in defense of peace, for disarmament. Let us achieve concerted action!

Let us build up a joint front to combat imperialist preparations for a new war!

Let us jointly defend democratic rights and freedoms and fight against the sinister forces of reaction and fascism, against racism and chauvinism, against monopoly domination, against the militarization of economy and political life.

The struggle of the peoples for their freedom and independence weakens the forces striving for war and multiplies the forces of peace.

Africa, whose peoples have suffered most from the scourge of colonial slavery and brutal exploitation, is awakening to a new life. As they establish their independent states, the peoples of Africa emerge in the arena of history as a young, increasingly independent and peace-loving force.

But colonialism, doomed as it is by history, has not yet been completely destroyed. Brute force and terrorism bar the road to freedom for the peoples of East Africa in the British and Portuguese colonies. A cruel racist regime reigns in the Union of South Africa. For more than six years the gallant people of Algeria have been fighting for the right to national independence, shedding their blood in a war forced upon them by the French colonialists, who are supported by their Atlantic accomplices. In the Congo, the imperialists use all kinds of underhand methods and bribery in an effort to overthrow the lawful government and transfer power to their obedient puppets. . . .

Brothers in countries which have freed themselves from colonialism and in countries which are fighting for their liberation:

The final hour of colonialism is striking!

We Communists are with you! The mighty camp of socialist countries is with you!

Together with you, we insist on the immediate and unqualified recognition of the right of all peoples to an independent existence.

May the riches of your countries and the efforts of the working people serve the good of your peoples alone!

Your struggle for full sovereignty and economic independence, for your freedom, serves the sacred cause of peace!

We, representatives of the Communist and Workers' Parties, call on all men, women and young people;

on people of all trades and all walks of life;

on all people, irrespective of political or religious creed, of nationality or race;

on all who love their country and hate war:

Demand the immediate prohibition of the testing, manufacture and use of nuclear weapons and all other weapons of mass annihilation.

Insist on the immediate conclusion of a treaty on general, complete and controlled disarmament.

May modern science and technology no longer serve the manufacture of weapons of death and destruction! May they serve the good of people and the progress of mankind!

May friendly co-operation and extensive commercial and cultural exchanges between all countries triumph over war alignments!

In our epoch *the peace forces are superior to the forces of war!*

The peoples will achieve the lofty and cherished goal of safeguarding peace if they pool their efforts and fight resolutely and actively for peace and friendship among nations. Communists will devote all their energies to this cause.

Peace will triumph over war!

EDITOR'S NOTE

Shortly after the issuance of this document of established marxism, as I suppose it may be called, the Yugoslavs responded with a very sharp reaction.[5] In their view, the appeal was not "one of the important Marxist-Leninist documents"; it was not significant as a "guide to action" for communist parties, either in or outside the Bloc. The Yugoslavs are quite naturally interested in it, first, from the point of view of its treatment of the Yugoslav way to socialism, which the statement fiercely denounced; secondly, and more generally, "from the point of view of the method in which the current problems affecting the activity of all the parties and movements which struggle for socialism are considered."

Mr. Vlahovic's pamphlet, of some 80 pages, concludes that "The effect of positive positions and conclusions in the Declaration on a number of questions is reduced by attacks against socialist Yugoslavia. . . . Obviously, these attacks encourage those forces in communist parties to whom the campaign against socialist Yugoslavia has become a component part of their internal political life in order to divert attention of the working people from their own problems. This is proved by the so-to-speak everyday attacks against our country in the press and over the radio in China and Albania, because the Moscow Declaration has legalized their present campaign against us."

While all this is indicative of the ideological battle between Yugoslavia and the Bloc, from our own point of view it is more important as it underlines two other points. First, "marxism" or "marxian-leninism" is not by any means "contained" within the soviet bloc. Second, even within that Bloc, as the very fact and the length of the Moscow meeting would seem to indicate, there are sharp differences of doctrine and of policy. We should not ignore the often savage and important differences of opinion, affecting actions directly which flourish within the Bloc, outside the Bloc and between the Bloc and the marxist outsiders.

5. Veljko Vlahovic, *A Step Backward* (Belgrade, 1961). Mr. Vlahovic is a member of the central committee of the League of Communists, and a member of the Executive board of the Alliance. Quotations are from pp. 16, 79-80.

EXCERPTS FROM THE MINUTES OF THE VIIITH
PLENUM OF THE POLISH UNITED WORKERS' PARTY [6]

Comrade Artur Starewicz ... As is well-known—the VIIth Plenum revealed clearly the source of the party's disease: the existence in our ranks and amongst the party leadership of retrograde tendencies, attempts to return to Stalinist methods in party and state, to strangle democracy, to exploit nationalist prejudices, to suppress popular initiative, to violate the rule of law. Some comrades have tried to deny the existence of a group in the Central Committee. Do they really think they are dealing with a bunch of idiots? We remember the series of well-co-ordinated speeches in which attacks, criticism and proposals were inter-related and supplemented each other. We all saw how this group behaved when tension rose to its highest pitch owing to the unexpected visit of a delegation of the presidium of the C.P.S.U., and when the members of this group, one after another, tried to spread the charge that the Warsaw party organization was preparing anti-Soviet demonstrations and God knows what else. Comrade Ruminski is our crown witness. It was he who on the first day of our deliberations—confident of the victory of that allegedly non-existent group—proclaimed in the lobbies that historic events always start with small groups, and that the Natolin group would now gain more support.

The main reasons for the deepening confusion and paralysis of the party and, above all of its leading cadres, were the threats of splitting the party, the anti-democratic sallies and personal attacks uttered by this group in the Central Committee....

We can no longer tolerate this disease in our party and our leadership: it threatens to produce incalculable harm to the cause of socialism in Poland.

Where the VII Plenum failed, the VIII Plenum must succeed. The party must destroy in its ranks those tendencies that would push it back into a blind alley: into obstructing the process of democratization, into throttling freedom of thought in the party, into administrative pres-

6. From *The Polish Road* translated and edited by A. Dressler (Leeds, 1957), pp. 34-41. Reprinted by permission of the International Society for Socialist Studies.

sure and bureaucratic government, into strangling criticism and into demoralizing the ranks of the party with rotten chauvinistic theories. The party must have a new leadership, a united leadership capable of action; a leadership that will tell the working-class and the nation the truth and nothing but the truth; a leadership that will resolutely and vigorously put into practice the decisions of the Central Committee, and that will be able to rally our whole party. . . .

In 1948 our party switched its political line when it became part and parcel of the centralizing system of the cult of the individual. Under the pressure of Stalinist policies, it rejected the Polish road to socialism (allegedly inconsistent with and opposed to the Soviet road) and followed the road of complete subjection to and mechanical imitation of the Soviet example in all spheres of life. . . .

We should not ignore the achievements of the past; apart from all mistakes, they are the fruit of great, self-sacrificing efforts of the working-class and of the whole nation. But under no circumstances can one agree with the evaluation given by Comrade Berman in his statement. Comrade Berman claims that "in the past we have pursued a fundamentally correct policy, searching for the most appropriate forms of building socialism in our country." What kind of a correct political line is this that leads to such deplorable results, to a political crisis in party and country, to the piling up economic difficulties? What appropriate forms of building socialism in our country are these that now must be revised because they could not stand the test of our vital requirements? Was not the essence of these forms precisely "that system of leadership which produced these centralizing and bureaucratic distortions which caused so much harm" referred to by Comrade Berman as if this system was unconnected with the party's policy?

The party's line during the last years has failed to put into practice the principles of socialism, it cannot be regarded as a correct line and neither the working-class nor the nation regard it as such.

Though the party's policy of industrializing the country was correct (and in this respect we have undeniably achieved successes), our methods based on Stalinist 5-year plans were wrong in many respects. Its greatest failure is not simply the result of certain disproportions and serious

errors due to the excessively centralized system of planning and control, but first and foremost of the unsocialist
attitude to the working-class.

The working-class was not master in its workshops; in
its name, control was exercised by the representatives of
the state—a bureaucracy often indifferent to the needs of
the masses. The needs of the masses, their standard of
living did not determine our economic planning—but, on
the contrary, they were determined by plans, which often,
at the expense of the masses, were based on wrong assumptions. This is why in spite of great successes in construction, the working-class is so exasperated and disillusioned. Though the general socialist perspective in the
transformation of the village was correct, the party's
policy, based as it was on Soviet patterns, was full of
serious mistakes. It is not just a matter of the pressure used
in the formation of producers' co-operatives. It is a matter
of far greater importance: the repetition of the mistakes
which even now are reflected in the attitude of the Soviet
peasantry; I am speaking about the irregular, perverted relations between state and village; the excessive extortion
of compulsory deliveries, and the very principle of compulsory deliveries, which has seriously reduced the exchange of goods and which has dealt a body blow at the
very heart of peasant economy; the policy that has starved
the village of credits; the destruction of the peasantry's
self-government, in all its manifold forms. The mistakes in
our agricultural policy have resulted not only in a decrease in productivity, they have caused great political
harm; today we have a situation in which the main line of
battle runs not between poor peasants and kulaks, but
between the united peasantry on the one hand and the
bureaucracy on the other. The inescapable result of all
this was the dissolution of a large number of producers'
co-operatives and considerable material loss to the state.

Serious errors were committed by the party in the political structure of our people's democracy. By imitating
mechanically Soviet models, a political system was created
that was formally democratic but which was in fact only
an empty shell without the true content of popular government. This system, which is reflected in our constitution, modeled on the so-called Stalin constitution of the
U.S.S.R., does not correspond to the relations of political

forces in our country and does not reflect the leading role of the working-class in a true workers' and peasants' democracy. . . .

The greatest political and moral damage was done by the large-scale violations of socialist legality and the terrible perversions and crimes of the security organs, Military Information and the judicial organs. These perversions and crimes were produced not by chance errors or by evil individuals, but above all by an erroneous policy that took as its starting point the Stalinist theory of the sharpening of the class struggle, of the inescapable identification of any form of opposition with imperialist diversionist activity, of the diversionist role of Tito and the C.P.Y.: these are immensely exaggerated, false and harmful views. They were due to the influence of the Beria-system, they were the result of pressure from outside and of its corollary: the placing of the security organs above party and state in accordance with then prevailing Soviet views. The persecution of innocent people, the inhuman methods of investigation, the framed trials and verdicts, and finally, the victims of these criminal practices who lost their lives—this whole tragedy . . . undermined the moral credit of our party and confidence in a number of its leaders.

How, in face of all these facts . . . can one claim that fundamentally the line of our party was correct?

Closely connected with all this is the problem of the relations between our party and the C.P.S.U., between Poland and the S.U. The abnormality of these relations, the serious violations of the principles of sovereignty, equality and mutual respect for the independence of parties, are the source of the many errors, distortions and losses of the past. This is also responsible for our failure to find our own solutions to the problems of the construction of socialism appropriate to the needs and interests of our nation. We put this quite frankly because it is impossible to strengthen solidarity with the S.U. and indispensable unity of the socialist camp without the destruction of the remnants of the cult of the individual, without returning to the Leninist principle in the relation between parties, without giving to each party full freedom to solve its problems in its own way, and to our party, in particular, the freedom to go its own, Polish road to socialism.

The Polish road to socialism cannot, of course, be opposed to the Soviet road to socialism. On the contrary, the unique national character and the independence of each country's road to socialism creates the strongest basis for the co-operation of all socialist parties and countries in their march toward their common goal. . . .

Comrade Roman Werfel—I want to speak only on a few points. In the first place about the character and the direction of the present thinking of the working-class, of our youth and the intelligentsia. Some comrades are disturbed by this movement. It seems to me that their attitude is wrong. The basic tendency of this movement is sound—it is a movement toward socialism.

What agitated the working-class, in particular in our great new enterprises, during the last few weeks? First of all, the problem of workers' councils. Not simply improvements in standards of living—but actually the problem of their participation in the management of their factories, of the whole national economy. . . . Surely, this is a development in the direction of Socialist democracy and not away from Socialism toward capitalism.

What agitates our youth? The most advanced elements of our youth want to change their organization, they want to call themselves: Communist Union of Youth. . . . Even if they are wrong—does it mean a retreat from socialism, doubts in communism, an attempt to return to capitalism? Of course not, it is a development toward socialism, against capitalism and reaction.

To be sure—the position of our intellectuals is more complex, they are strongly influenced by ideological concepts of liberalism. But even here we have a nucleus of convinced communists, and even amongst the catholics and liberals there are many who publicly call for participation in the construction of socialism. Some eminent intellectuals who ten years ago were indifferent and even hostile to the working-class movement and to socialism, today have accepted socialism and defend it. They say to their foreign colleagues: if you want to raise standards of culture you'll have to carry out a socialist revolution. These same people, of course, also say many things that are completely wrong and that shock us. But what is the main trend in this development? Again, I think, it is in the direction of socialism. We must grant that the past, all that we call "the cult of the individual" had made socialism odious to many people. We have all seen symptoms of indifference, even dislike. There was Poznan. And I think that it is a sign of the common-sense, of the sound class instincts of the popular masses, of the unconquerable strength of our socialist ideas that when the popular masses take the initiative, and we as a party fail to lead this tempestuous movement, their initiative is directed unambiguously to the left, toward socialism, toward the development of our democracy, of working-class democracy. . . .

I now turn to my second point: is it true, then, that we cut ourselves off from comrades in other countries, from the international working-class movement, from the communists of the whole world? It seems to me that none of us here yet fully understand the changes that have recently occurred in the international communist movement.

Some comrades (and especially those who are most angry) take an over-simplified view of how it was possible for Stalinist errors to warp our movement to such an extent. They speak about the influence of the so-called Beria system, or even about some kind of direct subjection to it. There is some truth in all that. But the point is, that as far as the mass of communists is concerned (who after all decided the development of our movement) we really believed that Stalin knew better even if sometimes some things seemed incomprehensible, and we were convinced that things were what they ought to be. . . .

Our attitude, of course, was based on certain facts. We looked upon the U.S.S.R. as the first socialist country in the world, the first country of the proletarian revolution. We were unable to see clearly—Stalin's tyranny did not permit us to see clearly—what was part of the spirit of the October revolution, of Marxism-Leninism; what were the distortions caused by the immensely difficult conditions of socialist construction in a country surrounded by imperialism, economically backward and physically destroyed; and finally, what were indefensible and inexplicable features of political degeneration.

After the 2nd World War the situation changed. The S.U. is no longer isolated. By her side stood the European countries of People's Democracies and a few years later People's China was victorious. The time had come to compare the experiences of the S.U. with the experiences of other countries, to consider which features . . . were different, specific, unique in each country. And then we had in all countries of People's Democracies anti-Yugoslav resolutions and everything connected with these resolutions. Why did we submit? I think, mainly because we were still convinced that any attempts at contradicting Stalin or even at preserving our own view would mean desertion into the camp of counter-revolution. As far as Poland is concerned, Comrade Gomulka showed political far-sightedness which many of us—including myself—lacked. After Stalin's death, and in particular, after the XX Congress, the situation changed thoroughly. Comrade Togliatti, when he spoke about the polycentrism of the international revolutionary working-class movement, was the first to define the new era. The S.U. remains a great socialist power. As before we shall guard and defend the unity of the international camp of socialism, the unity of the communists of all countries. But now the communists of *each* country will search—learning from comrades in other countries basing themselves on Marxism-Leninism, on its scientific achievements, and its dialectic—for the best means of building socialism in the conditions of their own country. . . .

We shall not isolate ourselves from the world revolutionary movement if we in Poland search for roads to socialism which in many respects will be different from both the Soviet and the Yugoslav, and the Chinese roads; all these roads will lead to the abolition of the exploitation of man by man through class struggle against the exploiters, through workers' government, and through the dictatorship of the proletariat. We shall be following the road that the most advanced communists have already taken and which tomorrow all communists will follow.

13. Marxism Outside the Bloc

EDVARD KARDELJ: *The Practice of Socialist Democracy in Yugoslavia* [1]

In Western Europe the following idea has grown up about Yugoslavia and her political position: In both ideology and political form, Yugoslavia until 1948 adhered to the Stalinist Soviet system. It was only in reaction to Soviet pressure in 1948 and subsequently that Yugoslavia was driven to combat bureaucratism and defend democracy. This opinion claims that in no other way could Yugoslavia create for herself an ideological and political base from which to resist this pressure. Having been forced to embark upon this course she now has no alternative but to move, sooner or later, toward the classic bourgeois forms of political democracy which prevail in Western Europe.

What is most noteworthy about this interpretation is that it inverts the entire sequence of events.

The fact is that the clash with the Soviet Union was not the *cause* but the *effect* of dissimilarity in tendencies of the internal developments of the systems of Yugoslavia and the Soviet Union. It was precisely this dissimilarity in internal tendencies which led to a corresponding dissimilarity in their foreign policies and which affected the relations between the two countries. Any other interpretation is contrary to the facts. It is true, the relations which developed between the two countries, after 1948, had the effect of strengthening the internal tendencies characteristic of the new Yugoslavia.

As a result, the developments internal to the new Yugoslavia caused a corresponding dissimilarity in the foreign policies of the two countries. The foreign and the domestic

1. 1954 speech in Oslo by the leading theoretician of the leading marxist country outside the Bloc. Used by permission.

aspects of these developments are two sides of the same coin. Therefore, any interpretation of the specific development internal to Yugoslavia as the result solely of the foreign political conflict is far from the truth. It makes it impossible to comprehend what has happened in Yugoslavia since 1948.

The basic question of how to proceed in the building of socialism confronted the socialists of Yugoslavia the moment the revolution proved victorious. The question resolved itself, in essence, to the form of management to be applied to the means of production which, whether by evolution or revolution, have become nationalized or socialized. The question of incentive for working men to further consciously the development of the socialized means of production was therefore posed at once. A collateral problem was thus raised of what political system should be erected during the transition from capitalism to socialism, in order to secure the most favorable conditions for the development of conscious activity by the workers.

As regards the theory and the principle involved in these questions, a clear answer had long ago been given by Karl Marx. This did not suffice, however, to solve the practical problem of determining the actual political form requisite if the inherent principle was to be realized in fact. Karl Marx himself, it seems, was adverse even to attempting to solve in advance the problems which future generations must encounter. He could not and did not present us with their definitive solutions. It is evident that at the start, he regarded the machinery of state as a principal instrument through which the proletariat would discharge the socialist role imposed upon it by history. Marx envisaged the proletariat replacing the old machinery of state by a new machinery of state in this very process. Later, . . . sensing the threat to socialism posed by bureaucratism, his attitude toward any centralized machinery of state independent of the people grew more reserved. He reached the belief that it should be replaced by the "proletariat organized as the state."

Russia, at the time of the revolution, was an appallingly backward country. It was this fact which, despite Lenin's attempt to direct developments in the opposite direction,

enabled the Stalinist principle to grow dominant. Expressed
in its simplest terms, this principle insists that the organizational form indispensable to vitalizing a nation's progress
to socialism is the centralized machinery of state. By
claiming that the apparatus of state and the will and consciousness of the working class are identical, Stalin reduced the warnings uttered by Marx and Lenin about the
dangers of bureaucratism to a mere admonition about red
tape, dawdling, and the dehumanizing of the administrative
apparatus. Stalin thus obscured the nature of bureaucratism
as a social-economic phenomenon.

Yugoslav socialism rejects this concept. It denies that
the independent and elemental actions of the economic
forces in social life can be arrogated by a centralized state
machinery having absolute control over all the economic
and productive resources of a people.

In stalinist theory, the state is claimed to be the national
consciousness incarnate, omnipotent. Consequently, stalinism claims the state can determine and direct the movement
of economic forces in even the most minute detail. The expression of consciousness in the regulation of human relations, stalinism insisted, was reserved almost exclusively to
state economic planning and centralized administrative
management of the economy. All other factors within the
economy must be subordinated to this centralized system.

The instruments of this system are mainly the following:
(1) directives issued from the supreme organs of the state
machinery to the lowest organs; (2) these lowest organs
transmit orders to each individual; (3) strict control of inferiors by superiors; (4) assignment of tasks; (5) punishment for failure in their performance.

This system is not aimed at the realization of the fundamental socialist principle: the emancipation of labor, the release of creative energies of man employing the social
instruments of production, the material and moral welfare
of the individual. . . .

Self-evidently, the stalinist system depends entirely upon
the functioning of the state apparatus. Recognizing this,
Stalin introduced a specific system of economic incentives
for members of the managerial cadre. The greater the success the apparatus could achieve, the higher the pay received
by the members of the administrative machinery. The purpose of this system of incentives was not to maximize the
creative potentialities of the workers but, above all else, to

stimulate the members of the apparatus to exercise control over the workers. As a result, the administrative state machinery grew to assume a very special *economic position* within the system of social relations.

Unless they are an expression of the common interests of men working together in freedom, direction and control are not themselves a creative force. Given socialization of the means of production, only the conscious will of the individual arising from his personal, material and moral interests can become such a creative force. The greater the consciousness of the worker that his interests are inseparable from those of the community and the greater the degree to which, through the organs of self-government, he participates as an equal in solving problems relating to his material and moral welfare and to that of the community, the more powerfully does the will of the individual find expression. What determines the quality of an individual's creative labor, physical or mental, is the quality and intensity of his will to create. This cannot be raised nor further intensified by control, inspection and external pressure. This is even truer after the means of production have been socialized than it was before.

The tasks of the Socialist society are: (1) to free the creative will of its individual members; (2) to secure its continuous social education and professional training; (3) to found it upon the individual and collective, the economic and the moral interests—and to encourage their realization. Consequently, the control and guidance by the superior social organs can prove positive and creative forces only if they are designed to secure favorable conditions for the realizations of these three objectives.

Therefore, centralization of power in the hands of the state, based upon the nationalization of industry can play a progressive role and earn the support of the masses only under special circumstances and for but a brief period. This period cannot extend beyond the abolition of the old relationship of exploitation. Nor is any progressive role left for it to play once there have been created the elementary material and political conditions upon which to build the new socialist relationships. However, the moment such a system of state becomes self-centered, as soon as a process of stagnation sets in, economic and political contradictions inevitably arise between the administrative machinery and the man. The individual begins to resist, consciously or unconsciously. He grows unwilling to produce more than the bare minimum demanded of him. Thus the working man is turned more and more into a helpless instrument of the machinery of state which, due to its monopolistic position in the management of economy, becomes increasingly bureaucratized. The effects of this kind of system are felt in both economic and political field. In economy they are manifested in slowing of growth of the pace in productivity of labor. The absence of incentives at the base of the economy militates against the development of the forces of production. The unavoidable consequence, as in any other system of monopoly, is toward stagnation, toward the decay of the productive forces. This situation, consequently, requires a corresponding organization of control and pressures, based on political despotism and universal suspicion.

In Western Europe, socialism has pursued quite a different course. Its orientation is toward strengthening and gradually through evolution consolidating the political and economic positions of the working class and socialism operating through the existing mechanism of classical bourgeois democracy. It is, of course, often a matter for debate whether this or that specific policy expressed through this medium represents some actual step toward socialism. In general, however, there is not the slightest doubt that evolution toward socialism through the classical European bourgeois system of political democracy is, for a number of countries, not only practicable but is being realized.

Two facts, however, command our attention. First, these countries are precisely the ones in which capitalism first appeared on the scene of history. They achieved a special economic position and a corresponding degree of economic power. Consequently, it was possible for them to attain a higher standard of living than prevailed in more backward areas. This had the effect of blunting the internal social antagonisms. It is for these reasons that the possibility of attaining socialism through an evolutionary process operating in the framework of the classical system of bourgeois political democracy is, in the main, confined to these highly developed countries. The democratic traditions of such nations tend to modify their social antagonisms while, at the same time, gradually strengthening the socialist elements within them.

In the more backward countries, however, which almost invariably are lacking in profound democratic traditions, and at the same time suffer much sharper internal antagonisms, it is less easily possible for developments to proceed in a similar way. In some cases it is altogether impossible. Moreover, in view of the extreme concentration of international capital which characterizes our epoch and an ever widening gap between developed and undeveloped countries, not one of the undeveloped countries can expect its evolution to be along classical capitalist lines. Therefore, in order that the socialist movements of undeveloped countries may solve the question of how to emancipate their working classes, they must first solve the question of how to free their countries from economic backwardness and political dependency. In their case, the accomplishment of this latter task is prerequisite to the building of socialism.

For the moment let us disregard the question of the level of development or underdevelopment of a given country. The fact still remains that certain countries whose political systems are incapable of compromise or of granting concessions to the labor movement find themselves as a result in a state of political and economic deadlock. Their internal antagonisms are sharpened extremely. This fact alone is sufficient to exclude a peaceful democratic solution of the internal antagonisms. Revolutionary conflicts are the outcomes of such situations. In effect, the old Yugoslavia was in exactly this condition. To claim, in view of these circumstances, that the revolutionary road of the labor movement cannot serve as the starting point for the development of socialism or to insist that classical bourgeois democratic forms are the sole practicable political framework within which to build socialism, is tantamount to creating a dogma no less injurious than that opposite dogma which seeks to impose the pattern of the October Revolution on all countries.

The historical inevitability of socialist revolutions is manifested by the fact that socialist revolutions have already occurred in several countries. This is fact. . . . Similarly, gradual evolution toward socialism through the forms of classical democracy has become a historical fact in a number of countries. To deny either of these facts is plainly ludicrous.

To dogmatize about one or the other is, today, an obstacle to the realization of a categorical imperative of present-day international socialism. This categorical imperative is the need to seek a way toward the internal unity of the international socialist movement. By this I do not mean unity in the sense of the ideological and practical uniformity of the type of the Cominform, but in the sense of constructive democratic co-operation capable of co-ordinating the individual international socialist trends toward a general progress to socialism. Unity of this description, accompanied by constructive critical exchange of experiences, can substantially contribute to making the socialist movement a vital factor in world affairs, flexible enough to adapt itself to existing and changing conditions, and capable of mobilizing and accelerating all factors tending toward the social progress of mankind. . . .

Ours is an age of transition. The political structure of the world is changing correspondingly. It is therefore wrong of us to go on inventing economic or political patterns to which all countries must conform. Critical as we may be toward the state-capitalist form, or toward the bureaucratic-administrative socialist systems, we nevertheless perceive that, for many backward countries in a given phase of development, even these systems may constitute a stride forward. It is possible that the sole alternative might be to mark time, to suffocate in internal antagonism, or to tolerate the nation's continued sinking into the morass of backwardness and dependency. Obviously, all these processes will proceed less painfully were the world to discover a form of economic assistance for speeding up the development of the undeveloped countries. However, it seems that this idea will not be realized in the immediate present.

In view of all these facts, it grows clear that any attempt to impose upon peoples or upon mankind any specific or single form of movement as the only possible one must necessarily have a reactionary result. Hence, I believe, efforts toward establishing a mutually tolerant coexistence and co-operation between countries with different systems are of momentous importance not only for the preservation of peace but also for securing the most favorable conditions for the further progress of mankind. It is only in such an environment that the most progressive socialist tendencies will be able to express themselves with full freedom.

However, the division of the world as we know it into

developed and underdeveloped countries is by no means the whole issue. For, whilst it is true that the system of classical bourgeois democracy could serve as an effective instrument during a phase, whether brief or protracted, in the elevation toward socialism, it is also true that the socialist results that came through its instrumentality must, at some point, begin reciprocally to exercise a modifying effect upon the whole old democratic mechanism. Otherwise, this political form, once suited to the continued progress of socialism, must become a brake upon it.

It is my considered judgment that, sooner or later, every democratic system which is trending toward socialism must find itself characterized by two dominant factors. The first of these is that the changed relations of production will create a corresponding demand for democratic forms of management of the economy, and this whether the socialization of the means of production has come about by evolutionary or revolutionary means. The second is that emancipation of the working class must connote enlarging and broadening the scope of the role of the individual within the general mechanism of social management.

The production and distribution of wealth represent the essential content of social life. Consequently, introduction of new democratic forms into the management and direction of the economy will impart to the democratic political mechanism a direction and form corresponding to its socialist economic basis. Economic democracy is an age-long concept. In the main, however, it has been regarded in the past either as a complement to or as parallel with classical political democracy. In my opinion, such a concept is untenable. It should be borne in mind that classical bourgeois political democracy is a specific form of economic democracy. Bourgeois democracy is rooted in the economic relationships arising from the private ownership of capital. It corresponds to the structure of such capitalist private ownership and to the economic needs of a society evolving upon this basis. *Therefore, the demand voiced in our time for economic democracy is, in reality, a demand for new democratic political forms designed to assist a freer development, a society whose point of departure is the socialization of the means of production.*

Our experience in the struggle for socialism enables us to assert beyond possibility of contradiction that "economic democracy" is the definitive form of the new political system emerging from the socialization of the means of production. At the same time, it is the only solution offered us for the growing difficulties of those democratic systems which, suffering increasing stagnation because of their outmoded forms, are incapable of adapting themselves to the new social reality.

As regards enlarging the role of the individual in social management, it seems to me unquestioned that this will determine the role and the power of the machinery of state. In this process, it will extend the influence and the sphere of activity of the organs of social self-government now regarded as of lowest rank, as closest to the masses. Also, the role by the autonomous and vertically united systems of self-governing bodies and organizations will grow in importance.

Self-evidently, this development cannot be without effect upon the existing system of political parties and their representative bodies, even the most democratic of parties indeed exercises restraint over the initiative of individuals. It causes political stagnation and unavoidably minimizes opportunities for direct creative action by the individual over questions of both personal and common interests. . . . The system of political parties has liberated society from the pressure of blind forces and has introduced greater stability into social relationships. It has accomplished this indispensable task by, in a certain sense, blunting the keenness of the essential antagonisms and, at times, by diverting them. . . . If, however, we assume the existence of the prevailing socialist economic relationships which have already developed in fact—not going so far into the future as to suppose the existence of a classless society—then we are already confronted with the fact of the minimization of open social antagonism which will be reduced to such an extent that the old systems or political parties become unnecessary and, in fact, a hindrance to the full utilization of the energies of society.

With the development of socialist relationships, therefore, we must assume that the mechanism of classical bourgeois democracy as we know it will gradually transform itself into a system of more direct democracy based upon life. . . . Then men will not be motivated by adherence to this or that party but by the attitudes they adopt, independently and as conscious social workers, to the concrete social problems confronting them. This is no less true of the socialist social systems whose starting point is revolution and whose return to classical bourgeois forms of democracy would signify repudiation of their revolution and surrender of their society into anti-democratic hands.

Even within such a system of direct democracy, it is true, community of concepts will still cause individuals to group themselves together for a common end. Such groupings, however, need not necessarily assume the character of rigid party formations. Futhermore, the essential difference between the mechanism of the *indirect* bourgeois democracy and the *direct* system of socialist democracy lies in the fact that bourgeois democracy, even in its classic form, asserts the centralized authority of the state while socialist democracy, based upon growing social self-management, represents the withering away of the state as the political instrument of a class. Whether the starting point is the classical mechanism of bourgeois democracy or the state mechanism produced by the socialist revolution, I believe that the growth of democracy leads inevitably to this end.

In the light of these facts, we reject the assumption that the growth of socialist democracy in Yugoslavia must inevitably lead to the mechanical re-establishment of the classical forms of bourgeois democracy. What we have accomplished so far is but the first step in our development. It is, nevertheless, a step toward the emergence of democratic forms organically reflecting the development of our economy upon a socialist basis.

Our approach to this question is thus a matter of principle. Even were this not so, it would be imposed upon us by practical political considerations. The working class of Yugoslavia is already managing the socialized means of production and comprises a good third of the population. Over 60% of our population, however, consists of small owner-producers. Moreover, socialism in our country is being built under conditions of unusually difficult international relations. This combination of circumstances means, in fact, that mechanical reversion to bourgeois democratic forms would be tantamount to our yielding up

the revolution and all it has attained. It would be as though
we announced ourselves ready to relinquish both our socialism and our national independence.

There are, within sections of the socialist movement,
some critics of our concepts who assert, in short; "We do
not deny that your revolution was justified and necessary. It
did away with an anti-democratic and reactionary system.
Nevertheless, now that the revolution is victorious, you
ought to establish the system of classical European democracy."

What this approach to our problem disregards is the
fact that no such thing as democracy existed in the old
Yugoslavia. This was not because of *deliberate refusal* of
the Yugoslav bourgeoisie to create it but because of its
sheer inability to do so. Democracy was precluded in the
old Yugoslavia by the extraordinary acuteness of her internal antagonisms. The anti-democratism of the Yugoslav bourgeoisie was a specific expression of the political
and economic relationships existing in the country.

Prewar Yugoslavia was one of the most backward countries in Europe. No more than 10% of the population was
engaged in manufactures, mining, or construction. About
75% of the population lived in villages, cultivating the
land with little assistance from modern implements or
technology. . . . It should be remembered that Yugoslavia is
a multi-national country, with great contrasts in economic
development between her different regions. The social-
economic and political structure of prewar Yugoslavia
therefore made impossible . . . further progress economically. . . .

Each of these economic and political characteristics of
our country exercised its separate effect—and continues to
do so to some extent—upon the development of our society
both before and after the revolution. True it is that the
revolution changed the character of state power and freed
the economic and political forces of social progress. This
did not bring about an automatic change in the economic
relationships of the country and, consequently, has not yet
liquidated the antagonisms arising from them.

It is obvious, therefore, that even if we were to approve,
in principle the establishment of the classical bourgeois
democratic system such an effort could not conceivably
succeed. It would plunge us into civil war or, possibly, deliver us up to the reactionary despotism of the classes we

have ousted from power. Even more probable is that it would lead directly to the establishment of a state-capitalist bureaucratism.

For all these reasons, the revolution alone could serve as the starting point of our progress toward new democratic forms. Furthermore, unless it did lead us toward direct democracy as a form of withering away of political monopoly, it would renounce its own content. *Once the revolution has become accomplished fact, no alternative point of departure exists from which to proceed. After the revolution, it is politically impossible to revert to some prerevolutionary form without the revolution ceasing to be a socialist revolution. . . .*

After the revolution, our decision to undertake the different task of industrializing our country even disregarding its international position flowed naturally from this reasoning. Some among our western critics are in the habit of suggesting that industrialization is some sort of dogmatic fixation of ours. We, however, realized from the start that the socialist forces of Yugoslavia would be able to hold on to their victory over contra-revolution and bureaucratism only if they grew strong enough economically to assume actual leadership over the entire economic development of the country and to introduce ever freer social relations. We could not accomplish this if we were to remain a socialist economic island stranded in a sea of undeveloped petty producer elements in the cities and villages. We could accomplish this only if the socialist forces grew powerful enough to eradicate the obsolete social relationships, primarily through economic action without resort to state compulsion. *We had, then, to proceed to the task of changing the material ratio of social forces in favor of socialism. . . .*

As a result of our efforts, postwar Yugoslavia has drawn appreciably closer to the state of development of the economically advanced countries of the world. Our efforts toward this end have demanded corresponding changes in political forms. Our economic backwardness left us vulnerable both to the residual forces of our capitalist past and to the danger of a growth of bureaucratism in opposition to these forces. Although the revolution had deprived them of power, the capitalist elements still possessed strength and were capable, under certain circumstances, of weakening the political stability of socialism to an appreciable extent. Our struggle against this latent opposition, coupled with our extraordinary efforts toward the acceleration of our economic progress, at first required a strong internal discipline and a considerable degree of political centralism and administrative management of the economy. Since this necessarily called for the creation of a powerful state apparatus, it also posed the danger of the growth of bureaucratism. . . .

Our own attitude is in distinct opposition to [the] stalinist principle. We assert that the revolution should not only substitute one state apparatus for another but that, simultaneously, it should also inaugurate the process of the withering away of the state as the instrument of authority generally. In the very nature of things, this cannot be a mere mechanical process of changing the juridical conditions. It can arise only as an organic result of the development of new material forces and new social relationships. Socialism as a social relationship will have become so strong and unshakable that class differences no longer manifest themselves only when a return to capitalist relationships has become as impossible and unthinkable as the revival of feudalism is conceded to be.

In short, the withering away of the state can occur only when socialism no longer needs the state as a prop to lean upon. Accordingly, the stronger the growth in the material power of socialist relationships and the more irreplaceable they become in the conduct of social life, the more unnecessary the state becomes in economic and political life or, to state it more correctly, the more it becomes transformed into a social mechanism no longer based on coercion but on common social interest and voluntary submission to a social discipline corresponding to the common interest.

What all this amounts to is that a centralized state apparatus "in the name of the working class" cannot be the chief prime mover in building socialist relationships nor act infallibly as a personified socialist consciousness. These socialist relationships can come into being only under the conditions of *social ownership of the means of production* and, even then, only as a result of both the conscious and the elemental, economic, social, and other activities and practices of men working, creating, reasoning, and building for the future under these very conditions. Men whom that activity is bringing into *new relationships* and upon whom is exerted the influence of these economic and social interests themselves become naturally oriented toward acting in a socialist manner within the framework of these relationships. Moreover, it is solely from this actual practice of socialism that the theoretical concepts of socialism can evolve further. In this context, of course, conscious socialist activity is an inseparable part of socialist development. "Society," as Karl Marx stated in the preface to the first German edition of *Capital*. ". . . can neither clear by bold leaps, nor remove by legal enactments, the obstacles offered by the successive phases of its normal development. But it can shorten and lessen the birth pangs."

In our view, this objective process must be matched by a corresponding organization of the mechanism of democracy evolving on the basis of the social ownership of the means of production. We believe that direct democracy alone provides a mechanism through which to secure the maximum possibilities of democratic self-government by working men and that this must operate through corresponding basic organs of management of production as well as of other fields of social life. It is this very function which is being borne by our workers' councils, our co-operatives, communes, the vertically united self-governing economic organizations and the autonomous social organs of the institutions of education, science, culture, health and other social services.

Simultaneously, the evolution and progressive expansion of these forms and their corresponding social activities are the form under which there is gradually being established the new democratic mechanism which is evolving organically out of the new social-economic basis and which, in the final analysis, represents neither more nor less than a form of the withering away of the state as an instrument of authority and coercion. In other words, once the means of production have become socialized, there must be built up an organized democratic machinery of social management such as will enable the working masses to come to the fore within it, not through the top levels of some political party, but directly in their daily life. . . . In no other way can we prevent the growth of bureaucracy or give full expression to the socialist creative initiative of the individual.

In such a social structure, it is not in the state administration in the narrower sense of the term but in the self-governing social institutions to which the working masses send their direct representatives that there is concentrated the task of consciously directing the socialist progress of the nation. The state administration must be a specialized apparatus subordinated to such self-growing social organs. It is among the masses themselves, not merely within a state apparatus, that the conscious fighters for socialism must strive to influence in the socialist directions the decisions reached in the appropriate democratic organs. It is through the masses, in other words, that we must try to insure that the decisions of the self-governing organs of society shall conform to the needs of socialism's defense against anti-socialist tendencies and to the needs of the continued expansion of socialism. These are the principles which lie at the base of socialist activity in Yugoslavia. . . .

To describe in brief how we have realized this principle in practice. The first question to decide was how to secure the free interplay of economic forces. This resolved itself to how best to insure that the working men employing the socialized instruments of production should be free as workers and as regards the expression of their initiative. . . . Responsibility for bringing about this reconciliation lies mainly in the *workers' councils*.

Within the framework of the general direction of our society and our national economic planning, each of our enterprises is a self-controlled operation. After deducting the costs of production—including the basic wages fund—the net income of these enterprises is regarded as a social income, i. e., it is regarded as both the individual net income of the enterprise and as part of the collective net income of the economy. In accordance with the provisions of the federal law and the federal plan, this net income is distributed in stated shares to the state, the commune, the enterprise concerned and to its workers and employees. That part of the net income which accrues to the individual enterprise is in part subject to distribution among the workers and employees to supplement their pay and in proportion to their output, the remainder being allocated to the capital funds at the free disposal of the enterprise. The enterprise invests this portion in expansion of and improvements upon its capital equipment, and in such social uses as housing and other purposes regarding which the workers' council is competent to decide independently.

Within this framework, the enterprise is wholly free in its activity. No administrative organ is competent to determine its policies. It engages in free competition on the open market, pursues its own independent development, and arranges the degrees and forms of the co-operation in which it engages with other equally independent enterprises.

Our enterprises are managed by working collectives through the workers' councils and managing boards. . . . Election is by secret ballot. . . . The workers' councils elect managing boards which carry out the decisions of the workers' councils in between their sessions and perform the current tasks of economic management of the enterprise. . . .

Thus, as regards Yugoslav socialism there exist no special state administrative boards within the state apparatus to which the individual enterprises or workers' councils are subordinated. However, enterprises are free to unite themselves within the framework of the chambers of industry and other economic chambers in order to enhance co-operation between them or to advance production. They may also create common economic and technical services and similar organizations leading to the same end.

The economic policy of the enterprises is determined by the workers' councils. Technical implementation of such policy is the responsibility of the manager and the body of technicians of the enterprise. . . .The manager, of course, may also advance proposals regarding the economic policy of the enterprise. Equally, the workers' council and the managing board may each offer observations and suggestions concerning the organization of labor in production. . . .

Yugoslavia has a free market within which enterprises compete one with another. Market success is determined by quality and price. The beneficial influence of competition upon pricing and quality, combined with considerable dependence of the material welfare of the whole working collective and even of the community upon the market success of the enterprise, provide a more potent stimulus toward quality and volume of production than could any form of administrative control. . . .

The workers are concerned to raise the productivity of labor since they are paid in proportion to the results achieved. They are interested in the over-all financial success of the enterprise since they share in its net income either directly as a supplement to their wages or indirectly through the allocation of that income to housing construction, health institutions, education, and the raising of the social standards of the local community, i. e., the commune.

Strong incentive is thus provided not only for the direct performance of labor but for active participation in the management of the enterprise and the government of the commune. The joint efforts of a democratic action by the workers' councils and free market competition make it possible for the working collectives to strive for maximum success subject to the limitations imposed by the prevailing material conditions. Our experience proves abundantly that the working collectives in the management of our enterprises can cope effectively with whatever tasks arise in the social management of production.

Transformation of the role of the trade unions is an actual consequence of this change in conditions. Once the workers' councils had begun to function in the enterprises, and the councils of producers in the communes ... the trade unions *as the instruments of economic struggle of the working class* in the main became unnecessary to the workers.

Nevertheless, the unions have retained significant social functions. First, the unions still retain a certain protective function. The agreement of the union, like that of the commune, is sought regarding the fundamental provisions of the basic wage regulations, so that the wage regulations assume some of the aspects of a collective contract. Through this participation in the enactment of basic wage regulations, the unions of the individual industrial branches are instrumental in securing a unified level of basic pay for identical work. In the implementation of the basic wage regulations, the unions also attend to the protection of the rights of the individual worker in relation to the organs of the enterprises or to other local factors. They strive for improved labor protection, for appropriate health and other measures, and so on.

Second, the unions contribute toward co-ordinating the direct economic interests of all workers with those of the individual working collectives. They do this by striving to secure uniformity of the means whereby the material and other rights of the workers are secured. Wherever individual working collectives show signs of pursuing possibly selfish ends at the expense of other collectives, the unions combat this.

Third, a primary function of the unions is the economic, vocational and other training of workers as well as their cultural development. The unions thus assist the workers to carry out their daily tasks, to participate in the organs of self-management of production and in the communes, and to reach full understanding of both their rights and their role in these spheres.

Fourth, the unions organize or foster the organization of canteens, social institutions, rest centers, hospitals, holiday resorts, physical culture establishments, etc. . . .

This is the general role and the organizational form of the basic organs of democracy in the fields of production, transport, trade and the economy in general. This system has been built on the basis of two fundamental concepts. The first is that no central leadership, however wise it may be, is capable of directing unaided economic and social development whether in general or in detail. . . .

The second basic premise is that the effort and initiative of the individual is not increased in proportion to the rigor of the directives, controls, and checks exercised upon him. . . .The pursuit of [the personal economic and social, cultural and material interests of the man who is doing the work, who is creating freely] should be that motive social force which will replace the capitalist free initiative of individual capitalists. . . . The social ownership of the means of production makes it possible for such initiative to become the substance of every man engaged in labor, provided that there exists the corresponding democratic mechanism of self-management by the producers.

The most vital problem of the new political system is how to co-ordinate the individual's interest of the working man with the collective interests of society in the system of social ownership of the means of production. Upon the solution of this problem also depends that of the requisite democratic political forms in the transitional phase of society's movement toward socialism. . . .

To us *the principle of self-government by the producers is the starting point of all democratic socialist policy, of every form of socialist democracy*. The revolution which does not open the door to such development must, inevitably, and for a longer or shorter time, stagnate in state-capitalistic forms, in bureaucratic despotism.

It follows that the means of democratic self-government must be so devised as to place the producer in a position to influence the social organs of decision. This form of organization, moreover, must be such that the producer is able to attain a complete sense of responsibility toward society. It must enable the producer to get insight into the economic and social relationships so that he can make decisions in compliance with real possibilities. It must be such, in short, that by *his consciousness and his material and other interests,* the working man grows capable of exercising an influence governed by his growing recognition of his individual and the social welfare.

It is to accomplish these ends that the social mechanism of a nation embarked on the building of socialism, and the democratic methods employed within that mechanism, should be adapted. In socialist Yugoslavia, this role is performed mainly by the commune which constitutes the foundation of our social edifice.

It must not be thought that the central organs of government in Yugoslavia retain no important functions. On the contrary, it is relative to the decisions of the central social and state organs as regards the distribution of the national net income or surplus labor that the effective and direct influence of the producer must be secured. The central organs of government serve to co-ordinate and canalize the entire economic development of the nation. Their functions are primarily those of allocating the national income to the different social funds and of securing the harmonious working of the system to a common end. It is in the central organs that there are enacted regulations for the implementation of social planning, etc. . . .

The decisive first step in the establishment of socialist democracy is the leap from the political monopoly of parties toward direct participation in decisions by each individual member of society. Such a democratic mechanism of social management must be decentralized in one direction in order gradually to replace the principle of *"government of people,"* by the principle of their self-government in tall spheres of social life and, primarily, in the economic field.

In the other direction, it will be appropriately centralized so as to secure the most effective social *administration of things,* i. e., of the common means of production and the material forces of society in general. Only a parallel and simultaneous development of both these processes, which is the antithesis of man's conversion into a slave of a centralized bureaucratic apparatus, can ever lead to that point at which the "administration of things" will cease to be a *social relationship* and will gradually transform itself into a *public social service* serving all free men.

Thus, we are not rejecting all centralization of social functions. . . . The social developments of our time call for a centralization of specific social functions not merely within individual nations but, in fact, in the international sphere as mankind is urged incessantly toward co-opera-tion and a universal solution to the world's problems. Our point of view, however, is that the point of departure of such a development must be the free producer engaged on the social means of production, i. e. the self-management of people brought together by common interest and not by the coercive power of the state. It is only in such a process that there can come about the withering away of the state as an instrument of coercion. This is not something we shall accomplish overnight but may prove to be a task even of generations.

In Yugoslavia, as I have already commented, the com-mune, headed by its people's committee, is the basis of such a mechanism of social democracy. It is supplemented by workers' councils and other direct organs of producer's self-government. . . .

The enormous social role and power of the commune lies, first of all, in its freedom of independent action in the field of economic development and, in the second place, in its organic connection with the workers' councils and with other democratic organs of self-government of the pro-ducers. Thus, the commune is not only a political but is first and foremost a social-economic organism with its political function destined gradually to grow weaker as its social-economic function gains in strength. In effect, it is through the commune that there will be effected distribu-tion of the surpluses from labor appropriate to its territory. In this way the commune becomes directly concerned with the constant expansion of the productive forces of its area.

The principal political and social-economic organs of the commune and the district are people's committees which are organized in such a way as to be able to discharge the above mentioned tasks. The people's committees of the communes are, ordinarily, unicameral bodies, election to them being by secret ballot by all adult citizens in the territory of the commune.

It is necessary that I enlarge somewhat upon the role played by the councils of producers in our system. These councils are elected by the direct producers alone, i. e., the workers and employees engaged in production, the working peasants, independent craftsmen and so on. These direct producers alone are eligible for election to them. . . . The central function of the councils is to correct the negative influence of old and outworn social relationships upon the new democratic organs of self-government and to do so in a democratic manner. This makes for progressive diminution of the need for adminstrative interference by the state in such relationships. Thus, the significance of the role of the councils of producers springs from the fact that, despite the present numerical inferiority of the working class, it confers a leading position on the working class within the whole social system. At the same time, it insures that latent bureaucratic tendencies shall not, under the guise of the dictatorship of the proletariat, win a victory over the proletariat itself and over its authority. Again it accomplishes this through the mechanism of democracy. . . .

At the head of the various administrative departments of the people's committees are councils which the people's committees elect from among citizens whose professional knowledge or other qualifications single them out as uniquely suited to contribute to the sound functioning of the administrative apparatus. These are not salaried officials, but unpaid citizens who offer their services voluntarily. The councils render decisions over matters of principle and over the more important aspects of the field of administration as regards the economy, education, health, internal policies and so on. It is also the responsibility of these councils to supervise the work of the staff. The decisions are effectuated through the secretaries of such councils and the specialized apparatus of the people's committee.

The nature of this organizational mechanism and the broad powers of the communes and districts present to each citizen the possibility of exercising great and direct influence upon the activity of the commune and the development of the whole social life. As the system grows in internal strength, this possibility is bound to be enhanced even further.

Moreover, the very fact that this mechanism exists and that the commune plays this role within it is causing the commune to become the most suitable form by which to integrate the collective social interests to the individual interests of the working man. The selfsame worker who, in the factory, participates in decisions regarding wages and the social standards of the individual is also enabled to participate in decisions reached by the commune on the other social needs of the community in which he resides. His voice is heard on the question of the further development of the productive forces requisite to increasing the commune's revenue, on the financing of education and sanitary improvements, and on all other questions. These are matters of as direct concern to the individual as is the question of his wages. Each and every unwarranted increase of personal consumption must necessarily be at the expense of the development of the forces of production and result in decreasing investment in other sectors vital to raising the general social standard.

This is a fact which every person living in the system of the commune has to think through for himself. Recognition of this collective interest of the commune, which is very close to the day-to-day thinking of the average working man, is thus becoming the most important corrective for blind pressures for increased individual income which otherwise might imperil the entire system of social self-government. . . .

Alongside the developments I have described it was also necessary for us to solve the question of social management in such non-economic domains as education, culture, science and health. The principle we applied to this problem was, again, that intervention by the state should gradually be reduced to a minimum, the focus of our activity being shifted to the creation of a corresponding mechanism of self-government.

In our universities, schools, scientific institutes, cultural and similar establishments, a beginning has been made in creating collective management organs whose composition is partly by representation of the people's assemblies or people's committees and partly by representation of the social institutions concerned. These organs of management (councils or committees) render independent decisions in principle based on law, while implementation of decisions or leadership in current activities is through boards and directors or the specialized leaderships of such institutions. Upon this foundation there is being evolved a system of self-governing administrative organs for these specific spheres of social life on a vertical or federal scale. . . .

In the further evolution of the organizational forms of our centralized social functions, an important part will fall to the special vertically united autonomous systems in individual fields of our social activity. I refer here to such forms as arise from the nation-wide association of enterprises, institutions, communes, and citizens in pursuit of common aims. Such organizations are represented by our economic chambers, economic associations, social insurance offices, professional associations, etc. These organizations will gradually take over an increasing number of functions now currently discharged by the centralized state organs. Through them, the principle of social self-government will assert itself in the field of common functions of nation-wide significance. Consequently, the development of communes and of such vertically linked self-governing organisms is the process by which, in the final analysis, we shall alter the physiognomy of the central state organs and the mode of their formation. It will be unwise of us today to venture further into the realm of prophecy.

*   *   *

Such, then, are the premises upon which our political and economic system is developing. It is a system which makes actually possible the direct participation of every citizen in management, promotes the contest of views, stimulates individual initiative, and fosters the free development of the forces of Socialism. Whilst accomplishing this, it is capable, as a unified system of socialist democracy, of defending itself against attacks from anti-socialist positions. It is precisely this fact which explains why it is also the form best fitted for carrying out the process of the gradual withering away of the different forms of political monopoly.

Herein, indeed, lies the essential difference between classical bourgeois and direct socialist democracy. The first is a *state form*. The second, in essence, is a *form of the withering away of the state....*

In Yugoslavia, however, which with prodigious effort has only begun to free itself from backwardness, this task is as yet far from accomplished today. We are not mere visionaries who mistake wish-thinking for objective reality. We need no urging to take stock of the actual interconnection of all the processes and developments of the material forces of our society. Our everyday practice is fairly accurately circumscribed by our material limitations. This means that the pace of development of our socialist democracy is also determined materially. Accordingly, we are under no illusion that we can bypass necessary stages through which our society must evolve, even though we open to ourselves the longer vistas of our further progress. On the contrary, it is these very perspectives which emphasize our conscious need to mobilize and organize those material factors capable today of bearing the burden at the present stage of our socialist development. This mission has to be performed by both the political organizations of the working class and its state. To renounce this mission would be tantamount to repudiating the revolution and socialism itself.

G. D. H. COLE: *The New Revisionism* [2]

What attitude should left-wing Socialists who set a high value on personal freedom and democracy take up toward Communism and the Communist parties whose advent has split the working-class movement into contending factions throughout the world? Many Socialists think it enough to assert and practice a thorough-going hostility to Communism and all its works, saying that Communism is a destroyer of democracy and of personal liberty, that it has imprisoned and maltreated millions of its citizens in "slave labor camps," and that it has revealed its true character in the innumerable purges and liquidations of its own leaders for political crimes of which no reasonable person be-

2. The views of a leading British Socialist after the death of Stalin. From *World Socialism Restated* (London, 1957), pp. 10-19, 44-48. Reprinted by permission of *The New Statesman* and the late Professor Cole.

lieves many of them to have been guilty. This is indeed a formidable indictment, from which it is impossible to escape by attributing all the evil that has been done to discredited individuals, such as Stalin or Beria; for it is evident that the entire Communist leadership has been involved, and that many essential features of Communist rule remain unchanged even now that it has become fashionable to denounce Stalin, as well as Trotsky, and to admit that serious "mistakes" have been made.

It is a plain fact of history that Communists, wherever they have held power, have been ruthless in suppressing opposition and in maintaining one-party dictatorial rule; that they have been callous about the infliction of suffering on anyone they have regarded as a political enemy or potential counter-revolutionary; that they have engaged in wholesale misrepresentation and often in plain lying about their opponents and have kept from their peoples the means of correcting their false statements by preventing them from acquiring true information; and that they have without scruple betrayed non-Communist Socialists who have attempted to work with them in the cause of working-class unity but have not been prepared to accept complete subjection to Communist Party control. It is no less a matter of history that after the First World War the Comintern, in pursuance of its campaign for world revolution, deliberately split the working-class movement in every country to which it could extend its influence, and thus opened the door wide to the various forms of Fascism that destroyed the movement in many countries—notably in Italy, Germany, and the Balkan States.

Nevertheless, though the indictment is heavy and unanswerable, it is not enough; for it ignores a number of vital facts. The first of these is that the Communists, whatever their vices, did carry through the Revolution in Russia and maintain it against all the efforts of world capitalism to encircle and destroy it, and that the Revolution in Russia did overthrow landlordism and capitalism and socialize the means of production, thus insuring that the vast increase in productive power which was achieved after the desperate struggles of the early years should accrue in the long run to the benefit of the workers and peasants and should lift Russia from primitive barbarism to a leading position among the world's peoples.

The second fact is that the Russian Revolution, though

it did not usher in the world revolution for which the Bolsheviks hoped, did largely help to set on foot the great movements for emancipation among the peoples of Asia and Africa which are rapidly transforming the world into a much more equal community and are helping to destroy imperialism and racial discrimination and to attack at its roots the exploitation of the underdeveloped countries by the more advanced.

The third fact is that, despite all the abuses of dictatorship in the Communist countries, it is unquestionable that the life of workers and peasants in Soviet Russia is immensely preferable to what they endured under Tsarism and that their status and opportunities for culture and good living—politics apart—have been immensely advanced.

In the light of these facts, deeply though I disapprove and hate many aspects of Communist rule and philosophy, I cannot regard Communism simply as an enemy to be fought. It is unrealistic to imagine that revolution could have been successfully carried through in Russia or in other parts of Eastern Europe and Asia by the methods of a "liberal" democracy of which no tradition, and for which no basis, existed in these societies, or that on the morrow of the Revolution they could have settled down under liberal-democratic regimes of the western type. Such regimes imply the existence of a readiness to accept the accomplished fact, and to accommodate oneself to it, that simply did not exist in Russia or China or in the other countries which have been conquered by Communism. To say that Russia or China ought not to have "gone Communist" is, in effect, to say that the Russian and Chinese revolutions ought not to have occurred at all; and, far from being willing to say this, I regard these two revolutions as the greatest achievements of the modern world. I do not mean that all the bad things that have been done in these countries since the revolutions have to be accepted as inevitable concomitants of the revolution. . . . But I am not prepared to denounce the revolutions because of the abuses that took place under them; to do so would be sheer treason to the cause of world Socialism. . . .

I have also, as a Socialist, to define my attitude both to present Communist trends in the Soviet Union—and in China as far as I understand them—and in Yugoslavia, and to the Communist parties of the countries not under Communist control—above all, France and Italy. As for the Soviet Union, I have naturally followed with deep attention the proceedings of the recent Communist Congress and the denunciations of the "personality cult"—and of Stalin as its exponent—and have observed that these attacks in no way involve any going back on the general principle of one-party dictatorship or any tolerance of opposition to the Party's policy. They only substitute collective for personal leadership; and it remains to be seen whether they imply any effective democratization of the Party itself, such as would allow policy to be determined from below, by rank-and-file opinion, rather than imposed by the collective leadership on the main body of the Party. I am not disposed to regard what has occurred as carrying with it any fundamental modification of Communist philosophy, though I hope it will because I am hopeful that the leaders will not be able to stop the process of destalinization just where they would wish it to stop. I am hopeful that they will find themselves carried by stages much further along the road of liberalization, as in effect the Yugoslavs have been since their break with the Cominform; and I believe it to be of the first importance that non-Communist Socialists should stand ready to welcome every sign of such liberalization and should not reject even relatively small advances out of hand.

As for Yugoslavia, where the one-party system remains but has been made compatible with a good deal of free discussion and with a considerable decentralization of power, I believe the time has come for non-Communist Socialists of the left to do their utmost to enter into friendly relations with the Yugoslav Communists and to endeavor to build a Socialist International broad enough to include them as well as the Socialists of the West and the Asian Socialists who are suspicious of the Socialist International in its present form. The Yugoslavs have been making most interesting and important advances in the direction of workers' control in industry and of democratic institutions of local government; and Western Socialists should be ready to learn from them as well as to criticize.

As for the Communist parties in the West, and especially in Italy and France, where they control the major part of the trade unions and are powerful electoral forces, it seems utterly clear that, in these countries, Socialism cannot possibly be achieved, or any substantial advance toward it made, without their collaboration; and it is accordingly imperative, not indeed to constitute with them an immediate United Front—for which the conditions are not yet ripe—but not to rule out the possibility of accommodation, and to seize on every chance of improving Socialist-Communist relations without sacrificing essential democratic principles. In Italy, a special problem presents itself because of the existence of a powerful Socialist Party—the Nenni Party—that works with the Communists in opposition to the much smaller Saragat Party that alone is recognized by the Socialist International. My sympathies are much more with the Nenni than with the Saragat Socialists; and in my view left-wing Socialists in other countries should be ready to co-operate and confer freely with the Nenni Party, which can be of great use in breaking down the barriers in the way of united international Socialist action.

In Great Britain, where the Communist Party is negligible as a political force, there is no case for an United Front—the more so because the Party is peculiarly sectarian and doctrinaire. But there is a case for recognizing the plain fact that the Communists are a quite considerable force in a number of trade unions and will continue to be a disruptive and trouble-making force as long as the attempt is made to ostracize them. I am not unaware of the mischief that a small, highly disciplined, unscrupulous minority out to make trouble can do to an organization consisting quite largely of rather apathetic adherents. Nevertheless, I am against the adoption of rules excluding Communists from trade union office, and still more against the tendency of some trade union leaders to brand every left-wing trade unionist as a Communist or "fellow traveler." I believe that the way to build a strong, democratic movement is to decentralize power and responsibility and to combat Communism, not by exclusions, but by increasing the numbers who can take an active part in trade union affairs and by carrying out a really big campaign of trade union education in economic and political matters.

For my own part, I reject the Communist philosophy, as inappropriate to the conditions of countries which possess, in any high degree, liberal traditions of free speech, free association, and freedom to change their institutions by peaceful means. I hate the ruthlessness, the cruelty, and the centralized authoritarianism which are basic characteristics of Communist practice; and I do not intend to mince my words in attacking them. But I also believe in the need for working-class unity as a necessary condition of the advance to Socialism; and I understand why, especially in countries subject to the extremes of reactionary class rule, so many Socialists, in reaction against the futility of impotent reformism, have rallied to the Communist cause. I want my fellow-Socialists to understand this too; for, unless they do, they will waste their energies in fighting against their fellow-workers instead of using them to further the victory of Socialism on a world-wide scale.

Karl Marx, who made many devastating and correct observations about the capitalist system, also believed that, as capitalism developed further, the workers would be condemned to "increasing misery," the middle classes flung down into the ranks of the proletariat, and the class-struggle more and more simplified by the elimination of those who were neither proletarians nor capitalist bourgeois exploiters. In these views he was mistaken. In the advanced capitalist countries there have been great advances in the standards of living and in the status and security of the main bodies of workers; there has been over the same period a great increase in the size of the middle class; the class-structure has become much more complex; and as a consequence the class-struggle has become less acute and Socialist and trade union movements for the most part much less revolutionary and much more interested in winning piecemeal reforms. Marxists sometimes argue that these things have occurred because the advanced countries, operating policies of economic and political imperialism, have thriven by exploiting the peoples of the less developed countries: so that the workers in the advanced countries have become in effect exploiters of colonial and quasi-colonial labor, and have in consequence taken on bourgeois characteristics. Today, it is argued, the real exploited proletariat consists of the workers and peasants of the less developed countries, out of whose product the workers, as well as the capitalists, of the advanced countries live relatively well by extracting the surplus value.

Although I fully agree that the peoples of the less developed countries are shamefully exploited, I have never been able to accept this argument. It is true enough that the economies of the advanced countries depend on the ever-increasing supply of raw materials and fuel from the colonial and quasi-colonial regions, and that the producers of these commodities are badly underpaid; but it is also true that the advanced countries, with the aid of scientific techniques, have immensely increased their productivity, and that the higher consumption of the workers in these countries has been mainly an outcome of this increase and of the pressure of their working-class movements to secure a share in it. Broadly speaking, working-class standards of living depend on the productivity of the various countries and on the strength and vitality of their working-class movements, much more than on the ability of the advanced countries to acquire the products of the less advanced on unduly favorable terms of exchange. It might even be to the advantage of the advanced countries to pay more for the products of the less advanced, because doing so would expand the world market for their own products and increase prosperity all round. But of course the capitalists of the advanced countries are not in the least likely to pay more than they have to: nor could those of any one country afford to pay more than their competitors in the others.

Imperialist exploitation is a marked feature of world capitalism, and justifies the resentment which it provokes in the less developed countries. But it is not the main explanation of the failure of Marx's prophecies about the "increasing misery" of the workers and the sharpening and simplification of class-antagonisms in the advanced capitalist countries to come true; and it is of great importance for Socialists to understand this, and to ask themselves how Marx came to go so badly wrong in forecasting the future.

Marx went wrong, in the main, not because he misrepresented the facts of the developing capitalist system as he observed them in the "Hungry Forties" of the nineteenth century, but because he assumed that the tendencies manifested by capitalism at that stage would continue in intensified form. Early machine-age capitalism did bitterly exploit its workers, while it was engaged in a fevered struggle to accumulate capital at their expense; and it did use mainly unskilled labor, destroying and undermining the old craft skills of the superior grades of workers. But as capital became more plentiful it became less necessary for the capitalists to hold wages down to bare subsistence level and more important for them to secure mass markets for their goods; and as the techniques of production advanced there was a growing demand for new kinds of skilled workers, who had to be paid more than the wages of common labor. Modern trade unionism developed mainly among these skilled workers, who presently grew strong enough to claim voting rights and a share in political influence. The class-structure became more complex as the numbers not only of skilled manual workers but also of blackcoats, technicians, managerial and professional workers sharply increased. After an interval the less skilled workers too began to assert their claims; and they too won better wages and voting rights, which they used to secure the first advances in the direction of the "Welfare State." Socialist parties—including those which proclaimed themselves Marxist—devoted themselves to promoting these improvements and became less revolutionary therewith. Finally, in our own day, capitalism, compelled to make large concessions to working-class opinion, devised ways and means of protecting itself against the recurrent crises that had hitherto beset it, and adopted in varying degrees the Keynesian and New Deal techniques which retrieved it from the terrible slump of the early 1930's; and American capitalism in particular, after coming near to collapse during these years, reconciled itself to a regime of high wages and recognition of trade unions which gave it a new lease of prosperity.

It is true that, despite these developments, world capitalism remains in a precarious position. American capitalism can sustain high production and employment only by giving an appreciable part of its product away to countries that cannot afford to pay for it because the Americans do not want their products; and in many countries less wealthy than the United States capitalism is kept going only by American aid. This, however, does not alter the fact that it *has* been kept going and that, far from showing signs of imminent collapse, it has made, on the whole, a remarkable recovery from the dislocations of war: so that it is now quite unrealistic to base Socialist policies on the easy assumption that Socialists need only await its dissolution and stand ready to inherit what it leaves behind.

True, this reconstructed capitalism operates only within a restricted area, dominated by the immense economic power of the United States. A large fraction of the world economy has passed out of its control and has gone over to a system of planned production under collective ownership—that is, to a sort of Socialism. The capitalist world now has to meet the increasing economic challenge of the Communist countries; and one of these—the Soviet Union —has proved its capacity to keep abreast of the very latest scientific developments and is training scientists and technicians on a scale unmatched by any capitalist country, even the United States. Economically, however, the impact of this challenge is for the present reduced by the barriers which largely divide the world into two separate trading blocs, with only very limited commercial exchanges between them—though there are signs that this isolation may break down as the Soviet Union becomes more able to provide capital exports to the less developed countries in rivalry with the capitalist suppliers of the West—for example, in the key regions of India and the Middle East.

The present division of the world into capitalist and Communist sectors—with disputed areas between—faces non-Communist Socialism with very serious problems; for if it sets out to fight Communism it finds itself allied with capitalism—above all, with American capitalism—against it. This, in view of the concentration of power in the hands of the United States, makes it very difficult to fight for Socialism either in the advanced western countries or in the underdeveloped countries that are the arena of dispute between the rival blocs. Western Socialism is in sore need to break free from its entanglement with capitalism and to endeavor to come to terms with the revolutionary movements in the underdeveloped countries. Its interest is to break down the barriers between East and West and to come to terms with the Soviet Union and China on a policy of co-operative world development—if the Communist countries are prepared to accept such a policy. There are at any rate some signs that they are moving toward such a position—witness the recent admission of the Soviet leaders that there may be variant ways of advance toward Socialism—an attitude very different from that of the Comintern in its early days. The Socialist policy must be one of promoting *détente* and disarmament and of seeking to use part of the resources released by disarmament for a common war on want, if possible under United Nations auspices. There are many obstacles in the way of such a policy, and particularly of American participation in it; for American help on any large scale is at present closely linked to military objectives, and it cannot be easy to persuade any American Congress to assist the development of Socialist or would-be Socialist—and much less of Communist—countries. Nevertheless, the attempt must be made; for United Nations assistance is much easier than American, or other directly national, assistance to reconcile with the natural suspicions of the less developed countries, which can all too easily topple over from legitimate anti-capitalism into hysterical xenophobia.

It is in any case indispensable to work actively for disarmament, both because of the ever more appalling prospects of war with modern weapons and because of the continually increasing cost of modern armaments, which constitutes an intolerable drag on the economy of every heavily armed country, except the United States. The Soviet Union has no less strong reasons than Great Britain or France to favor disarmament, which offers the prospect of a rapid increase in living standards to the long-suffering Russian peoples and is, for Great Britain, the necessary condition of putting an end to the long-continued crisis of the British economy and of stabilizing the balance of payments without a fall in the standard of life. Disarmament, moreover, is the indispensable condition of German reunion, which is impossible as long as East and West Germany are lined up on opposite sides in the "cold war." I am convinced, not only as a Socialist but also on grounds of plain commonsense, that the decision to rearm Western Germany was a prodigious error, on which it is imperative to go back; but there is now little prospect of going back on it except in conjunction with an agreement to reduce armed forces on both sides.

Disarmament, however, is unlikely to be brought about unless Great Britain and France make clear to the Americans their refusal to endorse a policy that finds excuses for rejecting every Soviet overture out of hand and that continues to insist on a boycott of West-East trade in just those kinds of goods of which both China and the Soviet Union stand in greatest need for their own peaceful development. The blockade does not greatly hurt the American capitalists; but it does great harm to both the British and the French economies. . . .

With disarmament—even partial disarmament—would go a *détente* that would do much to break down the iron curtain across Europe and to make possible the conversion of the present movement toward closer West European economic and political unity into a movement extending to the entire continent. No less, a *détente* between the two power blocs would do much to lessen Asian suspicions of Western imperialism, which have been seriously aroused both by S.E.A.T.O. and by the Treaty of Bagdad in the Middle East. It is overwhelmingly advantageous to Socialism as a world movement to end the system of rival power blocs preparing for total war. Indeed, unless this can be done, non-Communist Socialism will remain helpless and Communism will profit by its impotence in capturing the allegiance of the suffering peoples of the underdeveloped countries, to which non-Communist Socialism will be able to give no effective aid in their struggle for self-determination and economic freedom.

I want then to see the Socialists of the world working together, both in common action against capitalism and imperialism and the remnants of feudal and military domination and in free and intimate intercourse for the development of Socialist ideas and policies. Socialism, in its Communist forms, has made giant strides in the world since the Russian Revolution of 1917, and is making great strides today. Democratic Socialism too has made big advances, especially in Great Britain and Scandinavia; but in these countries it seems to be at a loss what to do next, and in the western world as a whole it appears to have got stuck, and to be no nearer winning over a majority of the people than it was a generation ago. Moreover, even in Great Britain, it is caught in the toils of a cold war which turns it into the ally of American capitalism against the Communist part of the world, and is thus both disabled by heavy spending on armaments from advancing further in the direction of social welfare and unable to struggle for Socialism with its hands free, for fear of antagonizing American opinion. Yet British Socialists are much more favorably placed than those of most of the western countries, who have been halted not only by the cold war but also by the increasingly organized political power of the Roman Catholic Church.

The great problem for western democratic Socialism is to find a way of escape from this containment. None, I feel sure, can be found while the cold war continues—or at all events, while Western Europe remains a party to it. We in Europe cannot prevent the American Government from continuing for as long as it wishes the policy of subordinating everything else to the thwarting of Communism in every part of the world, no matter how much support for black reaction such an international policy requires. We can, however, refuse to remain parties to such a conception of world strategy by breaking free from the bonds of N.A.T.O., S.E.A.T.O., and the alliance with America in the Middle East, and by insisting on testing out to the full the genuineness of the Communist desire for peace and mutual disarmament. We can become, like India under Nehru, neutral spectators of the American-Soviet conflict, free to set about the better management of our own affairs.

Such a policy of course involves risks. If the Soviet will to peace is not genuine—but I am sure in essence it is—we shall expose ourselves to the danger of military conquest by the Soviet Union, without any assurance that America will come to our aid. But I do not believe this danger to be real: if it had been, war would have broken out long ago, when the Soviet armies could have walked right over Europe practically unopposed. The one thing that seems quite certain in an uncertain world is that the people of the Soviet Union have a sheer horror of war, whatever may be the attitude of their leaders; and I cannot believe that their leaders either want war in such a situation or would dare to unloose it even if they did. This of course does not prevent them from stirring up trouble for the capitalist world wherever they can, especially in its colonial territories or in areas subject to economic imperialist penetration by it. But have they not the right to make trouble in these areas, as long as capitalist governments continue to hold them in subjection by force or to exploit them economically and include them in a power bloc against the Communist countries? I think they have; and I am not prepared to modify my anti-imperialism to suit the requirements of an anti-Communist crusade.

But, even apart from the danger of a Soviet war of aggression, can the western countries afford to do without American economic support, which is now given only on condition of their alignment with the anti-Communist bloc? The answer is that they can, if they both cut their armaments and develop their trade one with another and with the countries of the East, from which they are now largely cut off by the American veto on "strategic" exports. It is not to be supposed that the United States, in ceasing to aid

Western Europe with gifts, would cut off its nose to spite its face by renouncing trade with European countries or with the sterling area, any more than it has ceased to trade with India because India has refused to join its power bloc. ... Economically, American aid, tied tightly to cold war and heavy spending on armaments, is bought at far too high a price.

The first task for West European Socialists is to shake their countries free from cold war entanglements and to do their best to establish terms of friendly intercourse and trade with the Communist countries. The second is to re-invigorate their Socialism, so as to give it a stronger and wider appeal to the peoples as a viable means of ending class-rule and economic exploitation, and thus to defeat the enemies who thrive on its inhibitions and evident lack of will to carry its own precepts into effect.

This reinvigoration of Socialism involves three things. First of all, an appeal to idealism as well as to material interest, and a statement of ideal objectives in terms which the ordinary man can both understand and feel to go to the root of the matter. It needs to be an appeal couched in terms of comradeship and of the brotherly pursuit of the good life as requiring not merely a decent minimum standard of material living for all, but also a let up on the competitive struggle for riches as the key to power and prestige—an appeal to the spirit of social equality, based on a classless educational structure, and a recognition of the right of the common man to share in economic as well as in political self-government. It involves, besides, an appeal to work hard and to increase productivity, not simply in order to get higher earnings but also because higher production is urgently needed for the re-establishment of Great Britain's and of other western countries' economic independence, and in order to make possible further advances in education and the social services.

Secondly, the reinvigoration of Socialism involves taking sides absolutely with the rising national movements in colonial and other underdeveloped countries, and refusing to be side-tracked by summons to the defense either of the prerogatives of settlers or *colons* claiming racial superiority over subject or "inferior" peoples, or of the claims of imperialist countries to extract profits (or dollars) from the exploitation of colonial resources or of the resources of other underdeveloped countries, such as the oil-producing regions of the Middle East or of Central America. It is not enough to support reform movements in colonial areas, on condition that they stop short of demanding full independence, economic as well as political; for this is to treat them still as inferiors, whereas Socialists cannot fall short of demanding full equality.

Thirdly, Socialism cannot be reinvigorated unless the working-class movement in each country can be reunited solidly in its support. This means that in France the rift between the Socialist Party and the Communists must be somehow healed, and an united trade union movement re-established. It means, in Italy, that the Nenni Socialist Party must be recognized as the party which in fact commands, together with the Communist Party, the allegiance of the main body of the working class, and that, far from wishing the Nenni Socialists to break their links with the followers of Togliatti, European Socialists should welcome the alliance and seek to broaden it so as to include the Saragat Socialists as well. It involves that, instead of holding the Yugoslav Socialists at arm's length, the Socialist International should use every endeavor to establish closer relations with them. It involves giving all possible help to the Spanish Socialists to come together for a concerted onslaught on Franco's dictatorship. Finally, it involves combining intensified opposition to the political Catholicism of the right with a readiness to welcome into the fraternity of Socialism those Catholics who, especially in France, have shown their genuineness by their attitude to French imperialism in Indo-China and North Africa.

Political allegiances and the support given to parties and movements can change very rapidly when there are real reasons for men to change their minds. There is no good reason for taking the present stalemate in western democratic Socialism as a sign that its impetus has been permanently lost. The case for it remains unshaken: what has happened to it is that it has allowed itself to be temporarily diverted into an anti-Communist blind alley, which prevents it both from engaging in a whole-hearted struggle against capitalism and imperialism and from being able to offer to the peoples even a substantial further improvement in their welfare. Democratic Socialism is suffering at present from altogether too many inhibitions. It dare not frighten possible marginal supporters; and it dare not flout that so-called "public opinion" which is really newspaper opinion put about by the reactionary press. It dare not offend the Americans, for fear of being left to face the Soviet Union without their backing. It dare not do anything that might make the capitalism of is own countries inefficient, because it is not prepared to replace capitalism by a Socialist economy. It dare not get on better relations with the Communists, because it is afraid of falling under the domination of their stronger wills and greater zeal.

Such attitudes will never serve for the making of a new society, which is an arduous task, requiring above all courage and a readiness to take risks. A Socialism that dares not is bound to fail; for the fighting spirit which created the Socialist movement is no less needed to carry it through to its goal. The use of parliamentary and constitutional methods need not destroy this spirit—though it is all too apt to do so, when constitutional Socialism has become respectable and accepted as part of the national political set-up, and when trade unions no longer have to fight for the right to exist and have become part of the recognized machinery of the capitalist order. So many good trade unionists and Socialists have gone over to Communism in so many countries largely because democratic Socialism has thrown away its militancy as a response to the acceptance of its right to exist within the bounds of constitutional action. If in Great Britain and Scandinavia such defections have been small, that is because in these countries democratic Socialism has solid, though limited, achievements to its credit and is still living on that credit, despite its hesitations about its future course. It cannot go on for long living on its past. Nor can it find the way to a new advance on a merely national plan. What needs to be re-created and endowed with fresh vigor is a world Socialism that will put itself at the head of a world movement for emancipation, in advanced and backward countries alike, and will shake off, as a world movement, the fears and inhibitions that are holding it prisoner.

ERNESTO "CHE" GUEVARA: *Notes for the Study
of the Ideology of the Cuban Revolution* [3]

This is a unique Revolution which some people maintain contradicts one of the most orthodox premises of the
revolutionary movement, expressed by Lenin: "Without a
revolutionary theory there is no revolutionary movement."
It would be suitable to say that revolutionary theory, as the
expression of a social truth, surpasses any declaration of
it; that is to say, even if the theory is not known, the revolution can succeed if historical reality is interpreted correctly and if the forces involved are utilized correctly. Every
revolution always incorporates elements of very different
tendencies which, nevertheless, coincide in action and in
the revolution's most immediate objectives.

It is clear that if the leaders have an adequate theoretical knowledge prior to the action, they can avoid trial and
error whenever the adopted theory corresponds to the
reality. The principal actors of this revolution had no coherent theoretical criteria; but it cannot be said that they
were ignorant of the various concepts of history, society,
economics, and revolution which are being discussed in the
world today. Profound knowledge of reality, a close relationship with the people, the firmness of the liberator's
objective, and the practical revolutionary experience gave
to those leaders the chance to form a more complete theoretical concept.

The foregoing should be considered an introduction to
the explication of this curious phenomenon which has
intrigued the entire world: the Cuban Revolution. It is a
deed worthy of study in contemporary world history: the
how and the why of a group of men who, shattered by an
army enormously superior in technique and equipment,
managed first to survive, soon became strong, later became stronger than the enemy in the battle zones, still
later moved into new zones of combat, and finally defeated that enemy on the battlefield even though their
troops were still very inferior in number.

3. A selection from various sources by this marxist spokesman of an
underdeveloped country in full revolutionary cry. From *Studies on the
Left*, Vol. I, No. 3 (Madison, Wisc., 1960), pp. 75-85. Reprinted by permission of the publisher.

Naturally, we who often do not show the requisite concern for theory, will not run the risk of expounding the truth of the Cuban Revolution as though we were its masters. We will simply try to give the bases from which one can interpret this truth. In fact, the Cuban Revolution must be separated into two absolutely distinct stages: that of the armed action up to January 1, 1959, and the political, economic and social transformations since then.

Even these two stages deserve further subdivisions; however, we will not take them from the viewpoint of historical exposition, but from the viewpoint of the evolution of the revolutionary thought of its leaders through their contact with the people. Incidentally, here one must introduce a general attitude toward one of the most controversial terms of the modern world: Marxism. When asked whether or not we are Marxists, our position is the same as that of a physicist or a biologist when asked if he is a "Newtonian," or if he is a "Pasteurian."

There are truths so evident, so much a part of people's knowledge, that it is now useless to discuss them. One ought to be "Marxist" with the same naturalness with which one is "Newtonian" in physics, or "Pasteurian" in biology, considering that if facts determine new concepts, these new concepts will never divest themselves of that portion of truth possessed by the older concepts they have outdated. Such is the case, for example, of Einsteinian relativity or of Planck's "quantum" theory with respect to the discoveries of Newton; they take nothing at all away from the greatness of the learned Englishman. Thanks to Newton, physics was able to advance until it had achieved new concepts of space. The learned Englishman provided the necessary steppingstone for them.

The advances in social and political science, as in other fields, belong to a long historical process whose links are connecting, adding up, molding and constantly perfecting themselves. In the field of social and political sciences, from Democritus to Marx, a long series of thinkers added their original investigations and accumulated a body of experience and of doctrines. The merit of Marx is that he suddenly produces a qualitative change in the history of social thought. He interprets history, understands its dynamics, predicts the future, but in addition to predicting it (which would satisfy his scientific obligation), he expresses a revolutionary concept: the world must not only be interpreted, it must be transformed. Man ceases to be the slave and tool of his environment and converts himself into the architect of his own destiny. At that moment, Marx puts himself in a position where he becomes the necessary target of all who have a special interest in maintaining the old—similar to Democritus before him, whose work was burned by Plato and his disciples, the ideologues of Athenian slave aristocracy. Beginning with the revolutionary Marx, a political group with concrete ideas establishes itself. Basing itself on the giants, Marx and Engels, and developing through successive steps with personalities like Lenin, Stalin, Mao Tse-tung and the new Soviet and Chinese rulers, it establishes a body of doctrine and, let us say, examples to follow.

The Cuban Revolution takes up Marx at the point where he himself left science to shoulder his revolutionary rifle. And it takes him up at that point, not in a revisionist spirit, of struggling against that which follows Marx, of reviving "pure" Marx, but simply because up to that point Marx, the scientist, placed himself outside of the History he studied and predicted. From then on Marx the revolutionary could fight within History. We, practical revolutionaries, initiating our own struggle, simply fulfill laws foreseen by Marx the scientist. We are simply adjusting ourselves to the predictions of the scientific Marx as we travel this road of rebellion, struggling against the old structure of power, supporting ourselves in the people for the destruction of this structure, and having the happiness of this people as the basis of our struggle. That is to say, and it is well to emphasize this once again: the laws of Marxism are present in the events of the Cuban Revolution, independently of what its leaders profess or fully know of those laws from a theoretical point of view. . . .

Each of those brief historical moments in the guerrilla warfare framed distinct social concepts and distinct appreciations of the Cuban reality; they outlined the thought of the military leaders of the Revolution—those who in time would also take their position as political leaders.

Before the landing of the "Granma," a mentality predominated that, to some degree, might be called "subjectivist"; blind confidence in a rapid popular explosion, enthusiasm and faith in the power to liquidate the Batista regime by a swift, armed uprising combined with spontaneous revolutionary strikes, and the subsequent fall of the dictator. . . .

After the landing comes the defeat, the almost total destruction of the forces and their regrouping and integration as guerrillas. Characteristic of those few survivors, imbued with the spirit of struggle, was the understanding that to count upon spontaneous outbursts throughout the island was a falsehood, an illusion. They understood also that the fight would have to be a long one and that it would need vast *campesino* participation. At this point, the *campesinos* entered the guerrilla war for the first time. Two events—hardly important in terms of the number of combatants, but of great psychological value—were unleashed. First, antagonism that the city people, who comprised the central guerrilla group, felt toward the *campesinos* was erased. The *campesinos*, in turn, distrusted the group and, above all, feared barbarous reprisals of the government. Two things demonstrated themselves at this stage, both very important for the interrelated factors: to the *campesinos*, the bestialities of the army and all the persecution would not be sufficient to put an end to the guerrilla war, even though the army was certainly capable of liquidating the *campesinos'* homes, crops, and families. To take refuge with those in hiding was a good solution. In turn, the guerrilla fighters learned the necessity, each time more pointed, of winning the *campesino* masses. . . .

[Following the failure of Batista's major assault on the Rebel Army,] the war shows a new characteristic: the correlation of forces turns toward the Revolution. Within a month and a half, two small columns of eighty and of a hundred forty men, constantly surrounded and harassed by an army which mobilized thousands of soldiers, crossed the plains of Camagüey, arrived at Las Villas, and began the job of cutting the island in two.

It may seem strange, incomprehensible, and even incredible that two columns of such small size—without communications, without mobility, without the most elemental arms of modern warfare—could fight against well trained, and above all, well armed troops.

Basic [to the victory] is the characteristic of each group: the more uncomfortable the guerrilla fighter is, and the more he is initiated into the rigors of nature, the more he feels himself at home; his morale is higher, his sense of security greater. At the same time, he has learned to risk his life in every circumstance that might arise, to trust it to luck like a tossed coin; and in general, as a final result of this kind of combat, it matters little to the individual guerrilla whether or not he survives.

The enemy soldier in the Cuban example which presently concerns us, is the junior partner of the dictator; he is the man who gets the last crumbs left to him in a long line of profiteers that begins in Wall Street and ends with him. He is disposed to defend his privileges, but he is disposed to defend them only to the degree that they are important to him. His salary and his pension are worth some suffering and some dangers, but they are never worth his life: if the price of maintaining them will cost it, he is better off giving them up; that is to say, withdrawing from the face of guerrilla danger. From these two concepts and these two morals springs the difference which would cause the crisis of December 31, 1958. . . .*

Here ends the insurrection. But the men who arrive in Havana after two years of arduous struggle in the mountains and plains of Oriente, in the plains of Camagüey, and in the mountains, plains, and cities of La Villas, are not the same men, ideologically, that landed on the beaches of Las Coloradas, or who took part in the first phase of the struggle. Their distrust of the *campesino* has been converted into affection and respect for his virtues; their total ignorance of life in the country has been converted into a knowledge of the needs of our *guajiros;* their flirtations with statistics and with theory have been fixed by the cement which is practice.

With the banner of Agrarian Reform, the execution of which begins in the Sierra Maestra, these men confront imperialism. They know that the Agrarian Reform is the basis upon which the new Cuba must build itself. They know also that the Agrarian Reform will give land to all the dispossessed, but that it will dispossess its unjust possessors; and they know that the greatest of the unjust possessors are also influential men in the State Department or in the Government of the United States of America. But they have learned to conquer difficulties with bravery, with audacity, and above all, with the support of the people; and they have now seen the future of liberation which awaits us on the other side of our sufferings.

* The day Batista was overthrown.

More than a year has passed now since the flight of the dictator, corollary to a long civil and armed struggle of the Cuban people. The achievements of the Government in the social, economic and political fields are enormous; nevertheless, we need to analyze, to give to each term its proper meaning; and to show the people the exact dimensions of our Cuban revolution. This is because our national revolution (fundamentally agrarian, but with the enthusiastic participation of workers, people of the middle class, and today even with the support of industrialists) has acquired continental and even world importance, sheltered as it is by the unshakable decision of its people and the peculiar features which animate it.

We are not attempting a synthesis, however much one may be needed, of the sum total of laws passed, all of them of undeniable popular benefit. It will suffice to place upon some of them the needed emphasis, showing at the same time the logical sequence which from first to last leads us, in a progressive and necessary scale, from affairs of state to the necessities of the Cuban people.

Attention was first directed against the hopes of the parasitic classes of our country, when there were decreed, in rapid succession, the rent regulation law, the lowering of electrical rates, and the intervention of the telephone company with the subsequent lowering of rates. Those who hoped to see in Fidel Castro and in the men who made this revolution only some politicians of the old school, or some manageable dolts whose beards were their only distinctive trait, began to suspect that there was something deeper emerging from the depths of the Cuban people and that their prerogatives were in danger of disappearing. The word Communism began to hover about the figures of the leaders, the figures of the triumphant guerrillas, and as a consequence, the word Anti-Communism as the dialectically contrary position began to nuclearize all those whose unjust sinecures were hampered or taken away. . . .

The INRA advanced like a tractor or a tank of war, since it is both tractor and tank, breaking down in its passage the barriers of the *latifundia* and creating new social relationships out of land tenure. This Cuban Agrarian Reform has emerged with several characteristics important in America. It was indeed antifeudal, for besides eliminating the *latifundia*—under Cuban conditions—it suppressed all contracts which required that land rent be paid in spe-

cie, and liquidated the conditions of serfdom which were
primarily maintained among our great agricultural products
of coffee and tobacco. But this was also an Agrarian Reform which was made in a capitalist environment in order
to destroy the pressures of monopoly which work against
the potentialities of human beings, isolated or collectively,
to work their land honorably and to be productive without
fear of creditor or master. It had the characteristic from
the very first of assuring the *campesinos* and agricultural
workers, those to whom the land was given, of necessary
technical support, capable personnel and machinery, as
well as financial support by means of credits granted by
INRA or sympathetic banks; and the great support of the
"Association of Stores of the People," which has developed
extensively in Oriente Province and is in the process of
developing in other provinces, where state graineries are
replacing the ancient *garrotero,* paying a just price for
crops and giving a fair return as well.

Of all the characteristics which differentiate the Cuban
from the other three great agrarian reforms in America
(Mexico, Guatemala and Bolivia), that which appears most
important is the decision to carry it through to the end,
without leniencies or concessions of any sort. This integral Agrarian Reform respects no right which is not
the right of the people, nor is it directed against any particular class or nationality; the scales of the law tip alike
for the United Fruit Company or the King Ranch, and for
the Creole *latifundistas.*

Under these conditions, the production of the materials
most important for the country, such as rice, oleaginous
grains and cotton, is being developed intensively and is
being made central in the planning process; but the Nation is not satisfied and it is going to redeem all its
wealth. Its rich subsoil, the site of monopolists' struggle and pasture for their voracity, has for all practical
purposes been rescued by the petroleum law. This law, like
the Agrarian Reform and all the others dictated by the
revolution, responds to the undeniable needs of Cuba, to
the inescapable urgencies of a people which wants to be
free, which wants to be master of its economy, which
wants to prosper and to achieve progressively higher goals
of social development. But for this very reason it is a
continental example which is feared by the petroleum
monopolies. It is not that Cuba harms the petroleum

monopoly substantially or directly, for there is no reason to consider our country an emporium of that precious combustible, although there are reasonable hopes of obtaining a sufficient amount to satisfy internal needs. On the other hand, the palpable example of Cuba's law is seen by the sister nations of America, many of whom are the grazing-land of those monopolies, while others are impelled to internal wars in order to satisfy the necessities or appetites of competing trusts. It shows to them what is possible, indicating likewise the exact hour when one may think of carrying it out. . . .

By a simple law of gravity, the small island of 114,000 square kilometers and 6,500,000 inhabitants is assuming the leadership of the anti-colonial struggle in America, for there are important conditions which permit it to take the glorious, heroic and dangerous lead. The nations of colonial America which are economically less weak, those which are developing their national capitalism by fits and starts in a continual struggle, at times violent and without quarter, against the foreign monopolies, are gradually relinquishing their place to this small new power for liberty, since their governments do not find themselves with sufficient strength to carry the struggle to the finish. This is because the struggle is no simple matter, nor is it free of dangers nor exempt from difficulties. It is essential to have the backing of an entire people, and an enormous amount of idealism and the spirit of sacrifice, to carry it out to the end under the almost isolated conditions in which we are doing it in America. Small countries have previously tried to maintain this position; Guatemala, the Guatemala of the quetzal bird which dies when it is imprisoned in a cage, the Guatemala of the Indian Tecum Uman who fell before the direct aggression of the colonialists; and Bolivia, the Bolivia of Morillo, the prototype of martyrs for American independence, who yielded before the terrible difficulties of the struggle, in spite of having initiated it and having given three examples which are fundamental to the Cuban revolution: suppression of the army, the Agrarian Reform, and the nationalization of mines—a maximum source of wealth as well as of tragedy.

Cuba knows the previous examples, it knows the failures and the difficulties, but it knows also that it stands at the dawn of a new era in the world; the colonial pillars have been swept away before the impulse of the national and popular struggle, in Asia as in Africa. Now the tendencies to unification of the peoples are no longer given by their religions, by their customs, by their appetites, by their racial affinities or lack of them; it is given by the economic similarities of their social conditions and by the similarity of their desire for progress and recovery. Asia and Africa have shaken hands at Bandung, Asia and Africa are coming to shake hands with colonial and indigenous America by means of Cuba, here in Havana.

On the other hand, the great colonial powers have given ground before the struggle of the peoples. Belgium and Holland are but two caricatures of empire; Germany and Italy have lost their colonies. France debates in the midst of a war she has lost, and England, diplomatic and skilled, liquidates her political power while maintaining economic connections. North American capitalism has replaced some of the old colonial capitalisms in those countries which have initiated their independent life; but it knows that this is transitory and that there is no real rest to be found in the new territory of its financial speculations. The claws of the imperial eagle have been blunted. Colonialism has died in all those places of the world or is in process of natural death.

America is another matter. It was some time ago that the English lion removed his greedy paws from our America, and the nice young Yankee capitalists installed the "democratic" version of the English clubs and imposed their sovereign domination in every one of the twenty republics.

These nations are the colonial feudal-estate of North American monopoly, "right in its own backyard"; at the present moment this is their *raison d'être* and the only possibility they have. If all the Latin American peoples were to raise the banner of dignity, as has Cuba, monopoly would tremble; it would have to accommodate itself to a new politico-economic situation and to substantial cuts in its profits. But monopoly does not like to cut its profits and the Cuban example—this "bad example" of national and international dignity—is spreading among the American countries. Every time that an upstart people sets up a cry of liberation, Cuba is accused; somehow or other Cuba is guilty, guilty because it has shown a way, the way of armed popular struggle against the supposedly invincible armies, the way of struggle in difficult terrain in order to exhaust and destroy the enemy away from his bases; in short, the way of dignity.

* * *

One may outline then, the necessity of a direct aggression on the part of the monopolies, and there are many possibilities which will be shuffled and studied in the IBM machines with all their calculating processes. It occurs to us at this moment that one possibility is the Spanish variation. The Spanish variation would be that in which an initial pretext will be seized upon; exiles, with the aid of volunteers, volunteers who for example might be mercenaries or simply soldiers of a foreign power, well supported by water and air; very well supported in order to insure success, let us say. It might be also the direct aggression of a state, such as Santo Domingo, which will ask some of its people, our brothers, and many mercenaries to die on these beaches in order to provoke the act of war, the act which will obligate the candid fathers of monopoly to declare that they do not wish to intervene in this "disastrous" struggle between brothers, that they will concentrate on freezing and limiting it to its present dimensions, that their battleships, cruisers, destroyers, aircraft carriers, submarines, minesweepers, torpedo boats, and airplanes as well will keep guard over the seas and skies of this part of America. And it could happen that, unbeknownst to the zealous guardians of continental peace, a single ship will get past them which will bring nothing good for Cuba, which will manage to "elude" the "iron" vigilance. Also intervention might take place through some "prestige" organ of the Americas, in order to put an end to the "crazy war" which "Communism" will unleash in our island; or, if this mechanism of this American "prestige" organ will not suffice, there might be direct intervention in its name in order to bring peace and to protect the interest of citizens, creating the variant of Korea. . . .

Many things might be asserted against the feasibility of enemy victory, but two of them are fundamental: one external, which is the year 1960, the year of the underdeveloped peoples, the year of the free peoples, the year in which at last and for always the voices of the millions of beings who do not have the luck to be governed by the possessors of the means of death and payment are going to make themselves respected; but a further, and even more weighty reason, is that an army of six million Cubans will reach for their weapons as a single individual to defend their territory and their revolution, and that this will be a field of battle where the army will be nothing other than a part of the people, armed, and that following destruction in a frontal attack, hundreds of guerrillas with dynamic command, with a single central orientation, will carry on the battle in every part of the country, and that in the cities the workers will carry death from the walls of their factories or centers of work, and in the fields the *campesinos* will carry death to the invader from behind every palm or from every furrow dug by the new mechanical plows which the revolution gave them.

And throughout the world, international solidarity will create a barricade of millions protesting against the aggression. Monopoly will see how its rotted pillars tremble and how its curtain of lies elaborated by the press will be swept away in a breath like a spider web.

* * *

It would be well for you who are present, the inhabitants of Havana, to turn over this idea in your minds: the idea that in Cuba a new type of human is being created, a fact which cannot be adequately appreciated in the capital, but which may be seen in every corner of the country. Those of you who went to the Sierra Maestra on the 26th of July will have seen two things absolutely unheard of: an army with picks and poles, an army whose great pride it was to march in the patriotic festivities in Oriente Province in columns and bearing pick and pole, while their companions of the militia marched with their rifles. But you will also have seen something even more important; you will have seen some children whose physiques made you think that they were 8 or 9 years old, and who nevertheless were almost all 13 or 14 years old. They are the most authentic children of the Sierra Maestra, the most authentic children of hunger and misery in all their forms. They are the creatures of malnutrition.

In this small Cuba, with its four or five television channels and its hundreds of radio stations, with all of the advances of modern science, when those children went to school by night for the first time and saw the shining of the electric lights, they exclaimed: "The stars are very low tonight." And those children, whom some of you will have seen, are learning in the collective schools everything from the ABCs to a trade, and even the most difficult science: of being revolutionaries. These are the new human types which are being born in Cuba. They are being born in some isolated spot, at distant points in the Sierra Maestra, and also in the co-operatives and the work centers.

* * *

The more that the imperialist forces (which act from without) and the reactionary forces (who are their natural allies from within) increase their pressure against the Cuban revolution, the more profound will it become, responding to the voice of the people and adopting measures each time more drastic. . . . The ink is still fresh with which we have just finished printing Resolution Number Two in our Gazette, by which the North American banks are nationalized. And while it is still fresh, our *companero* Fidel is packing his knapsack to go to New York. And I say that he is packing his knapsack, first of all, because that is a fighting job and therefore merits such a literary figure of speech. But he is also packing it because the North American imperialists, submerged in barbarism, wish to deprive him even of the right of all members of the United Nations to live in the place where the United Nations is located, in the United States of America. And Fidel Castro has clearly announced that he is taking his knapsack and his hammock with the nylon awning, and we ought not to be surprised if tomorrow we see a photo of our delegation slinging its hammocks in the Central Park of the most barbarous nation on earth.

And it is logical that way. We slung our hammocks up in the mountains when Cuba was submerged in barbarism and we fought for her liberation. Therefore we can sling our hammocks today in the center of that barbarous civilization, defending the right of all peoples to achieve their liberty, their total economic independence and their freely chosen path.

But he will go preceded by this new measure which will deepen the struggle, a measure which will bring economic problems, but which we have adopted precisely in order to defend our dignity and our right to be free. For many years now imperialism has based its economic power on money, on the bank, and has little by little taken possession of the peoples and has twisted their economy, until it has converted these peoples into a simple appendage of the greater economy of imperialism.

That is how our potent sugar industry has developed; it did not fall from the sky, nor did it develop because of North American goodness, but because they dominated the great *centrales,* those of greatest productivity, and dominated the entire market and paid us a preferential price. This last they did because, sheltered by these prices, they would introduce into our country, by means of a law falsely called the law of reciprocity, all of the manufactured consumers' articles used by this people; the conditions were such that the competition of other countries, also producers of consumer goods, was impossible.

* * *

But the North American form of action requires accomplices. They could not, as in the ancient times of the Roman Empire, hurl their legions upon a conquered country and have there a proconsul representing the Empire. They needed a proconsul, but one with special characteristics, outfitted in the modern manner and at times suave of demeanor, but revealing always his imperialist entrails. And those proconsuls were at times ambassadors, sometimes they were bank presidents, and sometimes they were the heads of military missions; but always they spoke English.

It was precisely in the dark epoch of the sugar depression that the task of the banks was very important, since all depressions are always felt by the mass of the people, and in the moments of depression is when the great monopolies see their profits increased and when they consolidate their economic empire, absorbing all the small fry, all the sardines in this sea of economic struggle. Thus in that epoch the North American banks had an important task. It was the task of foreclosing for debts, according to the laws of the country, all those who could not resist the force of the depression; and they rapidly consolidated their empires. Always they belong to the vanguard of the great financial groups which in the United States dispute for power.

They belong to the Rockefellers, to the Mellons, to the Morgans and to all those who have deployed their tentacles among the three branches which sustain the power of the United States: finance, the army, and as a simple younger brother, the government. For the government of the United States represents, as its army also does, the finances of the United States; but these finances do not represent the North American people, they represent a small group of financiers, the owners of all the big enterprises, the owners of money, who also exploit the North American people. Clearly they do not exploit them in the same manner that they exploit us, the human beings of inferior races, the *mestizos* of America, Africa and Asia, for we have not had the good fortune of being born from blond, Anglo-Saxon parents. But they do exploit them and divide them; they too are divided into blacks and whites, and they too are divided into men and women, union and non-union, employed and unemployed. . . .

Because of this it is good to see that here the first stage of imperial division, or disunion has been absolutely conquered; that we no longer need to be ashamed of the color of our skin; that we no longer need to fear because of our sex or our social status that we will or will not obtain a job more or less remunerative. When the working class united, when the agricultural laborers of the country united, the first step toward definitive liberation was taken. For the old, the very old imperial maxim of "divide and conquer" remains, today as yesterday, the basis of imperialist strategy.

14. New Beginnings?

For Marx, the agency of historic change—the proletariat—is a built-in feature in the development of capitalism. Accordingly, socialism is not merely the ideal of any minority, and it cannot be imposed upon the population of a country. It is the next stage of history, the post-capitalist epoch, and it can occur only when the proletariat gains revolutionary consciousness. Virtually all specific theories of classic marxism are attempts to describe and to explain this central thrust. And around these points all marxists after Marx—both in doctrine and in practice—have revolved.

1

Two overwhelming facts have to do with the scene of the climactic event: first, in no advanced capitalist society has a revolution of proletarian or bolshevik type succeeded. Second, revolutions of a bolshevik type, in the name of marxism, have succeeded only in backward peasant societies having autocratic governments.

There is now no substantial reason to believe that marxist revolutions will come about in the foreseeable future in any major advanced capitalist society. In fact, the revolutionary potential—whatever the phrase may reasonably mean—of wageworkers, labor unions and political parties, is feeble. This is true of the generally prosperous post-World War II period; it was also true of the thirties when we witnessed the most grievous slump so far known by world capitalism.

Such facts should not *determine* our view of the future, but they cannot be explained away by references to the corrupt and corrupting "misleaders of labor," to the success of capitalist propaganda, to economic prosperity due to war economy, etc. Assume all this to be true; still the evidence points to the fact that, without serious qualification, wageworkers under mature capitalism do accept the system. Wherever a labor party exists in an advanced capitalist society, it tends either to become weak or, in actual policy and result, to become incorporated within the welfare state apparatus. Social democratic parties everywhere become merely liberal, a kind of ineffectual, permanent façade of opposition.

Revolutions in the name of marxism have succeeded, without outside aid, in three countries: Russia, China, and Yugoslavia. Contrary to Marx's expectations, each of these, at the time of its revolution, was an extremely backward society, having a predominantly peasant population and autocratic government. The installation of stalinist regimes in Albania, Rumania, Bulgaria, Poland, Hungary, East Germany, and Czechoslovakia, was not the result of any autonomous revolution, proletarian or non-proletarian. All but one—Czechoslovakia's—were imposed by Russian arms (on the heels of retreating Nazi armies). Thus, in Konstantinov's textbook,[1] we read:

> Hardly any of the people's democracies belonged to the type of country with a highly developed capitalist system ripe for socialism. They included countries such as Poland and Rumania, with only slight capitalist development, and with considerable relics of feudalism, where the agrarian problem played an overwhelming role. . . . Thanks to the Soviet army it was possible for the popular democratic regime to be constituted and established in these countries without any commotion or civil war worth mentioning. . . . In this way the victorious dictatorship of the proletariat in the form of a people's democracy, carried out the tasks of the bourgeois-democratic republic, set about dealing with the tasks of the socialist revolution, and tackled the construction of a socialist system. The existence of the Soviet Union and its help have been of decisive importance in the development of the people's democracies on their path to socialism.

2

The history of marxism is the history of nineteenth-cen-

1. Fyodor V. Konstantinov is the editor-in-chief of *Komunist*—the leading theoretical organ of the Communist Party in the Soviet Union; he is appointed by The Central Committee of the CPSU.

tury thinkers and twentieth-century politicians. It is also the history of twentieth-century men who are at once thinkers and politicians. Yet there is one feature of marxism that runs through the several epochs we have briefly examined. To put it in its most obvious form: the theoretical capacities of such politicians as Stalin, Mao Tse-tung, Khrushchev and those of the thinkers Marx and Engels—are simply not comparable. There is no need to prove this; one has merely to read them. But to understand why this is so, we must keep in mind three things:

(1) Marx was not addressing millions of people; the twentieth-century politicians are doing just that. (2) Marx was without political power; these men hold in their hands enormous power of party and state, army and science. (3) Marx wrote in a world situation in which there were no post-capitalist societies; these politicians are in the middle of a kind of "socialist construction" about which Marx had very little or nothing to say. So it is little wonder that these politicians are more tightly ideological and less freely theoretical; that they are less abstract and more practical; that their theoretical or "verbocratic" work has to do, first of all, with policy, with decision, with justification.

With respect to these differences, Lenin and Trotsky stand between the nineteenth-century thinkers and the twentieth-century politicians. Both are thinkers of high quality, and both are among the most accomplished politicians of the last hundred years. That is why today so many soviet intellectuals, and the Party generally, find in Lenin their image of the ideal man. For them, Lenin embodies "the unity of theory and practice." Beyond that he is The Representative Man of Marxism, and the ideal man of the communist future.

Politically, these judgments of Lenin's place in the history of marxism are correct. But the same intellectuals hold fragmentary and vulgar judgments of Trotsky, based upon the enormous ignorance and systematic distortion of the stalinist era (which still prevails). If the day should come when the Party published great editions of Trotsky's complete works, and discussed widely and freely both his theoretical contributions and his political roles in their revolution, that will surely be most propitious for new beginnings in soviet marxism. Such a day appears far off; only a fool would say that it will never come.

It is a signal characteristic of the history of marxism that its doctrines and its practices have been, in one way or another, closely knit. Even those powerful decisions that are not made openly but which become public only after the fact are subject to doctrinal review and debate. My opinion, already suggested, is that marxism is probably more of a guide in these ways in the Soviet Union than is liberalism in the United States:

First, the political facts of power make it so: the soviet elite are in a position of power—making it more possible for them to be guided by theory than are the American elite.

Second, American decision-makers are less educated in the liberal classics than are the soviets in marxian classics. The traditions, the training, the selection of the soviet elite are much more likely to be effected by theoretical positions and disputes. Ideas, in short, and not only slogans, do count for more in the USSR than they do in the US, both in the higher circles and among the underling population.

Third, the distortions and illusions of soviet marxism today should not blind us to the fact that many marxist classics occupy an official place in educational routines and in political ideology. Despite the doubletalk and obfuscation characteristic of Soviet ideology, its genuine marxist elements do contain more of value for understanding the social realities of the world today than do the abstractions, the slogans and the fetishes of liberalism.

3

In 1939, Joseph Stalin said: "We have no right to expect of the classical Marxist writers, separated as they were from our day by a period of forty-five or fifty-five years, that they should have foreseen each and every zigzag of history in the distant future in every country."

In 1960, Nikita Khrushchev said, more boldly: "We live in a time when we have neither Marx nor Engels nor Lenin with us. If we act like children who, studying the alphabet, compile words from letters, we shall not go very far. Based on Marxist-Leninist teaching, we must think for ourselves, we must thoroughly study life, analyze the present situation and draw conclusions that are useful to the common cause of communism." [2]

There are great differences between Stalin's position in the 1930's and Khrushchev's in the 1960's. Stalin could impose his view—on the USSR and upon communist parties throughout the world. Russia was then "the only socialist country" and Stalin controlled it firmly as well as the parties outside it. But Khrushchev's Russia is not "the only socialist country" and his control, even inside Russia, is certainly more political and less dictatorial than Stalin's. Alongside the Soviet Union, there is now China, geographically smaller but in population much larger and in a different phase and level of development. China today is in a stage of development somewhat similar to Russia's in the early thirties. Her ideologists interpret "leninism" in a different way than do those of the Soviet Union.

Those who think hopefully about the future of the soviet bloc point out that the standards of living and of education there are rising; that the international situation may well ease, and that the military security of the soviet countries are reaching the point of invulnerability. As these developments occur, these optimists hold, the people will make more fully legitimate the ruling system; thus democratic liberties and practices can increasingly prevail. Indeed, they say, a *more* genuine freedom will prevail, because it will include economic as well as political life. Whether or not types of institutions like those existing in "Western" democracies will come about seems to those who hold this view less important than the hope that a democratic content will prevail.

Since the death of Stalin, we have been reminded by events that marxism—however monolithic, irrational and dogmatic a creed under Stalin—is, after all, an explosive and liberating creed, and that the ends for which Marx hoped, and which are built into his thought, *are* liberating ends. The most serious error we can make in our effort "to understand communism" is to lump all the countries and doctrines that go by the name "marxist" or "marxism-leninism" together under some consistent evil called "communism." Although the Bloc is not splitting up it is far from homogeneous. It is neither immutable nor monolithic. The changes within it indicate neither the advent of communist society nor its disintegration. The major changes include the following:

First, within the Soviet Union, Khrushchevism means the resuscitation of the Party as the agency of rule. At different times, Stalin had used various agencies of control—different governmental bureaus, tractor stations, the secret police. The importance of Khrushchev lies in the revitalization of the Party as the prime agency.

Second, the Bloc is no longer *run* as it was, by one communist party—the Party of the Soviet Union. Other parties of other national units have more voice in "the general line of the socialist camp"—and more room for maneuver and divergence. There is greater variety in their relationships with the Soviet Union—and certainly not merely unilateral subordination to it. The growing power of China has had much to do with this change, but the very scale of the Bloc itself tends to move its members in this direction.

Third, there is greater flexibility in the attitude inside the Bloc toward new nations, such as Guinea and Cuba, which are extremely nationalist, and although influenced by marxist ideas, are by no means "people's democracies." Toward these countries there is not the either-or attitude that went with Stalin's domination.

Fourth, these three changes point to, and are deeply involved with, a fact of the first importance: the break-up of orthodoxy among marxists both inside and outside the Bloc. It should be mentioned in passing that this fact contrasts sharply with the increased rigidity of official liberalism in the United States.

We should also remember that ideology is coming to play an increasingly important role in the making of history, and that the varieties of marxism are among the major ideologies and political philosophies. Marxism must now embrace theories of soviet types of societies as well as of advanced capitalist and of underdeveloped countries. For many marxists, inside and outside the Bloc, it must at times be difficult to know just what is "orthodox" and what is not. We must hope that for intellectual and for political work the terrible and wonderful historical experiences of half a century of soviet history will become truly available inside the Bloc, as well as outside it.

The ideals which Marx expected to be realized in post-capitalist society have not been realized in the Soviet

Union. Their use has clearly been utopian and optative, for the Soviet Union has not been the fully industrialized society envisaged by Marx as *the* condition for a successful marxist revolution. It *is* approaching that condition. However brutal the means have been, stalinism has done the work of industrialization and modernization that was done by capitalism in other societies. And the ideals of classic marxism still form the official legitimation of the regime and of the organizations and practices that constitute it. So we must now confront these questions:

1. In Khrushchev's world, are the ideals of classic marxism merely an ideology, cynically used to justify otherwise naked power? Or are they taken seriously by the directing elite as a guide to policy, as the goals they really wish to accomplish?

2. If these ideals, which are those of the western humanist tradition, are taken seriously, what then are the conditions and what are the agencies in Soviet society under which and by which they might possibly be realized?

3. Is it merely wishful thinking to ask the question: Might not a society conforming to the ideals of classic marxism be approximated, *via* the tortuous road of stalinism, in the Soviet world of Khrushchev and of those who will follow him?

Such questions, I believe, are the most difficult and the most important questions that can be raised in the contemporary history of marxist thought.

Index to Selections

A

B

C